REGIONAL IDENTITIES AND CULTURES OF MEDIEVAL JEWS

THE LITTMAN LIBRARY OF
JEWISH CIVILIZATION

Life Patron
COLETTE LITTMAN

Dedicated to the memory of
LOUIS THOMAS SIDNEY LITTMAN
who founded the Littman Library for the love of God
and as an act of charity in memory of his father
JOSEPH AARON LITTMAN
and to the memory of
ROBERT JOSEPH LITTMAN
who continued what his father Louis had begun
יהא זכרם ברוך

'Get wisdom, get understanding:
Forsake her not and she shall preserve thee'
PROV. 4:5

The Littman Library of Jewish Civilization is a registered UK charity
Registered charity no. 1000784

REGIONAL IDENTITIES AND CULTURES OF MEDIEVAL JEWS

◆

EDITED BY
JAVIER CASTAÑO
TALYA FISHMAN
AND
EPHRAIM KANARFOGEL

London
The Littman Library of Jewish Civilization
in association with Liverpool University Press

The Littman Library of Jewish Civilization
Registered office: 14th floor, 33 Cavendish Square, London W1G 0PW

in association with Liverpool University Press
4 Cambridge Street, Liverpool L69 7ZU, UK
www.liverpooluniversitypress.co.uk/littman

Managing Editor: Connie Webber

Distributed in North America by Longleaf Services
116 S Boundary St, Chapel Hill, NC 27514, USA

First published 2018
First published in paperback 2024

Catalogue records for this book are available from the
British Library and the Library of Congress

ISBN 978-1-837640-53-9

Publishing co-ordinator: Janet Moth
Copy-editing: Agnes Erdos
Proof-reading: Andrew Kirk
Index: Sarah Ereira
Designed and typset by Pete Russell, Faringdon, Oxon.

Printed and bound by CPI Group (UK) Ltd, Croydon, CR0 4YY

Contents

Contributors

JAVIER CASTAÑO
Instituto de Lenguas y Culturas de Mediterráneo y Oriente Próxime, CSIC (Spanish National Scientific Research Council), Madrid*

MORDECHAI Z. COHEN
Professor of Bible and Associate Dean, Bernard Revel Graduate School of Jewish Studies, Yeshiva University

JONATHAN DECTER
Edmond J. Safra Professor of Sephardic Studies, Brandeis University

TALYA FISHMAN
Department of Near Eastern Languages and Civilizations, University of Pennsylvania

AVRAHAM GROSSMAN
Professor Emeritus of Jewish History, Department of Jewish History and Contemporary History, Hebrew University of Jerusalem

ELISABETH HOLLENDER
Seminar für Judaistik, Goethe-Universität, Frankfurt am Main

MOSHE IDEL
Emeritus Max Cooper Professor in Jewish Thought, Hebrew University of Jerusalem

EPHRAIM KANARFOGEL
E. Billi Ivry University Professor of Jewish History, Literature and Law at Bernard Revel Graduate School of Jewish Studies, Yeshiva University

Y. TZVI LANGERMANN
Department of Arabic, Bar-Ilan University

HANANEL MACK
Department of Talmud, Bar-Ilan University

* Professor Castaño played a key role in the conversations at the Katz Center for Advanced Jewish Studies of the University of Pennsylvania in 2012 from which this volume originated. Regrettably, he was unable to sustain his involvement, but the project benefited greatly from his guidance

PAUL MANDEL
Schechter Institute of Jewish Studies, Jerusalem

LUCIA RASPE
Privatdozentin at Goethe-Universität, Frankfurt am Main, and curator at the Jewish Museum Berlin

PINCHAS ROTH
Senior Lecturer, Talmud Department, Bar-Ilan University

MICHAEL TOCH
Emeritus Professor of Medieval History, Department of History, Hebrew University of Jerusalem

Note on Transliteration

Hebrew

THE TRANSLITERATION of Hebrew in this book reflects consideration of the type of book it is, in terms of its content, purpose, and readership. The system adopted therefore reflects a broad approach to transcription, rather than the narrower approaches found in the *Encyclopaedia Judaica* or other systems developed for text-based or linguistic studies. The aim has been to reflect the pronunciation prescribed for modern Hebrew, rather than the spelling or Hebrew word structure, and to do so using conventions that are generally familiar to the English-speaking reader.

In accordance with this approach, no attempt is made to indicate the distinctions between *alef* and *ayin*, *tet* and *taf*, *kaf* and *kuf*, *sin* and *samekh*, since these are not relevant to pronunciation; likewise, the *dagesh* is not indicated except where it affects pronunciation. Following the principle of using conventions familiar to the majority of readers, however, transcriptions that are well established have been retained even when they are not fully consistent with the transliteration system adopted. On similar grounds, the *tsadi* is rendered by 'tz' in such familiar words as barmitzvah. Likewise, the distinction between *ḥet* and *khaf* has been retained, using *ḥ* for the former and *kh* for the latter; the associated forms are generally familiar to readers, even if the distinction is not actually borne out in pronunciation, and for the same reason the final *heh* is indicated too. As in Hebrew, no capital letters are used, except that an initial capital has been retained in transliterating titles of published works (for example, *Shulḥan arukh*).

Since no distinction is made between *alef* and *ayin*, they are indicated by an apostrophe only in intervocalic positions where a failure to do so could lead an English-speaking reader to pronounce the vowel-cluster as a diphthong—as, for example, in *ha'ir*—or otherwise mispronounce the word.

The *sheva na* is indicated by an *e*—*perikat ol, reshut*—except, again, when established convention dictates otherwise.

The *yod* is represented by *i* when it occurs as a vowel (*bereshit*), by *y* when it occurs as a consonant (*yesodot*), and by *yi* when it occurs as both (*yisra'el*).

Names have generally been left in their familiar forms, even when this is inconsistent with the overall system.

Arabic

In Arabic transliteration, long vowels are indicated with macrons (*ā*, *ī*, *ū*). The hard and breathed consonants are indicated by a dot below the letter (*ḥ*, *ḍ*, *ẓ*, *ṣ*, *ṭ*). The letter *thā'* is indicated by *th*, *dhāl* by *dh*, *khā'* by *kh*, and *shīn* by *sh*. *Hamza* and *'ayn* are indicated by ' and ' respectively, with the exception of initial *hamza*, which is not marked. The definite article is represented throughout as *al-*, with no attempt to indicate elision, either following a vowel or preceding a sun letter. *Tā' marbūṭa* is indicated by *a*, except in the construct (*iḍāfa*), when it is represented as *at*. All Arabic words, apart from proper names standing alone, are italicized.

Introduction

TALYA FISHMAN

THOUGH THE EXISTENCE of Jewish regional cultures is widely known, the prominence of two groups, Ashkenaz and Sepharad, has tended to obscure the far richer variety of identities.[1] Both Ashkenaz and Sepharad are biblical toponyms adopted by medieval Jews: Ashkenaz by settlers in Carolingian Franco-Germany, and Sepharad by settlers in Islamic al-Andalus. It was only in the early modern period that each was transformed into an umbrella category, encompassing smaller regional identities within it. The historian Jonathan Ray has shown that Iberian Jews of the late fourteenth and the fifteenth centuries identified themselves not as Sephardim, but as Jews of a particular town or principality. 'Sepharad' as a catch-all identity was first used by the established residents of non-Iberian lands, who applied this label to Jewish newcomers from Spain. But while old-timers perceived the immigrants as members of a homogeneous unit, first-generation émigrés did not embrace a shared 'Sephardi' identity. Their descendants, on the other hand, were shaped by this form of 'othering' and by its accompanying governmental policies, which afforded uniformity of treatment to the Iberian Jewish émigrés, and indirectly incentivized their collaboration—economically, socially, and, in time, culturally.[2]

Joseph Davis's study of early modern halakhic codes demonstrates that Ashkenaz, too, became an umbrella category in the sixteenth century.[3] Yet the overlap between his conclusions and those of Ray is, in some ways, coinciden-

[1] R. Israel Brodie, former chief rabbi of the British Commonwealth, described the State of Israel as 'the melting-pot of the many "tribes" representing Jews of many countries who form the Ingathering of the Exiles'. He cited the prayer book created for all members of the Israeli military as an example of a 'conscious effort in *mizzug* [blending]', and affirmed that 'the differences between Sephardim and Ashkenazim . . . are but variations of the same common Judaism expressed in identical basic terms'; foreword to Zimmels, *Ashkenazim and Sephardim*.

[2] Ray, *After Expulsion*; cf. id., *The Sephardic Frontier*.

[3] Davis, 'The Reception of the Shulhan 'Arukh'.

tal, for their respective studies explore very different sorts of evidence, and from divergent perspectives. Employing the lens of social history to analyse archival material, Ray reveals that Sepharad as a 'big-tent' identity was, at first, unwelcome. By contrast, Davis's investigation of printed texts underscores the synergy between the codificatory aspirations of two rabbinic scholars and the standardizing powers of print. Davis suggests that the Sepharad–Ashkenaz binary that persists to this day may be traced to the composition of complementary law codes in the early modern period, and to their circulation in print. Unlike earlier codes, which were transmitted only in manuscript,[4] the Sephardi *Shulḥan arukh* by R. Joseph Karo of Safed (1488–1575) and its Ashkenazi complement, the *Mapah* by R. Moses Isserles of Kraków (1520–72), reached readers across vast swaths of territory. Combining sweep with rabbinic authority, they effaced differences in local practice and identity, forging overarching—and uniform—subcultures that had never before existed.[5] Nor was it exclusively rabbinic authority that extended the geographical scope of 'Ashkenaz'; Davis notes that the boundaries of this term were at times simply redrawn by entrepreneurial printers keen to enlist more readers.[6]

This opening excursus on the early modern transformations of Ashkenaz and Sepharad into composite regional identities explains why the sixteenth century is the *terminus ad quem* for the present volume. The other temporal bookend, the *terminus post quem*, is far more difficult to pinpoint. Its clearest marker, in fact, is geographical rather than chronological, for the emergence of Jewish subcultures (Ashkenaz and Sepharad among them) was linked to decline in the power of the rabbinic centres of the East, Palestine and Babylonia. The new, European, entities distinguished themselves from these older institutional bases, and from one another as well. Yet the paucity of documentary evidence prior to and around the first millennium makes it difficult to reconstruct their origins. With rare exceptions, little effort has been made to integrate epigraphic and archaeological evidence about the earliest European Jewish settlements into broader historiographical narratives.[7] Finally, scholarly attention has been deflected from the study of medieval Jewish sub-

[4] Davis notes (ibid. 264) that R. Jacob ben Asher contrasted customs of Ashkenaz and Sepharad in more than 100 passages in his *Arba'ah turim*.

[5] See Davis, 'The Reception of the Shulhan 'Arukh', 252.

[6] On the role of print in solidifying—or altering—the geographical boundaries of a subgroup, and the ability of Hebrew printers to 'expand a law code's announced authority', see ibid. 264.

[7] See e.g. Goldberg, *Crossing the Jabbok: Illness and Death in Ashkenazi Judaism*, 24–8.

cultures, their genesis and re-formation, by a twentieth-century theory that purported to explain their origins.

Up until the 1980s, students of Jewish history were taught that Ashkenaz and Sepharad were medieval satellites of the two centres of Jewish life in antiquity; Ashkenaz was portrayed as the heir to Roman Palestine, and Sepharad the heir to Sassanid Babylonia.[8] In its most far-reaching formulations the two-centre theory not only posited lines of genealogical filiation between Jewish communities of the ancient East and the medieval West; it ascribed ontological status to their differences. Writing in 1944, Benjamin Klar asserted that the ancient duality of Palestine and Babylonia was 'determinative' of 'the entire form and character of the Judaism of this place and of that, from the perspective of spiritual development and of the stance of the soul [*ha'emdah hanafshit*]'.[9] This ancient binary, wrote Klar, 'not only establishes the political destiny but also the spiritual face [*et partsufah haruḥani*] of Judaism over the course of 1,000 years'.[10]

In a 1976 essay reviewing the evidence adduced in support of the connection between Ashkenaz and Palestine, Avraham Grossman posed a forceful challenge to the two-centre theory. He acknowledged the Palestinian antecedents for Ashkenazi customs[11] and liturgical compositions,[12] but he also noted that medieval Ashkenazim never saw themselves as the heirs of only one of the eastern centres, and that Ashkenazi leaders corresponded with scholars in both Babylonia and Palestine.[13] Since 1976 the theory of Ashkenazi dependence on Palestine has been further discredited.[14]

In short, scholarly deconstructions of the last several decades have cleared the field for fresh investigations of the Jewish subcultures that emerged—and underwent transformation—in the Middle Ages. Scholars contributing to the present study were invited to consider how Jewish regional identities were fashioned, propagated, reinforced, contested, and reformed—and to reflect on

[8] The two-centre theory was propounded in many works, among them Bernfeld, 'The Land of Israel and Babylonia' (Heb.), 289 ff; Assaf, 'Babylonia and the Land of Israel in the Era of the Geonim' (Heb.); Assaf and Mayer (eds.), *Sefer hayishuv*, ii. 42–4.

[9] See Klar's afterword to *Megilat aḥima'ats*, 144.

[10] Ibid. 148. Statements like this have led some readers to assume that the historical judgement of Klar, and of Assaf before him, was clouded by the momentum of Zionism and its conceptual agenda.

[11] Grossman, 'The Relationship of Early Ashkenazi Jewry to the Land of Israel' (Heb.).

[12] Some of these were noted in the bibliography of Fleischer, *Hebrew Liturgical Poetry in the Middle Ages* (Heb.), 501–10.

[13] Grossman, 'The Relationship of Early Ashkenazi Jewry to the Land of Israel' (Heb.), 75.

[14] See, in particular, Soloveitchik, *Wine in Ashkenaz in the Middle Ages* (Heb.), ch. 9.

the developments, events, or encounters that made their identities manifest. They were asked to identify ways in which subcultural identities proved to be useful, and the circumstances in which these identities were deployed. The resulting volume spans the ninth to the sixteenth centuries, and explores Jewish cultural developments in western Europe, the Balkans, North Africa, and Asia Minor. In its own way, each contribution considers factors—demographic, geographical, historical, economic, political, institutional, legal, intellectual, theological, cultural, and even biological—that led medieval Jews to conceive of themselves, or to be perceived by others, as bearers of a discrete Jewish regional identity. Notwithstanding the singularity of each essay, they collectively attest to the inherent dynamism of Jewish regional identities.

*

Given their diversity, on the one hand, and their many points of overlap, on the other, a variety of organizational schemes might have been adopted for the presentation of these essays. In the end, the editors decided to arrange them in four units. Part I, 'Identity Claims', includes two essays that offer bird's-eye views. Each concerns claims that have been made about the lineage and history of medieval Jews, and each reflects on the political ramifications of these claims. The four essays in Part II, 'The Impact of Non-Jewish Cultures on Regional Traditions', explore how particular products of medieval Jewish culture were shaped by non-Jewish cultures, Christian or Muslim. The five essays in Part III, 'Geopolitical Boundaries and Their Impact on Jewish Regional Identities', focus on cases in which Jewish practices, orientations, or cultural developments were defined by territorial borders. The two essays in Part IV, 'Cultural Content as a Marker of Jewish Regional Identities', present little-known cultural phenomena that were characteristic of specific regions. Though readers may debate whether the geographically specific phenomena described warrant designation as Jewish 'subcultures', the prompting of thoughtful deliberation would be a welcome outcome.

Michael Toch's essay 'The Emergence of the Medieval Jewish Diaspora(s) of Europe from the Ninth to the Twelfth Centuries, with Some Thoughts on Historical DNA Studies' offers a broad introductory overview and poses large questions about identity, and about identity claims. Notwithstanding its title, this study's chrono-geographical mapping of Jewish migration and settlement spans the late Roman period to the thirteenth century, and includes in its scope not only Europe but Asia Minor, Mesopotamia, and North Africa. Toch traces Jewish migratory patterns and changes in the size of discrete Jewish populations; he sets these data in the context of broader demographic shifts and explains their causes. He also challenges several theories pertaining to specific Jewish populations, their size, and their origins. Toch asserts that the number of Jews in the Roman empire was considerably smaller than scholars have claimed—and that there are no grounds for regarding medieval Ashkenazim as the direct descendants of Jews in antiquity. He also rejects the claim that the earliest Jews of France were emigrants from Germany, and declares the Khazar theory of Ashkenazi Jewish origins utterly baseless. Providing a sense of Jewish numbers in medieval Europe, Toch suggests that there were around 1,000 Jewish communities in the Germanic empire by 1348.[15] He also presents a finding of historical geneticists, whose tracking of mitochondrial DNA, a maternal marker, has led them to claim that a mere four women, probably of Near Eastern ancestry, were the 'founding mothers' of Europe's considerable Jewish population a millennium later.

Nonetheless Toch challenges the methodology of historical geneticists who allow contemporary populations to serve as 'stand-ins' for those that lived a millennium ago. As the grounds for asserting congruence are flimsy to non-existent, such studies (and their alleged conclusions) are without value. Toch reserves his strongest criticism for contemporary writers who invoke data pertaining to the biological basis of Jewish identity in order to build political claims about rights to land.

Some questions posed by Toch pertain to the discipline of Jewish demography: What was the effect of apostasy on population numbers and what was the effect of exogamy? Were non-Jewish women more likely than men to marry into the Jewish community? Other questions concern the grounds for constructing Jewish identities (on any scale), the terminology used (race? ethnicity? culture? civilization?), and the functions these identities have served.

Like Toch's contribution, that of Avraham Grossman concerns what the historian Marc Bloch has labelled 'the idol of origins'.[16] Grossman's 'Medieval Jewish Legends on the Decline of the Babylonian Centre and the Primacy of Other Geographical Centres' offers a resounding 'yes' to Toch's question: Should the date of settlement guarantee a population's regional loyalty? As Grossman explains, some aspects of the foundation myths generated by several European Jewish populations in the eleventh and twelfth centuries were intended to impress Jews, and others to impress non-Jews.

As the Babylonian centre declined following Hai Gaon's death in 1038,

[15] He does not offer a definition of community. See the questions raised in the conclusion to this Introduction.

[16] Bloch, *The Historian's Craft*, 29–35.

legends from Spain, Italy, Ashkenaz, northern France, and Provence affirmed a 'transfer of learning' from the East to the West. Some did so through claims of providential occurrence, others through allegations of marriage into Hai Gaon's family. Foundational myths that affirmed filiation with ancient Palestine claimed aristocratic lineage, whether as descendants of the House of David in the First Temple era or as exiles from Jerusalem following the destruction of the Second Temple. The fact that some aetiological narratives cited in Grossman's study served to legitimize leadership of learning, and others administrative leadership, deserves further attention.

Grossman asserts that these legends were designed not only to justify disengagement from ancient eastern centres of rabbinic life, but also to affirm subcultural predominance. He cites in particular a rivalry over aristocracy of lineage that involved Ashkenaz and Sepharad. Other foundational accounts posited ancient origins for practices and disciplines associated with the locale.

As Grossman points out, Jews were no less concerned than contemporaneous Christians to extol their places of habitation; he assumes that the foundational myths produced by European Jews were in line with broader regional practices. Like Christians, Jews of different locales linked themselves to powerful leaders of the past, such as Charlemagne. Through such allegations the groups hoped to command respect, to stress their loyalty to the current ruler, and to affirm their entitlement to the sovereign's protection.

The essays in Part II illuminate the impact of non-Jewish cultures on Jewish regional traditions. This section opens with Paul Mandel's study of a striking literary-theological motif that surfaced in the writings of medieval Ashkenazi Pietists and was subsequently channelled into more mainstream rabbinic literature. 'The Sacrifice of the Souls of the Righteous Upon the Heavenly Altar: Transformations of Apocalyptic Traditions in Medieval Ashkenaz' traces the title theme from its biblical origins to its place in Second Temple writings, and from there to rabbinic and New Testament teachings. Mandel's essay, rich in texts, carefully draws attention to the motif's accrual of literary elements and theological meanings in these earlier stages of transmission, and in its later passage from Byzantium to Ashkenaz.

As a work of historical reconstruction, Mandel's essay pinpoints textual moments of interregional and cross-cultural exchange. It offers clear illustrations of the overlap between Christian and Jewish traditions during the first centuries of the Common Era, and illuminates the route of cultural transmission from the Byzantine East to Ashkenaz. In tracing the transformation of the motif, Mandel notes the shift in focus—from the souls of the deceased righteous, stored under the Throne of Glory, to the souls of martyred Jews. In the later iterations of the motif, attested in both liturgical and homiletical writings, the sacrifice of martyred souls on the altar of the Heavenly Temple atones for the sins of Israel, thereby hastening the End. Mandel relates the metamorphoses of this Jewish theme to developments in Christian martyrological theory and practice.

Hananel Mack's essay concerns a case in which the interreligious border may be said to have shaped a canon, in that it led Jews to withhold the transmission of certain cultural products. The corpus considered—the teachings of Rabbi Moses Hadarshan, a pioneering scholar of eleventh-century Narbonne—was meticulously assembled by Mack from direct and reworked citations in Rashi's Bible commentary, from citations preserved by the exegete R. Joseph Kara, from specific midrashic compilations, and from *Pugio Fidei* (The Dagger of Faith), an anthology of rabbinic traditions compiled in the thirteenth century by Ramon Martini in order to assist Christian polemicists in their disputations with Jews. Mack offers illustrative examples of R. Moses' teachings in three appendices to the essay. The first contains citations of his *peshat* teachings that were left unaltered; the second illustrates Rashi's alteration of R. Moses' *peshat* teaching, and the third presents two of his messianic homilies that are preserved in *Pugio Fidei*.

In his essay, entitled 'The Bifurcated Legacy of Rabbi Moses Hadarshan and the Rise of *Peshat* Exegesis in Medieval France', Mack asserts that this homilist was not only the first Jew on European soil to engage in *peshat*, or plain-sense, biblical exegesis, he was also the first European Jew to engage in *derash*, the homiletical exegesis of Scripture. While *derash* had been cultivated in ancient Palestine, the *derash* of R. Moses differed from earlier expressions in its sermonic style and messianic content. Yet, notes Mack, only one of these exegetical strands, *peshat*, had an afterlife among Jews; indeed, it was further developed by Jewish scholars in both Christian and Muslim lands. Mack considers the possibility that R. Moses Hadarshan's *peshat* teachings may have been indebted to the linguistic clarifications of Andalusian Jewish philologists such as Jonah Ibn Janāḥ, and he speculates on a possible connection between the French *pashtan* Menahem bar Helbo and the Iberian grandson of Samuel Hanagid.

Why did European Jews refrain from circulating—and building on—the *derash* approach pioneered by R. Moses? Mack speculates that, as Christian–Jewish relations worsened, medieval Jewish scholars made a conscious decision to abandon (and thus to bury) this approach to cultural production. As it turned out, writes Mack, their assumption that Jewish homilies of messianic content would be used against Jews by Christian polemicists was well founded; the *derash* teachings of R. Moses Hadarshan have only been preserved in Christian writings. Mack explicitly links the jettisoning of *derash* by medieval Jewish scholars to the explosion of *peshat* exegesis: 'Where the methods of *derash* could lead anywhere, even to the sanction of theological notions consonant with Christianity, search for Scripture's plain sense stood as a bulwark against such interpretative plasticity.'

While Mack's study pinpoints the origins of *peshat* exegesis in Europe, Mordechai Cohen notes that *peshat* as a concept meant something different to Jewish scholars living within different majority cultures. 'A New Look at Medieval Jewish Exegetical Constructions of *Peshat* in Christian and Muslim Lands: Rashbam and Maimonides' clarifies the divergent 'hermeneutical trajectories' of *peshat*, and links their differences to cultural elements in their broader societies. Cohen's detailed analysis of passages in the writings of R. Samuel ben Meir (Rashbam, *c.*1085–*c.*1158) of northern France, and of R. Moses ben Maimon (Rambam, 1135/8?–1204) of Egypt, demonstrates that their divergent understandings of *peshat* reflected vastly different assumptions about the relationship between exegesis and halakhah. Rashbam comfortably acknowledged that certain midrashic interpretations 'overrode' Scripture's *peshat* meaning and determined the law as it was to be practised. Maimonides, writes Cohen, 'made *peshuto shel mikra* [Scripture's plain sense] his legal foundation'.

Situating each figure within his broader cross-cultural environment, Cohen explains how Maimonides' understanding of *peshat* was linked to features of Islamic jurisprudence. Though he does not suggest any comparable debts to developments in Christian culture, he notes that Rashbam's perception of midrashic interpretation as the expression of the 'ultimate' meaning of Scripture bears a resemblance to the conceptual hierarchy of scriptural meanings expressed in the writings of his Christian contemporary, Hugh of Saint-Victor.

Where Cohen's essay helps to explain Maimonides' unique perspective on *peshat* by reconstructing its relationship to the terminology and features of *uṣūl al fiqh*, Talya Fishman's contribution links a Sephardi tradition about the written Talmud to an influential theory in medieval Arabic literary theory and practice. The riddle at the heart of her essay is a claim, transmitted by Andalusian rabbinic scholars, that 'our Talmud', when written, was fashioned as a work of applied law. 'The "Our Talmud" Tradition and the Predilection for

Works of Applied Law in Early Sephardi Rabbinic Culture' speculates about the origins of this poorly understood claim. Drawing on Leonard Levy's study of R. Isaac Alfasi, Fishman notes that this eleventh-century scholar, a linchpin between the rabbinic cultures of North Africa and al-Andalus, referred to the Talmud's anonymous stratum (the *setam*) as 'al-Talmūd'. If not an overt personification, this title designated a single voice that could be discerned in the text, notwithstanding the welter of speakers and conflicting perspectives. According to Levy, Alfasi regarded 'al-Talmūd' as a 'unitary, consistent editor who deliberately used a number of methods to signal' to sensitive readers the applied law as it was to be practised.

Setting this observation within the broader context of Arabic literary theory, Fishman conjectures that Alfasi regarded the *setam*, the Talmud's anonymous voice, as a *mudawwin*, the Arabic term ascribed to the recorder-narrator-editor whose hand fashioned and controlled the discourse in a written text. If Alfasi held such a perspective, writes Fishman, it would explain why Andalusian Jews (consumers of Alfasi's *Sefer hahalakhot*) described the *edited* text of the Babylonian Talmud as a guide to law-as-practised. It might also shed light on the known Sephardi preference for works of applied law, so different from the Ashkenazi tendency to engage the Talmud with its accumulated glosses and commentaries.

The essays that comprise Part III are less directly concerned with the impact of cross-cultural influences; instead, they highlight the role of geopolitical borders in shaping regional realities of medieval Jewish culture. Ephraim Kanarfogel's piece has some affinities with that of Jonathan Decter: where one demonstrates that there was no monolithic northern European subculture, the other illuminates the diversity of medieval Sepharad. Both studies, like that of Pinchas Roth, emphasize the impact of regionally specific institutions on the shaping of local Jewish identities. The other two essays in this section consider the impact of borders on cultural exchange. Elisabeth Hollender's study sheds light on a particular case of 'othering' which proved surprisingly dynamic. Lucia Raspe's piece maps a *sui generis* subculture that emerged when small numbers of Jews from different locales banded together in a territory previously devoid of Jewish life.

Kanarfogel's starting point is the general similarity in halakhic outlook that characterized medieval rabbis in Germany and northern France, and the porousness of their boundaries where intellectual exchange was concerned. 'From Germany to Northern France and Back Again: A Tale of Two Tosafist Centres' examines the cleavage between these regional identities at a particular moment of the High Middle Ages, and it attempts to explain its causes. Kanarfogel draws attention to differences in the cultures of rabbinic pedagogy and practice that prevailed in the title regions: the disparate etiquettes that characterized relationships between students and their *rashei yeshivah*, and the ways in which the regions named their institutions of talmudic learning. The role of responsa in their respective locales was also different: while scholars of both regions penned answers to legal enquiries, only those of Germany systematically collected responsa and referred to them in making judicial decisions.

A noticeable separation between the rabbinic cultures of the two regions occurred between 1175 and 1215. It was during this period that divergence in the styles and values of leadership became most apparent and that communication between the regions dwindled. After the 1230s there appears to have been a rupture in the formerly continuous German rabbinic leadership. Explaining these developments, Kanarfogel reconstructs the circles of scholarship through which the students of Rabbenu Tam, both French and German, transmitted his pedagogical and curricular approach following his death in 1171. According to Kanarfogel, the greatest divide between the rabbinic leaders of the regions appeared when those of Germany assumed professional responsibilities that were not expected of their French counterparts. As heads of talmudic academies, the rabbinic leaders in northern France had only circumscribed judicial responsibilities. They oversaw courts of divorce, and at least some were involved in the training of judges who would preside in courts devoted to matters of monetary and ritual law. (Even Rabbenu Tam, the quintessential dialectician, engaged in these practical matters, though, as Kanarfogel notes, subsequent generations have chosen to remember him differently.) By contrast, the judicial responsibilities of German rabbis included the adjudication and recording of cases. Even in instances where the rabbinic court was linked to a rabbinic academy, the court was deemed the dominant venue.

The conclusion to Kanarfogel's essay refers to the oblique role of the state in shaping leadership styles and ideals of rabbis in different regions. Where Ashkenaz and northern France were concerned, the geopolitical border indirectly determined whether rabbinic power would be expressed through the ability to discover new (and academic) interpretations of Talmud or through the rendering of legal decisions.

The essay by Pinchas Roth maps the cultural specificity of a different European region. 'Rabbinic Politics, Royal Conquest, and the Creation of a

Halakhic Tradition in Medieval Provence' reconstructs the coherent sub-cultural identity forged by Provençal rabbis, notwithstanding the pull exerted by immigrants from both Spain and northern France. Provence absorbed an influx of Andalusian Jews fleeing the Almohads in the first half of the twelfth century, and of Jews expelled from France in 1306; both immigrant populations brought with them their distinctive bodies of learning. Through careful analysis of several legal cases that occurred in Provence and that engaged both local rabbis and those from northern France, Roth sheds light on the clash of regional orientations, the differences between Jewish–Christian relations in the two locales, and the role played by the state in determining the legal conditions of its resident Jews. All the cases discussed are preserved (primarily in manuscript) in Provençal responsa of the late thirteenth and early fourteenth centuries. Several offer piquant and vibrant glimpses of everyday life, and all concern matters that were of social and financial consequence. Roth sets each of these carefully selected cases in its diachronic and synchronic context, across territories and across the Jewish–Christian divide. He highlights the battles between halakhists of southern and northern France, records their outcome and aftermath, and argues that the cultural 'onslaught' from the north 'was as instrumental in the formation of a Provençal Jewish identity as it was in the emergence of an Occitan Christian identity'.

Whereas the Jews of northern France described in Roth's essay cavalierly assumed that lands to the south had no pre-existing rabbinic culture, the poets discussed in Jonathan Decter's study were highly sensitive to differences in regional orientation. As he shows in 'Mediterranean Regionalism in Hebrew Panegyric Poetry', poets consciously tailored their writing style to suit addressees in different lands. Though the analysis of praise poems, a highly stylized genre, might seem unlikely to yield much in the way of historical or regional insight, Decter's study of Hebrew panegyrics illuminates the uses of poetry in constructing political legitimacy. The poems under consideration were composed in different regions of the Mediterranean—by Hai Gaon, Andalusian poets, and Judah Halevi of Christian Spain—and Decter mines them for their representational import. Decoding specific idioms of power, he reads them as clues to societal values and norms in the lands of their creators, and in the lands of their intended readers and hearers. He identifies the use of the vernacular, inclusion of biblical language, and invocation of place names as poetic features that convey specific cultural meanings. The language of political rituals embedded in the panegyrics and the honorifics chosen for the addressee are of particular significance. According to Decter, these did not simply establish relationships of patronage, financial transaction, and friendship (real or aspirational). Variations in the titles bestowed upon a leader—whether they alluded to communal authority or to aristocracy of lineage or of learning; whether they posited linkage to a non-Jewish court; whether they were formulated in the present or future tense—were used to negotiate and mark subtle changes in the hierarchies of interaction.

Elisabeth Hollender's essay, 'Attraction and Attribution: Framings of Sephardi Identity in Ashkenazi Prayer Books', examines a different genre of Hebrew poetry, *kinot*—liturgical poems lamenting the destruction of the Temple and, in some cases, more recent Jewish tribulations. Whereas Decter's research highlights the impact of borders on literary production, Hollender's study focuses on literary reception in cases where cultural exchange was neither planned nor anticipated. Her exploration of medieval Ashkenazi prayer manuscripts that—both knowingly and unknowingly—incorporate Sephardi *kinot* demonstrates that, from the late twelfth into the early thirteenth century, Ashkenazi worshippers craved these liturgical poems of lament, and particularly the 'Zionides' of Judah Halevi.

The admired *piyutim* were not only imported but also emulated. Ashkenazi *payetanim* created their own *kinot* in the Sephardi style, utilizing biblical language and adopting the metre and stanza forms of their Iberian models. Hollender's identification and analysis of eighty-three rubricating 'metatexts' for Sephardi *kinot* in Ashkenazi prayer manuscripts sheds light on the 'othering' that accompanied subcultural exchange. In the ultimate—if unwitting—expression of appreciation, some of the prefatory rubrics 'domesticated' the most prominent of the Iberian poets, transforming the Castilian R. Judah Halevi into the Ashkenazi Judah Kästlin. In this case, a confluence of factors—cultural appetite, scribal error, and the passage of time—had resulted in the complete erasure of borders.

Lucia Raspe's essay offers an unusual glimpse of the birth of a subculture. '*Minhag* and Migration: Yiddish Custom Books from Sixteenth-Century Italy' maps the genesis of a specifically Italian Ashkenazi identity in the late fourteenth century, precipitated by large-scale migration to Italy of Jews expelled from German towns and principalities. As Raspe points out, this crossing of geopolitical boundaries engendered no encounter between Jewish old-timers and newcomers, because the lands of settlement had no pre-existing Jewish communities. Coming from many different German locales and in small family units, no one group of émigrés prevailed over the others. Instead, notes Raspe, their commingling produced a unified—and original—

Ashkenazi identity that was unique to Italian lands and that endured into the later age of the ghetto.

Raspe's investigation of identity claims and identity formation focuses on Hebrew and Yiddish *sifrei minhagim*. Works of this quintessentially local genre set forth regional customs and relayed the regionally specific practices of the Jewish liturgical year. As the period studied coincides with the advent of print, Raspe was able to compare editions of the most popular Hebrew customaries of the time, *Sefer maharil* and the *Minhagim* of Isaac of Tirna, in both manuscript and print, with fifteen Yiddish manuscript adaptations of these works. While diachronic analysis enabled her to comment on changes in book culture and in the tastes of book owners, meticulous scrutiny of these works—for content, codicological features, organizational patterns, glosses, and other elements—made it possible to reconstruct a process of textual growth.

Several features of these Yiddish manuscripts are singled out for special attention. Raspe notes that a number of *minhagim* books were written explicitly for women, and she identifies elements in them that may reflect a gender-specific readership. Drawing attention to the sloppiness of some manuscripts (which mangled or omitted mandatory blessings), Raspe comments on their unreliability, and she raises questions about the ways in which the *minhagim* books were used. Lastly, she highlights the spirit of jocularity found in certain manuscripts, drawing attention to scribal wisecracks.

Contributions in the final part of this volume also illuminate regionally specific cultural creations, but they place less emphasis on the determinative role of borders. While aware of these frontiers, the authors conduct their investigation, as it were, from the inside out.

Like several other contributions to this volume, Tzvi Langermann's essay 'A Collection of Jewish Philosophical Prayers' is cartographically significant: its presentation and analysis of a novel trove of prayers adds new data to the map of medieval Jewish culture. A fifteenth-century Hebrew manuscript in a Byzantine hand lies at the heart of the study; the compositions it includes are ascribed to a range of authors, poets of Crete among them. On the basis of both content and form, Langermann characterizes them as prayers, though none offer clues as to when, where, or by whom they were recited. Each addresses God directly—as 'the Cause of Causes', for example—and each employs philosophical concepts and terminology. Some describe the wonder inspired by God's cosmic creation, its structures and processes; others the journey of the soul. All express deep longing for intimacy with the Divine.

Some compositions are subdivided into known structural units of prayer, and some instruct the worshipper to assume specific bodily postures of kneeling or prostration.

In his study of several philosophical prayers, Langermann identifies the provenance of their constituent elements and reconstructs likely pathways of evolution and transmission. He tracks translations from Hebrew to Arabic, literary amplifications, and attributions. He raises doubts as to Maimonides' authorship of any of the three prayers ascribed to him, noting that scholar's profound conservatism regarding liturgical language and his conviction that silent contemplation was the ideal form of worship. And he portrays a particular prayer, with its theme of yearning to abandon worldly life, as the literary product of boundary-crossings in language, genre, and religion—having made its way in stages from an unnamed Sufi ethical will to a Jewish philosopher in fourteenth-century Candia.

Linking a lengthy supplicatory prayer by Judah Halevi to a passage in his *Kuzari*, Langermann raises the possibility of autobiographical significance. The longest (and most intricate) excursus in the essay examines the relationship between overlapping prayers that are ascribed, in discrete iterations, to Zerahyah, Hippocrates, and Socrates.

Moshe Idel offers a map of a little-known development in 'Prophets and Their Impact in the High Middle Ages: A Subculture of Franco-German Jewry', an essay that consolidates and analyses sources that pertain to Jewish prophetic figures, prophetic techniques, and prophetic practices between 1150 and 1300. Idel explains that the phenomenon in question differed from other types of medieval Jewish prophecy in its focus on the prophet's actual voice as the medium of revelation. Though rabbinic tradition had proclaimed the cessation of prophecy following the destruction of the Temple, the medieval Jews involved in this phenomenon reinterpreted those teachings. Their affirmation of the ongoing vitality of prophecy relied heavily on the writings of Sa'adyah Gaon, which supplied scaffolding for the theological notion of immanentism, the belief that God is found in all. Idel identifies this phenomenon as a product of Franco-Germany that made its way to the Iberian territories of Catalonia and Castile.

The essay presents testimonies about the techniques employed by some of the eleven prophetic figures identified, and about the social settings in which these were used. Sources describe a range of esoteric practices that were intended to induce clairvoyance, facilitate divination, or enrol the help of higher powers through recitation of names or through exegetical tactics. Most striking are the descriptions of homilies given by prophets in Ashkenazi synagogues. According to Idel, the presence of other learned men on these occasions triggered collective prophetic experiences. He emphasizes that the human voice was all-important in such instances: through loud prayer, Israel was understood to effect God's coronation, and, in the fullness of time, God would return the crown to his people.

Idel traces this medieval phenomenon to rabbinic teachings about the annual appearance of the prophet Elijah on Yom Kippur, and he tracks its spread to other lands, through the travels of Ashkenazi prophets in the mid-thirteenth century and the circulation of the fourteenth-century law code, the *Arba'ah turim*. He discerns the influence of north European prophetism in several south European developments: the prophetic approach of Abraham Abulafia, R. Solomon ben Adret's critique of the Prophet of Avila, and the rise of messianism in Castile, Catalonia, and Sicily. Idel suggests that the gematria-laden exegeses of the prophetic sermons may have had an indirect effect on Spanish kabbalistic writings, though these exploited the symbolic use of numbers. The mediating link, he posits, was Ashkenazi Bible commentaries of the thirteenth century that relied on gematria and other 'radical hermeneutical forms'. Idel also hypothesizes that the importance of homilies in the Zohar may be linked to the sermonic component of Ashkenazi prophetism.

*

Historical sources and other Jewish writings create the impression that medieval Jews knew that there were acceptable 'ways of being Jewish' that were other than their own. Was there any counterpart, in the Middle Ages, to this allowance for diversity within a faith community?

Latin Christians of the West and Byzantine Christians of the East regarded one another as schismatics, and engaged in reciprocal acts of excommunication. Within the Catholic Church, deliberations over dogma and practice determined the boundaries between orthodoxy and heresy. Of course significant differences in identity distinguished medieval Christians of discrete regions; these found expression in their disparate languages, foods, and styles of clothing,[17] and in their distinctive styles of painting, architecture, literature, music, and at times even theological orientation. Yet, as groupings, these highly perceptible regional identities do not seem to be categorically akin to Jewish subcultures.

[17] In his study of ethnicity, Fredrik Barth refers to certain cultural diacritica as 'the non-articulating sectors of life'; *Ethnic Groups and Boundaries*, 32.

The Islamic world offers a different canvas for comparison. From the eighth century to the present, Muslims have acknowledged the existence of multiple *madhāhib* (schools of jurisprudence) and have accepted that their disparate rulings are of equal validity. Unlike Jewish subcultures, however, these schools are associated only with law, and not with other cultural areas. (This may explain one scholar's—contested—suggestion that Karaites and Rabbanites be thought of as Jewish *madhāhib*.)[18]

Apart from asking whether Jewish subcultures were unique groupings in the medieval world, the search for parallels or comparisons highlights the murkiness of the very category around which this volume is centred. Terms such as 'regional identity', 'ethnicity', and 'subculture' may be understood from context, but none is precise, and each, in its own way, falls short of describing the phenomenon in question.

Many problems of methodology[19] that have been sidestepped here are treated in more general studies of ethnicity,[20] ethnogenesis,[21] and ethnohistory;[22] these consider, among other things, the role that 'ecological' adaptation plays in group definition and in the assignment of nomenclature.[23] At the same time, the present collection takes an important first stride, raising anew questions about origins and transformations. Its constituent essays break new ground, some in their reliance on underexplored, or until recently unknown, data from the Cairo Genizah and other manuscript collections; others in foregrounding matters of gender. The essays in this volume, together with other studies of premodern Jewish subcultures, point to many other topics that warrant further scrutiny in conversation with historians, anthropologists, and sociologists who explore the formation and re-formation of group identities.

[18] Rustow, *Heresy and the Politics of Community*, pp. xxviii–xxix. This framing was subjected to criticism in Polliack, 'The Karaite Inversion of "Written" and "Oral" Torah', 283–4.

[19] Different approaches to the study of ethnicity are reviewed and criticized in Heather, 'Ethnicity, Group Identity and Social Status'.

[20] See e.g. Barth, *Ethnic Groups and Boundaries*; Wimmer, *Ethnic Boundary Making*.

[21] On the process of ethnogenesis and the manners in which it was portrayed in antiquity see Geary, *Myth of Nations*, 44; cf. Heather, 'Ethnicity, Group Identity and Social Status'.

[22] Ethnohistory chronicles cultural accretion and change; it attempts to explain why certain cultural elements were borrowed or appropriated when they were. See Geary, *Myth of Nations*; Heather, 'Ethnicity, Group Identity and Social Status'; and Barth, *Ethnic Groups and Boundaries*, 12.

[23] Noting that ecology is 'the history of adaptation to an environment', Barth (*Ethnic Groups and Boundaries*, 12–13) uses the term 'ecological circumstances' to explain why people of a single ethnic group who share a cultural tradition but live in different places present different characteristics.

Bibliography

ASSAF, SIMHA, 'Babylonia and the Land of Israel in the Era of the Geonim' (Heb.), *Hashilo'aḥ*, 34–35 (1918), 286–95, 442–52.

—— and L. A. MAYER (eds.), *Sefer hayishuv*, vol. ii (Jerusalem, 1944).

BARTH, FREDRIK, *Ethnic Groups and Boundaries: The Social Organization of Culture Difference* (Long Grove, Ill., 1969).

BERNFELD, SHIMON, 'The Land of Israel and Babylonia' (Heb.), *Hashilo'aḥ*, 4 (1898), 289–302.

BLOCH, MARC, *The Historian's Craft*, trans. Peter Putnam (New York, 1953).

DAVIS, JOSEPH, 'The Reception of the Shulhan 'Arukh and the Formation of Ashkenazic Identity', *AJS Review*, 26/2 (2002), 251–76.

FLEISCHER, EZRA, *Hebrew Liturgical Poetry in the Middle Ages* [Shirat hakodesh biyemei habeinayim] (Jerusalem, 1975).

GEARY, PATRICK, *Myth of Nations: The Medieval Origins of Europe* (Princeton, NJ, 2002).

GOLDBERG, SYLVIE ANNE, *Crossing the Jabbok: Illness and Death in Ashkenazi Judaism in Sixteenth- through Nineteenth-Century Prague*, trans. C. Cosman (Berkeley, Calif., 1996).

GROSSMAN, AVRAHAM, 'The Relationship of Early Ashkenazi Jewry to the Land of Israel' (Heb.), *Shalem*, 3 (1981), 57–92.

HEATHER, PETER, 'Ethnicity, Group Identity and Social Status', in I. Garipazanov, P. Geary, and P. Urbanczyk (eds.), *Franks, Northmen and Slavs: Identity and State Formation in Early Medieval Europe* (Turnhout, 2008), 17–49.

Megilat aḥima'ats, ed., with afterword, Benjamin Klar (Jerusalem, 1944).

POLLIACK, MEIRA, 'The Karaite Inversion of "Written" and "Oral" Torah', *Jewish Studies Quarterly*, 22 (2015), 243–302.

RAY, JONATHAN, *After Expulsion: 1492 and the Making of Sephardic Jewry* (New York, 2013).

—— *The Sephardic Frontier: The Reconquista and the Jewish Community in Medieval Iberia* (Ithaca, NY, 2006).

RUSTOW, MARINA, *Heresy and the Politics of Community: The Jews of the Fatimid Caliphate* (Ithaca, NY, 2008).

SOLOVEITCHIK, HAYM, *Wine in Ashkenaz in the Middle Ages: Yeyn Nesekh—a Study in the History of Halakhah* [Hayayin biyemei habeinayim: yein nesekh—perek betoledot hahalakhah be'ashkenaz] (Jerusalem, 2008).

WIMMER, ANDREAS, *Ethnic Boundary Making: Institutions, Power, Networks* (Oxford, 2013).

ZIMMELS, HIRSCH JAKOB, *Ashkenazim and Sephardim: Their Relations, Differences and Problems as Reflected in the Rabbinical Responsa*, 3rd edn. (London, 1976).

PART I

Identity Claims

CHAPTER ONE

The Emergence of the Medieval Jewish Diaspora(s) of Europe from the Ninth to the Twelfth Centuries, with Some Thoughts on Historical DNA Studies

MICHAEL TOCH

INTRODUCTION

Continuously debated from the nineteenth century onwards, the genealogy of the European Jewish diaspora has been relevant to the concerns of Jews and non-Jews alike. Were the different constituents of this diaspora part of one Jewish people, or were they, rather, distinct cultures to begin with? Can a single thread of origin be detected for the Jews living in different parts of Europe? From what chronological point were Jews found in their countries of residence? Were their settlements as old as those of their non-Jewish neighbours, or were they newcomers (and thus, perhaps, less deserving of 'full citizenship')? What is the weight of non-Jewish origins, as in the case of the Khazars, reputed by some to be the forefathers of Ashkenazi Jewry? How central are such considerations to the self-image of Jews, or to the ways in which others perceive them?

Informed answers to these large questions (and others) require a return to the issues of origins, migrations, and the chronology of settlement, which in turn have a bearing on the topic of Jewish–Christian relations. Is anti-Judaism an essential constituent of European culture, or rather a historically contingent development? Later stages of Jewish existence in medieval Europe were clearly marked by Christian hostility, but was this also true of earlier stages? This essay explores the available evidence, taking recent DNA studies into consideration.

The above questions have engaged the attention of historians for a long while. Over time, specialists in economics, Yiddish linguistics, halakhah, and other fields have joined the discussion, and, most recently, scholars of historical genetics. The topic has also aroused the interest of individuals who might charitably be called 'non-professionals': publicists and writers of different persuasions, often with clearly visible axes to grind. It would seem that some professional historians also have their agendas, even if these are more difficult to make out.

By now there exists a 'majority view' on the origins of European Jewry, to wit: the Jewish nuclei of medieval Europe defined themselves religiously, culturally, and linguistically as parts of the broader entity of a Jewish people that was historically anchored in the ancient Middle East.[1] Against this mainstream approach, a persistent contrarian strain postulates non-Jewish origins for both Ashkenazi and Sephardi Jews, claiming that medieval communities consisted mainly of converts from other faiths, most notably the Khazars.[2] A similar assertion has been made for the Jewish communities of central and northern France, where converts of late antiquity and the early Middle Ages were thought to have been numerous enough to produce the substantial Jewish population that came into view in the eleventh century.[3]

Running parallel to this mainstream–fringe dichotomy of views on the origins of European Jews, there is a similar one concerning the dating of their settlement. Most scholars, myself included, see the Jewries of northern Europe as recent arrivals, that is, from the ninth and tenth centuries; they cannot be presumed to be the descendants of Jews of late antiquity, whose presence in northern Europe is hazy (and sparsely attested). The Jews of the Mediterranean south, by contrast, are seen to possess a much longer history; Italian Jewry has been described as a population that 'has lived in one of the Diaspora countries for a millennium or more'.[4] This statement can also be made of Byzantine Jews; indeed, there is a considerable overlap between the two groups in most regions of southern Italy. In contrast to this majority view

[1] A convenient but somewhat dated presentation of this majority view is found in Roth (ed.), *The World History of the Jewish People*, ii: *The Dark Ages*.

[2] In place of the huge and usually contentious literature on the subject see now Golden et al. (eds.), *The World of the Khazars*. For Yitzhak Schipper's hypothesis on the Khazar origins of Polish Jewry and its scholarly criticism, see the sympathetic account by Litman, *The Economic Role of Jews in Medieval Poland*. For a linguistic reworking of this notion see Wexler, *The Ashkenazic Jews*. Yet one more polemic denying Jewish nationhood, ostensibly on Khazar grounds, is Sand, *The Invention of the Jewish People*. For the agendas of contemporary eastern European proponents of the Khazar thesis see Shnirelman, 'The Story of a Euphemism', 353–72. For the Israeli polemic see Penslar, 'Discussion: "When and How Was the Jewish People Invented?"' (Heb.).

[3] Bautier, 'L'Origine des populations juives de la France médiévale'.

[4] Gil, *Jews in Islamic Countries in the Middle Ages*, 579.

there is a different perspective, dating back to the nineteenth century and recently expressed with renewed vigour, which claims a significant continuity of Jewish presence not only in Mediterranean lands, but also in territories north of the Alps—in northern Gaul and even in Germany. Here, too, present-day concerns can be discerned behind scholarly claims. The desire to present the city of Cologne as 'the cradle of Ashkenazi Jewry' in a yet-to-be-built Jewish museum (that might anticipate a torrent of Jewish tourists) is one such example.[5] A less disturbing assertion is that the sudden bloom of cultural creativity in twelfth- and thirteenth-century Normandy must necessarily be explained by 'a lengthy prehistory of Jewish settlement and legal rights . . . apparently beginning during the period of Roman colonization of Gaul'.[6] There is little to no evidence for either claim.

I

A short sketch of the political and economic background of Europe may help set up the essential timeline. All regions of Mediterranean Europe (Byzantium, Italy, southern France, and Iberia) experienced an economic and demographic crisis between the sixth and eighth centuries, in which the prime victim was the urban population—which included Jews. By contrast, from the ninth century onwards, and, in some places, from the tenth, each region witnessed demographic and economic recovery in different ways, sometimes slow and sometimes more rapid.[7] Viewed through the lens of political geography, this period corresponds to the mid-Carolingian period in France, northern Italy, and Catalonia, to the period of the Byzantine *reconquista* in the Mediterranean, and to the formation of a Muslim state in Iberia. In terms of settlement structure, it was the time of hesitant re-urbanization in the south (as in the cases of Venice and Amalfi), and of entirely new semi-urban and urban formations in the north. This can be seen, for example, in the numerous commercial *wik* settlements on the north-western seaboard and in England. It seems that Jews, along with other urban and commercial groups, had little incentive to settle or expand in the crisis-ridden European regions of the first medieval centuries, and very good reasons to do so from the ninth century onwards. This is indeed the picture that detailed examination of the evidence has found for this period: a double movement—repopulation in the south and

[5] For details and critique see Toch, *The Economic History of European Jews*, 295–8.

[6] Golb, *The Jews in Medieval Normandy*, 33; for a reasoned critique see Toch, *The Economic History of European Jews*, 305–6.

[7] Among the vast literature see McCormick, *Origins of the European Economy*.

immigration to the north.[8] Except for Iberia, I have not found evidence for the migratory moves from the Islamic world into Europe that have been alleged in a recent book.[9]

In more detail, the history of Jewish settlement in the different regions of late antique and early medieval Europe can be characterized as follows:[10] under ancient Roman rule Jews became a significant ingredient of some town populations of the Eastern Empire (later Byzantium). Of the 100 sites of archaeological evidence for Jewish life in the Balkans, Greece, and Asia Minor, more than half are on, or near, the shores of the Mediterranean and the Black Sea, or on islands in the Mediterranean. Of the inland archaeological sites, the large majority are in Asia Minor, mostly on the ancient trans-Anatolian highway leading from Smyrna (Izmir) and Ephesus on the Aegean coast to Mesopotamia, by way of Iconium (Konya). Though the archaeological evidence is considerable, it in no way supports the still-held belief in a vast Jewish population in the late antique Roman empire—a notion that has lately come under well-deserved criticism.[11]

Both in the number of communities and in geographical scope, Jewish settlement in medieval Byzantium was still much below its zenith in late antiquity. As for the earlier medieval period (sixth to ninth centuries), it is difficult to decide whether it reflects an actual demographic low, or only a dearth of sources. I tend to accept the first view. In the tenth to twelfth centuries, there appear to have been half as many Jews in the region as there were in late antiquity. Still, given the earlier premise—of a dramatic drop in the Jewish population, along with those of other urban and commercial groups in the sixth to eighth centuries—this ratio might also imply remarkable recovery. The evidence bears witness to a further distinctive and apparently persistent feature: the patterns of geographical migration among Jews in Byzantium. Two basic demographic phenomena mark Byzantine Jewry. Firstly, Jewish presence in the Eastern Empire was continuous from late antiquity into the High Middle Ages, ebbing and surging at a pace apparently consistent with that of the population at large. Secondly, there was a migratory flow and geo-

[8] Toch, *The Economic History of European Jews*, *passim*.

[9] Botticini and Eckstein, *The Chosen Few*, 173–5.

[10] For details and references the reader is directed to the chapters making up the first part and the appendices of Toch, *The Economic History of European Jews*, where the evidence for each place of settlement is laid out and critically appraised.

[11] Wasserstein, 'The Number and Provenance of Jews in Graeco-Roman Antiquity'; McGing, 'Population and Proselytism'. For the historiographical context see the aptly titled study by Kraabel, 'The Roman Diaspora'.

graphical dissemination of Jews throughout the realm of Byzantium. Such movement and communication encompassed not only the whole empire, but also southern Italy, North Africa, and the Middle East—including Palestine and Egypt. Jewish communities in Byzantium maintained some contact with the latter regions even after the Arab conquest and, apparently, with renewed vigour from the late tenth century onwards. The overarching perception is one of ongoing small-scale moves rather than of the 'folk migrations' usually associated with the movement of populations.

Italy presents a complex picture. Home to a sizeable Jewish population in antiquity, particularly in Rome, Italy, too, saw a general decline in Jewish settlement and in numbers at the beginning of the Middle Ages. In only a small minority of locations, such as Rome and some towns in the south, was there a continued Jewish presence into the Middle Ages. A similar disparity between the south and the rest of the country characterized the many places where Jews first settled during the Middle Ages. Until the eleventh century many of these settlements lay in regions ruled by Byzantium. Both culturally and demographically, southern Italian Jewry was greatly influenced by, if not directly derived from, its Byzantine counterpart; to some extent, this was due to migration.

On the Iberian peninsula, the sparse Jewish population of Roman late antiquity seems to have barely survived into subsequent Visigothic times. By contrast, the data available from the late tenth and early eleventh centuries reflect a different order of magnitude, both in the number of places inhabited and in population numbers. This appears to parallel the general upward demographic curve in al-Andalus, and is clearly linked to a more favourable Arab regime and to immigration from North Africa. It is difficult to assess whether the emergent Sephardi Jewry displayed any similarities or continuity with the Jews of the Roman and Visigothic periods, given that little is known about them. In the Christian north, Barcelona and Gerona were the earliest places of residence, dating from the late ninth century, when the Carolingians colonized Catalonia. During the tenth century Jews settled in Leon-Castile's capital, and elsewhere in the region during the eleventh. Jews do not appear to have settled in the kingdoms of Aragon and Navarre prior to the eleventh or early twelfth centuries. The emergence of a highly intolerant Muslim regime in the south of the peninsula caused significant numbers of Jews to flee to the Christian north. According to one opinion, there were also Jewish migrants from France. Population growth apparently reached its apogee towards the end of the thirteenth century and the beginning of the fourteenth, making Iberian Jewry the largest of all Europe.

In fourth-century Gaul, Jews appear to have had a transient presence along the Roman borders, and slightly later in a few other towns as well, primarily in the south. Only in Arles, Narbonne, and possibly Marseilles did Jewish habitation continue without interruption between the ninth and eleventh centuries. As in other parts of Europe, there was considerable overall growth in the post-Carolingian era. The new communities in northern Gaul became the western branch of Ashkenazi Jewry, and were present in Île-de-France, Maine-Anjou, Burgundy, Champagne, Lorraine, and Normandy. As elsewhere, it was during the third quarter of the thirteenth century that the numbers were greatest and the distribution widest. Though this was surely due in some measure to immigration, it is nonetheless difficult to pinpoint; the influx most likely came from the Mediterranean south. There is little room for a hypothesis, raised some years ago, which posited that the French part of Ashkenazi Jewry was composed of the descendants of immigrants from Germany.[12] Given the very small number of Jews in these communities, population expansion can better be explained by internal growth.

In Germany, Jewish life for a long time was a small-scale affair, wholly dependent on immigration. In the ninth century Jewish migrants to Germany cannot have made up more than a few dozen families; in the tenth century they may have numbered a few hundred. In the course of the eleventh century there was a marked growth in the number of Jews, nourished not only by internal demographic growth but by ongoing immigration from France, and to a lesser degree from Italy.[13] It appears that converts from Christianity, though present, contributed only a handful of individuals to the early Jewish population. Over the next 200 years the pace of settlement quickened; by the early fourteenth century the number of locations and the geographical scope of Jewish presence had attained a peak that remained unmatched until the nineteenth century. From the beginning of Jewish settlement to 1348, around 1,000 Jewish communities were established in the different regions that comprised the medieval German empire.

In eastern Europe, the sizeable Roman-era Jewish settlement along the

[12] Schwarzfuchs, 'L'Opposition Tsarfat–Provence'.

[13] See Grossman, *The Early Sages of Ashkenaz* (Heb.), 424–35; id., 'The Relationship of Early Askhenazi Jewry to the Land of Israel' (Heb.); Berger, 'Research on the Early Ashkenazi Rabbinate' (Heb.); Fishman, *Becoming the People of the Talmud*, 91–120. Haym Soloveitchik has now put forward an intriguing hypothesis, claiming the following: 'Given their command of Babylonian Aramaic, their ignorance of and indifference to the [Talmud] Yerushalmi, and their exclusive preoccupation with the Bavli, the founding fathers of Ashkenazic halakhah clearly hailed from Babylonia rather than from Palestine' ('The "Third Yeshivah" of Bavel', 163).

shores of the Danube and the Black Sea did not continue into the early medieval period. The earliest evidence for renewed presence in the tenth and eleventh centuries suggests that it was transient, made up of traders coming mostly from western Germany, and less frequently from the east—the lands of the Turks. These merchants crossed Bohemia, Hungary, and Poland on their way to and from Russia, and some remained active in their lands of origin. A stable community, possibly of Khazar origin, apparently settled in Kiev in the tenth century. In the eleventh century Jews inhabited a few communities in Bohemia, Hungary, and Poland. Outside of these, further settlement did not occur before the twelfth and thirteenth centuries. Eastern Europe was thus populated by Jews considerably later, and at considerably lower density, than all other regions of Europe. The sources tell us little about a possible pre-Ashkenazi stratum, whether Byzantine, Turkish-Khazar, or Slavonic. In the fourteenth century Jews moved more deeply into Slavonic regions from long-settled Bohemia; this was also the case for Jews from Silesia and Pomerania who had migrated eastwards from Germany during the thirteenth century.

II

According to my interpretation, the Middle Ages saw the foundation of two of the three major divisions that make up the Jewish people to this day: Ashkenazim of central and eastern European extraction and Sephardim of Spanish and Portuguese origin, along with later residents of the Ottoman empire from the Balkans to North Africa. Other Jewish groupings predate the Middle Ages; these include parts of Italian Jewry, Yemenite Jews, Jews of the Caucasus area, and the Jewish populations of the Middle East, most notably in Israel-Palestine, Babylonia (Iraq), and Egypt, who were numerically and culturally dominant throughout the Middle Ages. According to established historiography, the cultures and populations of the medieval Jewish diaspora stemmed from religious centres in the Land of Israel-Palestine and in Babylonia. Against this mainstream narrative, which portrays the development of Jewries as an ongoing process, there is a persistent, often polemical narrative that gives pride of place to genetic origins. It postulates non-Jewish origins for both Ashkenazi and Sephardi Jews, claiming that these communities consist mostly or entirely of converts from other faiths or ethnicities, most famously from the long-lost Turkish Khazars of the eighth to tenth centuries. This debate has attained more public presence due to its resonance with contemporary political claims. Shlomo Sand, for example, has of late questioned Ashkenazi origins, and tied this topic to discussions about the legitimacy or illegitimacy of the Jewish claim to the Land of Israel. In the heat of political argument, the issue of Ashkenazi origins has moved from the esoteric fringes into the centre of public disagreement. Other contentions concern the very nature of Judaism and Jewishness: are the Jews a tribe solely defined by descent, or a civilization defined by culture, religion, and history? Such questions have become relevant today among diaspora Jews who are troubled about their own cohesiveness and about their relationship to Israelis at a time when Israeli identity appears to be receding in favour of Jewish identity. Against this backdrop, DNA studies have been embraced as a way to bring an objective perspective to a debate that looks increasingly unmanageable.

A number of questions arise with regard to the migration movements that brought the medieval diaspora into being. Beyond what can be gleaned from the written and archaeological sources, there are many more open problems that might possibly profit from the analysis of DNA data. The following is a list of the most important questions.

1. Was there a continuity of Jewish settlement from Roman late antiquity into the Middle Ages, as is apparent in Byzantium, southern Italy, southern France, and eastern Spain? Or did the European diaspora come into being exclusively through migration?
2. As sketched above, the historical record supports the Jewish settlement of northern Europe by migration. If so, what were the points of origin of the Jews who eventually became Ashkenazi? Textual evidence suggests two routes: one moves from Italy to the Rhine valley and from there into eastern France and central Germany; the other begins in southern France and follows the Rhône river into eastern France and western Germany. Can either or both of these routes be confirmed by genetic evidence?
3. When did the foundational migrations take place, and how large were the populations involved?
4. Where did the Sephardim come from? Though some have claimed continuity from antiquity, I believe that Sephardi Jewry was as much a creation of the Middle Ages as was Ashkenazi Jewry. What remains to be explained is the geographical, and thus also cultural, origins of this population. Can DNA studies confirm my hypothesis that Sephardi Jewry derives, in the main, from North Africa?

5. What was the impact of proselytism, most notably the putative mass influx of the Khazars? More realistically, what was the numerical impact of conversion to Judaism by individuals from different European backgrounds? Can we gauge the impact of apostasy, a phenomenon that runs like a red thread throughout diaspora history, on Jewish demography?
6. It is clear from DNA studies that there are huge differences between the male and female ancestry lines of Jewish populations. Does this data have bearing on the notion, widespread in DNA scholarship, that generally females 'were taken' from non-Jewish populations?
7. Behind most of the genetic history of Jews lurks the question of endogamy versus exogamy. Can DNA studies illuminate this matter and offer clues as to when and how Judaism became a 'closed' demographic system?

These points pose a programme for future research. I have no illusion that I can answer all or even some of the above questions. The sad fact is that DNA studies today are beset with some problematic methodological tendencies. The basic method of historical genetics is to compare a contemporary, living population with a historical population in order to assess whether they are related—and if so, how closely. It is even standard to use 'stand-in populations' in these studies. Thus a contemporary ethnic or national group is allowed to serve as a proxy or surrogate for a historical group that no longer exists. Another problem concerns 'genetic depth': if a specific earlier population can be identified, how far into the past are researchers entitled to search? Is any attention paid to the other populations that came into contact with the one under consideration? Current DNA analysis examines contemporary populations of different Jewish diasporas, asking the participating individuals about their place of origin, that of their parents, and sometimes of their grandparents. The resulting data has been used to construct group categories such as 'Ashkenazi', 'eastern or western Ashkenazi', 'Sephardi', and so on. This practice is said to be based on 'informed consent' and 'self-designation'. One study that attracted a lot of media attention drew its material from a 'sample of 174 males, made up of self-defined Sephardic Jewish males either from the Iberian Peninsula itself or from countries that received major migrations of Sephardic Jews after the expulsion of 1492–1496, as follows: Belmonte [a place in Portugal where a community of crypto-Jews is said to have survived into the twentieth century], Portugal (16); Bulgaria (49); Djerba (13); Greece (2); Spain (3); Turkey (91)'. Sephardi identity was established by an individual's 'self-designation' and by the fact that the individual's parents had resided in a country that had been home to Sephardi exiles some 500 years earlier, in the late fifteenth and early sixteenth centuries. The comparison of the DNA of these subjects to the DNA of today's inhabitants of Iberia led the researchers to conclude that 19.8 per cent of the latter population possess Jewish ancestry.[14] Clearly there is a problem if the study population is sampled in such cavalier fashion. An even more problematic study constructed its target Jewish population by searching DNA databanks for people with ancestors 'bearing first names that appeared to be Jewish, such as Aaron or Avraham, provided that the last names also appeared to be Jewish'.[15] The author, otherwise highly regarded, was unaware of the intensive research carried out on Jewish names by Alexander Beider, for instance, with twenty-five articles between 1991 and 2014. In short, the very question of how one constructs a study population of contemporary Jews is itself problematic.

The identification, framing, and construction of the target historical population of Jews can be even more challenging. The inherent difficulty of this project is exemplified in a recent study (released with media fanfare) which alleged to have definitely clinched the question of the origin of Ashkenazi Jewry, declaring them descendants of the Turkish Khazars.[16] In this study modern Palestinians were deemed to be the descendants of 'proto-Judeans', ancient inhabitants of the region, but not the forebears of modern-day Jews. Contemporary Georgians and Armenians were deemed the descendants of 'proto-Khazars'. As one critic has noted: 'this paper screams of the problem with taking a mass of data and using legitimate methods, and coming out with very specific results because of the way the parameters are set'.[17]

Basic flaws in identifying the make-up of the population to be studied are at times compounded by naive assumptions about historical data and laziness in its treatment. From the DNA study of Iberia quoted before:

> history records that Ibiza, found to have a high apparent Sephardic Jewish ancestry proportion in our study, had an insignificant Jewish population compared to its neighbors, yet had previously been an important Phoenician colony. [This was in the ninth to eighth century BCE!] Likewise, Minorca is recorded as having a substantial Jewish population, yet here, it shows no Sephardic Jewish ancestry.

[14] Adams et al., 'The Genetic Legacy of Religious Diversity and Intolerance'.
[15] Klyosov, 'Origin of the Jews via DNA Genealogy', 61.
[16] Elhaik, 'The Missing Link of Jewish European Ancestry'.
[17] Khan, 'Ashkenazic Jews are Probably not Descended from the Khazars'.

The lone source for these claims is a guidebook for tourists.[18] Only one of over twenty-five DNA studies on the genetic history of Jews went to the trouble of including a historian among its authors. It is unfortunate that many DNA scientists derive their understanding of historical context from the reference works that are most easily accessible—which are often the most superficial and/or outdated. Some reflect views that are glaringly eccentric to most historians. An example is the citation of Shlomo Sand's *Invention of the Jewish People* as a standard reference on the Khazars. In other words, most DNA studies are poorly informed about historical context and sloppy in their construction of populations. Probably most damaging to historically oriented DNA research is the near-total ignorance of the Jewish migration movements of the nineteenth and twentieth centuries. Most contemporary western Ashkenazi Jews are but two generations removed from the eastern Ashkenazi population.[19]

It is hoped that many of these problems will be addressed in future studies. What can the existing body of DNA scholarship contribute to the questions posed above, given the current state of the field? Thanks to the definitive disproval of the Khazar theory by both genetic and historical arguments, the mainstream view of the origins of the Ashkenazi diaspora has been affirmed. Thus, 'DNA analysis of Ashkenazi Jews together with a large sample from the region of the Khazar Khaganate corroborates the earlier results that Ashkenazi Jews derive their ancestry primarily from populations of the Middle East and Europe, that they possess considerable shared ancestry with other Jewish populations, and that there is no indication of a significant genetic contribution either from within or from north of the Caucasus region.'[20] When all is said and done, the accepted wisdom is still acceptable. There is no evidence that Ashkenazi Jews are descended from central Asian 'Jews with swords', and there is every reason to think that they simply came from central Europe.

Once the Khazar theory is discounted there is no evidence for large-scale proselytism that would have added whole ethnicities to European Jewry. This does not mean that there were no proselytes from surrounding populations; however, historical sources teach that these were individuals, not whole populations.

[18] Foss, *Ibiza and Minorca*.

[19] If both my paternal and maternal grandparents arrived in Vienna around 1890, is my DNA to be included in the sample of western Ashkenazi Jewry or does it rather belong somewhere else?

[20] Behar et al., 'No Evidence from Genome-Wide Data of a Khazar Origin for the Ashkenazi Jews'.

Work has been done pertaining to proselytism, gender differences, and the larger questions of endogamy and exogamy. These findings need to be integrated into an—admittedly provisional—historical framework. Most intriguing are the findings concerning maternal ancestry, which can be followed through mitochondrial DNA. Three different studies differ as to paternal ancestry lines, but concur that 'most Jewish communities were founded by relatively few women, that the founding process was independent in different geographical areas, and that subsequent genetic input from surrounding populations was limited on the female side'.[21] One study concludes that 'four founding mtDNAs [mitochondrial DNAs], likely of Near Eastern ancestry, underwent major expansion(s) in Europe within the past millennium'.[22] In contrast to this last point, a third study, the most recent one, maintains that 'all four major founders . . . have maternal ancestry in prehistoric Europe, rather than the Near East or Caucasus'.[23] These are the 'four founding mothers' or matriarchs of Ashkenazi Jewry celebrated by the media a few years ago. The figure four need not be taken literally, but the consequence of these findings is significant. Firstly, they point once again to the very small dimensions of the earliest nucleus of northern European Jewry. Secondly, they provide evidence that no consensus exists yet on the 'gentile' or 'Jewish' character of female ancestry, meaning that the question remains moot as to whether 'many Jewish communities outside Israel were founded by single men who married and converted local women'.[24]

One study has noted a close genetic resemblance between contemporary Ashkenazi Jews and modern Italians, a resemblance that indeed accords with the historical presumption that Ashkenazi Jews started their migrations from Italy, and with historical evidence that conversion to Judaism was common in ancient Rome.[25] The findings of other genetic researchers—that the DNA of most Jews seems to link them with other Jews more than with any other group—have not been disproven.[26]

Not much more can be gained from DNA studies of the last two decades, and we shall have to wait for techniques that allow for finer resolution of temporal and spatial data. The origins of Sephardi Jewry have been the object

[21] Thomas et al., 'Founding Mothers of Jewish Communities'.

[22] Behar et al., 'The Matrilineal Ancestry of Ashkenazi Jewry'.

[23] Costa et al., 'A Substantial Prehistoric European Ancestry'.

[24] *New York Times* headline of 8 Oct. 2013.

[25] Zoossmann-Diskin, 'The Origin of Eastern European Jews'; but see above, n. 10.

[26] Stampfer, 'Are We All Khazars Now?' See also his exhaustive study of the textual evidence, 'Did the Khazars Convert to Judaism?'

of very few studies—actually not more than two, and, as mentioned, both are marred by grave methodological errors. Even less work has been done for other Jewish diasporas. This is yet another area in which the study of Ashkenazi Jewry dominates.

It is evident that DNA studies do not, as yet, provide the master key to historical questions. What can be realistically said today is that 'a major contributing factor to the genetic divergence between Jewish groups may have been admixture with local host populations, while, at the same time, threads of Eastern Mediterranean ancestry remain evident'.[27] Even with DNA studies, Judaism is and remains a largely cultural category. As has been noted, 'Ethnic identity is not essential or primordial; as a component of social identity it is flexible, situational, and may change and develop over time. Ethnicity is not genetic, although groups may identify by kinship ties that are both real and fictitious.'[28] Genetically described populations reflect probabilistic clusters of markers inscribed in human DNA. They are not a concretization of race.

[27] Klitz et al., 'Genetic Differentiation of Jewish Populations'.
[28] Brody and King, 'Genetics and the Archaeology of Ancient Israel'.

Bibliography

ADAMS, SUSAN A., et al., 'The Genetic Legacy of Religious Diversity and Intolerance: Paternal Lineages of Christians, Jews and Muslims in the Iberian Peninsula', *American Journal of Human Genetics*, 83/6 (2008), 725–36.

BAUTIER, ROBERT-HENRI, 'L'Origine des populations juives de la France médiévale: Constations et hypothèse de recherche', in X. Barrai i Altet et al. (eds.), *La Catalogne et la France méridional autour l'an mil* (Barcelona, 1991), 306–16.

BEHAR, DORON, et al., 'The Matrilineal Ancestry of Ashkenazi Jewry: Portrait of a Recent Founder Event', *American Journal of Human Genetics*, 78 (2006), 487–97.

—— et al., 'No Evidence from Genome-Wide Data of a Khazar Origin for the Ashkenazi Jews', Human Biology Open Access Pre-Prints, Paper 41; <http://digitalcommons.wayne.edu/humbiol_preprints/41>.

BERGER, DAVID, 'Research on the Early Ashkenazi Rabbinate' (Heb.), *Tarbiz*, 53 (1984), 479–87.

BOTTICINI, MARISTELLA, and ZVI ECKSTEIN, *The Chosen Few: How Education Shaped Jewish History, 70–1492* (Princeton, 2012).

BRODY, AARON J., and ROY J. KING, 'Genetics and the Archaeology of Ancient Israel', *Human Biology Open Access Pre-Prints,* Paper 44, <http://digitalcommons.wayne.edu/humbiol_preprints/44>.

COSTA, MARTA D., et al., 'A Substantial Prehistoric European Ancestry amongst Ashkenazi Maternal Lineages', *Nature Communications*, 8 Oct. 2013, DOI: 10.1038/ncomms3543.

ELHAIK, ERAN, 'The Missing Link of Jewish European Ancestry: Contrasting the Rhineland and the Khazarian Hypotheses', *Genome Biology and Evolution*, 5 (2013), 61–74.

FISHMAN, TALYA, *Becoming the People of the Talmud: Oral Torah as Written Tradition in Medieval Jewish Cultures* (Philadelphia, 2011).

FOSS, ARTHUR, *Ibiza and Minorca* (London, 1975).

GIL, MOSHE, *Jews in Islamic Countries in the Middle Ages* (Leiden, 2004).

GOLB, NORMAN, *The Jews in Medieval Normandy* (Cambridge, 1998).

GOLDEN, P. B., et al. (eds.), *The World of the Khazars: New Perspectives* (Leiden, 2007).

GROSSMAN, AVRAHAM, *The Early Sages of Ashkenaz: Their Lives, Leadership and Works (900–1096)* [Ḥakhmei ashkenaz harishonim: koroteihem, darkam behanhagat hatsibur, yetsiratam haruḥanit mereshit yeshivatam ve'ad ligezerat tatnu (1096)] (Jerusalem, 1981).

——'The Relationship of Early Askhenazi Jewry to the Land of Israel' (Heb.), *Shalem*, 3 (1981), 57–92.

KHAN, RAZIB, 'Ashkenazic Jews Are Probably Not Descended From The Khazars', *Discover*, 8 Aug. 2012.

KLITZ, W., et al., 'Genetic Differentiation of Jewish Populations', *Tissue Antigens*, 76 (2010), 442–58.

KLYOSOV, ANATOLE A., 'Origin of the Jews via DNA Genealogy', *Proceedings of the Russian Academy of DNA Genealogy*, 1 (2008), 54–232.

KRAABEL, ALF THOMAS, 'The Roman Diaspora: Six Questionable Assumptions', *Journal of Jewish Studies*, 33 (1982), 445–64.

LITMAN, JACOB, *The Economic Role of Jews in Medieval Poland: The Contribution of Yitzhak Schipper* (Lanham, Md., 1984).

MCCORMICK, MICHAEL, *Origins of the European Economy: Communications and Commerce AD 300–900* (Cambridge, 2002).

MCGING, BRIAN, 'Population and Proselytism: How Many Jews Were There in the Ancient World?', in John Raymond Bartlett (ed.), *Jews in the Hellenistic and Roman Cities* (New York, 2002), 88–106.

PENSLAR, DEREK, 'Discussion: "When and How Was the Jewish People Invented?" and the End of the New History' (Heb.), *Zion*, 76 (2011), 481–506.

ROTH, CECIL, (ed.), *The World History of the Jewish People*, 2nd series, vol. ii: *The Dark Ages* (Tel Aviv, 1966).

SAND, SHLOMO, *The Invention of the Jewish People* (London, 2009).

SCHWARZFUCHS, SIMON, 'L'Opposition Tsarfat–Provence: La Formation du Judaïsme du Nord de la France', in Gérard Nahon and Charles Touati (eds.), *Hommage à Georges Vajda* (Louvain, 1980), 135–50.

SHNIRELMAN, VICTOR, 'The Story of a Euphemism: The Khazars in Russian Nationalist Literature', in P. B. Golden et al. (eds.), *The World of the Khazars: New Perspectives* (Leiden, 2007), 353–72.

SOLOVEITCHIK, HAYM, 'The "Third Yeshivah" of Bavel and the Cultural Origins of Ashkenaz—A Proposal', in id., *Collected Essays*, vol. ii (Oxford, 2015), 150–201.

STAMPFER, SHAUL, 'Are We All Khazars Now?', *Jewish Review of Books* (Spring 2014), last page.

—— 'Did the Khazars Convert to Judaism?', *Jewish Social Studies*, 19/3 (Spring/Summer 2013), 1–72.

THOMAS, MARK G., et al., 'Founding Mothers of Jewish Communities: Geographically Separated Jewish Groups were Independently Founded by Very Few Female Ancestors', *American Journal of Human Genetics*, 70 (2002), 1411–20.

TOCH, MICHAEL, *The Economic History of European Jews: Late Antiquity and Early Middle Ages* (Leiden, 2012).

WASSERSTEIN, ABRAHAM, 'The Number and Provenance of Jews in Graeco-Roman Antiquity: A Note on Population Statistics', in Ranon Katzoff (ed.), *Classical Studies in Honor of David Sohlberg* (Ramat Gan, 1996), 307–17.

WEXLER, PAUL, *The Ashkenazic Jews: A Slavo-Turkic People in Search of a Jewish Identity* (Columbus, Ohio, 1993).

ZOOSSMANN-DISKIN, AVSHALOM, 'The Origin of Eastern European Jews Revealed by Autosomal, Sex Chromosomal and mtDNA Polymorphisms', *Biology Direct*, 5/57 (2010), DOI: 10.1186/1745-6150-5-57.

CHAPTER TWO

Medieval Jewish Legends on the Decline of the Babylonian Centre and the Primacy of Other Geographical Centres

AVRAHAM GROSSMAN

During the eleventh and twelfth centuries the Babylonian centre of Jewish study gradually went into decline and Jewish centres in Christian Europe grew stronger, particularly in France, Germany, Spain, and Provence. As was customary in contemporaneous Christian societies, Jews sought reasons to extol the virtues of their own locale. Inasmuch as individuals in medieval societies felt the need to belong to an ancient sacred tradition, various centres in Christian Europe sought to establish a connection to the charismatic Charlemagne,[1] and cities and countries in the Islamic world also produced literatures praising their region. The eleventh-century legends and folk tales extolling the virtues of different Jewish centres in Europe may be set within this context, and against the backdrop of the decline of the Babylonian centre following the death of R. Hai Gaon (1038). Rivalry between Spain and Ashkenaz was especially fierce at this time, with each centre striving to outdo the other.

SPAIN

Spanish Jewish scholars claimed that the decline of the Babylonian centre was the result of the same divine decree that had designated Spain as its successor. Making good use of the verse in Obadiah (1: 20) concerning 'the exiles from Jerusalem who are in Sepharad', they identified Sepharad with Spain, and claimed that it was chosen from among all the lands of Jewish exile because Jewish inhabitants of Jerusalem had reached Spain as early as the First Temple period. As R. Samuel Hanagid claimed, 'Sepharad has been a place of Torah study from the time of the First Temple and the exile of Jerusalem to

[1] Folz, *Le Souvenir et la légende de Charlemagne*.

this day.'[2] This argument was bolstered by the fact that the Aramaic translation of that verse identifies Sepharad as Aspamia (Aramaic for the Latin Hispania), and other medieval centres of Jewish life accepted this identification without question. Comparison of two commentaries on the verse in Obadiah, that of Abraham Ibn Ezra—who praises Spain—and that of Rashi, who is forced to concede Spain's superiority, indicates that this source was used effectively to extol the pre-eminence of Spanish Jewry.

The well-known story of the four captives in R. Abraham Ibn Daud's *Sefer hakabalah* (1160) recounts the fate of four eminent Torah scholars who were taken captive after setting sail from Italy and sold to Jewish communities in Egypt, Spain, and North Africa, where they proceeded to teach Torah. The narrator ascribes the events to a heavenly design, aimed at transferring elsewhere the centre of Jewish learning that had been based in Babylonia. The story lavishes praise on one of the captives, R. Moses ben Hanokh, and stresses his meteoric rise in Spain, a land said to have been devoid of Torah study for many generations. Ibn Daud was prepared to portray Spanish Jewry as having been ignorant and lacking in any Torah learning in the early Middle Ages before the arrival of R. Moses ben Hanokh from Italy, where his family had long resided, for a claim to rapid transformation in this arena bore rhetorical witness to an act of providence. Whether or not the chronicler fabricated this detail, descendants of R. Moses who were familiar with their own family history were still living in Spain in Ibn Daud's time.

Other traditions in Spain reflected a contrary agenda: by portraying Spanish Jews as having gained their knowledge directly from the exiles of Jerusalem, these narratives sought to present Spain as a divinely chosen place from time immemorial, and as one that needed neither Babylonia nor Italy. Yet the historical truth is that the Jewish intellectual centre in Spain underwent rapid growth in the time of R. Hisdai Ibn Shaprut, in the mid-tenth century.

R. Samuel Hanagid relayed the tradition that Jewish scholars of Spain had received their knowledge from R. Natronai Gaon of Babylonia: 'It was he who wrote down the Talmud for the scholars of Spain without consulting a book.'[3] A similar legend was repeated by R. Judah al-Barceloni: 'A well-known tradition in Spain, handed down by their fathers, is that R. Natronai Gaon, of blessed memory, came to them from Babylonia by "shortening the way" [*kefitsat haderekh*]. He taught them Torah and then returned; he came

[2] The *nagid*'s words are quoted by R. Judah ben Barzilai of Barcelona in *Sefer ha'itim*, 267.

[3] *Sefer hilkhot hanagid*, ed. Margaliot, 2.

not by convoy, nor was he seen along the way.'[4] The Jews of Spain adduced this tale not only to highlight their connection to the centre in Babylonia, but also to emphasize the miracles that were performed for R. Natronai. The claim that founders of the Jewish community in Spain had arrived there in the First Temple period served to counter the Babylonian scholars' claim that they themselves were descendants of the exiles of Jerusalem in the time of King Yehoyakim.

As late as the fifteenth century, R. Isaac Abravanel, following R. Abraham Ibn Ezra, claimed that the prestigious families of Spanish Jewry outnumbered the members of the exilarch's family in Babylonia, descendants of King David. According to him, the exilarch's family was 'not numerous, but [they were] special people'. Abravanel also cited a leading eleventh-century Spanish scholar, R. Isaac Ibn Ghiyyat, as having said that 'two families of the line of King David' had come to Spain and grown in number; Abravanel emphasized that his own family was one of them.[5]

Offering an interesting explanation for the superiority of Spanish Jewry in rhetoric and for the beauty of the poetry it produced, R. Moses Ibn Ezra described these as their heritage from the Land of Israel. While Jews in other medieval centres were descendants of exiles from other cities and villages, those of Spain were the descendants of exiles from Jerusalem itself:

> There is no doubt that inhabitants of Jerusalem, to whom we, the diaspora of Spain, trace our ancestry, were exceptionally skilled at dazzling language, and [were] experts in the science of rhetoric, more so than inhabitants of other towns and villages . . . Another verse hints at this very clearly . . . 'The law will go forth from Zion and the word of God from Jerusalem' [Isa. 2: 3].[6]

ITALY

The Jewish sages of Italy underscored their deep attachment to the Land of Israel by referring to the many Jews who had been exiled from Jerusalem to cities in Italy. The *Chronicle of Aḥima'ats* (1054) characterizes some of these exiles as 'Torah scholars, the wise and learned', as mystics, and as outstanding composers of liturgical poetry whose *piyutim* are included in the prayer book. The point of these claims is that the exiles who came to Italy belonged to the upper crust of the ancient population of Jerusalem—a claim that echoed in

[4] *Commentary on Sefer yetsirah* (Heb.), 150. [5] Abarbanel, commentary on Zech. 12: 7.

[6] Ibn Ezra, *Shirat yisra'el*, 62. I have presented herein some of the legends and traditions recounted by the sages of Spain. For more see Beinart, '¿Cuando llegaron los judíos a España?'

the foundation traditions of Spanish Jewry.[7] The French Tosafist R. Jacob Tam quoted a well-known saying among Italian Jews: 'The law will go forth from Bari, and the word of God from Otranto'. Playing on Isaiah 2: 3, 'The law will go forth from Zion, and the word of God from Jerusalem', this formulation portrays Italy as the centre of Jewish life following the destruction of Jerusalem.

The *Chronicle of Aḥima'ats* also stresses the attachment of this Jewish population to the academies of the Babylonian geonim. Sources attesting to these ties were collected by Benjamin Klar, and additional sources have been found since.[8] According to one legend, Abu Aaron, son of the Babylonian exilarch, came to Italy and established an academy called the Sanhedrin Yeshiva; from here his teachings spread among the sages of Italy. This narrative indicates that Italy was chosen from among the other medieval Jewish centres as the place of exile and haven for the son of the Babylonian exilarch; in this sense it was second only to Babylonia. It is no coincidence that the Jews of Italy underscored their affiliation with both famed centres of Judaism of a previous era, the Land of Israel and Babylonia. These claims implied that Italian Jewry was intimately connected to all the ancient sources of the Jewish people. Consequently it had no need to draw directly upon the spiritual heritage of either historic centre, since it had its own sacred, ancient, and illustrious traditions.

The centre in Italy was much admired by Ashkenazi Jewry as well. As early as the eleventh or early twelfth century, the scholars of Ashkenaz consulted those of Italy regarding the Ordinance of Restricted Residence (*ḥerem hayishuv*). The Tosafists had great respect for the erudition of R. Hananel of North Africa because, among other things, he had acquired knowledge from the scholars of Italy. Over the twelfth century this regard gradually diminished.

[7] Abraham Schechter believed that Babylonia and Italy competed for intellectual hegemony in the 10th and early 11th centuries, but there is no real proof of this; see Schechter, *Studies in Jewish Liturgy*. Reuven Bonfil, in 'Between Erets Yisra'el and Babylonia' (Heb.), suggests that in Italy primacy passed from the Land of Israel to Babylonia in the mid-9th century. I am of the opinion that this development took place in the course of the 10th century, since at the end of the 9th century the Babylonian Talmud had not yet entered Jewish works in Italy. See, too, Bonfil, *History and Folklore in a Medieval Jewish Chronicle*, ch. 2; Grossman, 'When Did the Hegemony of Erets Yisra'el Cease in Italy?' (Heb.).

[8] *Megilat aḥima'ats*, ed. Klar, 45–50. See, too, the original in an Oxford manuscript on the sages of Italy who studied at the academy of R. Hai Gaon in Pumbedita: Bodleian MS 1101, fo. 184*a*; Neubauer, 'Ancient Words from Oxford' (Heb.), 41.

ASHKENAZ

The Pietists (*ḥasidim*) of Ashkenaz traced their mystical traditions to Abu Aaron, son of R. Samuel Hanasi of Babylonia. According to them, when Abu Aaron came to Lucca, Italy, he revealed 'all his secrets' to a certain R. Moses, who subsequently emigrated to Germany.[9] This version of the legend reflects an earlier tradition of Italian Jews, which traces their sacred leader's migration from Babylonia to Ashkenaz, a centre more worthy than any other of continuing the Jewish mystical tradition. According to another Pietist tradition in Ashkenaz, R. Gershom Me'or Hagolah had gained his knowledge from R. Hai Gaon.[10] There is no hint of this claim in any of R. Gershom's own writings; his teacher and mentor, he clearly states, was R. Leontine.[11]

According to another legend designed to legitimate the religious and intellectual heritage of Ashkenaz, R. Gershom had married R. Hai Gaon's sister.[12] Claims of this sort are found in other traditions as well.[13] One, which tells of mass immigration from Persia (including Babylonia) to Ashkenaz in the wake of the Islamic conquest, lacks historical basis but is designed to link Ashkenazi Jewry to the illustrious heritage of Babylonian Jewry.

According to a different legendary tradition, R. Meshulam of Ashkenaz went to Babylonia and visited the head of the academy at his home. When the visitor turned out to be more erudite in Torah than his host, the latter offered his daughter's hand to him in marriage. R. Meshulam declined, however; he returned to Germany and became a leader of the community.[14] While the first two traditions proudly portrayed German Jewry as linked to the Babylonian community, this last legend depicts it as superior to that of Babylonia. In the eleventh or early twelfth century a fierce dispute erupted over the wording of the blessing to be recited at the betrothal ceremony, with each side tenaciously defending its own custom, perceived as sacred and ancient. We see, then, that the legends of foundation and primacy had practical ramifications as well.

Three medieval traditions link the Jews of northern France to Babylonia. The first depicts R. Elijah ben Menahem of Le Mans as having been chosen

[9] This tradition is cited and discussed in Dan, *The Esoteric Theology of Ashkenazi Hasidim* (Heb.), 14–20.

[10] Cited by R. Solomon Luria in a responsum (*She'elot uteshuvot maharshal*, no. 29).

[11] See ibid. for the tradition that R. Gershom had studied with R. Hai; for his studies with R. Leontine see Grossman, *The Early Sages of Ashkenaz* (Heb.), 113–16.

[12] Zimmer, 'R. Azriel Trabot's *Sefer haposekim*' (Heb.), 245.

[13] See e.g. Duby, *Les Trois Ordres*; Heers, *Le Clan familial au Moyen Age*.

[14] Zfatman, *The Jewish Tale in the Middle Ages* (Heb.), 97–111.

by God to succeed R. Hai Gaon of Babylonia. The author—R. Elijah himself—says that, according to talmudic tradition, in every generation God chooses a worthy leader for the Jewish people to succeed the previous leader. Given his own close relationship with R. Hai, claims R. Elijah, it was he who was worthy of becoming the Gaon's successor. In fact, R. Elijah did visit R. Hai's academy, where the latter bestowed upon him the title of *aluf* (leader).[15] R. Elijah does not allude to any ties with the geonim of the Land of Israel, although he does mention his lengthy stay there, and describes his ascent to the Mount of Olives on the festival of Hoshana Rabah. Nonetheless it is not clear whether ties with the Land of Israel in this period made a convincing claim for the transposition of regional authority.

Another tradition, apparently legendary in nature, recounts that R. Elijah married R. Hai's sister. A third one claims that R. Shemayah Hashoshani went from France to Babylonia, bringing with him ancient prayer rites. Earlier modern scholars believed that the figure in question was a French sage from Soissons; in fact, he was originally from Babylonia or Persia.[16]

Fewer legendary accounts of the grandeur of French Jewry were produced in the second half of the eleventh century. Rashi failed to mention any; he evidently eschewed this cultural practice.

PROVENCE

The Jews of Provence claimed that the founders of their community were linked to Babylonian geonim from the time of Charlemagne. According to their tradition, Charlemagne had petitioned the king of Babylon 'to send a Jew from among the Jews in his land of royal blood, of the House of David', to lead the Jews of Provence. The esteemed R. Makhir, 'great and wise . . . of royal blood, of the House of David', presumably an eighth-century figure, was dispatched. He and his descendants led the Jews of Provence for many generations, and are said to have wielded their influence over other Jewish centres as 'lawmakers and judges all over the world, like the exilarchs'.[17] It is difficult to find even a slim historical basis for statements claiming that a prominent Jew had emigrated from Babylonia to Provence and become a leader of the com-

[15] On the identity of the author and the significance of this source see Grossman, *The Early Sages of France* (Heb.), 88–98.

[16] For a discussion of the man, his origins, his literary legacy, and sources relating to his receiving traditions from the East, see Grossman, *The Early Sages of France* (Heb.), 366–81.

[17] Neubauer, *Mediaeval Jewish Chronicles*, i. 82.

munity. However, distinguished Jewish families of Provence did bear the title 'Prince' (*nasi*). The association of R. Makhir and his descendants with the exilarchs of Babylonia—rather than with the geonim—underscores the attempt to draw a connection to the House of David. This was even a source of pride for R. Menahem Hame'iri (d.1316) in the fourteenth century: 'Pre-eminence passed from one generation to the next . . . this tradition is upheld by the greatest of our princes in Narbonne.'

As in the reference to Charlemagne, the claim to Davidic lineage affirmed the authority and legitimacy of the Provençal Jewish community and its leaders. In Ashkenazi communities the immigration of the founding Kalonymos family was also seen as Charlemagne's doing.[18] Moreover, an Egyptian Jewish tradition preserved in Joseph ben Isaac Sambari's *Divrei yosef* recounts a similar story. At the instigation of the queen, Egypt's king 'sent forth messengers to the land of Babylon with the message: "I have heard that in your kingdom there are Jews of the House of David . . . send me one of them." They sent him a wise man, a descendant of the princes in that land; the king appointed him over Egypt; henceforth was the *negidut* [leadership] established in Egypt.'[19] The striking similarities between this legend—intended to establish the legitimacy of Jewish leadership in Egypt and to extol the virtues of the local community—and the corresponding Provençal one indicate that Jewish foundational myths shared certain themes.

And just as a Provençal legend claims that a Jew had risked his life to save Charlemagne, German Jewish narratives claim that a Jew had risked his own life to save the life of Emperor Otto II during his war against the Saracens in Sicily.[20] The story also appears in the chronicle of Thietmar, bishop of Merseburg between 1009 and 1018.[21] We may presume that these foundational myths are all interconnected, and were influenced by common practice in contemporary European society as well as by the desire to convince non-Jewish neighbours of the ancient origins of the local Jewish community. These legends served a twofold purpose: apart from glorifying the local Jewish centre, they stressed the Jews' loyalty to their land and sovereign—for which they rightly deserved the ruler's protection.

[18] See Grossman, *The Early Sages of Ashkenaz* (Heb.), 29–48.

[19] Sambari, *Sefer divrei yosef*, 139–40.

[20] Grossman, *The Early Sages of Ashkenaz* (Heb.), 36–8.

[21] See Thietmar of Merseburg, *Thietmari Merseburgensis episcopi Chronicon*, 765. Perhaps the tale has some historical basis, since it is unlikely that a bishop would fabricate a story about a Jew risking his life to rescue his Christian sovereign.

CONCLUSION

Several of the foundation legends considered above affirm connections between the newer centres of Jewish learning and the Babylonian geonim, either through teachings or through familial links to R. Hai. Though he represents the last of the geonim, the institution of the geonate actually survived several generations beyond Hai's death. None of these medieval sources attempt to establish links to the geonim of the Land of Israel. While the communities of Spain and Italy do attribute the emergence of their centres to the immigration of Jews from the Land of Israel during the First Temple (Spain) or Second Temple (Italy) period, this motif serves to accentuate their *direct* link to the heritage of Israel as early as Temple times, albeit with no relation whatsoever to medieval reality. The Jewish communities of Babylonia, Spain, and Italy repeatedly reiterated the claim that they had inherited the true, sacred tradition of Israel, specifically that of Jerusalem.[22]

Translated from the Hebrew by Sara Friedman

[22] BT *San.* 38*a*. Cf. the words of Pirkoi ben Baboi in praise of the Babylonian Jews and their learning, describing them as having been exiled to Babylonia twelve years before the destruction of the First Temple: Lewin, 'Genizah Fragments from *Sefer hama'asim*' (Heb.), 394–7.

Bibliography

BEINART, HAIM, '¿Cuando llegaron los judíos a España?', *Estudios*, 3 (1962), 1–32.

BONFIL, ROBERT (Reuven), 'Between Erets Yisra'el and Babylonia' (Heb.), *Shalem*, 5 (1987), 1–30.

—— *History and Folklore in a Medieval Jewish Chronicle* (Leiden, 2009).

DAN, JOSEPH, *The Esoteric Theology of Ashkenazi Hasidim* [Torat hasod shel ḥasidei ashkenaz] (Jerusalem, 1968).

DUBY, GEORGES, *Les Trois Ordres ou l'imaginaire du féodalisme* (Paris, 1978).

FOLZ, ROBERT, *Le Souvenir et la légende de Charlemagne dans l'empire germanique médiéval* (Geneva, 1973).

GROSSMAN, AVRAHAM, *The Early Sages of Ashkenaz: Their Lives, Leadership and Works (900–1096)* [Ḥakhmei ashkenaz harishonim: koroteihem, darkam behanhagat hatsibur, yetsiratam haruḥanit mereshit yeshivatam ve'ad ligezerat tatnu (1096)] (Jerusalem, 1981).

—— *The Early Sages of France: Their Lives, Leadership and Works* [Ḥakhmei tsarfat harishonim: koroteihem, darkam behanhagat hatsibur, yetsiratam haruḥanit] (Jerusalem, 1995).

—— 'When Did the Hegemony of Erets Yisra'el Cease in Italy?' (Heb.), in Ezra Fleischer, Mordechai Friedman, and Joel Kraemer (eds.), *Mas'at Moshe: Studies in Jewish and Islamic Culture, Presented to Moshe Gil* [Masat mosheh: meḥkarim betarbut yisra'el ve'arav mugashim lemosheh gil] (Tel Aviv, 1998), 143–57.

HEERS, JACQUES, *Le Clan familial au Moyen Age* (Paris, 1974).

IBN EZRA, MOSES, *Shirat yisra'el*, ed. Ben-Zion Halper (Jerusalem, 1966/7).

JUDAH BEN BARZILAI OF BARCELONA, *Commentary on Sefer yetsirah* (Heb.), ed. David Kaufmann (Berlin, 1885).

—— *Sefer ha'itim*, ed. I. Shor (Kraków, 1903).

LEWIN, B. M., 'Genizah Fragments from *Sefer hama'asim livenei erets yisra'el*' (Heb.), *Tarbiz*, 2 (1931), 406–10.

LURIA, SOLOMON, *She'elot uteshuvot maharshal* (Jerusalem, 1983).

Megilat aḥima'ats, ed. Benjamin Klar (Jerusalem, 1974).

NEUBAUER, ADOLF B., 'Ancient Words from Oxford' (Heb.), *Hamagid*, 18 (1874).

—— *Mediaeval Jewish Chronicles*, 2 vols. (Oxford, 1887).

SAMBARI, JOSEPH BEN ISAAC, *Sefer divrei yosef*, ed. Shimon Shtober (Jerusalem, 1994).

SCHECHTER, ABRAHAM I., *Studies in Jewish Liturgy* (Philadelphia, 1930).

Sefer hilkhot hanagid, ed. Mordecai Margalioth (Jerusalem, 1962).

THIETMAR OF MERSEBURG, *Thietmari Merseburgensis episcopi Chronicon*, Monumenta Germaniae Historica: Scriptores rerum Germanicarum 3 (Leipzig, 1935).

ZFATMAN, SARA, *The Jewish Tale in the Middle Ages: Between Ashkenaz and Sepharad* [Bein ashkenaz lisefarad: letoledot hasipur hayehudi biyemei habeinayim] (Jerusalem, 1993).

ZIMMER, YITZHAK, 'Azriel Trabot's *Sefer haposekim*' (Heb.), *Sinai*, 76 (1975), 237–52.

PART II

The Impact of Non-Jewish Cultures on Regional Traditions

CHAPTER THREE

The Sacrifice of the Souls of the Righteous upon the Heavenly Altar: Transformations of Apocalyptic Traditions in Medieval Ashkenaz

PAUL MANDEL

Dedicated to the memory of the victims of terror in Jerusalem, Marheshvan 5775, all righteous souls

A SURPRISING MOTIF found in early medieval rabbinic traditions, and which appears in some manuscripts of the Babylonian Talmud and elsewhere, concerns the sacrifice of 'the souls of the righteous' (*nishmoteihen shel tsadikim*) upon the heavenly altar. Comparison of this motif, its background and transmission, with other traditions concerning the 'souls of the righteous' in rabbinic literature and with precedents in texts of the Second Temple period reveals a channel of influence not previously noted. This channel is connected to early Enochic traditions, apocalyptic texts of the Second Temple period, and early Christian cultural traditions and beliefs. The present study indicates that there was a nexus between Christian and Byzantine Jewish traditions which became manifest in the development of motifs and textual sources during the first centuries of the Common Era, and was later expressed in medieval Ashkenazi texts. Further evidence is thus provided for lines of cultural transmission between Byzantine works, traditions of the East, and the cultural milieu of medieval Ashkenaz.[1]

Previous versions of this essay were presented at the Annual Departmental Conference of the Talmud Department, Bar-Ilan University, in June 2012, and at the Seventh Enoch Seminar on 'Enochic Influences on the Synoptic Gospels' at Camaldoli, Italy, in July 2013.

[1] Despite reservations regarding the scope of the Byzantine–Italian connection to early Franco-German Jewish culture of the medieval period, there is no doubt that Italy served as a channel of transmission to Ashkenazi scholarly culture of liturgy, *piyut*, and esoterica (*torat*

THE REPOSITORY OF SOULS IN HEAVEN AND BENEATH THE HEAVENLY THRONE

In the Hebrew Bible the soul or spirit (*nefesh*, *ruaḥ*) of a person, denoting both 'breath' and, more generally, 'life-force', is understood to be in God's hands: 'Into Your hand I entrust my spirit [*ruḥi*]' (Ps. 31: 6); 'In His hand is every living soul [*nefesh kol ḥai*], and the breath [*ruaḥ*] of all mankind' (Job 12: 10). In later Jewish thought, in concert with belief in the continued existence of the soul after death, individual souls were often said to reside in a 'treasury' or 'store-room' (*otsar*) which is in proximity to, or 'with', God, as in the following midrashic comment on the phrase *elohei haruḥot lekhol basar* in Numbers 27: 16 (and cf. Num. 16: 22):

R. Eleazar the son of R. Yose Hagelili says: As long as man lives, his soul is deposited with the Maker; when he dies it is laid in a store-room, as is written: 'May the life of my lord be bound up in the bundle of life with the Lord your God' [1 Sam. 25: 29].[2]

Abigail's apt invocation to David is understood here and elsewhere in rabbinic sources to refer to eternal life.[3] This verse became a *locus classicus* for the idea that righteous souls are preserved ('bound up'), while the souls of the wicked are 'bound and thrown'. Compare the following passage, in which the souls of the righteous are stored 'under the Throne of Glory' (*taḥat kisé hakavod*), as opposed to those of the wicked:

R. Eliezer says: The souls of the righteous are concealed [*genuzot*] under the Throne of Glory, as it is written: 'May the soul of my lord be bound up in the bundle of life with the Lord your God'. But [the souls] of the wicked are bound and discarded, as it is written: 'and He shall fling away the soul of your enemies as from the hollow of a sling' [1 Sam. 25: 29].[4]

hasod) from Byzantine Palestine and as the place of composition for works read and studied by later Ashkenazi scholars. See Grossman, 'The Relationship of Early Ashkenazi Jewry to the Land of Israel' (Heb.); id., *The Early Sages of Ashkenaz* (Heb.), 424–40; Ta-Shma, 'The Library of the Ashkenazi Sages' (Heb.); id., 'Towards a History of the Cultural Links between Byzantine and Ashkenazi Jewry' (Heb.); Geula, 'Lost Aggadic Works' (Heb.), i. 318–36.

[2] *Sifrei on Numbers*, *piska* 139 (ed. Horovitz, p. 185), and cf. *Mekhilta derabi yishma'el*, *shirta* 10 (ed. Horovitz and Rabin, pp. 149–50) and elsewhere.

[3] See *Targum yonatan ben uzi'el* ad loc., where the biblical phrase 'bound in the bundle of life' is translated as 'stored in the depository of eternal life before God' (*geniza bigenaz ḥayei alma kadam adonay elahakh*).

[4] BT *Shab.* 152*b*. Cf. *Avot derabi natan*, version A, ch. 12 (ed. Schechter, p. 50), and see also ibid., ch. 26, p. 82: 'All who are buried in Erets Yisra'el are as if they are buried under the altar, since all of Erets Yisra'el is worthy of being an altar; and all who are buried under the altar are as if they are buried under the Throne of Glory.'

The heavenly throne depicted in Ezekiel 1: 26 and elsewhere in the Bible features prominently in Second Temple Jewish literature as part of a more general description of the heavenly Temple, mentioned explicitly in Isaiah 6: 1. Thus God's heavenly throne is depicted in 1 Enoch 14: 9–23 and in the Enoch 'Similitudes' (1 Enoch 39–41).[5] A 'heavenly city', denoting the heavenly Jerusalem, is mentioned in Fourth Ezra 7: 26 ('the hidden city'); it appears as the New Jerusalem descended from heaven in Revelation 3: 12 and 21: 2, and in that book a heavenly altar is also mentioned (6: 9 and 8: 3).[6] The same theme occurs in both early and late rabbinic literature, for instance in the following passages:

'The place [*makhon*] for Thee to dwell in' [Exod. 15: 17]—corresponding to [*mekhuvan*] Thy dwelling place. This is one of the statements to the effect that the throne below corresponds to, and is the counterpart of, the throne in heaven. And so it says, 'The Lord is in His holy Temple, the Lord, His throne is in heaven' [Ps. 11: 4]. And it also says, 'I have surely built Thee a house of habitation, a place for Thee to dwell in forever' [1 Kgs 8: 13].[7]

[5] See also the Qumran scroll *Songs of the Sabbath Sacrifice* (4Q405), 20 ii and 23 i; these depictions frequently appear in the later *merkavah* literature. See Newsom, *Songs of the Sabbath Sacrifice*; on the sacrifices offered by the celestial beings see ibid. 371–2.

[6] See Stone, *Fourth Ezra*, 202, 213–14 and n. 47 there. On Rev. 6: 9 see below. On the heavenly Jerusalem see Heb. 8: 1–6, 9: 23–4. Cf. the longer recension of the Testament of Levi 3: 5 (in *The Old Testament Pseudepigrapha*, ed. Charlesworth, ii. 789), where the sixth firmament contains 'the angels of the presence of the Lord, those who minister and make propitiation to the Lord for the "sins of ignorance" of the righteous, and they offer to the Lord a pleasant odour, a reasonable and bloodless offering' (the latter phrase reflecting a common Christian set of terms). The passage is missing in the shorter recension and would seem to reveal a Christian motif. In the same work (5: 1) a heavenly Temple and divine throne are depicted. See also 3 Baruch (Greek and Slavonic recensions), chs. 11–12, where the archangel Michael accepts 'the prayers of men' (Slavonic recension) or 'the virtues of the righteous and the good works which they do' (Greek recension), bringing them before God (although no altar is mentioned); cf. also 3 Baruch 14: 1–2. The various sources for the tradition of the heavenly Temple, including most of those mentioned in this essay, were collected by V. Aptowitzer in 'The Heavenly Temple in the Aggadah' (Heb.).

[7] *Mekhilta derabi yishma'el, shirta* 10 (ed. Horovitz and Rabin, pp. 149–50). The rabbinic derivation is based on a reading of the word *makhon* ('dwelling') as *mekhuvan* ('corresponding to'). See the similar interpretation in JT *Ber.* 4: 5 (Venice edn., 8*c*). Cf. BT *Ta'an.* 5*a*: '"In your midst—the Holy; I will not come into the city" [Hos. 11: 9]: Rabbi Yohanan said: Thus said the Holy One, blessed be He: I will not enter the Jerusalem above until I enter the Jerusalem below.' The support for the existence of the two corresponding cities is adduced from Ps. 122: 3: 'Jerusalem, built as a city that is [as one] connected with it together.' Cf. also *Ber. Rab.* 55: 7 (*Midrash Bereshit Rabba*, ed. Theodor and Albeck, p. 591) and *Midrasch Tehillim*, ed. Buber, 30: 1.

R. Simon said: At the time the Holy One, blessed be He, told Israel to set up the Tabernacle, He hinted to the angels that they should also make a Tabernacle above. [T]he[y] did not; rather, [only] after the Tabernacle had been erected below was the Tabernacle erected above, as it says, 'And it came to pass on the day that Moses had completed'—*hamishkan* is not written here but *et hamishkan*; [the particle *et*] signifies the Tabernacle on high.[8]

THE HEAVENLY ALTAR AND THE SACRIFICE OF THE SOULS OF THE RIGHTEOUS

A description of the celestial Temple appears in the Babylonian Talmud, *Ḥagigah* 12*b*, where the Palestinian sage Resh Lakish lists the seven firmaments of heaven. In the fourth firmament, named Zevul, resides the heavenly Jerusalem, Temple, and altar:

R. Judah said: There are two firmaments . . . Resh Lakish said: Seven, and they are: Vilon, Rakia, Sheḥakim, Zevul, Ma'on, Makhon, Aravot. . . . Zevul, in which is Jerusalem and the Temple and the built altar. And Michael, the great prince,[9] stands and offers a sacrifice on it, as it is said, '[Then Solomon declared: The Lord has chosen to abide in a thick cloud;] I have now built for You a stately House [*beit zevul*], a place [*makhon*] where You may dwell forever' [1 Kgs 8: 12–13]. And from where [is it known] that it is called Shamayim? As it is written: 'Look down from *shamayim* and see, from Your holy *zevul* and Your glorious place' [Isa. 63: 15].[10]

[8] *Pesikta rabati, piska* 5 (ed. Friedmann, p. 22*b*), on Num. 7: 1; see too *Pesiqta Rabbati: A Synoptic Edition*, ed. Ulmer, i. 76. The text follows the reading of the Parma manuscript. This passage, along with others surrounding it from *Pesikta rabati*, was inserted into the text of *Tanḥuma*, 'Naso' in the Mantua edition (1563) and appears in the current print editions of *Tanḥuma*, 'Naso' in par. 18 (ed. Buber, 38 n. 131.) The parallel text of *Bemidbar rabah*, 12: 12, contains an addition mentioning the heavenly Tabernacle as 'the abode of "the youth" [*hana'ar*] whose name is Metatron, where he sacrifices the souls of the righteous to atone for Israel during their exile'; this late addition is based on the tradition discussed in the present study; see below, n. 41.

[9] Concerning Michael as 'the great prince' who has responsibility for the people of Israel, see Dan. 12: 1. See above, n. 6, on earlier traditions concerning Michael's activity in a heavenly setting.

[10] The text presented here is as attested in the printed editions of BT *Ḥagigah*: Pesaro (1514), Venice (1521), and later. The same text, with only minor variants, is found in the following manuscripts: Göttingen 3, British Library Harley 5508 (cat. Margoliouth, no. 400), Munich 6, Munich 95, Oxford Bodleian Opp. Add. fo. 32, and the citation in *Hagadot hatalmud* ad loc. A variant text found in other text witnesses is discussed below. The statement describing the heavenly altar and Michael's sacrificial activity appears also in BT *Zev.* 62*a* and *Men.* 110*a* (based on an exegesis of 2 Chron. 2: 3), with no further detail.

This is the text as it appears in the *editio princeps* of the Babylonian Talmud and in all subsequent printings. However, in his marginal glosses, printed in the standard editions of the Talmud (*Hagahot habaḥ*), R. Joel Sirkes of sixteenth-century Poland presented an emendation in which the following line is inserted after the citation of the verse from 1 Kings 8:

What does he [the angel Michael offer as] sacrifice? Could you possibly consider that there are sheep there [in heaven]? Rather, he offers as sacrifice the souls of the righteous [*nishmatan shel tsadikim*].[11]

The additional line is also adduced by R. Sirkes's Polish contemporary, R. Samuel Eidels (Maharsha), who cites it from *Ein ya'akov*, R. Jacob Ibn Habib's aggadic anthology of the Talmud. Though absent from the majority of text witnesses to the tractate, the line is found in all editions of *Ein ya'akov* from the first printing (Salonica, 1516) onwards, and is attested in an early Spanish print of BT *Ḥagigah* (1482) as well as in two Ashkenazi manuscripts of the tractate.[12] The large degree of similarity in the language of these texts, combined with the absence of the line in the majority of talmudic text witnesses of the Talmud, demonstrates that the emended version, first attested (among extant sources) in an Ashkenazi talmudic manuscript of the thirteenth century, served as the basis for the text of the fifteenth-century Spanish print, and was subsequently copied in *Ein ya'akov* and also cited as an amendment to the printed talmudic text in the sixteenth century.

The motif of the sacrifice of the souls of the righteous upon the heavenly altar is cited in the *Tosafot* on *Menaḥot* 110*a* (s.v. *mikha'el sar hagadol*) as an alternative exegetical tradition, but it is not presented as a textual variant, and indeed the tradition does not appear in any known text of the talmudic passage there:

'And Michael the great prince stands and offers a sacrifice on it': [There are] conflicting [aggadic] interpretations: There are those who say [that the sacrifices are] the souls of the righteous, and there are those who say, sheep of fire. This [i.e. the first tradition] is [in accordance with] what we recite in the Eighteen Benedictions in [the blessing] Avodah: 'And the fire-offerings of Israel and their prayers accept speedily with love.' Others say that [at the beginning of this phrase] is connected with the previous phrase: 'Restore the [sacrificial] service to the sanctuary of Your house, and the fire-offerings of Israel.'

The same tradition is cited by the prominent scholar of the German Pietists

[11] I thank Jerome Gellman for bringing this emendation to my attention.

[12] The manuscripts are Vatican ebr. 134 (13th century) and Vatican ebr. 171 (15th century).

(Hasidei Ashkenaz), R. Judah Hehasid (d.1217), in the context of a discussion concerning the travels of the soul after a person's death. As in the comment of the *Tosafot*, R. Judah associates the Avodah blessing of the Amidah (Eighteen Benedictions) with the motif of the heavenly sacrifice of the souls of the righteous:

The soul of a man sits on the nose of the dead until [the body] putrefies, and afterwards it is transferred to Dumah, who brings it to *ḥatser mavet* (Death Court), which is a large court in front of which lie the rivers of Eden and vegetables, and it grazes for a year. The souls of the righteous take pleasure in the stream for one year. Afterwards Michael offers it [i.e. the soul] as incense on the heavenly altar, and from the flame of the altar it rises and heals, through [the agency of] the Tree of Life, and is bound into the bundle of life beneath the Throne of Glory: *bitseror* ['in the bundle'] in *gematria* is [equivalent to] *bekisé hakavod* ['in the Throne of Glory']. And the souls of the righteous, those that gave their souls for this Torah—'a man who dies in the tent' [Num. 19: 14]—are kindled as incense with the spices of the Garden of Eden, and with the scent it rises to the Throne. . . . Michael is the high priest above, and he offers the souls of the righteous as incense. Therefore we say in the blessing Avodah: 'Restore the [sacrificial] service to the sanctuary of Your house'. The fire purifies like a *mikveh* [purification pool], as it is written, 'All that cannot withstand fire you shall pass through water' [Num. 31: 23].[13]

It is noteworthy that, in R. Judah's account, the sacrifice of the souls of the righteous is understood to be part of the general purgatorial process that these

[13] Judah Hehasid, *Sefer gematriyot* 114 (ed. Stal, i. 123–7). This passage finds a parallel in *Midrasch Tehillim*, ed. Buber, 11, fos. 51*a*–52*a*. However, as Buber notes (n. 46 in his edition), the entire passage there is attested only in MS Parma (de Rossi 1232; designated by Buber as MS *aleph*) and in the similar text of the MS that Buber received from Solomon Zalman Hayim Halberstam (designated as MS *vav*; see *Midrasch Tehillim*, ed. Buber, introduction, 81–6), and is missing in all other text witnesses to that work. As I. Ta-Shma has noted, these two manuscripts contain numerous additions that stem from an Ashkenazi recension of *Midrash tehilim*; among these additions many deal with the theme of martyrdom (Ta-Shma, 'The Library of the Ashkenazi Sages' (Heb.), 303 and n. 23). See Ta-Shma concerning the early Ashkenazi custom, associated with this passage, of refraining from eating or drinking in the late afternoon of the sabbath, in id., *Early Franco-German Ritual and Custom* (Heb.), 201–4, and esp. 202–3 and 207; Ta-Shma suggests a Palestinian source for these customs. It would seem that the motif was transmitted to German scholars from Italy; see Geula, 'A Sermon and *Piyut* for the Sabbath Afternoon' (Heb.), 177 and n. 23. Rabbi Judah's description of the righteous (*tsadikim*) as ones who 'gave their souls for this Torah' should not be understood to refer to martyrdom, but rather to the dedication of one's life to the study of Torah; see the source of this statement in BT *Ber.* 63*b*, BT *Shab.* 83*b*, BT *Git.* 57*b*, and cf. *Sifrei on Deuteronomy* 306 (ed. Finkelstein, p. 337); see also the phrase *natan nafsho alav* in *Mekhilta derabi yishma'el, shirta* 1 (ed. Horovitz and Rabin, p. 117), and *Ber. Rab.* 82: 8 (*Midrash Bereshit Rabba*, ed. Theodor and Albeck, p. 985).

souls undergo; the fire, like the water of a ritual immersion pool (*mikveh*), acts as a purifying element for the souls, after which they may continue to be bound up 'under the Throne of Glory [*kavod*]'.

R. Judah's student R. Eleazar ben Judah of Worms (Eleazar Roke'ah, d.1238) wrote similarly in his work on esoterica, *Sodei razya*:

Michael . . . is the intercessor for Israel, and he is priest to the Most High God, and offers the souls of the righteous as sacrifice upon the altar which is in Zevul. . . . He offers a sacrifice of fire on God's altar, and burns incense on the altar of incense, and offers up offerings of flame on the altar of offering, as it says, 'I have surely built a house of Zevul for You' [1 Kgs 8: 13]. . . . Until the Temple was destroyed, Michael the High Priest would sacrifice [an offering] similar to that of Israel for God's acceptance. After the destruction God said to him: Do not offer to Me the image of an ox, sheep, or goat, for I will not enter the Temple above until I have built the House in My name, as is written: 'In your midst—the Holy One; I will not come into the city' [Hos. 11: 9];[14] and it is written: 'I have now built for You a lofty House, a place where You may dwell forever' [1 Kgs 8: 13]; 'a place where You may dwell'—this is Jerusalem, which is built 'as a city that is connected together' [Ps. 122: 3] . . . the altar below, opposite the altar in Zevul. And from the day that the altar below was destroyed God said: I do not desire the image of an ox or a sheep to be offered on the altar above, but rather the souls of the righteous and the young children who have not sinned.[15] And these rise immediately as sweet incense every day, without delay, along with the prayer. This is what we say in [the blessing] Retseh: 'And the offerings of Israel and their prayers accept favourably, speedily, with love.' And that altar [above] will descend to the Temple, which will be rebuilt speedily, in our days.[16]

In this account the act of sacrificing the souls of the righteous began at the time of the Temple's destruction and will continue after the rebuilding of the Temple, when the heavenly altar becomes one with the earthly one.[17]

The liturgical discussion found in the *Tosafot* on *Menaḥot* is also mentioned by R. Jacob ben Asher (d.1349). He, too, recognized the alternative version describing the heavenly sacrifice of the souls of the righteous as an aggadic tradition (*midrash*) and not as a talmudic variant:

In the Midrash it states: Michael the great prince offers the soul[s] of the righteous upon the altar above, and on this basis they established [the prayer] 'and the fire-

[14] Rabbi Eleazar integrates here a passage from BT *Ta'anit* 5*a* based on the verse from Hosea (see above, n. 7).

[15] Concerning the motif of the 'children who have not sinned', see the text from *Seder arakim* cited in n. 29 below.

[16] *Seder alpha beta*, letter *samekh*, in *Sodei razya* (ed. Eisenbach, i. 82). (In his explanations for the letter *samekh*, R. Eleazar dedicates most of the discussion to the angel Michael because of

offerings of Israel [accept with favour]'. There are those [however] who construe [this phrase as connected] to [the phrase] before it, and this is its interpretation: 'Restore the [sacrificial] service to the sanctuary of Your house and the fire-offerings of Israel.' [The following phrase,] 'and accept their prayers with favour', is the beginning of [another] sentence.[18]

The above examples demonstrate that the motif of the sacrifice of the souls of the righteous on the heavenly altar was familiar to Ashkenazi scholars, who understood the sacrifice to affect all righteous souls. According to Eleazar of Worms, moreover, these sacrifices, which began with the destruction of the Temple, were to continue in the messianic future, following the rebuilding of the Temple.

THE REPOSITORY OF THE SOULS OF THE RIGHTEOUS IN THE APOCALYPTIC TRADITION

The apocalyptic book of 1 Enoch, written originally in Aramaic around the third century BCE, is a source for the tradition placing the souls of the righteous in a heavenly repository. In chapter 22 Enoch is shown four caves in the side of a mountain which function as a necropolis; an angel explains to him

the *gematria* of *samekh* as 120, which is equivalent to the sum of the numerical value of characters in the phrase *zehu mikha'el* [זהוא מיכאל], see ed. Eisenbach, i. 82.) See *Sefer arugat habosem*, ed. Urbach, i. 52, where this passage from Eleazar Roke'ah is cited, as well as an otherwise unknown text from Judah Hehasid's *Sefer hakavod*, which repeats the statement in *Sefer gematriyot*: 'Some say that he sacrifices the souls of the righteous, so that if there is the smallest amount of sin in them it will be atoned for, and afterwards they will be bound up in the bundle of life.' In his edition of Judah Hehasid's work, Stal cites the parallels to this motif; see nn. 14–15 (*Sefer gematriyot*, i. 126) and his extended discussion in the supplemental note (*Sefer gematriyot*, ii. 791–3, *ma'amar* 17).

[17] As Stal points out (*Sefer gematriyot*, i. 125 n. 15), the citation of the passage from the Amidah in Judah Hehasid's *Sefer gematriyot* seems to be abbreviated. The essential part, as in the passage of Eleazar Roke'ah and the *Tosafot*, is the phrase following the cited text: 'and the offerings of Israel and their prayers accept favourably, speedily, with love'.

[18] Jacob ben Asher, *Arba'ah turim*, 'Oraḥ ḥayim', 120. In his commentary ad loc., *Beit yosef*, R. Joseph Karo offers two interpretations of the phrase *ishei yisra'el* according to the alternative tradition:

> The interpretation is: 'the offerings of Israel' [אשי ישראל—*ishei yisra'el*]—that is, the men [*anshei*] of Israel who are offered as sacrifice by Michael. Or rather, [the term] comes from the phrase 'a savoury fire-offering' [אשה ריח ניחוח—*isheh re'aḥ niḥo'aḥ*], that is, it is the 'sacrifices of Israel', which are their souls, that are offered as sacrifice by Michael; [these] and the prayers of Israel accept with favour.

that three of the caves are dark and serve different types of non-righteous individuals. One is for those who did not receive punishment in their lives and await Judgement Day; another holds murdered souls, who may 'bring suit' to avenge their death;[19] a third contains the souls of those who were 'companions of the lawless', who will neither receive judgement nor be raised up.[20] The one cave which is lit and contains a fountain of water is for the souls of the righteous as they await their reward:

Then Raphael answered: . . . These hollow places [are intended so] that the spirits of the souls of the dead might be gathered into them. . . . until their judgement day [when God will mete out the recompense due to each]. . . . Then I asked about [all] the hollow places: Why are they separated one from the other? And he answered me and said: These three were made so that the spirits of the dead might be separated; and this [one] has been separated for the spirits of the righteous, where the bright fountain of water is. This [one] was created for [the spirits of the] sinners, when they die and are buried in the earth and judgement has not been executed on them in their life. Here their spirits are separated for this great torment until the great Day of Judgement . . . that there might be a recompense for their spirits. . . . And this [one] has been separated for the spirits of those that make suit, who bring a plea regarding their destruction, when they were murdered in the days of the sinners. And this [one] was created for the spirits of the men who were not pious but sinners, who were godless, and they were companions of the lawless. Their spirit will not be punished on the Day of Judgement, nor will they be raised from there.[21]

The same motif is found in the text of Fourth Ezra, a work written after the destruction of the Temple, near the end of the first century CE. In this version 'the souls of the righteous in their treasuries' await the final judgement and their resurrection, and plead with the heavenly host concerning the duration of their stay there and their future reward:

Then I [Ezra] answered and said, 'How long and when will these things be? For our years are few and evil.' He [the angel] answered me and said, 'You do not hasten faster than the Most High, for your haste is for yourself, but the Highest hastens on behalf of many. Did not the souls of the righteous in their treasuries ask about these matters,

[19] Cf. the passage in 1 Enoch 22: 5–7 and 12 (and cf. also 9: 10) concerning Abel and others who make suit against their murderers, and see *1 Enoch 1: A Commentary*, ed. Nickelsburg, 308.

[20] See ibid. 308–9. The most plausible explanation for this class of sinners connects them to those who had already received punishment in their lifetime, as in the case of the generation of the Flood.

[21] 1 Enoch 22: 3–13; *1 Enoch 1: A Commentary*, ed. Nickelsburg, 300–9. Cf. the Aramaic text of the Qumran fragment of Enoch 22: 3–7, 4Q206, 2 ii (*nafshat*).

saying, "How long are we to remain here? And when will come the harvest of our reward?"'[22]

In the above texts the repository of the souls of the dead is not mentioned as being in the proximity of the heavenly throne, although, as mentioned above, the image of God's throne appears in that text. However, the author of *Sefer haheikhalot* (also known as 3 Enoch), a later Hebrew apocalyptic text written in post-talmudic times, does connect these motifs; it places the souls near God's throne and describes their attempt to intercede before God. In this work the angel Metatron shows R. Ishmael the souls of the righteous, 'which fly above the Throne of Glory before God'. Here the souls include not only those righteous who have died 'and have returned [to their heavenly abode]', but also unborn righteous souls.[23] Another passage in 3 Enoch describes the 'brilliant right hand of God', which is 'drawn back' because of the destruction of the Temple, alluding to the text of Lamentations 2: 3: 'He has drawn back His right hand from before the enemy; He has burned up Jacob like a flaming fire, consuming all around.' This image symbolizes God's decision not to use his 'outstretched arm' to deliver his people during this period. The author of 3 Enoch relates further that 'all the souls of the righteous, those who are worthy to see the joy of Jerusalem', appear before this divine arm with praise, and 'ask for mercy from before it [her]' three times every day: 'Awake, awake, clothe yourself with splendour, O arm of the Lord' (Isa. 51: 9).[24] Thus, in this later apocalyptic text the souls of the righteous serve an important intercessory function: they request mercy for Jerusalem during the period of God's wrath. However, according to the continuation and culmination of this text, God's decision to 'stretch out His hand' against the nations of the world and deliver his people is due to the absence of any righteous individual in that generation who can entreat God to action (as did Moses and Samuel under similar

[22] Stone, *Fourth Ezra*, 4: 33–5, and see on the 'treasuries of the souls' 7: 32 (pp. 90, 85, 95, 101; cf. the discussion there, pp. 96, 219–20, 241). Although a number of passages in 4 Ezra mention the souls of the righteous in these repositories, the meaning seems to be that all souls reside there as they await final judgement, 'until the number of those like yourselves is completed' (4: 36); cf. ibid. 99, 220. Cf. also Rev. 6: 9–10 and the discussion below.

[23] 3 Enoch 43. See Schäfer, *Synopse zur Hekhalot-Literatur*, section 61 (30–1); see the verse cited there as proof-text (Isa. 57: 16), which mentions souls (*neshamot*) as coming from God. On the complex nature of 3 Enoch see Alexander, 'The Historical Setting of the Hebrew Book of Enoch', and more recently Herrmann, 'Jewish Mysticisms in Byzantium'.

[24] 3 Enoch 48 (and cf. also ch. 44); cf. Schäfer, *Synopse zur Hekhalot-Literatur*, section 68 (34–5). See the subsequent verses in Isaiah, especially 51: 11: 'So let the ransomed of the Lord return, and come with shouting to Zion, crowned with joy everlasting. Let them attain joy and gladness, while sorrow and sighing flee.'

circumstances). God thus decides to act 'for His own sake', citing the verse: 'For My sake, My own sake, do I act, lest [My name] be dishonoured; I will not give glory to another' (Isa. 48: 11).[25]

In contrast to the earlier apocalyptic literature, in 3 Enoch the righteous souls take advantage of their proximity to God in order to intercede on behalf of the destroyed Jerusalem. Nonetheless even the righteous souls cannot significantly influence God's actions on behalf of Israel; in the end God must act by himself.

THE SACRIFICE OF THE RIGHTEOUS SOULS IN MEDIEVAL JEWISH WORKS

In the early sources from the Second Temple and rabbinic periods, the motifs of the heavenly abode of the righteous souls and the heavenly Temple remain independent and are unlinked. The sacrifice of the souls of the righteous upon the heavenly altar, cited by medieval Ashkenazi scholars and scribes, is thus a unique and surprising motif, unparalleled in rabbinic literature. It cannot be considered talmudic in origin; the emendations to BT *Ḥagigah 12b* reflect the grafting of an external source onto the talmudic passage concerning the heavenly altar.

A passage linking the two motifs appears in the introduction to a work known by several titles: *Seder arakim*, *Sidur shel midot tovot*, or, based on its *incipit*, 'God in His wisdom has established the Earth' (Prov. 3: 19).[26]

From here [is deduced] that God created the world as one born of woman [is born]. He began from the place [where] the Temple [was to be built]. . . . There God created the Temple below and the Temple on high. During the time that the Temple stood, a priest would sacrifice and bring incense in the Temple below, and Michael, the High Priest, would stand and sacrifice in the Temple above. And when the Temple was destroyed, the Holy One, blessed be He, said to Michael: 'Michael! Since I have destroyed my house and burned my sanctuary, do not sacrifice the image of an ox or of a lamb or of a goat.' [Michael] said to Him: 'Lord of the universe! Your children—what shall become of them [i.e. how will they receive atonement]?' The Holy One, blessed be He, said to him: 'Sacrifice [lit. bring] before Me [the merits and the prayers

[25] 3 Enoch 48; cf. Schäfer, *Synopse zur Hekhalot-Literatur*, sections 69–70 (35).

[26] *Seder arakim*, included as section 6 in *Kevod ḥupah*, ed. Horowitz, 19–21; repr. in *Otsar midrashim*, ed. Eisenstein, i. 70–2. Another version, known as Midrash 'God in His wisdom established the earth' (Prov. 3: 19), was published in *Bet ha-Midrasch*, ed. Jellinek, v. 63–9, no. 14. Cf. also *Midrash konen*, in *Bet ha-Midrasch*, ii. 23–39, no. 3, and see ibid., introduction, pp. xii–xiv. On the manuscript versions of this text see below, n. 29.

and[27]] *the souls of the righteous that are concealed beneath the throne of Glory* and the schoolchildren [*tinokot shel beit raban*]; and through them I shall atone for the sins of Israel.' For as long as there was this joy below, there was this joy above; now that that which is below mourns, so it mourns above. And when that which is below is rebuilt, so it will be rebuilt above.[28]

This aggadic work, attested in Ashkenazi and Italian manuscripts from the thirteenth century onwards,[29] is part of a genre of Hebrew books that deal with esoteric topics such as the heavens, Eden, and God's abode, and which may have originated in Byzantine southern Italy between the eighth and tenth centuries, during a period of Hebrew and scholarly renaissance.[30] In the above text the motif of the sacrifice of the righteous souls and their place 'under the Throne of Glory' resembles the tradition reflected in the talmudic emendation discussed earlier. Here, however, the sacrifice is limited to the time of the Temple's destruction, during which God himself ordains it as a temporary measure; in lieu of the sacrifices offered by Israel, now defunct, the souls of the righteous are 'brought before' God, along with other meritorious works, as expiation for Israel's sins. In contrast to the explanation of Eleazar of Worms mentioned above, this activity is not to continue forever; it will cease upon the rebuilding of the Temple, when expiation can again be offered for

[27] The bracketed words are found in Jellinek's text.

[28] Emphasis mine. The final line, from 'For as long as there was this joy below . . . so it will be rebuilt above', appears in Jellinek's text as 'And when I rejoice below I rejoice above'.

[29] The text of *Seder arakim* in Horowitz's edition is based on the text as found in two manuscripts: Parma Palatina 2295 (cat. de Rossi, no. 563/21, fos. 124ᵛ–126ᵛ; see cat. de Rossi, *Codices Hebraici Biblioth.*, ii. 85–8) = cat. Richler, no. 1541/24 (see Richler, *Hebrew Manuscripts in the Biblioteca Palatina*, 458–60), written in Ashkenazi script on parchment, dating from the 13th or 14th century; and British Library Add. 27089 (cat. Margoliouth, no. 1076; fos. 112ᵛ–114ʳ), written on paper in Mestre (Venice) in an Italian hand 'strongly influenced by the German style' from the 15th or 16th century (see Margoliouth, *Catalogue of the Hebrew and Samaritan Manuscripts in the British Museum*, iii. 462, section VII, and cf. ibid. 464–5, section XV; see also the introduction to *Seder arakim* in Eisenstein, *Otsar hamidrashim*, i. 70). The text of Midrash 'God in His wisdom established the earth' was transcribed by Jellinek from MS Munich 117 (see Steinschneider, *Die hebräischen Handschriften der K. Hof- und Staatsbibliothek in München*, 74–5; fos. 209ᵛ–212ʳ), written in a 'German-Italian' hand in 1435 (see Jellinek's introduction in *Bet ha-Midrasch*, vol. v, p. xxix). The two texts are separate recensions of one book, known to Eleazar of Worms by the latter title; he cites it in his *Sodei razya*, letter *bet* (ed. Eisenbach, i. 23). It should be noted that the phrase *tinokot shel beit raban* in the passage is typical of the Babylonian Talmud and thus reflects the author's acquaintance with the linguistic style of that work.

[30] On this genre and other specific examples of it, as well as on its transmission in the German milieu of the 12th and 13th centuries, and in particular by the leaders of the German Pietists, see Geula, 'Lost Aggadic Works' (Heb.), i. 318–36, esp. 325–6, 330–1. Cf. Ta-Shma, 'On the History of Cultural Relations between Byzantine and Ashkenazi Jews' (Heb.).

Israel through the normal channels: 'when the [Temple] is rebuilt below, the [Temple] will be rebuilt above'.[31]

The alternative view, offered by Judah Hehasid and Eleazar of Worms, that the sacrifice of the souls of the righteous on the altar will endure forever, is found in later versions of the above-cited tradition. The following passage, found in the work entitled *Midrash* (or *Seder*) *gan eden*, includes a description of the peregrination of the souls that is similar to the explanation of Judah Hehasid in his *Sefer gematriyot*:

When the souls rise to the Garden of Eden on high on the sabbath eve, several announcements are made both above and below. And all [the souls] disrobe from that garb and rise higher.[32] And there, in the firmament Aravot [!], Michael, the great prince, stands with the altar before him, and he offers all the souls of the righteous on that altar. And then, with that same scented spirit [*re'aḥ mevusam*[33]] with which they would perform their deeds in this world, the Holy One, blessed be He, causes its spirit to come to Him . . . And at the same time that Michael offers the souls as sacrifice, He causes the spirit to come to Him and brings it in.[34]

The following composite text, interpolated into a late recension of the tenth-century oriental work *Midrash aseret hadiberot* (Midrash on the Ten Commandments), contains similar language to that of the talmudic interpolation ('Is it sheep that he offers?') and to the motif mentioned by

[31] Stal emphasizes that the immediate sense of both Judah Hehasid and Eleazar of Worms is that the sacrifice is not related to the destruction but is everlasting (cf. Judah Hehasid, *Sefer gematriyot*, ii. 793, *ma'amar* 17). It should be noted that both authorities make specific mention of the altar (*mizbe'aḥ*) as this appears also in the talmudic emendation discussed above, while in the passage from *Seder arakim* it is the Temple that is the locus of the sacrifice.

[32] In the Oxford MS: 'from those garbs'.

[33] So in Jellinek; the manuscript has *ruaḥ*, which may be the correct reading.

[34] The work *Seder gan eden* was transcribed by Jellinek in *Bet ha-Midrasch*, iii. 13–40, no. 11 (version B); it is cited by R. Bahya ben Asher (Spain, d.1340). The work appears as a sequel to the book entitled *The Testament of Rabbi Eliezer*, also known as *Orḥot ḥayim*; these are first printed in a volume as an appended text preceding the astronomical work *She'erit yosef* (Salonica, 1521; see Steinschneider, *Catalogus Librorum Hebraeorum*, ii. 1527, no. 6002). I have compared Jellinek's text of *Seder gan eden* with that found in MS Oxford Mich. 266 (see Neubauer, *Catalogue of the Hebrew Manuscripts in the Bodleian Library*, i. 504, no.1409/4; fo. 152r), from which I cite corrections and variants in the following notes. Gershom Scholem noted the existence of parallels in language and content between the two parts of this work, *Orḥot ḥayim* and *Seder gan eden*, and the Zohar, and concluded that they share the same author, Moses de León; see Scholem, *Major Trends in Jewish Mysticism*, 183 (and 393 n. 103), 200 (and 396 n. 145), 241–2 (and 407 n. 127); id., 'Sources of *Ma'aseh rabi gadi'el hatinok* in the Kabbalistic Literature' (Heb.), 294–5. Cf. Zohar, 'Vayera' 80*a*–*b*.

R. Eleazar, who claims that with the future rebuilding of the Temple the heavenly altar will descend to earth, enabling the continuation of the sacrifice of the souls of the righteous:

Moreover the Holy One, blessed be He, created seven firmaments . . . above Shehakim is Zevul, and in Zevul there is a built altar, and Michael, the prince of Israel, is the high priest, and he stands and offers sacrifice on [the altar] each and every day. And what sacrifices does he offer? Is it sheep that he offers?[35] Rather, the sages said: Michael, the prince of Israel, is the high priest in heaven; from the day of the destruction of the Temple, may it be rebuilt speedily in our days, [during which time] the [service of the] priests was discontinued, what has he been sacrificing? The souls of the righteous, until [the time that] the Temple is rebuilt, when the Holy One, blessed be He, will bring down [*yorid*][36] the Temple in Zevul to the earthly Jerusalem.[37]

It is reasonable to assume that this version reflects the tradition of the sacrifice of the souls of the righteous in the heavenly Temple as it had been altered by the medieval German rabbis,[38] whereas the passage in *Seder arakim* is evidence for the motif as found outside the German milieu, possibly in southern Italy. In the latter, sacrifice of the souls of the righteous is limited to the period of the destruction of the Temple, and will cease with the rebuilding of the earthly Temple, at which time animal sacrifices will again be offered on the altar, and, it may be assumed, the parallel activity will be resumed in the Temple above using 'heavenly' animals.

[35] The sentence 'Is it sheep that he offers?' is missing in the Oxford manuscript due to a *homoioteleuton* (*makriv–makriv*).

[36] Jellinek mistakenly reads *morid* ('brings down', present tense). The sentence is missing in the Oxford manuscript.

[37] *Midrash aseret hadiberot* as presented in *Bet ha-Midrasch*, ed. Jellinek, i. 62–90; the cited text appears on p. 64. This version, clearly a composite, is a later adaptation of the aggadic passage in *Seder arakim*; it appears only in the versions of *Midrash aseret hadiberot* related to the Polish print (Lublin, 1572, which also includes the above-mentioned *Orḥot ḥayim*), among these an Ashkenazi manuscript of the 16th century (MS Oxford Bodleian 268/3; see Neubauer, *Catalogue of the Hebrew Manuscripts in the Bodleian Library*, i. 52–3). From A. Shapira's analysis of the textual transmission of *Midrash aseret hadiberot* (*Midrash aseret hadibrot: Text, Sources and Interpretation* (Heb.), 99–117, and see esp. 103), the secondary and interpolated nature of this text is evident. R. S. Boustan, however, assumes that the text is part of the original version of *Midrash aseret hadiberot*; see his *From Martyr to Mystic*, 168–9, and see below, n. 42.

[38] On the appearance of traditions of the German Pietists in the zoharic literature, see Ta-Shma, *Early Franco-German Ritual and Custom* (Heb.), 217–20.

ORIGIN OF THE MOTIF OF THE SACRIFICE OF THE SOULS OF THE RIGHTEOUS

The purpose of the sacrifice of the souls of the righteous has yet to be explained. Though the righteous souls that appear in early and late Jewish apocalyptic texts (1 Enoch, 4 Ezra, and 3 Enoch) play a role as intercessors before God during the time of destruction, such intervention bears little resemblance to the active sacrifice of the souls themselves as appearing in the medieval texts. How does the sacrifice of the righteous souls effect expiation, and why would these souls need to be sacrificed upon an altar? Would not their very existence suffice as a plea for mercy?

A solution to this enigma may be obtained by tracing the origin of the motif as found in the Byzantine Jewish work 'Tale of the Ten Martyrs', composed probably in Palestine in the late Byzantine period (sixth to ninth centuries). Basing himself on a tale that appears in *Heikhalot rabati*, the author recounts the ascent of R. Ishmael, one of ten sages designated by the king for execution, to the Holy Throne. While there, he asks the angel Metatron for confirmation of the divine decree of death ordered by the authorities for him and his colleagues. Metatron repeats the accusation that Joseph's ten brothers had incurred guilt by selling Joseph. He announces that their punishment is indeed God's decree,[39] adding that God had not found ten individuals more worthy than R. Ishmael and his colleagues. At this point in the narrative R. Ishmael notices the heavenly altar and asks Metatron about it:

Rabbi Ishmael said [to Metatron]: What is this before you? He said to him: An altar. He said to him: Is there a sacrifice and an altar on high? He said to him: All that is below is on high, as it is written, 'I have now built for You a lofty House, a place where You may dwell forever' [1 Kgs 8: 13]. He said to him: And what do you sacrifice on this altar? Do you have oxen and goats and sheep? He said to him: We have no oxen or goats or sheep here; rather, we sacrifice on it the souls of the righteous before God. When R. Ishmael heard this, he said: Now I have learned that which I have never previously heard. Immediately he descended and found his colleagues fasting and

[39] As noted already by S. Zeitlin ('The Legend of the Martyrs', 4–5), the motif of the atonement for the sin of Joseph's brothers originated in the book of Jubilees (3rd century BCE). The story of the martyrs is also related briefly in *Heikhalot rabati*; see P. Schäfer's synoptic edition of *Heikhalot rabati*, 50–2, paragraphs 105–9 (*Synopse zur Hekhalot-Literatur*, 50–2). An early list of ten sages who lived during the Hadrianic persecutions and who were 'consumed' upon God's initiative (cf. Lam. 2: 1) is first mentioned in the 5th-century aggadic *midrash*, *Eikhah rabati* on Lam. 2: 1 (ed. Buber, p. 100), although there is no specific mention there of their martyrdom, nor are they called *harugei malkhut*, the term used elsewhere to designate the martyred sages of that period.

praying. They said to him: What is with you [i.e. what can you tell us]? He said to them: Go and wash and purify yourselves and wear your [death] shrouds, for the decree is from God.[40]

From R. Ishmael's response it is clear that it is precisely this exchange that has enabled him to finally grasp the significance of the evil king's decree and its justification. Metatron's description of the sacrifice of the souls of the righteous on the heavenly altar has led to R. Ishmael's understanding of his own death and that of his colleagues as an act of martyrdom; the 'righteous' are those whose deeds, performed during their earthly existence, enable them to atone, through their death, for Israel's sins. It is for this reason that he concludes that he and his fellow sages must themselves become martyrs: they are the 'righteous souls', and their martyrdom will serve as an atonement for Israel's sins during the period of the Temple's destruction. This constitutes a remarkable development in the transmission of motifs concerning the souls of the righteous in the apocalyptic tradition. In the earlier sources all righteous souls, without distinction, are portrayed as entreating God for mercy, but here it is only the martyred, those who, by their very act of martyrdom, had fulfilled a necessary function for the benefit of the people of Israel, who are sacrificed by Metatron as expiation for Israel. The *tsadikim*, according to this tradition, are thus not merely righteous individuals (i.e. all those who have lived pious lives) but, more precisely, martyrs.[41] It may have been the intention of the author of the 'Tale of the Ten Martyrs' that the image shown to R. Ishmael by Metatron on his heavenly journey would serve only as a symbolic, one-time lesson for him and his colleagues. In contrast, the sacrifice of the souls of the

[40] *Die Geschichte von den Zehn Märtyren*, ed. Reeg, 40*–1*, versions II, IV, and V; see also *Midrash eleh ezkerah*, in *Beth ha-Midrasch*, ed. Jellinek, ii. 66.

[41] It is not surprising that the tradition of Metatron's sacrifice of the souls of the righteous on the heavenly altar is cited in *Bemidbar rabah* 12: 12 (on Num. 7: 1), in an interpolation to a passage taken from *Pesikta rabati* (see above, n. 8). There the activity surrounding the heavenly altar is connected explicitly to Metatron (named 'the youth' (*hana'ar*), as is common in the *heikhalot* texts), and it is he, not the angel Michael, who offers up the souls of the righteous 'to atone for Israel in the days of their exile'. This is clearly adapted from the aggadic tradition of the 'Tale of the Ten Martyrs' and is grafted onto the earlier passage of *Pesikta rabati* concerning the heavenly altar. On the identification of Michael and Metatron see Alexander, 'The Historical Setting of the Hebrew Book of Enoch', 163 (and see the references there). *Parashiyot* 1–14 of *Bemidbar rabah* were probably composed in the 12th century, perhaps in Provence (see Mack, *Prolegomena and Example to an Edition of Midrash Bemidbar Rabba, Part 1* (Heb.), 191–3, 221). This passage thus reflects an independent chain of tradition, parallel to the one investigated here, and probably derives from texts that originated in the southern Italian milieu and were subsequently transmitted to Provence.

righteous before God in *Seder arakim* is initiated, upon God's directive, as part of an ongoing act of atonement during the entire period of the destruction of the Temple.[42]

The idea that a Jew who dies a martyr's death is rewarded with life in the World to Come is common in rabbinic texts and in those of the Hasmonean period;[43] the idea that such deaths procure merit for others is relatively rare.[44] However, the image of the active sacrifice of martyrs by a heavenly being for the purpose of expiation is not found elsewhere in Jewish texts of the period.[45] The motif found in the 'Tale of the Ten Martyrs' is new and unique; it is this motif that is reflected in the later medieval passages cited above, where it is presented as an event occurring for the express purpose of expiation during the Temple's absence. The motif underwent further transformation in the hands of Judah Hehasid and his pupil Eleazar of Worms, who blended the idea of expiation for others with that of the personal cleansing of each individual righteous soul. In this manner the heavenly offering of the righteous souls came to be seen as part of the soul's natural progression en route to its final destination, 'bound in the bundle of life beneath the Throne of Glory'. Rabbi Eleazar implies that in the future Temple this heavenly activity will be brought down to the earthly sphere, and the heavenly purification of the righteous souls will continue to take place in the earthly Temple.

CHRISTIAN ORIGIN OF THE MOTIF

The motif found in the 'Tale of the Ten Martyrs' may be seen as characteristic of that idiosyncratic work. Recent studies have suggested that the story

[42] R. S. Boustan has discussed the tradition of the sacrifice of the righteous on the heavenly altar at some length, especially in the context of the passage in the 'Tale of the Ten Martyrs', and covers much of the material discussed here; see Boustan (Abusch), 'Rabbi Ishmael's Miraculous Conception', 339–40; and id., *From Martyr to Mystic*, 165–73. See the review and critique of the latter by I. Rozen-Zvi in *Zion*, 73 (2008), 211–16; cf. Zeitlin, 'The Legend of the Martyrs', 1–16. Boustan considers the composition of the 'Tale of the Ten Martyrs' to predate that of *Heikhalot rabati*, although this is not the scholarly consensus.

[43] See 2 Macc. 7; BT *AZ* 18*a* (the death of Rabbi Hanina ben Teradyon); *Ber.* 61*b* (the death of Rabbi Akiva).

[44] See 2 Macc. 7: 37, and especially 4 Macc. 6: 29.

[45] In BT *Git.* 57*b* the mother of the seven martyred sons mentions that she has 'built seven altars', implying an initiative on her part in the martyrdom of her sons. However, her statement reflects the biblical motif of Abraham's aborted sacrifice of Isaac, and should be understood as only a rhetorical modelling of that act; indeed, the sons are not brought to their death by their mother, but rather they are martyred as a result of their own refusal to acquiesce to the king's demands.

reflects surprising knowledge and influence of Christian martyrological texts.[46] Early intimations of the theme of the sacrifice of righteous souls upon the Temple altar may be found in the New Testament book of Revelation (6: 9–10), where the slaughtered Lamb opens the fifth of seven seals on the heavenly scroll:

When he broke the fifth seal, I saw under the altar the souls of those who had been slaughtered for the word of God and for the testimony they had given; they cried out with a loud voice, 'Sovereign Lord, holy and true, how long will it be before You judge and avenge our blood on the inhabitants of the earth?' They were each given a white robe and told to rest a little longer, until the number would be complete both of their fellow servants and of their brothers and sisters, who were soon to be killed as they themselves had been killed.

Written during the period immediately after the destruction of the Second Temple, this passage makes use of the apocalyptic motif of souls entering a plea and demanding justice,[47] but it is concerned specifically with those individuals who have been 'slaughtered for the word of God'; it is these that the Lamb finds under the altar. This altar is not the heavenly one, however; it refers to the actual altar of the Jerusalem Temple at whose base many were slain, priests and other 'righteous individuals' among them. The image undoubtedly reflects a fresh and raw memory for those living just after the destruction of Jerusalem and the Temple in 70 CE.[48] In this context the plea of the martyrs does not differ significantly from that of other righteous individuals in the apocalyptic traditions surveyed above. They cry out to God for justice and demand that it be brought swiftly, and God responds by saying that 'the measure must be fulfilled'.[49] Although the New Testament passage states that God will wait until enough martyrs have been slain, it does not suggest

[46] Hillel Newman, in a lecture given at the Fourteenth World Congress of Jewish Studies in Jerusalem, 2005, demonstrated a close parallel between the tradition in the 'Tale of the Ten Martyrs' concerning Rabbi Akiva's burial under the *tetrapylon* of Caesarea and a Christian martyrological narrative of the 7th century. My own research has revealed possible Christian martyrological traditions embedded in that work; see Mandel, 'Was Rabbi Akiva a Martyr?' On other Christian sources in the 'Tale of the Ten Martyrs' see Boustan (Abusch), 'Rabbi Ishmael's Miraculous Conception'; id., *From Martyr to Mystic*, 171–3, and see below, n. 51.

[47] See above, n. 22.

[48] In her commentary on Revelation, Josephine Massyngberde Ford remarks: 'The idea [of the blood of sacrificial offerings at the base of the altar] may have been derived from the fact that the blood of a sacrifice, which was considered the life of the victim, ran down to the base of the altar; thus the life would literally be under the altar' (*Revelation*, 110).

[49] See 1 Enoch 22: 10–13, 47: 2, and Fourth Ezra 4: 33–7; cf. above, n. 22.

that these souls are being actively sacrificed on a heavenly altar, as portrayed in the 'Tale of the Ten Martyrs'. Moreover, here it is not for the purposes of expiation or atonement for Israel that the souls entreat God; rather, as in the early apocalyptic texts,[50] they seek justice and demand that their murder be avenged.

The notion that the sacrifice of a person serves as expiation is, of course, familiar to Christian thought and theology. The institution of the Sacrament of the Eucharist, also called the Sacrament of the Altar, is, indeed, intimately connected with the tombs of Christian martyrs. Not only were the early basilicas of fourth-century Rome built over the catacombs which enshrined the tombs of the martyrs, but, according to early Christian custom, the eucharistic meal was celebrated on an altar erected at the tombs of martyrs on the anniversary of their death.[51] This custom reflects the symbolic nature of the celebration of the Christian saviour's sacrifice over the remains of those who sacrificed themselves in his name and who thereby provided an imitation

[50] See 1 Enoch 9: 10 and 22: 12.

[51] According to the collection of papal biographies entitled *Liber Pontificalis*, it was Pope Felix I (269–74) who decreed that the mass be celebrated over the tombs of the martyrs (*missa ad corpus*): 'He instituted the celebration of masses over the sepulchres [or: memorials] of the martyrs' ('Hic constituit supra sepulcra [variant: memorias] martyrum missas celebrare') (*Liber Pontificalis* 27.2, ed. Mommsen, 37; English translation in *The Book of the Popes*, ed. Loomis, 33). (The Latin *memoria* designates here a monument or church erected in dedication to a martyr, often above the martyr's grave.) While the ascription to the 3rd-century bishop is most likely not historically accurate (see Loomis's introduction to *The Book of the Popes*, pp. xvi–xvii), the prescription reflects a custom attested in the 4th century; see Redmond, 'Altar 3. In the Liturgy', 347, and see the note in *The Book of the Popes*, 33 n. 2. On celebratory commemorations observed on the anniversary of the death of Christian martyrs from the Decian persecution (mid-3rd century), see Cyprian, *Epistles*, in *Patrologia Latina*, ed. Migne, iv. 323A, Epistle xxxiv (Eng. trans. in *The Ante-Nicene Fathers*, v. 313, listed there as Epistle xxxiii; see 301 n. 3 on the reason for the different numbering of the epistles), and also in *Patrologia Latina*, ed. Migne, iv. 328C, Epistle xxxvii (English translation in *The Ante-Nicene Fathers*, v. 315, listed there as Epistle xxxvi). The theme of the souls of the righteous offered as a sacrifice in Paradise appears explicitly in the Christian apocryphal work *The Questions of Bartholomew*, where Jesus requests his apostles to wait for him since 'today a sacrifice is offered in paradise ... [for] there are souls of the righteous which today have departed the body and will go to paradise, and unless I be present they cannot enter into paradise' (*The Questions of Bartholomew*, 1: 28, in Elliott, *The Apocryphal New Testament*, 657). Scholarly consensus places the composition of this work, written originally in Greek, in Egypt between the 2nd and 6th centuries (see ibid. 652). The dating is significant for determining when the motif was introduced in the Jewish sources, although the narrative uses of the motif differ in each work (there is no indication of martyrdom in the Christian text) and the relationship between the sources is unclear. On the textual problems of the *Questions of Bartholomew*, see Kaestli, 'Où en est l'étude de l'"Évangile de Barthélemy"?' Cf. Boustan, *From Martyr to Mystic*, 171.

of his death through their own, and it embodies the idea of martyrdom as the pinnacle of religious significance and achievement.

The idea of personal sacrifice as expiation is also found in the later Jewish texts considered here. Martyrs are understood to ensure not only their own expiation and reward in the world to come; they also facilitate (vicarious) atonement for the people of Israel, particularly at times when God's wrath is evident, for example during the period of the destruction of the Temple. As the actual altar of the Temple, upon which animal sacrifices were offered, was the traditional locus for the procurement of atonement for individuals as well as for the people of Israel as a whole, it could naturally become a symbol for national atonement, whether in its earthly form or as a part of the heavenly Temple. The motif concerning the sacrifice of human souls upon the heavenly altar in lieu of 'images' of animal sacrifices, as described in the early medieval Jewish texts, thus mirrors, from a historical perspective, the Christian altar upon which the Eucharist was celebrated, where vicarious atonement was said to have been attained through the sacrifice of the souls of the righteous.

CONCLUSION

While ancient Jewish texts from the biblical and rabbinic periods on refer to a heavenly Temple with its altar that corresponds to the earthly Temple of Jerusalem, and also to repositories where dead souls await final judgement or recompense, these two themes remained separate. In the apocalyptic texts righteous souls entreat God and plead for personal or communal reward; in rabbinic texts, the heavenly altar could mirror the earthly one as the location for the offering of 'heavenly' animal sacrifices. But the two elements were combined in a new, radical image in the Byzantine 'Tale of the Ten Martyrs', in which the souls of the righteous are sacrificed upon the heavenly altar in lieu of the regular heavenly animal sacrifices. From an awareness of this special sacrifice on high R. Ishmael and his colleagues are convinced of the necessity of their martyrdom for the expiation and atonement of Israel's sins. The motif may have had its origins in real executions of priests and other Jews at the Temple's altar in the year 70 CE, to which the book of Revelation seems to allude. The present study suggests that the image gained special force and meaning against the background of early Christian martyrological theology and practice, for the placement of eucharistic altars above the graves of martyred saints gave expiatory meaning to their sacrificial deaths. Byzantine Jewish tradition transposed this Christian theme: when sacrificed on the heavenly altar, the souls of righteous martyrs effected expiation for all Israel in the post-destruction period. The theme of atonement, implicit in the 'Tale of the Ten Martyrs', becomes explicit in the later aggadic text *Seder arakim*, possibly transmitted in southern Italy. There the sacrifice of the righteous souls is demanded by God as a substitute for the expiation that had previously been effected through animal sacrifices (real and virtual) on the Temple altar. According to this source, the need for such expiatory sacrifices would end, and animal sacrifices would resume, with the rebuilding of the Temple.

Though this tradition reached medieval Ashkenaz with other Palestinian-Italian aggadic traditions and was cited by leaders of the German Pietists of the twelfth and thirteenth centuries, they reformulated it and framed the sacrifice of the righteous—and not merely the martyrs—as an instrument for the personal purification of the individual soul, a step in the journey towards its final 'binding' under the heavenly throne.

It remains to be determined whether the Christian influence proposed here was literary in nature, or was, rather, the result of a more general cultural influence. Did the author of the 'Tale of the Ten Martyrs' have direct access to Christian martyrological texts which proliferated during the third to sixth centuries, or is the incorporation of the martyr-sacrifice motif into this text indicative of more widespread cross-cultural influences in Byzantine Palestine? Whatever the motif's origins, the popularity of the 'Tale of the Ten Martyrs' account, and its robust lines of transmission, facilitated the re-implantation of the motif in later aggadic texts of Byzantine Italy, as well as its spread from there to scholars of medieval Ashkenaz, whose disciples and scribes saw fit to broaden the significance of the motif to reflect nuanced interpretations of the daily prayer liturgy, and to emend accordingly the talmudic passage in tractate *Ḥagigah* concerning sacrifices upon the heavenly altar.

Bibliography

1 Enoch 1: A Commentary on the Book of 1 Enoch, Chapters 1–36; 81–108, ed. G. W. E. Nickelsburg (Minneapolis, 2001).

3 Enoch: Or, the Hebrew Book of Enoch, ed. H. Odeberg (Cambridge, 1928).

Avot derabi natan, ed. S. Schechter (Vienna, 1887; repr., ed. Kister, Jerusalem, 1997).

ABRAHAM BEN AZRIEL, *Sefer arugat habosem, kolel perushim lapiyutim*, ed. E. E. Urbach, 4 vols. (Jerusalem, 1963).

ALEXANDER, PHILIP S., 'The Historical Setting of the Hebrew Book of Enoch', *Journal of Jewish Studies*, 28 (1977).

APTOWITZER, AVIGDOR, 'The Heavenly Temple in the Aggadah' (Heb.), *Tarbiz*, 2 (1930), 137–53, 257–87.
Bemidbar rabah, in *Midrash rabah* (Vilna, 1887).
Bet ha-Midrasch: Sammlung kleiner Midraschim und vermischter Abhandlungen aus der ältern jüdischen Literatur, ed. A. Jellinek, 6 vols., 2nd edn. (Jerusalem, 1938).
The Book of the Popes (Liber Pontificalis) I: To the Pontificate of Gregory I, trans. and ed. Louise R. Loomis (New York, 1916).
BOUSTAN, RA'ANAN S. (ABUSCH), *From Martyr to Mystic: Rabbinic Martyrology and the Making of Merkabah Mysticism* (Tübingen, 2005).
——'Rabbi Ishmael's Miraculous Conception: Jewish Redemption History and Anti-Christian Redemption', in A. H. Becker and A. Y. Reed (eds.), *The Ways That Never Parted: Jews and Christians in Late Antiquity and the Early Middle Ages* (Tübingen, 2003), 307–43.
DE ROSSI, GIOVANNI BERNARDO, *MSS. Codices Hebraici Biblioth.*, 3 vols. (Parma, 1803).
ELEAZAR OF WORMS, *Sodei razya*, ed. A. Eisenbach, 2 vols. (Jerusalem, 2004).
FORD, JOSEPHINE MASSYNGBERDE, *Revelation: A New Translation with Introduction and Commentary*, Anchor Bible 38 (Garden City, NY, 1975).
Die Geschichte von den Zehn Märtyren, ed. G. Reeg (Tübingen, 1985).
GEULA, AMOS, 'Lost Aggadic Works Known Only from Ashkenaz: *Midrash Abkir*, *Midrash Esfa* and *Devarim Zuta*' [Midreshei agadah avudim hayedu'im me'ashkenaz bilevad: avkir, esfah, udevarim zuta], Ph.D. diss., 2 vols. (Hebrew University of Jerusalem, 2006).
——'A Sermon and *Piyut* for the Sabbath Afternoon Service in Byzantine Synagogues' (Heb.), in A. Reiner et al. (eds.), *Ta Shma: Studies in Judaica in Memory of Israel M. Ta-Shma* [Ta-shema: sefer zikaron le-y. m. ta-shma] (Alon Shevut, 2011), 171–94.
GROSSMAN, AVRAHAM, *The Early Sages of Ashkenaz: Their Lives, Leadership and Works (900–1096)* [Ḥakhmei ashkenaz harishonim: koroteihem, darkam behanhagat hatsibur, yetsiratam haruḥanit mereshit yeshivatam ve'ad ligezerat tatnu (1096)] (Jerusalem, 2001).
——'The Relationship of Early Ashkenazi Jewry to the Land of Israel' (Heb.), *Shalem*, 3 (Jerusalem, 1981), 57–92.
Hagadot hatalmud (Constantinople, 1511).
HERRMANN, KLAUS, 'Jewish Mysticisms in Byzantium: the Transformation of Merkavah Mysticism in *3 Enoch*', in R. Boustan, M. Himmelfarb, and P. Schäfer (eds.), *Hekhalot Literature in Context* (Tübingen, 2013), 85–116.
IBN HABIB, JACOB, *Ein ya'akov*, 2 vols. (Salonica, 1516).
JACOB BEN ASHER, *Arba'ah turim*, 21 vols. (Jerusalem, 1990–4).
JUDAH HEHASID, *Sefer gematriyot*, ed. Y. I. Stal, 2 vols. (Jerusalem, 2004).
KAESTLI, JEAN-DANIEL, 'Où en est l'étude de l'"Évangile de Barthélemy"?', *Revue biblique*, 95 (1988), 5–33.

Kevod ḥupah, ed. C. M. Horowitz (Frankfurt am Main, 1888).

Liber Pontificalis (Pars prior), ed. T. Mommsen (Berlin, 1908; repr. Munich, 1982).

MACK, HANANEL, 'Prolegomena and Example to an Edition of Midrash Bemidbar Rabba, Part 1' [Midrash bemidbar rabah ḥelek I: parashiyot bemidbar venaso—mavo vedugmah], Ph.D. diss. (Hebrew University of Jerusalem, 1991).

MANDEL, PAUL, 'Was Rabbi Akiva a Martyr? Palestinian and Babylonian Influences in the Development of a Legend', in T. Ilan and R. Nikolsky (eds.), *Rabbinic Traditions between Palestine and Babylonia*, Series of Ancient Judaism and Early Christianity 89 (Leiden, 2014), 306–53.

MARGOLIOUTH, GEORGE, *Catalogue of the Hebrew and Samaritan Manuscripts in the British Museum*, 4 vols. (London, 1899–1935).

Mekhilta derabi yishma'el, ed. H. S. Horovitz and I. A. Rabin (Frankfurt am Main, 1928–31).

Midrasch Eikha [Lamentations] *Rabati*, ed. S. Buber (Vilna, 1899).

Midrasch Tanḥuma, ed. S. Buber (Vilna, 1885).

Midrasch Tehillim, ed. S. Buber (Vilna, 1891).

Midrash Bereshit Rabba, Critical Edition with Notes and Commentary, ed. J. Theodor and C. Albeck, 3 vols. (Berlin, 1912–36; 2nd edn. Jerusalem, 1965).

Midrash tanḥuma (Mantua, 1563 (facs. edn. Jerusalem, 1970); Warsaw, 1875).

NEUBAUER, ADOLF, *Catalogue of the Hebrew Manuscripts in the Bodleian Library and in the College Libraries of Oxford*, 2 vols. (Oxford, 1886, 1906).

NEWSOM, CAROL, *Songs of the Sabbath Sacrifice: A Critical Edition* (Atlanta, 1985).

The Old Testament Pseudepigrapha, ed. J. H. Charlesworth, 2 vols. (New York, 1983).

Otsar midrashim, ed. J. D. Eisenstein, 2 vols. (New York, 1915).

Patrologia Latina [*Patrologiae cursus completus*. Series Latina], ed. J.-P. Migne, 221 vols. (Paris, 1844–90).

Pesikta Rabbati, ed. M. Friedmann (Vienna, 1880).

Pesiqta Rabbati: A Synoptic Edition of Pesiqta Rabbati Based upon All Extant Manuscripts and the Editio Princeps, ed. R. Ulmer, 3 vols. (Atlanta, 1997).

The Questions of Bartholomew, in J. K. Elliott, *The Apocryphal New Testament* (Oxford, 1993), 652–72.

REDMOND, R. X., 'Altar 3. In the Liturgy', *The New Catholic Encyclopedia* (New York, 1967), i. 347–51.

RICHLER, BENJAMIN (ed.), *Hebrew Manuscripts in the Biblioteca Palatina in Parma* (Jerusalem, 2001).

ROBERTS, ALEXANDER, and JAMES DAVIDSON (eds.), *The Anti-Nicene Fathers: Translations of the Writings of the Fathers Down to A.D. 325*, 10 vols. (Grand Rapids, Mich., 1978–81; repr. of *Anti-Nicene Christian Library*, Edinburgh, 1867–72).

ROZEN-ZVI, ISHAY, Review of Ra'anan S. Boustan, *From Martyr to Mystic* (Heb.), *Zion*, 73 (2008), 211–16.

SCHÄFER, PETER, *Synopse zur Hekhalot-Literatur*, Texte und Studien zum Antiken Judentum 2 (Tübingen, 1981).

SCHOLEM, GERSHOM, *Major Trends in Jewish Mysticism* (New York, 1941).

——'The Sources of *Ma'aseh rabi gadi'el hatinok* in the Kabbalistic Literature' (Heb.), in D. Sadan and E. E. Urbach (eds.), *A Gift to Agnon: On the Author and His Books* [Le'agnon shai: devarim al hasofer usefarav] (Jerusalem, 1966).

SHAPIRA, ANAT, *A Midrash on the Ten Commandments: Text, Sources and Interpretation* [Midrash aseret hadiberot: tekst, mekorot uferush] (Jerusalem, 2005).

Sifrei on Deuteronomy, ed. L. Finkelstein (New York, 1969).

Sifrei on Numbers, ed. H. S. Horovitz (Leipzig, 1917; repr. Jerusalem, 1966).

STEINSCHNEIDER, MORITZ, *Hebräischen Handschriften der K. Hof- und Staatsbibliothek in München* (Munich, 1895).

—— *Catalogus Librorum Hebraeorum in Bibliotheca Bodleiana*, 3 vols. (Berlin, 1931).

STONE, MICHAEL EDWARD, *Fourth Ezra: A Commentary on the Books of Fourth Ezra* (Minneapolis, 1990).

TA-SHMA, ISRAEL M., *Early Franco-German Ritual and Custom* [Minhag ashkenaz hakadmon] (Jerusalem, 1999).

——'The Library of the Ashkenazi Sages in the Eleventh and Twelfth Centuries' (Heb.), *Kiryat sefer*, 60 (1985), 298–309.

——'Towards a History of the Cultural Links between Byzantine and Ashkenazi Jewry' (Heb.), in Ezra Fleischer et al. (eds.), *Me'ah She'arim: Studies in Medieval Jewish Spiritual Life, in Memory of Isadore Twersky* [Me'ah she'arim: sefer hazikaron liprof. yitsḥak twersky] (Jerusalem, 2001), 61–70.

ZEITLIN, S. 'The Legend of the Martyrs and Its Apocalyptic Origin', *Jewish Quarterly Review*, 36 (1945–6), 1–16.

CHAPTER FOUR

The Bifurcated Legacy of Rabbi Moses Hadarshan and the Rise of *Peshat* Exegesis in Medieval France

HANANEL MACK

BEFORE THE ELEVENTH CENTURY the most obvious examples of *peshat*, that is, plain-sense Bible interpretations, were produced by Jewish linguists of the Islamicate world, who were familiar with developments in quranic exegesis as well as with Arabic lexicography and grammar. The origin of *peshat* exegesis among the Jews of Christian lands is far more difficult to determine. The earliest known *pashtan* (plain-sense exegete) in non-Islamic Europe was R. Moses, of eleventh-century Provence, yet his moniker Hadarshan ('the homilist') leaves the impression that he was better known at one time for his homiletical interpretations of Scripture. In fact, R. Moses Hadarshan was the pioneer of both *peshat* and *derash* (homiletical) exegesis on European soil. Yet, strikingly, his literary legacy is characterized by a dramatic bifurcation. Though perhaps inadequately recognized, R. Moses' *peshat* traditions proved foundational; they were cited by scholars such as Rashi and R. Joseph Kara, better-known builders of *peshat* biblical exegesis from the last quarter of the eleventh century onwards. Yet most of R. Moses' *derash* teachings—for which he had earned the sobriquet 'the Homilist'—were in the end abandoned by medieval Jews. This sermonic material surfaced later—in a thirteenth-century assemblage of rabbinic writings compiled by Christians, to be used in converting the Jews. Exploration of R. Moses' poorly known oeuvre, both the *peshat* and the *derash*, and reconstruction of his bifurcated literary legacy, will shed light on two interrelated developments in medieval French Jewish culture. One was the tendency to marginalize, avoid, and perhaps even suppress inherited traditions of messianic content so that they would not appear on the Jewish bookshelf or in Jewish curricula. The other development, far better known, was the robust cultivation of *peshat* exegesis by Jewish Bible scholars in medieval France.

As is the case with others in a long line of early medieval Jewish authors, Provençal scholars among them, little is known about R. Moses' life, his teachers, and his training in Torah.[1] We are not certain who helped him acquire the knowledge and the proficiency that facilitated his production of a body of interpretations and *midrashim*, and we cannot speculate about the chronological order of his creations, or about possible shifts in his approach. It is also impossible to assess quantitatively his collected writings from the evidence at hand. What has been retrieved thus far are eighty-two *derash* interpretations of biblical passages, mostly preserved in Christian sources,[2] and forty-five *peshat* interpretations, preserved in Jewish sources. All are poorly known, having been recovered only recently.[3]

In the first section of this essay I consider the role of R. Moses Hadarshan in the history of *derash*, and present two of his homiletical passages of messianic content, along with brief philological analyses. In the second section I present selections of his *peshat* teachings, survey what is known about their transmission, and recapitulate speculative theories about a possible Andalusian influence. The third and final section offers a speculative hypothesis about R. Moses' bifurcated literary legacy. Endeavouring to explain the avoidance of his homilies (and even the citation of his name) in later medieval Jewish writings, this hypothesis may also account for the intellectual energy that was invested in the pursuit of *peshat* scriptural exegesis.

I

R. Moses Hadarshan was hardly the father or progenitor of homily as a method of study and exegesis; *derash* interpretations of Torah had been widespread in the Jewish world from antiquity. But R. Moses' exegesis and preaching are in no way a direct continuation of the homiletical material found in the classical midrashic literature and the two Talmuds.[4] His approach is also unlike that of the geonim and the medieval exegetes in the lands of Islam and the Mediterranean basin who followed their path. In this sense, R. Moses

[1] Possible influences on R. Moses' teachings from Italian and Byzantine sources as well as from those of the Islamic east are discussed in Mack, *The Mystery of Rabbi Moses Hadarshan* (Heb.), 72–92.

[2] Rashi does cite some *derash* interpretations of R. Moses Hadarshan that have no messianic content. See e.g. Rashi's comments on Num. 7: 19–23, 'one silver plate'. And see Mack, *The Mystery of Rabbi Moses Hadarshan* (Heb.), 133–41.

[3] All known passages are collected and discussed in Mack, *The Mystery of Rabbi Moses Hadarshan* (Heb.).

[4] Ibid. 109–14.

Hadarshan was a pioneer of *derash*—both in planting creative homiletical interpretation in European soil and in developing his own method of preaching. Some of his homilies have been preserved in *Midrash bamidbar rabah*,[5] *Midrash bereshit rabati*,[6] *Midrash agadah*,[7] and in Rashi's commentary on Scripture.[8] None of these sermonic materials are of messianic content—a crucial fact to which I return below. Casuistic interpretations and sermons by the Tosafists and their associates also evince similarities with the homiletical style of R. Moses; the same is true of certain compositions from the circle of the Rhineland Pietists.

Though, as stated above, none of R. Moses' homilies that survive in the above-mentioned midrashic collections have a messianic content, much of his exegesis is concerned with messianic themes. The two pieces presented here with analysis focus on passages in the book of Genesis. Both have been preserved in *Pugio Fidei*, a thirteenth-century anthology of rabbinic texts compiled by the Dominican monk Ramon (Raimundus) Martini. Designed for medieval Christian polemicists to use in the mission to convert the Jews, *Pugio Fidei* has been described as 'the most learned, comprehensive, and damaging work of anti-Jewish polemic composed by a Christian in the Middle Ages'.[9] The first piece is R. Moses' commentary on the Joseph story in Genesis:

'And Reuben said to them, Shed no blood! Cast him into that pit out in the wilderness, but do not touch him yourselves' [Gen. 37: 25]. As it is written, 'You would even cast lots over an orphan, or barter away your friend' [Job 6: 27]. [With regard to] this, Scripture said, 'We have become orphans, fatherless' [Lam. 5: 3]. R. Berakhyah said: The Blessed One said to Israel: You said, 'We were orphans, with no father'. So too, the saviour whom I will establish from your midst will have no father, as it says, 'Behold, a man called the Branch [*tsemah*] shall branch out from the place where he is' [Zech. 6: 12], and it says, 'For he has grown by His favour like a tree crown' [Isa. 53: 2]. And of him David said, 'From the womb, from the dawn, yours was the dew of youth' [Ps. 110: 3].[10]

In this homily R. Moses blends four components: the image of the messiah as a human with no corporeal father; Isaiah's prophecy of the tortured and

[5] Ibid. 171–87. [6] Ibid. 188–94. [7] Ibid. 195–7.

[8] See e.g. his comments on several sections in the book of Numbers: the offerings of the *nesi'im* at the dedication of the altar in the Tabernacle, the second census, and elsewhere. See too Mack, *The Mystery of Rabbi Moses Hadarshan* (Heb.), 133–41.

[9] Cohen, 'The Second Paris Disputation' (Heb.), 557–79.

[10] *Bereschit Rabba, R. Mosis Haddarshan*, in *Pugio Fidei*, ed. Karpzov, 759.

suffering servant; the verse 'Indeed, My servant shall prosper' (Ps. 52: 13 ff.);[11] and Psalm 110, which describes God's relationship to the one who sits to his left, and to Melkhitsedek—verses that have played a significant role in Christian tradition and theology through the ages.[12] R. Moses applies the verse from Job to the figure of Joseph, the orphan and friend, who was cast into the pit and sold. The homily appears in *Midrash eikhah rabati* on the verse 'We have become orphans' (Lam. 5: 3). Yet neither the Vilna nor the Buber edition of that work has the verse from Job or the concluding verses from Zechariah, Isaiah, and Psalms. By including them in his homily, R. Moses Hadarshan interpreted the biblical portent of the saviour in a manner that later Christian exegetes developed more fully. The same is true of his reference to 'the Branch' (*tsemah*). In discussing the name(s) of the messiah, the *midrashim* and the Talmuds offer various opinions, all based on scriptural verses.[13] The words of R. Joshua ben Levi are adduced both in the Jerusalem Talmud (*Ber.* 2: 4; 5*a*) and in *Midrash eikhah rabati* 1: 51.[14] According to R. Joshua, the name of the Messiah is Tsemah, in keeping with the verse 'Behold, a man called the Branch' (Zech. 6: 12). Of all the other names of the messiah identified by the rabbis—Shiloh, Yinon, Haninah, and Menahem among them—Tsemah was the only one which was not homiletically derived. Unlike the others, Tsemah appears in Scripture as the revealed name of the man mentioned by the prophet Zechariah.

A second messianic homily by R. Moses Hadarshan is divided between two chapters in *Pugio Fidei*. The first part concerns the discrepancy between the portraits of the messiah presented in the prophecies of Zechariah and Daniel:

'He tethers his ass to a vine' [Gen. 49: 11]: when King Messiah comes to Jerusalem to deliver Israel, he reins in his donkey and rides on it and comes to Jerusalem, comporting himself humbly,[15] as it is written, 'poor [*ani*], riding on an ass' [Zech. 9: 9].

'His ass's foal to a choice vine' [Gen. 49: 11]: when he comes to gather Israel, as it says, 'his ass's foal to a choice vine', he will ride on his ass's foal, and thus it says, 'Rejoice greatly, daughter of Zion' [Zech. 9: 9]. And has it not already been said of the Messiah, 'One like a human being came with the clouds of heaven' [Dan. 7: 13]?

[11] Because this chapter was used by the apostate Pablo Christiani in the Barcelona Disputation of 1263, Nahmanides dedicated a special section to it. See *Kitvei haramban*, i. 321–6.

[12] Ps. 110 is one of the most widely cited scriptural sections in the New Testament. See the words of R. David Kimhi at the end of his commentary on this psalm.

[13] See BT *San.* 98*b*.

[14] *Eikhah rabah*, ed. Buber, 88.

[15] In a marginal note to the Karpzov edition: as a poor person (*ke'ani*).

If [the children of] Israel merit, then with the clouds of heaven; if they do not merit, 'riding on an ass' [Zech. 9: 9].

The second part of the homily focuses on Jacob's blessing to Joseph:

'He washes his garment in wine' [Gen. 49: 11]: when the Messiah comes, he will be dressed in purple, beautiful to behold, and it will resemble wine. 'His robe in blood of grapes'[16] [Gen. 49: 11]: the garment of King Messiah will be of fine wool, red like blood, and will be a weave of other colours. And he will be at the head of Israel, as it is written, 'he washes his garment in wine', corresponding to 'Why is your clothing so red?' [Isa. 63: 2] And 'his robe in blood of grapes', corresponding to 'your garments like those of the one who treads grapes' [Isa. 63: 2].[17]

Both segments of this homily overlap with known passages in rabbinic writings. A discussion of the incompatibility between Zechariah's 'poor, riding on an ass' and Daniel's 'One like a human being came with the clouds of heaven' is presented by R. Alexandri in the name of R. Joshua ben Levi in the Babylonian Talmud (*San.* 98*a*). Both the question and the response regarding these divergent portraits of the messiah follow a similar question and answer concerning the verse '[I the Lord] will speed it in its time' (Isa. 60: 22). The continuation of the narrative relates R. Joshua ben Levi's encounter with the messiah, who was sitting among the poor at the gates of Rome; this theme, too, may follow from Zechariah's verse about the impoverished messiah.

Other passages in rabbinic literature also offer homiletical explanations of the verse 'poor, riding on an ass' (Zech. 9: 9) as referring to the messiah. Two are found in *Bereshit rabah*. One is '"I have acquired cattle and asses" [Gen. 32: 6]: an ox is one anointed for battle . . . the donkey is the King Messiah, as it says, "poor, riding on an ass".'[18] The second is, '"He tethers his ass to a vine" [Gen. 49: 11]: the one of whom it is written, "poor, riding on an ass".'[19] A third rabbinic passage appears in *Pesikta rabati*: '"poor [*ani*] etc." [Zech. 9: 9]: this is the messiah. And why is his name Ani [from the verb *la'anot*, to torture]? Because he was tortured all those years in prison.'[20]

The second part of the homily is familiar from the Aramaic translations of Jacob's blessing to Judah. Targum Onkelos presents the messiah as the subject of the prophecy 'the sceptre shall not depart from Judah' (Gen. 49: 10). Onkelos translates the second part of the next verse, 'He tethers his ass to a

16 The masoretic text reads *sutah* (rather than *kesuto* as is found here).

17 *Bereschit Rabba, R. Mosis Haddarshan*, in *Pugio Fidei*, ed. Karpzov, 850.

18 *Bereshit rabah* 75: 6 (*Midrash Bereshit Rabba*, ed. Theodor and Albeck, pp. 892–3).

19 *Bereshit rabah* 99: 8 (*Midrash Bereshit Rabba*, ed. Theodor and Albeck, p. 1280).

20 *Pesikta rabati* 34. This is found on fo. 179*b* in the Ish-Shalom edition.

vine, his ass's foal to a choice vine; he washes his garment in wine, his robe in blood of grapes', in the following manner: 'His garments will be of fine purple, his woollen robe of the colour crimson and [other] dyed colours.' The Targum ascribed to Jonathan renders the verse as follows: 'How handsome is King Messiah . . . He arranges orders of battle with his enemies . . . his garments are rolled in blood, as if [in] a winepress.' The Targum then repeats the same phrase in Hebrew.[21] The messiah's clothes are red from the blood of the battles with his enemies, and their colour is similar to the 'blood of grapes'. This links the blessing to Joseph with the martial verses in Isaiah 63.[22]

It is difficult to know whether medieval Jews would have associated the messiah's purple cloak with the garment forced on Jesus by the Romans to taunt the 'King of the Jews'.[23] As residents of Christian Europe, they most probably would have known that church ecclesiastics were garbed in clothing that was the colour of grapes.

II

The *peshat* teachings of R. Moses Hadarshan, recovered from writings of other eleventh- and twelfth-century scholars, demonstrate his overarching exegetical concern: to make the text of Scripture clearer and more accessible to its readers and hearers. The examples presented below include comments on peculiar spellings and terms and on disjunctive narratives.

Rashi invokes R. Moses when he comments on the peculiar spelling *letsonakhem* (with a seemingly superfluous *alef*; Num. 32: 24), meaning 'to your flocks', in the words that Moses addressed to the tribes of Gad and Reuben. Acknowledging this anomaly, Rashi writes, 'This word is from the form of "Sheep [*tsoneh*] and oxen, all of them" [Ps. 8: 8], where there is no *alef* between the *tsadi* and *nun*. Thus, the *alef* that appears after the *nun* appears in place of the *alef* of *tsoneh*. I learned this from the *Yesod* of R. Moses Hadarshan.'[24] Elsewhere he includes R. Moses' comment about a measurement mentioned in Scripture whose precise meaning is unknown. In reporting the death of his wife Rachel, the patriarch Jacob noted that she had died on his return from

[21] See *Targum yonatan*, ed. Rieder.

[22] Several sources in Jewish tradition relate the messiah's purple clothes, the colour of which 'resembles wine', to the clothing of God. See the index in Yuval, *Two Nations in Your Womb*, s.v. *porphyrion*. Yuval stresses the double role of the *porphyrion*, which was the basis of both Jewish and Christian legends.

[23] Mark 15: 17, 20.

[24] It is perhaps possible to maintain that Rashi's *peshat* interpretation emerged indirectly from an otherwise unknown *derash* by R. Moses that focused on the unusual word *tsonakhem*.

Padan Aram, 'while I was journeying in the land of Canaan, when still *kivrat ha'arets* from Efrat' (Gen. 48: 7). Rashi adduces two explanations for this opaque phrase. One is the Aramaic explanation of Onkelos, who wrote that *kivrat ha'arets* was 'the measurement of what can be ploughed in a day'. The other was the explanation of R. Moses Hadarshan, according to whom the term designates 'the measure of the land, and this is 2,000 cubits, like the measure of the sabbath boundary'. In citing both interpretations, Rashi offers variant *peshat* traditions. Though quantitatively different, both attempt to clarify Scripture's plain sense. Other teachings of R. Moses adduced by Rashi are close to the *peshat* of the verse, and are based on the Arabic language.[25] Rashi may well have been following in the footsteps of R. Moses when he invoked the vernacular to comprehend and explain Scripture's plain sense.

Other *peshat* comments of R. Moses attempt to explain interruptions in the flow of the scriptural narrative. One such instance is when Jacob recounts his return to his father's house from Padan Aram. The travel account is disrupted by the announcement 'And Deborah, the nursemaid of Rebecca, died' (Gen. 35: 8). Commenting on this non sequitur, Rashi writes: 'Why is the matter of Deborah in [the matter of] Jacob's home? For since Rebecca said to Jacob, "then I will fetch you from there" [Gen. 27: 45], she sent Deborah to him at Padan Aram to [get him to] leave, and she [i.e. Deborah] died on the way. I learned this from the words of R. Moses Hadarshan.' As the origins of this particular teaching by R. Moses may lie in aggadah, Rashi's decision to include it in his commentary may be seen as an illustration of his—acknowledged—propensity to integrate 'aggadah that resolves words of Scripture—"a phrase well turned" [cf. Prov. 25: 11]'.[26]

Elsewhere Rashi poses a question about a scriptural riddle in overtly homiletical terms, then proceeds to adduce a *peshat* teaching of R. Moses Hadarshan that is contrastingly prosaic. In this case it was the Frenchman from the north who sermonized, underlining the text's decidedly non-plain meaning, and his Provençal predecessor who crunched numbers, hoping in this manner to provide data that would make the narrative of Scripture more credible. To give one example, Rashi opens his commentary on the weekly

[25] See e.g. Rashi's comments on Ps. 45: 12; 68: 17; Prov. 5: 19. It is quite possible that R. Moses knew Arabic, and some have suggested that he knew Persian as well, although this claim is much more speculative. See Mack, *The Mystery of Rabbi Moses Hadarshan* (Heb.), 75–7.

[26] See Rashi's comment on Gen. 3: 8: 'There are many *midreshei agadah* which the rabbis have already organized in their proper place in *Bereshit rabah* and in other midrashic collections. I have come, however, to present *peshuto shel mikra*, along with *agadah* that resolves the words of the biblical text, all in the proper context.'

Torah portion of 'Masei' ('Journeys'; Num. 33: 1) with a question:

Why were these journeys written down? To inform us of God's kindnesses. For even though He decreed that they be carried and moved through the desert, you should not say that they were being moved and carried from journey to journey all forty years, without rest. After all, these are only forty-two journeys. From them, subtract fourteen which occurred in the first year, before the decree, [that is] during their travel from Ramses to Ritma, from whence the spies were sent, as it says, 'After that the people set out from Hatserot' [Num. 12: 16]; 'Send men etc.' [Num. 13: 2]. And here it says, 'They set out from Hatserot and they encamped at Ritma' [Num. 33: 18], which, you have learned, is in the desert of Paran. Beyond this, subtract eight journeys that occurred after the death of Aaron—from Hor Hahar to the Plains of Moab, in the fortieth year. We find that for the duration of thirty-eight years, they made only twenty journeys. This is from the *Yesod* of Rabbi Moses.

This is not the only case in which R. Moses' *peshat* orientation stands in marked contrast to the interpretative claims of Rashi and his students—his grandson Rabbenu Tam among them.[27]

As we have seen, some citations from R. Moses Hadarshan refer to his *Yesod*, a work which is no longer extant. But others of his teachings may have been passed down by his son, R. Judah Hadarshan, whose exegetical comments on Scripture are best known through a collection compiled by his student, R. Menahem bar Helbo.[28] R. Menahem appears to have been a (perhaps older) contemporary of Rashi's, and was probably from Provence.[29] All the

[27] An example appears in Munich MS 5, where R. Moses understands the word 'light' in Elihu's remarks (Job 36: 30–1) as referring to actual light. This interpretation stands in marked contrast to that set forth in the homily of R. Yohanan in *Bereshit rabah* 26: 7 ((*Midrash Bereshit Rabba*, ed. Theodor and Albeck, 255), where references to light are understood as rainfall. This—certainly non-*peshat*—interpretation is repeated in the commentary on *Bereshit rabah* attributed to Rashi, in Rabbenu Tam's commentary on Job, and in the commentary on Job attributed to Rashi's student (*Sefer iyov mibeit midrasho shel rashi*, ed. Shoshana).

[28] See Geiger, *Sefer parshandata*, 20, *ma'amar sheni*; Poznanski, *Introduction to the Biblical Exegetes of France* (Heb.), p. xii; id., 'R. Menahem bar Helbo's *Pitronim*' (Heb.), 390; *Sefer arugat habosem*, ed. Urbach, iv. 8 n. 33; Grossman, *The Early Sages of France* (Heb.), 340 n. 301.

[29] The conjecture about R. Menahem bar Helbo's Provençal origins is supported by the appearance of a vernacular term, of presumably Provençal origin, in a manuscript version of Rashi's commentary which lists R. Menahem as one of the tradents. The word in question is *nafradura* (נפרדורא), which, according to Poznanski, is French. Mosheh Katan, however, suggests that it is from the Provençal; see Katan, *A Treasury of Foreign Words* (Heb.), 68 (entry 4214). On the manuscript passage where R. Menahem's name is mentioned see Poznanski, 'R. Menahem bar Helbo's *Pitronim*' (Heb.), 431 and n. 3. The same comment does not appear in the printed edition of Rashi's commentary on Job.

extant scriptural commentaries by R. Menahem are of the *peshat* type,[30] and are known as *pitronot*. Though S. A. Poznanski, who collected most of these *pitronot*, concluded 'that their composer himself wrote them in a book; not that his students who heard them recorded them in their master's name',[31] it is clear that the *pitronot* were also transmitted orally. Two of R. Menahem's most prominent pupils—his nephew R. Joseph ben Simon Kara[32] and Rashi —refer in writing to his oral teachings.[33] He also served as a communal teacher and preacher,[34] perhaps following in the footsteps of earlier preachers of Narbonne, R. Moses and R. Judah.[35]

It is almost certain that Rashi never had a face-to-face encounter with R. Moses Hadarshan.[36] There is no evidence of the intimate familiarity and warm interpersonal relations that characterize Rashi's connection with his masters, talmudic scholars of Mainz and Worms, and with his students in France.[37] He may have learned the traditions of R. Moses both from R. Menahem and from R. Joseph Kara,[38] for the latter was active in Worms

[30] According to Grossman, R. Menahem made every effort to interpret Scripture according to its *peshat*; see *The Early Sages of France* (Heb.), 343.

[31] See Poznanski, 'R. Menahem bar Helbo's *Pitronim*' (Heb.), 391. Sixty years before Poznanski published R. Menahem's *pitronim*, Abraham Geiger wrote of his hope to engage in research on the writings of that sage. See his letter no. 7 to Senior Sachs (dated 13 Adar II, 1853), which appeared in *Kerem ḥemed*, 8 (1854), 41–51 (p. 50): 'perhaps if God grants it I will also be able to wave my hand over [and write about] our other French scholars, whose works are hidden and covered in the dust of the repositories of books that fell into disuse. Menahem bar Helbo has been cast away, and the newer generations did not know Joseph Kara or Joseph Bekhor Shor.' See too Poznanski, 389–439.

[32] Grossman has written extensively on R. Joseph Kara in *The Early Sages of France* (Heb.), 254–346. It is possible that the descriptive title 'Kara' was ascribed to R. Menahem bar Helbo as well. See Berliner, 'On the History of Rashi's Commentaries' (Heb.), 204.

[33] See Rashi's commentary on Isa. 10: 24; Ezek. 12: 3; Joseph Kara's commentaries on 1 Sam. 13: 21 and Judg. 2: 17.

[34] On R. Menahem bar Helbo as a preacher of ethics see Kara's commentary on 1 Kgs 8: 32.

[35] R. Joseph Kara, who set his interpretations in writing, also served as a communal preacher. See Mondschein, 'Was R. Abraham Ibn Ezra Familiar with R. Joseph Kara's Torah Commentaries?' (Heb.), 257–60.

[36] Rashi was born in 1040 (or 1041); see Grossman, *The Early Sages of France* (Heb.), 122. The years of R. Moses' birth and death are not known, but certain data make it reasonable to assume that he died around the middle of the 11th century. See Mack, *The Mystery of Rabbi Moses Hadarshan* (Heb.), 38.

[37] This image has been espoused to a large extent in popular and literary treatments of Rashi and in academic studies as well. A description of the relationship between Rashi and his teachers on the one hand and between him and his students on the other appears in Grossman, *The Early Sages of France* (Heb.), 121–53.

[38] This is especially so if we accept Grossman's view that R. Menahem preceded Rashi.

and Troyes from at least the eighties of the eleventh century.[39] R. Joseph Kara transmitted traditions of R. Judah Hadarshan, his uncle's teacher, both in his biblical exegesis and in his commentaries on *piyut* (liturgical poetry). R. Moses Hadarshan,[40] his son R. Judah,[41] R. Menahem bar Helbo, and his nephew R. Joseph Kara[42] all wrote commentaries on *piyutim* composed by the early Palestinian liturgist R. Eleazar Hakalir.

R. Simon bar Helbo, brother of R. Menahem and father of R. Joseph Kara, may also have been a student of R. Moses Hadarshan and a transmitter of his teachings—to Rashi and, of course, to his own son Joseph. In his commentary on the verse 'Ephraim thinks, Ah, I have become rich; I have got power' (Hos. 12: 9–10), Rashi cites a *midrash agadah* in the name of 'R. Simon, may the memory of the righteous be for a blessing';[43] the same *midrash agadah* is also cited by R. Joseph Kara, in his commentary on the book of Joshua, in the name of R. Simon. As the content and style of this teaching are compatible with those found in the sermons of R. Moses Hadarshan, it is not far-

[39] See Grossman, *The Early Sages of France* (Heb.), 340–6; M. Cohen, 'A Possible Source for the Concept of *Peshuto shel Mikra*' (Heb.), 372.

[40] Three commentaries on *piyutim* by R. Moses are known, as is at least one by his son, R. Judah. These commentaries are cited and discussed in Mack, *The Mystery of Rabbi Moses Hadarshan* (Heb.), 296–300.

[41] R. Judah's interest in *piyut* is well explained by the fact that he spent time in Ashkenazi yeshivas, where the study of *piyut* occupied a prominent place. See Mack, *The Mystery of Rabbi Moses Hadarshan* (Heb.), 47–56.

[42] R. Joseph Kara ends his interpretation of R. Eleazar Hakalir's *piyut* for Yom Kippur, 'Shoshan emek ayumah', writing, 'This is how it was interpreted by my father's brother, R. Menahem bar Helbo, in the name of R. Judah bar Moses Hadarshan, may the memory of the righteous be a blessing.' It is cited by Urbach in his introduction to *Sefer arugat habosem*, iv. 3–4 (n. 5).

[43] Rashi writes on this verse:

> R. Simon propounded a *midrash agadah* [on the phrase] 'I have gotten power'—I have found a document of obligation which grants me dominion over Israel [as the verse in Gen. 50: 18 states], 'And [Joseph's] brothers also went and fell before him saying, "We are before you as servants."' Jerabam ben Nevat, who was from the tribe of Ephraim, flattered himself saying, I have become rich and powerful because I have a document [which states] that all of Israel are my slaves since my father had acquired them [cf. Gen. 50: 18], and what a slave acquires is acquired by his master, and all their money is therefore mine. Therefore, I will incur no sin if I take all that is theirs, for they are my servants. What is written after this, 'And I am the Lord your God from the land of Egypt' [Hosea 13: 4]—the greatness that your ancestor [Joseph] achieved in Egypt derived from Me, God said. The verse [uttered by Joseph] 'you will be my slaves' you remembered, but 'I am the Lord your God' [Exod. 20: 1] in the Ten Commandments you forgot, because you erected two calves, one in Beit El and the other in Dan.

fetched to conjecture that the source of the homily in Narbonne was the school of R. Moses. In short, it was not only through the citations in Rashi's commentary that the *peshat* approach and insights of R. Moses came to be known to Jews in northern France. *Peshat* was a serious endeavour in Provence well before the twelfth-century 'explosion' in plain-sense exegesis.

In speculating about the influences and concerns that impelled R. Moses and his exegetical heirs to engage in *peshat* exegesis, scholars have wondered about possible Provençal or French contacts with Andalusian Spain, home to Jewish linguists, grammarians, and lexicographers.[44] Avraham Grossman has suggested that the Spanish Jewish heritage may have influenced the development of the *peshat* school in France,[45] but Eliezer Touitou thought it unlikely.[46] Touitou has hesitantly suggested that the absence of such contact could be explained on linguistic grounds; after all, he notes, the Sephardi scholars composed their works in Arabic, which the French could not read. The language barrier noted by Touitou might shed light on the silence of French scholars regarding Andalusian writings on subjects such as philosophy, the sciences, and grammar. However, it cannot account for the paltry use that French Jews made of the Hebrew (and Aramaic) writings of Jewish scholars of southern Europe, from both Muslim Spain and Provence. These compositions included works of halakhah, interpretations of oral Torah, and biblical exegesis.[47]

[44] See e.g. Grossman, *The Early Sages of France* (Heb.), 563. I have dealt with the presence and influence of teachings from the Jews of the East and from Italian Jewry in Moses Hadarshan's writings, and I have also considered the possibility that R. Moses was born in Italy, or lived there for an extended period of time (Mack, *The Mystery of Rabbi Moses Hadarshan* (Heb.), 79–89). However, I did not find any evidence for parallel Spanish influences on his work.

[45] See Grossman, *The Early Sages of France* (Heb.), 323. Regarding the ascent of the *peshat* approach as early as the 11th century see ibid. 462–8; and see also Touitou, 'The Historical Background of Rashi's Commentary on Lection *Bereshit*' (Heb.), 97–105; and M. Cohen, 'A Possible Source for the Concept of *Peshuto shel Mikra*' (Heb.), 354 n. 7.

[46] See Touitou, 'The Historical Background of Rashi's Commentary on Lection *Bereshit*' (Heb.), 46–7.

[47] The relative absence of Andalusian influence on French rabbinic culture, not only in the 10th and 11th centuries but later as well, constitutes a riddle that has been widely discussed in contemporary scholarship. Ya'akov Sussman has considered the literary and cultural relationship between the rabbinic scholars of Provence and their colleagues in northern France and Germany in 'Rabad's Commentary on Tractate *Shekalim*' (Heb.), 131–70. At the outset (starred footnote on p. 131) Sussman notes that he had completed his study many years earlier but had delayed publishing it 'because I hoped that I would be able to clarify this great historical problem [of the relationship between rabbinic scholarship in Germany, Provence, and Italy] along firmer and clearer lines'. Although the problem has not been fully resolved, there is no doubt that Sussman's essay contains a large amount of highly important material that will form the

Some years ago Mordechai Cohen cautiously suggested that the introduction to *Sefer harikmah* by the Andalusian R. Jonah Ibn Janāḥ (990–1050) may have been a possible source for Rashi's concept of biblical *peshat*.[48] Though he thought it unlikely that Rashi read *Sefer harikmah*, even in translation, Cohen pointed out that there were notable parallels between the teachings of Ibn Janāḥ and those in the exegesis of Rashi's school.[49]

A passage that appears in a manuscript of Rashi's commentary on the book of Job suggests yet another avenue for thinking about possible lines of Andalusian influence on the *peshat* exegetes of Provence and their northern French students. Citing the tradents of a particular teaching, this passage states that the tradition was transmitted to Rashi 'in the name of R. Joseph [Kara], in the name of R. Menahem [bar Helbo], who said it in the name of R. Azariah'.[50] Avraham Grossman has noted this passage, but he was of the opinion that there was no other information about R. Azariah.[51] Yet in fact Yehosef, the son of R. Samuel Hanagid (993–1056), had a son named Azariah, renowned for his intelligence. (We know of no other scholar named R. Azariah who lived in south-west Europe in those generations.[52]) When a mob in Granada assassinated Yehosef (1035–66), Azariah fled to R. Isaac Ibn Ghiyyat (1038–89) who was based in Lucena in Al Andalus.[53] As Ibn Ghiyyat died in 1089, and Azariah predeceased him, it would have been chronologically possible for R. Menahem bar Helbo to have learned the interpretation in question from Azariah, the son of Yehosef and grandson of Samuel Hanagid. Unfortunately we have no knowledge of whether the Spaniard R. Azariah had ever travelled to Provence, or whether R. Menahem had spent time in southern Spain. We also find no similar type of interpretation in Muslim Spain of the eleventh century.

cornerstone of any subsequent treatments. A more recent summary, written in brief bullet-point form, is provided by Sussman ibid. 154 n. 99.

[48] Cohen's comment stemmed from his observation that Nahmanides had relied on Ibn Janāḥ's teachings when he wrote his animadversion to Maimonides' *Sefer hamitsvot*. See M. Cohen, 'A Possible Source for the Concept of *Peshuto shel Mikra*' (Heb.), 373.

[49] Ibid.

[50] Rashi's manuscript commentary on Job 9: 17, discussed in Poznanski, 'R. Menahem bar Helbo's *Pitronot*' (Heb.), 431 and n. 3. This comment does not appear in the printed edition of Rashi's commentary to Job.

[51] See Grossman, *The Early Sages of France* (Heb.), 343 n. 314.

[52] There is no connection between the European scholars discussed here and either Daniel ben Azariah, the Gaon of Erets Yisra'el between 1051 and 1062, or his father Azariah.

[53] According to Abraham Ibn Daud, author of *Sefer hakabalah*, R. Isaac Ibn Ghiyyat recognized Azariah's ability 'and wished to establish him as the head of the community of Lucena and

III

Rashi greatly admired R. Moses Hadarshan's interpretations, both *peshat* and *derash*, and he attested to this by incorporating many of them into his own writings, where he cited the preacher by name.[54] It may be assumed that, on the whole, Rashi was in agreement with R. Moses' exegetical approach, for he criticized interpretations that did not seem right to him.[55] To be sure, Rashi's exegetical method is more complex than that which emerges from an analysis of R. Moses' teachings. But Rashi's 'high road', about which he declared, 'I have only come [to explain] the *peshat* of Bible and the aggadah which explains [a difficulty] in Scripture, "a phrase well turned" [Prov. 25: 11]', is based, in no small measure, on the path paved by R. Moses Hadarshan.

Yet the number of citations from R. Moses in the writings of scholars who followed Rashi is very small. It is striking that the best-known French *peshat* exegetes who further developed Rashi's method of exegesis—R. Samuel ben Meir, R. Joseph Kara, R. Joseph Bekhor Shor, and R. Eleazar of Beaugency—largely avoided R. Moses' name in their writings, even in places where his influence was recognizable.

How can this discrepancy in medieval Jewish attitudes towards R. Moses Hadarshan be explained? We may conjecture that biblical scholars after the time of Rashi were familiar with a significant part of R. Moses' writings but deliberately marginalized his work. Even if they took interest in his teachings, they refrained from mentioning them—and even avoided mention of his name. Following Rashi's death, I suggest, Jewish scholars placed the figure of R. Moses 'out of bounds' because, in their times, the overt messianic content of his homiletical teachings had come to pose a danger to Jews in western Europe. The Christian anti-Jewish religious polemic which arose in the late eleventh century[56] was only beginning in Rashi's time;[57] it later took the form

the other communities of southern Spain even though he was a young man'. As Azariah passed away at a young age, R. Isaac's plan never came to fruition.

[54] As a general rule, Rashi and his students do not mention many exegetes who preceded them. See Mordechai Cohen, and his citations from Sarah Kamin and Sara Japhet.

[55] See e.g. Rashi's comment on Prov. 26: 10.

[56] See Mack, *The Mystery of Rabbi Moses Hadarshan* (Heb.), 99–101, and id., 'Why Have R. Moses Hadarshan's Books Disappeared?' (Heb.). On the role of R. Joseph Kara as an interlocutor with Christians see Grossman, 'Exile and Redemption in the Teachings of R. Joseph Kara' (Heb.).

[57] Judah Rosenthal and Avraham Grossman have noted the presence of polemical elements in Rashi's biblical commentaries. See Rosenthal, 'Anti-Christian Polemic in Rashi's Bible Commentary' (Heb.). In his view Rashi was not sufficiently sensitive to the ways in which

of public disputations, whose consequences for the Jews were grave. Long before the final arrangement of *Pugio Fidei*,[58] Jewish scholars appear to have recognized that Christians (Jewish apostates among them) who were committed to the conversion of the Jews could use R. Moses' messianic homilies as missionizing tools. While other rabbinic passages could be invoked to ridicule the Jews, R. Moses' messianic homilies could be used to prove the veracity of Christian beliefs from Jewish scholarly writings, and to attack Jews for ignoring their own beliefs. This theory alone may explain why there is almost no mention of R. Moses Hadarshan's name in rabbinic literature between the beginning of the twelfth century and the end of the fifteenth.[59]

We may similarly conjecture that if the teachings of R. Moses were intentionally suppressed, readers of the Bible would have been conscious of an exegetical vacuum, and would have been eager to fill this by developing *peshat* explanations that were insulated from homily. Whereas the methods of *derash* could lead anywhere, even to the sanction of theological notions consonant with Christianity, search for Scripture's plain sense stood as a bulwark against such interpretative plasticity. If these speculations are correct then the wariness of *derash* and the emphasis on *peshat* that characterized the Jewish culture of medieval France would have been bound together in one moment of history. It is this moment that is illuminated by the bifurcated literary legacy of

messianic interpretations could be appropriated by Christians. According to Sarah Kamin and Avraham Grossman, however, Rashi was indeed sensitive to this, as is apparent in a number of his comments on Psalms and the Song of Songs. It could be argued that he became more aware of this issue in his later years. See Kamin, 'Rashi's Commentary on the Song of Songs' (Heb.); Grossman, 'Rashi's Commentary on the Book of Psalms' (Heb.); and more recently Grossman, 'He Dispersed in the Hour of Gathering' (Heb.), 228–30 and nn. 21, 26–8.

[58] Claims about the time of Jesus' appearance in *Pugio Fidei* that are based partly on gematria seem to have been written in 1278 (*Pugio Fidei*, ed. Karpzov, 395), but the final editing of the work took several additional years.

[59] At the end of the 15th century R. Isaac Abarbanel mentions R. Moses in *Yeshuot meshiḥo*, and even cites about twenty of his *derash* teachings. Composed after the expulsion of the Jews from Spain, this work provided encouragement to Jews who had fled. It also responded (belatedly) to the claims presented by the apostate Joshua Halorki at the Tortosa disputation in 1413–14. In the course of the disputation Halorki had made use of those sections of the writings of R. Moses Darshan that were included by Ramon Martini in *Pugio Fidei*. Some eighty-five years later Abarbanel argued with Halorki and cited the passages from R. Moses that Halorki had adduced. All of the sections cited by Abarbanel are found in *Pugio Fidei*, with only minor changes. At several points Abarbanel noted that he did not have R. Moses' original work; apparently he had not seen it when he was in Spain and Portugal. This reinforces the broader impression that R. Moses' work was largely absent from the 'Jewish bookshelf' during the medieval period.

R. Moses Hadarshan, the European Jew who pioneered both modes of biblical exegesis.

APPENDIX

Rabbi Moses Hadarshan is recognized as the founding figure of Hebrew biblical exegesis in the world of medieval Latin Christendom, yet his teachings are barely known. Nowadays, his *peshat* interpretations are retrievable only through their citation in a range of medieval Hebrew texts, and his *derash* teachings through their citation in medieval Christian sources. Given the importance of R. Moses' writings to several rich arenas of research—medieval Jewish biblical exegesis, Jewish–Christian polemics, and the origins of rabbinic Jewish culture in Christian Europe—several of his teachings are made available in this appendix.

Section I contains six selections from the words of R. Moses Hadarshan which explain Bible in accordance with *peshat*. The source in which R. Moses' comment was embedded is noted in parentheses at the end of each selection. Section II offers a homiletical (*derash*) teaching of R. Moses. We may assume that it was preserved in Rashi's Bible commentary because it bears no messianic content.

I. R. Moses Hadarshan's *Peshat* Interpretations

1. *Psalm 60:4*

'You have made the land quake; You have torn it open. Mend its fissures, for it is collapsing.'

I saw in the words of Dunash that this is in the Arabic language. But he did not explain it. And in the *Yesod* of R. Moses Hadarshan, they explained it as a term of tearing, and cited a proof: 'and You rent it with windows' [Jer. 22: 14], translated in the Targum, 'and You cracked them'. (Rashi's commentary)

2. *Psalm 45:2*

'an expert [*mahir*] scribe'

I saw in the *Yesod* of R. Moses Hadarshan that *mahir* [lit. swift] means 'expert' in Arabic. (Rashi's commentary)

3. *Psalm 68:17*

'Why do you lie in wait [*teratsdun*], O jagged mountains?'

I saw in the *Yesod* of R. Moses Hadarshan that *r-ts-d* means ambush in Arabic. (Rashi's commentary)

4. *Proverbs 26:10*

'A master can produce anything, but he who hires a fool is as one who hires transient passers-by.'

In the words of R. Moses, I saw [regarding] 'A master can produce anything'—a rich man has many activities. And if a merchant is foolish in his labour, he is like the merchant whose damaged work is seen by all passers-by, [and they] instruct [him] about how he can make it possible/fix it, and how he should act. But this is a vapid comment [cf. Dt. 32: 47], and is not germane here. (Rashi's commentary)

5. *Job 24:10*

'They go about naked for lack of clothing, and the hungry carry sheaves.'

I found a different interpretation in the *Yesod* of R. Moses Hadarshan: 'and the hungry carry sheaves—for those steal these from them, and they remain famished.' [Rashi: 'and they would remain famished' (Munich MS 5)]. (This saying appears in Rashi's printed commentary on Job, without the name of R. Moses Haharshan, following the opening words 'And it is also interpreted'.)

6. *Job 34:1–2*

'And Elihu said in reply: Listen O wise men to my words; you who have knowledge, give ear to me.'

Because he had provoked them earlier, when he said, 'I thought, let age speak; let advanced years declare wise things' [Job 32: 7], and he says, 'But truly, it is the spirit in men' [Job 32: 8]. He sensed that he had sinned against them, and he began to speak in a more low-key manner, 'Listen [give heed], O wise men, to my words; you who have knowledge, give ear to me.' For before this matter it is written, 'And he was angry with his three friends' [Job 32: 3]—his wisdom disappeared from him. Thus said the sages, 'A person's anger causes him to lose his wisdom. And once he becomes calm and his anger subsides, he begins with soft words' [BT *Pes.* 66*b*]. From the *Yesod* of R. Moses Hadarshan. (Munich MS 5)

II. A Homily by R. Moses Hadarshan, Cited in Rashi's Commentary on Numbers 7: 19–23, 'one silver plate'

The sum of its letters [i.e. 'silver plate'] is 930, corresponding to the years in the life of the first man.

'Its weight is 130' [there]: because when he brought progeny into worldly existence, he was 130 years old, as it says, 'And Adam lived 130 years and sired etc.' [Gen. 5: 3].

'A single basin of silver' [there]: 520 in gematria, in connection with Noah, who brought progeny into the world when he was 500 years old. And because of the decree of the Flood, which was decreed twenty years before his progeny—as I have explained with reference to [Gen. 6: 3], 'and his days were 120 [years]'.[60] For this reason it said, 'a single basin of silver', and it did not say 'one silver basin' as was said regarding the plate, to say that even the letters in *eḥad* ['a single'] join in the count.

'Seventy shekels' [there]: corresponding to the seventy nations that descended from his children.

'One ladle' [Num. 7: 20], where *kaf* can mean 'ladle' or 'palm', corresponding to the Torah, which was given from the hands of God.

'Ten [shekels of] gold' [there]: corresponding to the Ten Commandments.

'Filled with incense' [there]: The gematria of *ketoret* [incense] is 613 commandments, as long as you switch the [letter] *kof* with [the letter] *dalet*, using the *atbash gardak* system.

'One bull' [Num. 7: 21]: corresponding to Abraham, of whom it was said, 'He took a calf of the herd' [Gen. 18: 7].

'One ram' [there]: corresponding to Isaac [as in Gen. 18: 7]—'and he took the ram'.

'One lamb' [there]: corresponding to Jacob [as in Gen. 30: 40]—'and Jacob separated the sheep'.

'Kid' [Num. 7: 22]: to atone for the selling of Joseph, as it says, 'And they slaughtered a kid' [Gen. 37: 31].

'And for the sacrifice of well-being, two oxen' [Num. 7: 23]: corresponding to Moses and Aaron, who established peace between [the children of] Israel and their Father in heaven.

'Five rams, five he-goats, and five yearling lambs' [there]: three types, corresponding to Priests, Levites, and Israelites, and corresponding to Torah, Prophets, and Hagiographa. Three sets of five, corresponding to the five *ḥumashim* [books of Torah]; and the five commandments written on one tablet, and five written on the second. Until here, in the *Yesod* of R. Moses Hadarshan.

The account of the tribal chiefs' sacrifices for the dedication of the altar is repeated in the Torah twelve times, and it concludes with a cumulative

[60] There is little doubt that this was added by Rashi, as Berliner noted, and they are not the words of R. Moses himself as Zunz suggests. See *Perush rashi al hatorah*, ed. Berliner, 292–3 n. 5.

summary of the details of the sacrifices (Num. 7: 84–8). Most preachers and exegetes refrained from engaging all these details, and certainly did not discuss all dozen occurrences. The exception was R. Moses Hadarshan, who homiletically interpreted each of the dozen cycles in all their detail, along with the details of their summaries—and whose homiletical explanations were preserved, with his name concealed, in *Midrash bemidbar rabah* (*parashot* 13–14). Rashi's words here are based on the homilies of R. Moses. Yet one who analyses the large corpus of these homilies in *Bemidbar rabah* will be convinced that Rashi had subjected the words of the homilist to a radical reworking. This is the manner in which the homily that appears before us was created, a composite of the homilies of R. Moses Hadarshan on several of the lections pertaining to the offerings of the tribal chiefs—particularly the chiefs of Issachar and Asher—and of the words of Rashi himself.

Bibliography

ABRAHAM BEN AZRIEL, *Sefer arugat habosem, kolel perushim lapiyutim*, ed. E. E. Urbach, 4 vols. (Jerusalem, 1963).

BERLINER, ABRAHAM, 'On the History of Rashi's Commentaries' (Heb.), in id., *Selected Writings* [Ketavim nivḥarim], vol. ii (Jerusalem, 1969), 179–226.

COHEN, JEREMY, 'The Second Paris Disputation and the Jewish–Christian Debate in the Thirteenth Century' (Heb.), *Tarbiz*, 68 (1999), 557–79.

COHEN, MORDECHAI, 'A Possible Source for the Concept of *Peshuto shel Mikra*' (Heb.), in Avraham Grossman and Sara Japhet (eds.), *Rashi: His Image and His Works* [Rashi: demuto viyetsirato] (Jerusalem, 1980), iii. 353–80.

GEIGER, ABRAHAM, *Sefer parshandata* (Leipzig, 1856).

GROSSMAN, AVRAHAM, *The Early Sages of France: Their Lives, Leadership, and Works* [Ḥakhmei tsarfat harishonim: koroteihem, darkam behanhagat hatsibur, yetsiratam haruḥanit] (Jerusalem 1995).

——'Exile and Redemption in the Teachings of R. Joseph Kara' (Heb.), in Reuven Bonfil et al. (eds.), *Culture and Society in Medieval Jewish History: An Anthology of Studies in Memory of H. H. Ben-Sasson* [Tarbut veḥevrah betoledot yisra'el biyemei habeinayim: kovets meḥkarim lezikhro shel h. h. ben-sason] (Jerusalem, 1989), 269–301.

——'He Dispersed in the Hour of Gathering: On Rashi's Sense of Mission' (Heb.), in A. Reiner et al. (eds.), *Ta Shma: Studies in Judaica in Memory of Israel M. Ta-Shma* [Ta shema: sefer zikaron le-y. m. ta-shma] (Alon Shevut, 2011), 221–34.

——'Rashi's Commentary on the Book of Psalms and the Jewish–Christian Debate' (Heb.), in *Essays Presented to Mosheh Ahrend* [Meḥkarim mugashim lemosheh ahrend] (Jerusalem, 1996), 59–74.

KAMIN, SARAH, 'Rashi's Commentary on the Song of Songs and the Jewish–Christian Debate' (Heb.), in Sarah Kamin, *Jews and Christians in Biblical Exegesis* [Bein yehudim lenotsrim beparshanut hamikra] (Jerusalem, 1992), 31–61.

KATAN, MOSHEH, *A Treasury of Foreign Words—the French Words in Rashi's Commentaries on Scripture* [Otsar hale'azim—hamilim hatsarfatiyot shebeperushei rashi latanakh] (Jerusalem, 1984).

MACK, HANANEL, *The Mystery of Rabbi Moses Hadarshan* [Misodo shel rabi mosheh hadarshan] (Jerusalem, 2010).

——'Why Have R. Moses Hadarshan's Books Disappeared?' (Heb.), *Alpayim*, 32 (2008), 149–76.

Midrash Bereshit Rabba, Critical Edition with Notes and Commentary, ed. J. Theodor and C. Albeck, 3 vols. (Berlin, 1912–36; 2nd edn. Jerusalem, 1965).

MONDSCHEIN, AARON, 'Was R. Abraham Ibn Ezra Familiar with R. Joseph Kara's Torah Commentaries?' (Heb.), *Tarbiz*, 73 (2004), 239–70.

NAHMANIDES, MOSES, *Kitvei haramban*, ed. C. D. Chavel (Jerusalem, 1973).

Perush rashi al hatorah, ed. A. Berliner (Frankfurt, 1908).

Pesikta rabati, ed. M. Ish-Shalom (Vienna, 1880).

POZNANSKI, S. A., *Introduction to the Biblical Exegetes of France* [Mavo al ḥakhmei tsarfat mefarshei hamikra] (Jerusalem, 1965); originally published as *Introduction to the Commentaries of R. Eliezer of Beaugency on Ezekiel and the Twelve Prophets* [Mavo leferushei r. eliezer mibelgenzi liyeḥezkel utrei-asar] (Warsaw, 1909)].

——'R. Menahem bar Helbo's *Pitronim* to Scripture' (Heb.), in *Sefer hayovel lenaḥum sokolow* (Warsaw, 1904), 389–439.

Pugio Fidei, ed. J. B. Karpzov (Leipzig, 1687).

ROSENTHAL, JUDAH, 'Anti-Christian Polemic in Rashi's Bible Commentary' (Heb.), in J. Rosenthal, *Studies and Sources* [Meḥkarim umekorot] (Jerusalem, 1967), 101–16.

Sefer iyov mibeit midrasho shel rashi, ed. A. Shoshana (Jerusalem, 2000).

SUSSMAN, YA'AKOV, 'Rabad's Commentary on *Shekalim*? A Bibliographical and Historical Riddle' (Heb.), in E. Fleischer et al. (eds.), *Me'ah She'arim: Studies in Medieval Jewish Spiritual Life in Memory of Isadore Twersky* [Me'ah she'arim: sefer hazikaron liprof. yitsḥak twersky] (Jerusalem, 2000), 151–61.

Targum yonatan, ed. D. Rieder (Jerusalem, 1984).

TOUITOU, ELEAZAR, 'The Historical Background of Rashi's Commentary on Lection *Bereshit*' (Heb.), in Zvi Arie Steinfeld (ed.), *Rashi: Investigations into His Works* [Rashi: iyunim biyetsirato] (Ramat Gan, 1993).

——*'Exegesis in Perpetual Motion': Studies in the Pentateuchal Commentary of Rabbi Samuel ben Meir* ['Hapeshatot hamitḥadshim bekhol yom': iyunim beferusho shel rashbam al hatorah] (Ramat Gan, 2003).

YUVAL, ISRAEL JACOB, *Two Nations in Your Womb* (Berkeley, Calif., 2006).

CHAPTER FIVE

A New Look at Medieval Jewish Exegetical Constructions of *Peshat* in Christian and Muslim Lands: Rashbam and Maimonides

MORDECHAI Z. COHEN

Peshat (plain-sense) exegesis is one of the major achievements of medieval Jewish learning. Generally contrasted with Midrash (the creative and at times fanciful rabbinic mode of interpretation), *peshat* came, from the eleventh century onwards, to connote a philological-contextual and historically sensitive reading of the Hebrew Bible. With the advent of modern historical-critical Bible scholarship, the prestige of *peshat* increased dramatically, as it came to be regarded as a precedent for 'scientific' analysis of the Bible. According to this perspective, certain medieval exegetes arrived, with varying degrees of success, at 'the *peshat*'—taken to be *the correct sense* of Scripture.

Yet this 'homogenized' account of *peshat* oversimplifies a set of dynamic hermeneutical trajectories in different centres of Jewish learning, each grappling with unique cultural and intellectual challenges. This essay offers a case study of two boldly original constructions of *peshat*, one devised by Rashbam (Samuel ben Meir, *c.*1080–1160) in northern France, a subculture of Ashkenaz, the other by Moses Maimonides (1138–1204), a scion of Jewish learning in Muslim Spain (al-Andalus, Sepharad). Rashbam—a great talmudist whose grandfather Rashi (1040–1105) had opened the gates of *peshat* interpretation in northern France—has long been celebrated as a *pashtan* (practitioner of *peshat*) who broke the shackles of midrashic interpretation, especially in his bold reinterpretation of the halakhic sections of the Pentateuch. By contrast, the great philosopher Maimonides, no less a talmudic scholar than Rashbam, is generally not viewed as a Bible exegete, and certainly not as a *pashtan*. Yet recent scholarship illuminates his key role in the tradition of Jewish Bible exegesis, and his unique contributions to the development of Jewish interpretative theory. In fact, he drew upon an earlier Andalusian hermeneutical tradition to devise a radical model of *peshat* that privileged it above midrashic interpretation—precisely where sensitive matters of halakhah are concerned. By comparing these two hermeneutical constructions, I aim to demonstrate that the medieval quest to define 'the *peshat* of Scripture' was not simply about what the sacred text 'really says'. It was, rather, an arena in which Jewish interpreters in diverse cultural contexts, each reflecting contemporaneous Jewish and non-Jewish intellectual currents, sought to make sense of the Bible—religiously and rationally. A comparative analysis of the *peshat* hermeneutics of these two sages highlights key differences between the ways in which Jews in Christian and Muslim lands perceived the workings of Bible interpretation and the relationship between these perceptions and their respective approaches to Jewish law (halakhah).

These differences bear upon the very translation of the term *peshat*. Until recently it was standard to render *peshat* as the literal sense, and *derash*, that is, midrashic interpretation, as denoting a figurative, symbolic, or otherwise non-literal reading. Yet in many cases the midrashic reading is more literal than what the medieval exegetes termed *peshat*, which can entail a figurative reading.[1] Scholars therefore prefer other translations of the term, such as 'the plain' or 'simple' sense, or they argue that *peshat* has no English equivalent and is best rendered 'the text as it is, [interpreted] according to its language, syntax, context, genre, and literary structure, within a rational approach'.[2] This account seems quite apt in the case of Rashi's school, and also illuminates Rashbam's usage. Yet for Maimonides and others in the Sephardi orbit there are other crucial components to the concept of *peshat*.

RASHBAM'S CONSTRUCTION OF *PESHAT*

Displaying remarkable dedication to 'the *peshat* of Scripture' (*peshuto shel mikra*), Rashbam interprets the Torah (Pentateuch) without consideration of the talmudic rabbis' biblical exegesis. His distinction between the two interpretative modes is highlighted in the following programmatic statement:

Our rabbis taught us that 'a biblical verse does not leave the realm of its *peshat*',[3] even though the essence [*ikar*] of the Torah comes to teach and inform us of the *hagadot*

[1] See Cohen, 'Emergence of the Rule of *Peshat*'; Garfinkel, 'Clearing *Peshat* and *Derash*', 131–2. See also the example cited at n. 4.

[2] Japhet, 'The Tension between Rabbinic Legal Midrash and the "Plain Meaning"', 403. Compare Kamin, *Rashi's Exegetical Categorization* (Heb.), 11–22.

[3] BT *Shab.* 63*a*; *Yev.* 12*a*, 24*a*.

[traditions, lore], *halakhot* [laws], and *dinim* [regulations] through the hint[s] of the *peshat* [*remizat hapeshat*] by way of redundant language, and through the thirty-two hermeneutical rules of R. Eliezer . . . and the thirteen rules of R. Ishmael. Now the early generations, because of their piety, tended to delve into the *derashot*, since they are the essence [*ikar*], and therefore [they] were not accustomed to the deep *peshat* of Scripture . . . Now our master, Rabbi Solomon, the father of my mother, luminary of the diaspora who interpreted Torah, Prophets, and Writings, aimed to interpret the *peshat* of Scripture. And I, Samuel, son of Meir his son-in-law [of blessed memory], debated with him personally, and he admitted to me that if he had the opportunity, he would have to write new commentaries according to the *peshat* [interpretation]s that newly emerge [*hamitḥadeshim*] every day.[4]

Rashbam emphasizes the independence of the *peshat* of Scripture from 'the *hagadot*, *halakhot*, and *dinim*' that make up the creed and laws of rabbinic Judaism. The latter are extrapolated from 'the hint[s] of the *peshat*', using the midrashic hermeneutical methods (*midot*) ascribed to the early sages Rabbi Eliezer and Rabbi Ishmael.[5] As an accomplished talmudist, Rashbam was quite familiar with these midrashic methods. Reflecting on the curriculum of study in his Ashkenazi milieu, he notes that the mainstay of Bible interpretation was a rehearsal of how the rabbis of the Talmud had applied these *midot* to yield the rubric of rabbinic Judaism ('the *hagadot*, *halakhot*, and *dinim*')—until Rashi began to take note of 'the *peshat* of Scripture'. According to Rashbam, Rashi himself recognized that more work remained to be done by his students, among them Rashbam.

Rashbam boldly applied his conception of *peshat* without regard for rabbinic interpretation, even in the realm of halakhah, as the following example illustrates. The rabbis (BT *Men.* 34*b*–37*b*) took Exodus 13: 9, 'And this shall serve you as a sign on your hand and as a reminder between your eyes—in order that the teaching of the Lord may be in your mouth—that with a mighty hand did the Lord free you from Egypt', as a source for every Jewish male's obligation to don phylacteries (*tefilin*). Following the Talmud, Rashi writes that the phylacteries are the 'sign' placed literally on the arm and head as a reminder of the Exodus.[6] But Rashbam remarks:

'As a sign on your hand': According to its deep *peshat*, it will always be on your mind, as if it were written on your hand. Like [the verse] 'Place me as a seal on your heart, as

[4] Rashbam (Samuel ben Meir), commentary on Gen. 37: 2, in *Perush hatorah*, 49. All translations of Hebrew and Arabic sources quoted in this essay are my own.

[5] On these lists of midrashic methods see Kahana, 'The Halakhic Midrashim', 13–16; Enelow, 'The Midrash of Thirty-Two Rules of Interpretation'.

[6] Commentary ad loc. in *Raschi: Der Kommentar des Salomo B. Isak*, 127.

a seal on your arm' [S. of S. 8: 6]. 'Between your eyes'—like an ornament or a gold chain that is customarily put on the forehead for decoration.[7]

Whereas Rashi took these phrases literally, Rashbam interpreted them figuratively, knowing that Scripture often employs metaphorical locutions. The appearance of similar poetic imagery in Song of Songs 8: 6 served him as an apt example of this stylistic tendency.[8] He argues that this verse does not refer to anything actually placed on the hand or between the eyes, but is, instead, Moses' exhortation to the Israelites to preserve the memory of the Exodus, as if it were imprinted 'on . . . [the] hand' and an adornment 'between . . . [the] eyes'. Rashbam regarded this meaning as the 'deep *peshat*' because it best accords with the context of this verse. The rabbinic interpretation breaks the connection between Exodus 13: 9 and the surrounding pericope (13: 3–10), which is devoted exclusively to the annual celebration of Pesach in commemoration of the Exodus. Rashbam's reading preserves the contextual unity of the pericope by construing Exodus 13: 9 as a command to continuously keep the Exodus from Egypt in mind.[9]

The audacity of Rashbam's interpretation can be gauged by the harsh criticism it elicited from the *pashtan* Abraham Ibn Ezra (1089–1164). Born and educated in Spain, where he achieved renown as a Hebrew poet, Ibn Ezra emigrated to Rome in 1140. There he encountered Rashi's commentaries, which he dismissed as midrashic.[10] He spent the remainder of his life travelling in Italy, Provence, northern France, and England, composing commentaries and grammatical works that epitomized 'the way of *peshat*' that had been pioneered by Sa'adyah Gaon (882–942, Egypt and Iraq) and refined by subsequent grammarians and Bible commentators in Muslim Spain.[11] In his

[7] Rashbam on Exod. 13: 9, in *Perush hatorah*, 98. This would seem to be an adaptation of the interpretation of the 10th-century Andalusian linguist Menahem ben Saruk. See his *Maḥberet*, 200*, s.v. *taf*.

[8] See his gloss ad loc. in *Perush rav shemuel ben meir (rashbam) leshir hashirim*, 277.

[9] On the expression 'its deep *peshat*' (*omek peshuto*) and others like it in Rashbam's lexicon—*ikar peshuto* (its essential *peshat*), *amitat peshuto* (its true *peshat*)—see Kamin, *Rashi's Exegetical Categorization* (Heb.), 268. On literary context as a critical ingredient in the northern French concept of *peshat* see R. Harris, 'The Literary Hermeneutic of R. Eliezer of Beaugency', 280–301.

[10] See Mondschein, '"Only One in a Thousand of His Comments may be Called *Peshat*"' (Heb.).

[11] Those works, written in Arabic, were not accessible to Jewish readers in Christian lands. The 10th-century Andalusian grammarians Menahem ben Saruk and Dunash Ibn Labrat are exceptional in this regard: they wrote in Hebrew and their works were widely used in Rashi's school. See Haas, 'Rashi's Criticism of Mahberet Menahem' (Heb.).

long commentary on Exodus 13: 9, Ibn Ezra cites 'those who disagree with our holy forebears and say that "as a sign . . . and reminder" is [metaphorical]'.[12] In his view 'it is in its literal sense, to make phylacteries of the hand and phylacteries of the head'. As he remarks, 'since the Sages, of blessed memory, transmitted thus, the first interpretation is void, for it does not have trustworthy witnesses as the second interpretation has'.[13]

Well aware of the Karaite charge that Rabbanite Jews had fabricated a system of halakhah that diverged from the one explicitly mandated by the Bible, Ibn Ezra endeavoured to reach a compromise between his philological sensibilities and the halakhic traditions and interpretations of the rabbis.[14] Where he could not reconcile the halakhic midrashic interpretation and his own philological analysis, he classified the former as an *asmakhta*, that is, a mnemonic device to preserve details of the halakhah that were originally transmitted only through an oral tradition.[15] But there is a line that Ibn Ezra would not cross: as in the above-mentioned case, he would under no circumstances advance a *peshat* interpretation at odds with the halakhah itself. This sort of consideration was of no concern to Rashbam, who writes, for example, in his commentary on Genesis 1: 5:

'And there was evening and there was morning, one day.' The evening of the first day arrived and the light faded away, and then there was morning . . . that is, the dawn arrived. At that point, one of the six days that God spoke of in the Ten Commandments [cf. Exod. 20: 8] was complete.[16]

Though in talmudic law it is well established that the time span of any 'day', sabbath included, is from sundown to sundown, Rashbam argues that a 'day' in the Bible begins at dawn and concludes at dawn. The halakhic implications of this interpretation were noticed by Ibn Ezra, who penned his *Epistle of the*

[12] See Ibn Ezra, *Perush hatorah*, ii. 87.

[13] See his short commentary on Exod. 13: 9, ibid. 264. The short commentary was written in Italy in the early 1140s, the long one in northern France a decade later. On the historical question of when Ibn Ezra could have become aware of Rashbam and his commentaries, see Mondschein, 'Concerning the Relationship of the Commentaries of R. Abraham Ibn Ezra and R. Samuel ben Meir to the Pentateuch' (Heb.); Simon, *The Ear Discerns Words* (Heb.), 102–11. In any case, he would have known this figurative interpretation from Menahem ben Saruk; see n. 7.

[14] He will thus often argue for the philological cogency of a rabbinic interpretation, even though it would not have naturally been his first choice from a purely linguistic perspective. See Simon, *The Ear Discerns Words* (Heb.), 82–133.

[15] On this concept in the geonic-Andalusian tradition see Cohen, *Opening the Gates of Interpretation*, 42–3, 80–1, 254–5; J. M. Harris, *How Do We Know This?*, 76–85.

[16] *Perush hatorah*, 5.

Sabbath to refute it and defend the traditional timing of the sabbath—from sundown to sundown.[17]

Though there are other instances in which Rashbam offers *peshat* interpretations at odds with the halakhah,[18] he undoubtedly adhered to halakhah in practice. His enterprise of *peshat* interpretation—including his non-halakhic and even anti-halakhic readings—was never intended to be a guide for Jewish practice. As he remarks in another of his programmatic statements:

> I have not come to expound *halakhot*, though they are essential, as I have explained in Genesis [above], for the *hagadot* and *halakhot* can be inferred from the redundancies of Scripture, and some are found in the commentaries of Rabbi Solomon my grandfather . . . I, on the other hand, have come to interpret the *peshat* of Scripture, interpreting the *dinim* [regulations] and *halakhot* according to the way of the world [*derekh erets*]. Yet the *halakhot* [as interpreted by the rabbis] remain primary, as our rabbis said: 'halakhah overrides Scripture' [BT *Sot.* 16*a*].[19]

Rashbam dedicated his efforts to the *peshat* of Scripture, but acknowledged that the halakhah stems from midrashic interpretation.

Sara Japhet characterizes Rashbam's hermeneutical outlook by noting his distinction between two layers in the interpretation of the Pentateuch: 'The *peshat* uncovers the original meaning of the Torah, and has the full authority of the original statement, whether by God or by Moses. The Midrash is indeed "hinted at" in the biblical text, but its authority and binding power derive from later exegesis, that of the rabbis.'[20] Yet, as Japhet and other scholars, such as David Weiss Halivni, have noted, Rashbam's position is rather baffling. For if the laws and ordinances are not expressed in the biblical text, which was authored by God himself, and were derived by the rabbis merely from 'hints of the plain meaning', why should they have the authority of biblical law?[21] Put simply, why doesn't the divergence Rashbam identifies between *peshat* and *derash* lead to a revision of the talmudic system of halakhah?

Ephraim Kanarfogel has illuminated this matter by considering Rashbam's talmudic intellectual background. Rashbam was an important Talmud

[17] See Simon, *The Ear Discerns Words* (Heb.), 73–81.

[18] See e.g. Japhet, 'The Tension between Rabbinic Legal Midrash and the "Plain Meaning"'; Lockshin, 'Tradition or Context'.

[19] Commentary on Exod. 21: 1, in *Perush hatorah*, 113. In Rashbam's parlance the expression 'according to the way of the world' connotes a rational, philological-contextual interpretation sensitive to the Bible's literary style. See Touitou, *Exegesis in Perpetual Motion* (Heb.), 134–46.

[20] Japhet, 'The Tension between Rabbinic Legal Midrash and the "Plain Meaning"', 421–2.

[21] See ibid. 422; Weiss Halivni, *Midrash, Mishnah, and Gemara*, 105–15.

commentator and one of the leading early Tosafists, working alongside his younger brother Rabbenu Tam—the chief figure in the Tosafist school. As Kanarfogel demonstrates, the Tosafists, developing an outlook that seems to have originated in early eleventh-century Ashkenaz, believed in and actively pursued the possibility of 'multiple truths in Torah study'.[22] Strictly speaking, this doctrine implies that a number of interpretations of the halakhah may be equally legitimate even though they are mutually exclusive. But Kanarfogel argues that this multiplicity was extended to validate different interpretative approaches in Torah study (analytical, midrashic, mystical, etc.), not unlike the multiplicity of disciplines that were brought together in the leading cathedral schools of northern France in the twelfth century and in the nascent universities in the thirteenth. It is for this reason, Kanarfogel argues, that Rashbam was not troubled by the contradiction between his own interpretations of *peshuto shel mikra* and the way the very same verses were interpreted in the Talmud—which he himself accepts for halakhic purposes in his Talmud commentaries.

And yet a certain tension still remains within Rashbam's system, even if he adhered to a 'multiple-truth' doctrine that legitimized the application of multiple, mutually exclusive interpretative methodologies to the biblical text. After all, one could still ask: Why is the halakhah determined using the midrashic method and not the 'truth of the *peshat* of Scripture'?[23] This tension is illustrated by the debate between Rashbam and Ibn Ezra regarding the opening verses of Leviticus 21, which present the laws concerning priestly defilement for close relatives:

> (1) And the Lord said to Moses, Speak to the priests, the sons of Aaron, and say to them: There shall be none defiled for the dead among his people, (2) Except for his close kin [*she'er*], for his mother, for his father, for his son, for his daughter, for his brother, (3) and for his sister, a virgin, who has had no husband. (4) A husband may not defile himself amongst his nation and so profane himself. (Lev. 21: 1–4)

A priest is generally prohibited from contracting ritual impurity through contact with a dead body, but verses 2–3 make an exception for specific family relations. Though only six are mentioned explicitly in these two verses, talmudic tradition assumes that there are 'seven close relatives' for whom a person is obligated to mourn[24]—and the priest permitted to defile himself—stating

[22] Kanarfogel, *The Intellectual History and Rabbinic Culture of Medieval Ashkenaz*, 26–35.

[23] Rashbam actually uses this expression (*amitat peshuto shel mikra*) in his commentary on Lev. 13: 10.

[24] There is a debate among talmudic commentators whether the obligation to mourn is

that 'his *she'er* is his wife'.[25] Yet verse 4, prohibiting 'a husband' from becoming defiled, seems to contradict this. The Talmud resolves the contradiction in the following way: a priest may defile himself by coming into contact with the dead body of his 'proper' (halakhically permitted) wife, for example to bury her, as indicated by verse 2, whereas verse 4 teaches that a priest may not defile himself for a wife who is halakhically unfit for him (for example a divorced woman), with whom he has 'profaned himself'.[26]

In a statement that reflects his geonic-Andalusian philological background, Ibn Ezra notes that 'by way of *peshat* the wife is never called *she'er*'. He thus posits that the Talmud's reading of this word is an *asmakhta*, that is, an *ex post facto* link to a scriptural locution.[27] Yet this position does not accommodate the message of verse 4. As Ibn Ezra remarks:

> It would have seemed to us that . . . the meaning of 'A husband [*ba'al*] among his nation' is that a husband may not defile himself for his wife. However, when we considered the fact that our rabbis transmitted [the law] that he may defile himself for his wife . . . [we had to conclude that] this interpretation is invalid.[28]

Ibn Ezra here lets us into the laboratory of his mind, revealing how he would have interpreted these laws on his own: verses 2–3 permit the priest to become ritually defiled for six blood relatives, and verse 4 clarifies that he may not do so for his wife. He then explains why this path was closed to him. Though he was willing to classify the rabbinic interpretation of 'his *she'er*' in verse 2 as an *asmakhta*, he would not allow a reading of a biblical passage (verse 4) that contradicts the halakhah attached to it.

In stark contrast to Ibn Ezra's willingness to suppress his philological insight to accord with the halakhah, Rashbam writes in his commentary on

biblical or rabbinic. Maimonides—following Isaac Alfasi—maintains that there is a biblical obligation to mourn, but only on the day of the death and burial (whereas the week-long mourning period is of rabbinic origin); see *Mishneh torah*, 'Hilkhot evel', 1: 1, with the commentaries of Radbaz and the *Kesef mishneh*. The expression 'seven close relatives' (*shivah kerovim*) does not appear explicitly in the Talmud, but it does in the early post-talmudic literature, e.g. the *She'iltot* of R. Aha of Shabha and *Halakhot gedolot*; see Brody, *The Textual History of the She'iltot* (Heb.), 160–1.

[25] BT *Yev.* 22*b*.

[26] Ibid. Not surprisingly, this resolution is adopted by Rashi in his gloss on the verse. It is also mentioned by Rashbam (see n. 29).

[27] See his alternative introduction in *Perush hatorah*, i. 141, 'Fourth Way'. This follows Sa'adyah's construal of the word *she'er*, which was subsequently adopted in the Andalusian tradition. See Zucker, *Rav Saadya Gaon's Translation of the Torah*, 387.

[28] Ibn Ezra, *Perush hatorah*, iii. 72.

verse 4: '"A husband may not defile himself amongst his nation": No husband in the priestly class [lit. in the 'nation' of priests] may defile himself for his wife; "and so profane himself"—because in doing so, he profanes his priesthood.'[29] Rashbam offers an interpretation that contradicts the halakhah; according to the *peshat*, he notes, the Torah forbids a priest to bury his wife.

Modern scholars, as mentioned above, raise the obvious question: if the *peshat* 'uncovers the original meaning of the Torah, and has the full authority of the original statement',[30] then how could the rabbis advance a different interpretation and apply the law (halakhah) accordingly, in violation of the Law stated by God himself? This very problem would be addressed by Maimonides—to whom we now turn.

MAIMONIDES: HALAKHIC CONSTRUCTION OF *PESHAT*

Generally speaking one might say that Maimonides drew exactly the conclusion that arises naturally from Japhet's analysis of Rashbam. As a master codifier of the talmudic legal system, it was critical for Maimonides to distinguish between laws that are *de'oraita* (of biblical authority) and those that are *derabanan* (of rabbinic authority only). This basic dichotomy appears in the Talmud and is one of the most important legal distinctions for any halakhic codifier or decisor to make with respect to any given law or case.[31] While halakhically observant Jews regard laws of both biblical and rabbinic authority as binding, there are significant theoretical differences between the two categories, which at times manifest themselves in practice.[32] But Maimonides was the first to endeavour to establish a systematic way of determining which laws belong to each of these two categories. Refitting the talmudic maxim 'a

[29] Rashbam, *Perush hatorah*, 163.

[30] Japhet, 'The Tension between Rabbinic Legal Midrash and the "Plain Meaning"', 421–2.

[31] See Elon, *The Principles of Jewish Law*, 9–10.

[32] Violation of biblical law may incur the most severe punishments, such as death, whether execution by the court or 'death at the hands of heaven' (*mitah biyedei shamayim* or *karet*—lit. 'cutting off'); but the violation of rabbinic law never incurs more than 'flogging for rebelliousness' (*makat mardut*). Although Jewish courts in the diaspora, as a rule, did not actually dispense these punishments, their stratification signalled the demand for more stringent observance of biblical law and the permissibility of leniency with respect to rabbinic law in extenuating circumstances. A talmudic rule of thumb, regularly invoked by halakhic decisors throughout the Middle Ages and beyond, is that where a doubt arises, one rules stringently in the case of a biblical law but leniently in the case of a rabbinic law. See BT *Beits.* 3*b*, *AZ* 7*a*. Accordingly, within responsa literature establishing whether a law is rabbinic or biblical is foundational and will often determine the direction of the decision ultimately rendered. See e.g. Maimonides, *Teshuvot harambam*, ii. 567, no. 308.

biblical verse does not leave the realm of its *peshat*[33] for this codificatory purpose, he made a categorical distinction between *halakhot* that stem from the text of the Pentateuch itself (that is, from *peshuto shel mikra*) and which are therefore *de'oraita* and those that resulted from the rabbis' midrashic extrapolation—what Rashbam had referred to as 'the hint[s] of the *peshat*'—which are *derabanan*.

Maimonides summarized this bold position in a Hebrew responsum, written late in his career:

No matter derived by analogy [*hekesh*], *a fortiori* reasoning [*kal vaḥomer*], comparison of similar expressions [*gezerah shavah*], or through any of the thirteen *midot* by which the Torah is interpreted is biblical, unless the sages say so explicitly . . . There is nothing [i.e. no commandment] that is biblical [in origin] except for that which is explicit in the Torah, such as the prohibition of blending linen and wool, the prohibition of crossbreeding seeds, the sabbath, and the forbidden sexual unions, or something that the rabbis said is from the Torah, and those are but three or four things.[34]

Maimonides also refers to his expansive discussion of this matter in the *Sefer hamitsvot* (Book of the Commandments), a Judaeo-Arabic composition he penned at the age of 30 as a blueprint for his monumental code of Jewish law, *Mishneh torah*. The Talmud had asserted that there are 613 commandments,[35] and Maimonides enumerates them in his *Sefer hamitsvot*. Its introduction sets forth fourteen principles that he used in determining which *halakhot* were to be enumerated as biblical commandments and which were to be excluded from this count. He had to justify his list because it differed from that found in the introduction to the *Halakhot gedolot*, an enumeration influential in his day.[36]

Maimonides' First Principle, 'It is not proper to count . . . *derabanan* laws',[37] is directed against geonic-era enumerations—including that of *Halakhot gedolot*—that incorporated rabbinically instituted laws, such as kind-

[33] BT *Shab.* 63*a*; *Yev.* 12*a*, 24*a*.

[34] Maimonides, *Teshuvot harambam*, ii. 632, no. 355; *kal vaḥomer* and *gezerah shavah* are actually two of the thirteen *midot*. On the exceptions to this rule see Cohen, *Opening the Gates of Interpretation*, 340–2, and below, n. 44.

[35] See BT *Mak.* 23*b*. The Talmud does not provide a list of the 613 commandments, and this prompted a number of medieval authors to compose such lists. Some authors in the Andalusian tradition came to question the exactness of this number, for example Judah Ibn Balam and Abraham Ibn Ezra. See Ibn Ezra, *Yesod mora vesod torah*, 32–3.

[36] This list of the 613 commandments—published as *Hakdamat sefer halakhot gedolot*—may have been written by another author and later appended to *Halakhot gedolot*, a work by the 9th-century author Simon Kayara. See Sklare, *Samuel ben Hofni Gaon*, 183, 222.

[37] *Sefer hamitsvot*, 9.

ling the Hanukah lights and reading the scroll of Esther.[38] As David Sklare has noted, the geonim at times blurred the line between rabbinic and biblical commandments because they emphasized that the rabbis of antiquity had been faithful transmitters of the oral tradition, and not independent legislators.[39]

Maimonides, on the other hand, makes this distinction sharply: 'Nothing rabbinic may be counted in the sum of 613 commandments because this sum is based entirely on the texts [*nuṣūṣ*] of the Torah.'[40] His focus on 'the texts of the Torah' signals a revolutionary biblical orientation in the discipline of halakhah, which, in Rabbanite circles, was previously centred on the Talmud. The implications of this new orientation emerge with full force in his Second Principle: 'It is not proper to count anything known through one of the thirteen *midot* by which the Torah is interpreted or [through] a redundancy.'[41] Yet he writes: 'We have already explained in the introduction to our *Commentary on the Mishnah* that most of the precepts of the Law [*sharī'a*[42]] are derived through the thirteen *midot* by which the Torah is interpreted.'[43]

Like Rashbam, Maimonides knew that the vast majority of the laws that make up the intricate system of halakhah are derived midrashically. Yet, unlike Rashbam, he asserted that this had crucial taxonomical implications. As a rule, he stated, laws so derived are of rabbinic authority only. Laws of biblical authority must stem from the biblical text itself: 'Anything for which you do not find a source text [*naṣṣ*] in the Torah and you find that the Talmud deduces it through one of the thirteen *midot* . . . .[44] [you must conclude that] it is a rabbinic law, since there is no [biblical] source-text indicating [*yadullu*] it.'[45]

He also referred critically to the enumeration in the *Halakhot gedolot* and in works of like-minded authors: 'When they found a *derash* on a verse

[38] This is attested not only in *Halakhot gedolot*, but also in the enumerations of Sa'adyah, Hefets ben Yatsliah (late 10th century), and Solomon Ibn Gabirol (11th century). See Zucker, 'Studies and Notes' (Heb.), 97–100.

[39] Sklare, *Samuel ben Hofni Gaon*, 159–60. This tendency is reflected in Ibn Ezra; see *Yesod mora vesod torah*, 113 (with editors' note).

[40] *Sefer hamitsvot*, 12.

[41] Ibid.

[42] The Arabic term *sharī'a* (usually rendered Torah by the medieval Hebrew translators) means 'religious law' and is used by Maimonides here to denote Jewish law in the general sense. See Kraemer, 'Naturalism and Universalism in Maimonides' Thought', 49–51.

[43] *Sefer hamitsvot*, 12.

[44] In part of the passage omitted here, Maimonides acknowledges that, in some cases, the *midot* were used to confirm laws actually known from transmitted interpretations. In such cases the law should be considered *de'oraita* and should be included in the enumeration. See Cohen, *Opening the Gates of Interpretation*, 288–9.

[45] *Sefer hamitsvot*, 13.

that . . . requires performing certain actions or avoiding certain things, all of which are undoubtedly rabbinic, they counted them in the sum of the commandments, even though the *peshat* of Scripture does not indicate any of those things.'[46] According to Maimonides, those authors actually violated a teaching of the rabbis:

> the principle that the [sages], peace be upon them, taught us, and which is their dictum: 'A biblical verse does not leave the realm of its *peshat*'.[47] And when they found a verse from which many matters are deduced by way of commentary and inference . . . the Talmud in many places enquires: 'The verse itself, of what does it speak?'[48]
>
> And had he [the author of *Halakhot gedolot*] counted . . . everything known through one of the thirteen *midot* by which the Torah is interpreted, the number of commandments would reach many thousands.[49]

On the basis of the talmudic rule of *peshat*, Maimonides argues that the rabbis ascribed biblical authority only to what 'the verse itself speaks of', and not to teachings inferred from it by way of *derash* or any of the thirteen *midot*. He understood this to be the meaning of the principle 'the [biblical] authority of a verse does not go beyond its *peshat*'. In other words, *peshuto shel mikra* is the sole 'indicator' (Arab. *dalīl*[50]) of biblical law.

Though Maimonides invokes talmudic authority here, his own perspective constitutes a substantial innovation, since the sages of the Talmud never used the '*peshat* maxim' to demote midrashically derived laws to rabbinic status. Generally speaking the very concept of *peshat* as an exegetical mode is a post-talmudic innovation, as recent scholarship has demonstrated.[51] The medieval commentators endowed the talmudic *peshat* maxim with new meaning, construing it as a fundamental exegetical principle. In the Talmud itself, as Weiss Halivni has observed, the maxim is rather vague and marginal, and even the very meaning of the term *peshat* is less than clear, leaving it open for later authors to employ in new ways as they saw fit.[52]

The idea of demoting certain laws just because they are derived midrashically was nothing less than scandalous within the medieval rabbinic world,[53] as is evident, for example, in the following reaction by the great

[46] Ibid. 14.

[47] BT *Shab.* 63*a*; *Yev.* 12*a*, 24*a*.

[48] As Kafih here notes, this expression is a paraphrase rather than a precise quote of any specific expression in rabbinic literature.

[49] *Sefer hamitsvot*, 14.

[50] On the significance of this term (drawn from Muslim jurisprudence) in Maimonides' hermeneutical system, see below.

[51] See Kamin, *Rashi's Exegetical Categorization* (Heb.), 11–110; Cohen, *Opening the Gates of Interpretation*, 14–17.

[52] See Weiss Halivni, *Peshat and Derash*, 52–79.

[53] It was so scandalous that Maimonides' talmudic defenders had to posit that he never

Catalan talmudic scholar, Nahmanides (1194–1270):

The Second Principle . . . is shockingly beyond my comprehension, and I cannot bear it, for . . . if so . . . then the truth is the *peshat* of Scripture alone, not the matters derived midrashically, as he mentions from their dictum, 'a biblical verse does not leave the realm of its *peshat*'. And as a result we would uproot the thirteen *midot* by which the Torah is interpreted, as well as the bulk of the Talmud, which is based on them.[54]

Maimonides was not insensitive to the disparity between his novel approach and the spirit of talmudic thought which Nahmanides later highlighted. Indeed, further in the Second Principle he emphasizes the binding authority of laws that are midrashically derived:

Do not think that we refrain from counting them because they are not certain [i.e. authoritative], or that we question whether the law derived from such a *midah* is valid or not. Rather, the reason is that all of the laws [so] derived are derivatives from the principal [law]s [*furūʿ min al-uṣūl*; lit. branches from the roots] that were explicitly stated to Moses at Sinai, and they are the 613 commandments.[55]

For Maimonides, the derivation of new laws—'branches from the roots'—through legal inference was essential to the halakhic system. Yet, since such derivatives are based on inference rather than on *peshuto shel mikra*, their authority is rabbinic rather than biblical.

Maimonides' construal of the Talmud's *peshat* maxim in the Second Principle forms part of a comprehensive hermeneutical-historical theory of halakhic development that was already manifest in his earliest major work, the *Commentary on the Mishnah*. According to his introduction to that work, the 613 laws of Torah were received at Sinai in the Written Torah, along with their original divine interpretation, the Oral Torah.[56] The latter was transmit-

actually meant what he wrote in the Second Principle. In a tradition dating from the 14th century, various pro-Maimonidean talmudic scholars suggested reinterpreting his words to mean that the laws derived through the *midot* are indeed of biblical force, and that when Maimonides classifies them as rabbinic he only means to say that they cannot be enumerated among the original 613 commandments given at Sinai; but in all other respects they enjoy biblical authority. For a detailed survey of this tradition, see Neubauer, *Maimonides on the 'Words of the Scribes'* (Heb.), 30–75. This, of course, is not how Nahmanides understood the matter (as indicated in his critique cited in the text that follows immediately below), and modern scholars generally agree that Maimonides indeed meant to deprive such laws of *de'oraita* status; see Neubauer, *Maimonides on the 'Words of the Scribes'* (Heb.), 24–30, 81–6; Weiss Halivni, *Peshat and Derash*, 83.

[54] *Sefer hamitsvot im hasagot haramban*, on Maimonides' *Sefer hamitsvot*; critique of the Second Principle, 44–5.

[55] *Sefer hamitsvot*, 15.

[56] Maimonides, *Hakdamot harambam lamishnah*, 327–8 (Arab.), 27–8 (Heb.). On his understanding of the Oral Law given at Sinai, the original interpretative tradition as an integral part of *peshuto shel mikra*, see Cohen, *Opening the Gates of Interpretation*, 293–304, 335–46.

ted so meticulously across the generations that none of its details were ever forgotten or debated.[57] The numerous debates attested in the Talmud, he explains, had emerged from the subsequent application of the midrashic *midot*, for their deployment was subjective:

Whatever ... the elders received [from Moses] was not subject to discussion or disagreement. But the derivative [law]s [*furūʿ*] not heard from the Prophet were subject to discussion, the laws being extrapolated [*tustakhraju*] through analogy [*qiyās*], using the thirteen *midot* by which the Torah is interpreted.[58]

The Arabic terminology used here is from the field of *uṣūl al-fiqh*, Muslim jurisprudence, upon which Maimonides drew to clarify the interpretative process applied in the Talmud.[59] In Muslim jurisprudence the key question asked is always: what is the source or 'indicator' (*dalīl*) of a given law? This question makes a basic distinction between (*a*) one of the 'essential' laws, termed *uṣūl* (roots); (*b*) the 'indicator', whose *naṣṣ* (text) is stated clearly in the foundational texts (the Quran and hadith); and (*c*) derivative laws termed *furūʿ* (branches), which are extrapolated from those texts by way of analogy (*qiyās*) and other forms of legal reasoning.[60]

Bernard Weiss explains this distinction in a way that illuminates Maimonides' thinking about the halakhic process:

The Arabic term *uṣūl* literally means 'roots'. The rules [i.e. laws] that the jurists produce are called, on the other hand, 'branches' [*furūʿ*] ... The work of the jurists is thus described by means of agricultural metaphors. Only the roots (that is, the sources) are given; the branches ... are not, but rather must be made to appear; and for this human husbandry is required. The jurist is the husbandman who must facilitate the growth of the law ... out of the roots.

In carrying out this task, the jurist must first explore ... the meaning of the texts in order to determine what rules are contained within that meaning. This task requires him to employ the skills of a philologist and to be well versed in Arabic lexicography, morphology, syntax, and stylistics ... When he is satisfied that he has harvested whatever rules of law lie within the text's meaning thus conceived, he may then

[57] See *Hakdamot harambam lamishnah*, 339 (Arab.), 40–1 (Heb.), and the citation below at n. 63. Halbertal, *People of the Book*, 59–61.

[58] *Hakdamot harambam lamishnah*, 328 (Arab.), 28–9 (Heb.).

[59] On Maimonides' adaptation of Muslim legal hermeneutical terms and concepts in this context, see Cohen, *Opening the Gates of Interpretation*, 247–51, 264–76. The discussion below is a summary of my conclusions there.

[60] See Weiss, *The Search for God's Law*, 151–7; id., *The Spirit of Islamic Law*, 38, 66–8, 122–7; Hallaq, *The Origins and Evolution of Islamic Law*, 119, 122–8; Schacht, *An Introduction to Islamic Law*, 59–61, 114–15.

. . . attempt to see what further rules may be gleaned by way of *qiyās* with rules already determined.[61]

Maimonides seems to have adapted this mode of thinking in explaining the stratification of the halakhic system. For him the laws conveyed by *peshuto shel mikra*, that is, the biblical text itself (according to its transmitted interpretation), are the *uṣūl*, from which further laws, the *furū'*, are derived using the *midot*, in a process he refers to as 'extrapolation' (*istikhrāj*—bringing out, extracting).

For Maimonides the Muslim legal concept of *istikhrāj* perfectly described the essential method of the creative halakhic interpretative process.[62] As he remarks in the introduction to his Mishnah commentary,

And when Joshua, peace be on him, died, he transmitted to the elders the interpretation that he had received [from Moses] and [the laws that were] extrapolated [*ustukhrija*] . . . After that, those elders transmitted what they had received to the prophets, peace be upon them, and the prophets one to another. And there was no time lacking in in-depth study of halakhah [*tafaqquh*] and [legal] creativity [*tantīj*, or bringing forth new things, drawing new conclusions]. And the people of each generation made the words of those who had come before them a principle [*aṣl*], and [new laws] would be extrapolated [*yustakhraju*] from it, and new conclusions would be drawn [*yuntaju natā'ij*]. And [as for] the [original] transmitted principles [lit. roots; *al-uṣūl*] [i.e. from Moses], there was no disagreement about them.[63]

Maimonides believed that only a small core of laws was given at Sinai, whereas the bulk of halakhah was left to be extrapolated through the *midot*. In using the Arabic terms *tantīj* (drawing forth new conclusions) and *istikhrāj* (extrapolation), he highlights the creativity involved in this interpretative operation. And in using the term *tafaqquh* (a derivative of *fiqh*, religious law), he highlights its centrality for the halakhic process.[64] Indeed, this sort of creative interpretation is the highest form of 'the study of the law' (*talmud torah*)

[61] Weiss, *The Spirit of Islamic Law*, 22–3.

[62] Though some have argued that Maimonides was original in this respect, this sort of dynamic model of halakhic development can be traced to others in the Andalusian tradition. See Cohen, *Opening the Gates of Interpretation*, 252–7, 265 n. 86. Cf. Halbertal, *People of the Book*, 59. It has been suggested that Maimonides' dynamic model of halakhah can be traced to Alfarabi, who defines the science of *fiqh* as the derivation (*istinbāṭ*) of new laws from the original ones (*uṣūl*). See Ravitsky, 'Maimonides and Alfarabi on the Development of the Halakhah' (Heb.), 219–20. Cf. Cohen, *Opening the Gates of Interpretation*, 267 n. 93.

[63] *Hakdamot harambam lamishnah* (Arab.), 36–7 (Heb.).

[64] See Cohen, *Opening the Gates of Interpretation*, 266.

in Maimonides' thought.[65] In this respect he, like Rashbam, regarded the laws derived through 'the hint[s] of the *peshat*' and through the midrashic *midot* as 'the essence of Torah' (to borrow Rashbam's terminology). Yet Maimonides distinguished between laws so produced, which are of rabbinic authority only, and those conveyed by *peshuto shel mikra*, which have biblical authority.

Three examples may illustrate the boldness of Maimonides' application of the Second Principle.

1. The institution of marriage is taken for granted in two legal passages of the Pentateuch, which deal with specific cases; each begins with the phrase 'If a man marries [lit. takes] a woman and cohabits with her' (Deut. 22: 13, 24: 1). The Mishnah records that 'a woman is betrothed [lit. acquired] in three ways . . . with money, with a document, or by intercourse' (*Kid.* 1: 1). The Talmud (*Kid.* 4*b*–5*a*) makes no distinction between these modes of acquisition, but midrashically links all three to biblical verses. By contrast, Maimonides, in his *Commentary on the Mishnah*, stratifies them; he notes that betrothal 'with money' and 'with a document' are derived midrashically—by way of *gezerah shavah* (similar expressions) and *hekesh* (analogy). On the other hand, he writes,

> betrothal by intercourse is the type stated most clearly . . . [and is] explicit in the Torah, and this is the most binding of them, and this is the one considered [lit. called] betrothal on the basis of Torah [*de'oraita*], as it says, 'If a man marries a woman and cohabits with her' [Deut. 22: 13, 24: 1]—by way of intercourse, she becomes a married woman.[66]

Maimonides' novel claim would be harshly criticized by later talmudic scholars, including Rabad (R. Abraham ben David) of Posquières (*c.*1120–97/8) and Nahmanides, and he himself later modified this position.[67] Nonetheless the boldness of his initial claim demonstrated the radical implications of the Second Principle and its potential impact on the talmudic system of law.

[65] See ibid. 466–72; Twersky, *Introduction to the Code of Maimonides*, 489–93.

[66] *Mishnah im perush r. mosheh ben maimon*, iii. 280–1. As Kafih notes, Maimonides—in his own autograph copy of the Mishnah commentary—later crossed out the words 'considered [lit. called] betrothal *de'oraita*' and added the words 'stated in the Torah' (a phraseology with less radical implications) in the margin, evidently to reflect his later, modified view (see n. 67).

[67] See Maimonides, *Teshuvot harambam*, no. 355, and *Mishneh torah*, 'Hilkhot ishut', 1: 2, with the critical gloss (*hasagah*) of Rabad ad loc.; see also Nahmanides, *Sefer hamitsvot im hasagot haramban*, 34–5, on the Second Principle, and Cohen, *Opening the Gates of Interpretation*, 414–17.

2. The prohibition in Exodus 22: 30, 'You shall not eat flesh that is *terefah* [lit. torn to pieces by beasts] in the field', was taken in the Talmud as prohibiting the eating of a diseased animal. Mishnah *Ḥulin* 3: 1 lists the defects referred to as *terefot* and gives the following general rule: 'If an animal with this defect could not continue to live, it is a *terefah*.' In biblical Hebrew, however, the root *t-r-f* denotes an animal tearing another animal to pieces; hence what this verse explicitly prohibits is the eating of an animal mortally wounded ('torn to pieces') by beasts.[68] In *Sefer hamitsvot*, Negative Commandment 181, Maimonides writes: 'We are prohibited from eating an animal torn up by beasts, and that is His dictum: "You shall not eat flesh torn up by beasts in the field" . . . [which is] the obvious sense of the text'.[69] He goes on to address the standard way in which the term *terefah* is used in the Talmud: 'As for an animal in which occurred one of the *terefot* [defects, illnesses] derived through *qiyās*, it is prohibited to eat, even if slaughtered properly. And one who slaughters it properly and eats of its flesh is given lashes for violating a rabbinic law.'[70]

According to what Maimonides would term *peshuto shel mikra*, Exodus 22: 30 only prohibits eating the flesh of an animal attacked ('torn up') by beasts; by contrast, the flesh of animals suffering from the defects classified in the Mishnah as *terefot* is forbidden rabbinically because that prohibition is derived through *qiyās*.[71]

Maimonides was not alone in his philological construal of the biblical Hebrew word *terefah*; he followed in the wake of Sa'adyah, and was followed, in turn, by Nahmanides.[72] Yet his halakhic ruling was unique and difficult to square with the tenor of the many talmudic discussions of *terefot*. (As Nahmanides points out in his critique of *Sefer hamitsvot*, the Talmud treats *terefot* as a *de'oraita* prohibition.[73]) It was in the spirit of this talmudic outlook that Ibn Ezra, in *Yesod mora*, included the verse in question among those that must be understood in light of the halakhic tradition of the rabbis.[74] Had it not

[68] Sa'adyah renders *terefah* using the Arabic word *muftaras* (an animal torn up by beasts) in his *Tafsīr* on this verse; *Oeuvres complètes*, ed. Derenbourg, 114. Nahmanides, likewise, defines *terefah* as an animal 'torn up by a lion or bear, killed by them in the field' in his commentary on Lev. 22: 8 in *Perush haramban al hatorah*, ii. 138–9.

[69] *Sefer hamitsvot*, 270.

[70] Ibid. 270–1. On the textual complexities of this passage of *Sefer hamitsvot* see Cohen, *Opening the Gates of Interpretation*, 419 n. 92.

[71] For reasoning behind the *qiyās* process here, see *Mishneh torah*, 'Hilkhot ma'akhalot asurot', 4:6–9. Gersonides applies the same reasoning in his commentary on that verse; see *Perushei hatorah lerabenu levi ben gershom*, 294.

[72] See n. 68 above.

[73] See Nahmanides, *Sefer hamitsvot im hasagot haramban*, 46–7.

[74] See Ibn Ezra, *Yesod mora vesod torah*, 6: 2, 133.

been for the rabbinic tradition, he would have interpreted it as a prohibition limited to the consumption of an animal torn up by beasts. But in light of the rabbinic definition of *terefah*, Ibn Ezra—characteristically—suspended his own judgement. Maimonides alone took the daring step of arguing in *Sefer hamitsvot* that *peshuto shel mikra* conveys only the limited prohibition of eating the flesh of an animal torn up by beasts; he relegated the other types of *terefot* mentioned in the Mishnah to the status of rabbinic law.[75]

3. The positions of Ibn Ezra and Rashbam on Leviticus 21: 1–4, the verses listing the relatives for whom a priest may and may not become defiled, were discussed above. Maimonides takes the next logical step and adjusts the talmudic halakhah in accordance with this understanding of *peshuto shel mikra*: 'These are [the relatives] that a person must mourn according to Torah law: his mother, father, son, daughter, brother, and sister. And [we learn] from their words [i.e. rabbinic law] that a man mourns his married wife and likewise a wife her husband.'[76]

He makes his reasoning clear in a subsequent discussion:

> The law of mourning is so powerful that [the prohibition of] defilement is waived for close relatives so that [the priest] can be occupied with them [i.e. their burial] . . . as it says, 'Except for his relative [*she'er*] that is close to him: for his mother [and for his father, for his son, and for his daughter, and for his brother, and for his sister who is a virgin and has had no husband,] to her he shall be defiled', which is a positive commandment.[77]

Like Ibn Ezra, Maimonides seems to have regarded the talmudic gloss 'his *she'er* is his wife' as *derash*; the addition of the wife to the six close relatives is therefore merely rabbinic in his opinion. But this leads to a halakhic difficulty, since talmudic law dictates that a priest may defile himself for his wife—which, according to Maimonides, is biblically prohibited. To resolve this problem Maimonides devised a novel understanding of the halakhah itself:

> A priest must defile himself for his wife. And this is only from the words of the scribes [*midivrei soferim*, i.e. a rabbinic enactment].[78] They accorded her the status of a

[75] It is possible that Maimonides eventually retracted this extraordinary position. See Henshke, 'The Basis of Maimonides' Concept of Halakhah' (Heb.).

[76] *Mishneh torah*, 'Hilkhot evel', 1: 2.

[77] Ibid. 2: 6.

[78] On the term *midivrei soferim* as used by Maimonides see Neubauer, *Maimonides on the 'Words of the Scribes'* (Heb.). It is clear that in this and similar contexts Maimonides uses it in the sense of a rabbinic enactment, as opposed to a biblical law.

'corpse left unburied' [*met mitsvah*]. Since he is her sole heir, no one else would be more diligent about burying her than the husband.[79]

The Mishnah stipulates that even the high priest himself may contract ritual impurity in order to fulfil the *mitsvah* of burying an abandoned corpse.[80] By subsuming the deceased wife within this halakhic category, Maimonides exercised an option that was not available to Ibn Ezra. He could remain true to his understanding of *peshat* and still affirm, with the rabbis, that a priest could defile himself to bury his wife.

COMPARING THE TWO LEGAL-HERMENEUTICAL CONSTRUCTIONS

The seemingly programmatic maxim, 'a biblical verse does not leave the realm of its *peshat*', appears only three times in the Talmud, and in two of them it introduces exceptions to the rule.[81] Talmudic interpretation, on the whole, is midrashic. The concept of *peshat* only gradually gained currency from the tenth century onwards, when the emerging sciences of Hebrew grammar and philology, developed by Jews in the Islamicate milieu, were applied to the biblical text itself. Its prestige would reach a pinnacle in the Andalusian school; Ibn Ezra conceived of *peshat* as the single correct—and authoritative—sense of the biblical text.[82] But where Ibn Ezra made no attempt to spell out the halakhic implications of his hermeneutical insight, Maimonides was able to do so. His presentation of the sources of the halakhah reflects the new *peshat–derash* hierarchy. In practice, Maimonides was largely bound by the halakhah as presented in the Talmud, and his actual legal innovations are few and far between.[83] But he attempted to effect a dramatic conceptual transformation: whereas *derash* is the central generator of law in the Talmud, Maimonides made *peshuto shel mikra* his legal foundation.[84] By harnessing the sophisti-

[79] *Mishneh torah*, 'Hilkhot evel', 2: 7. The notion that the rabbis declared the wife of a priest a *met mitsvah* is not entirely Maimonides' innovation, as it is found in the Talmud (BT *Yev.* 89*b*), but there it is applied in only an exceptional case (an orphaned minor girl betrothed by her mother or elder brothers, whose authority to do so is only rabbinic).

[80] Mishnah *Nazir* 7: 1.

[81] See Weiss Halivni, *Peshat and Derash*, 52–79.

[82] See Cohen, *Opening the Gates of Interpretation*, 31–85.

[83] Moreover, he sometimes retracted his more radical applications of the Second Principle. See above, nn. 67 and 75.

[84] See Cohen, *Opening the Gates of Interpretation*, 429–45. It should be noted that Maimonides' position was either rejected or interpreted away by subsequent halakhic authorities (see above, n. 53, and at n. 54), and so he was not actually successful in transforming the halakhic system in accordance with his radical position.

cated legal hermeneutical thought of Muslim jurisprudence—the differentiation between text, which conveys the 'roots', and legal analogy, which yields the 'branches'—he was able to create a logical stratification of talmudic law in accordance with the primacy of *peshat* in the Andalusian outlook.[85]

Sara Japhet's formulation, devised for Rashbam, would seem especially apt to describe the Maimonidean model: '"Peshat" . . . uncovers the original meaning of the Torah, and has the full authority of the original statement . . . of God . . . and the Midrash, which is . . . "hinted at" in the biblical text . . . its authority and binding power derive from later exegesis, that of the rabbis.'[86] It is important to distinguish here between two points. The first is exegetical: *peshuto shel mikra* is the sole original meaning of the words of the Pentateuch. The second point is metatextual: *peshat* carries unique authority since it reflects the will of God, 'author' of the Torah. Maimonides embraces both points: for him *peshuto shel mikra* is the sole original sense of the biblical text, and it also has the highest legal authority—with *derash* relegated to a lower legal status, as it yields laws of rabbinic authority only.

I would agree with Japhet that her first point characterizes Rashbam's bold conception that the *peshat* alone represents the direct sense of the biblical text itself. However, the comparison with Maimonides reveals that Rashbam did not subscribe to the second point. He did not grant special legal authority to *peshuto shel mikra*. In fact, he specifically states that it carries no weight in determining the halakhah, which is based on midrashic interpretation. Paradoxically, Rashbam understood Midrash—and the system of talmudic halakhah based upon it—to be the product of the rabbis' post-biblical interpretation. But at the same time he believed that *derash*, not *peshat*, was the determinant of the halakhah that the Talmud classified as being of biblical force, and that it carried the authority of the will of God himself.

How could Rashbam hold such a paradoxical view? How could the midrashic interpretations devised by the rabbis override the direct sense of the Pentateuch?

The solution to this dilemma depends on a clearer understanding of the traditional hermeneutical assumptions regarding the Bible inherited by both Jews and Christians. As James Kugel has shown, the fundamental axiom of early Jewish and Christian interpreters was that the Bible is essentially a cryp-

[85] It seems likely that the factor motivating Maimonides in this regard was the increasingly privileged status of *peshuto shel mikra* in the geonic-Andalusian school in the 12th century. For a consideration of other possible motivating factors, including the need to combat Karaite views, see Cohen, *Opening the Gates of Interpretation*, 487–90.

[86] Japhet, 'The Tension between Rabbinic Legal Midrash and the "Plain Meaning"', 421–2.

tic text, the deeper meaning of which lies beneath its surface. While Jews and Christians differed substantially over its precise nature, both assumed that the deeper meaning of the Bible is the more important, even truer, one.[87] For Christian interpreters—from the time of Paul to the Middle Ages and beyond—the Christological 'spiritual' senses transcended and superseded the 'literal' sense, to which the Jews were said to adhere stubbornly.[88] But in actuality, Jewish interpreters in late antiquity and the early medieval period applied the operations of *derash* to the biblical text to reinterpret it substantially, and hardly took it in its literal sense. As Rashbam records: 'the early generations, because of their piety, tended to delve into the *derashot*, since they are essential [*ikar*], and therefore they were not accustomed to the deep *peshat* of Scripture'.[89]

Growing interest in Scripture's literal sense among medieval Christian interpreters—such as Hugh of Saint-Victor (*c.*1096–1141), his student Andrew of Saint-Victor (*c.*1110–75), Herbert of Bosham (1120–94), and, most notably, Nicholas of Lyre (d.1349)[90]—hardly implied its superiority over the spiritual senses. Quite the contrary, the literal-historical sense remained subsidiary within a scheme that continued to grant supremacy to the Christological 'spiritual' interpretation of the Hebrew Bible. What was new about this development was the insistence of the Victorines and their successors on preserving the integrity of the literal and historical sense of Scripture; this was the foundation on which the spiritual senses could be properly built.[91] As Rashbam's contemporary Hugh of Saint-Victor remarked:

First of all, the student of sacred Scripture ought to look among history, allegory, and tropology for that order sought in the disciplines—that is, he should ask which of these three precedes the other in the order of study . . . In the construction of buildings . . . first the foundation is laid, then the structure is raised upon it . . . [Likewise] you will [not] be able to become perfectly sensitive to allegory unless you have first been grounded in history.[92]

[87] Kugel, *The Bible As It Was*, 18–19.

[88] See Whitman, 'Antique Interpretation', 41–5; Fredriksen, 'Allegory and Reading God's Book'.

[89] See above, n. 4.

[90] See Smalley, *The Study of the Bible in the Middle Ages*; Evans, *The Language and Logic of the Bible*; Coulter, '*Historia* and *Sensus Litteralis*'; van Zwieten, 'The Place and Significance of Literal Exegesis in Hugh of St. Victor'; van 't Spijker, 'The Literal and the Spiritual: Richard of Saint-Victor'; van Liere, 'Andrew of St. Victor, Jerome, and the Jews'; de Visscher, *Reading the Rabbis*; Klepper, *The Insight of Unbelievers*; Minnis, *Medieval Theory of Authorship*.

[91] See Lubac, *Exégèse medievale*, ii. 47–50.

[92] Hugh of Saint-Victor, *Didascalicon*, Book VI, chs. 2–3; English edn.: *The Didascalicon of*

We call by the name 'history' not only the recounting of actual deeds, but also the first meaning of any narrative which uses words according to their proper nature [i.e. literally]. And in this sense of the word . . . all the books of either Testament . . . belong to this study in their literal meaning.[93]

In speaking of the literal sense as 'foundation', Hugh invokes the authority of Gregory the Great in his *Moralia in Job*:

just as you see that every building lacking a foundation cannot stand firm, so also is it in learning. The foundation . . . is history, from which . . . the truth of allegory is extracted . . . As [Gregory advised:] 'lay first the foundation of history; next, by pursuing the "typical" meaning, build up a structure in your mind to be a fortress of faith'.[94]

Gregory's work was highly influential, and his characterization of the historical sense as the 'foundation' for the spiritual senses was repeated in the early Middle Ages, for example by Bede (673–735), Rabanus Maurus (780–856), and Rupert of Deutz (1075–1129).[95]

Just as Hugh's interest in the literal-historical sense is part of a hermeneutical system that grants primacy to the Christological spiritual senses, Rashbam seems to have regarded the midrashic reading of the Bible as a reflection of its ultimate meaning. Echoing the hierarchy of valuation he ascribed to the 'early ones', he acknowledged that 'the essence of Torah comes to teach and inform us—through the hint[s] of *peshat*—the *hagadot*, *halakhot*, and *dinim* by way of redundant language and through the thirty-two hermeneutical rules of R. Eliezer . . . and the thirteen rules of R. Ishmael'.[96] It would appear that Rashbam conceived of the Pentateuch as a text intentionally studded with irregularities that hint at deeper meanings, which the rabbis were authorized to extract using the special interpretative keys entrusted to them—the midrashic *midot*. In doing so, Rashbam believed, the rabbis were not merely drawing their creative inferences from the text (as Maimonides would say),

Hugh of St. Victor, trans. Taylor, 135–6. See also Minnis, Scott, and Wallace (eds.), *Medieval Literary Theory*, 74.

[93] Hugh of Saint-Victor, *Didascalicon*, Book VI, ch. 3 (trans. Taylor, 138). See also Minnis, Scott, and Wallace (eds.), *Medieval Literary Theory*, 76.

[94] Hugh of Saint-Victor, *Didascalicon*, Book VI, ch. 3 (trans. Taylor, 138). See also Minnis, Scott, and Wallace (eds.), *Medieval Literary Theory*, 76–7. The citation from Gregory's *Moralia in Job* is from section iii of the dedicatory epistle to Leander. See *Didascalicon*, trans. Taylor, 223 n. 9.

[95] See Lubac, *Exégèse medievale*, i. 434–9, who traces this image to Origen and Jerome.

[96] See above, at n. 4.

but were actually discovering the deep intentions implanted in the Bible by God himself. In sum, it would appear that Rashbam never questioned the traditional assumption that the essential meaning of the Pentateuch lies beneath its surface, as expounded in midrashic teaching.

The new step Rashbam takes is to differentiate consistently between the deeper midrashic sense of the Bible and *peshuto shel mikra*, which he seems to conceive as its 'pre-midrashic' or 'pre-halakhic' sense.[97] In his estimation the 'early ones'—the interpreters predating Rashi—refrained from expending effort on this lesser aspect of scripture, which does not truly reflect its essence—or God's true intention. Ultimately, then, for Rashbam it is the midrashic interpretation that carries divine authority, and it, rather than *peshuto shel mikra*, determines the halakhah.

Rashbam's revolutionary exegetical methods propelled the philological-contextual analytical mode of analysis (pioneered by Rashi) to new heights. But from a hermeneutical perspective he seems to have been conservative, embracing the traditional hierarchy that privileged—and granted supreme authority to—the midrashic interpretation of Scripture, based on the assumption that the Bible is a cryptic text. He lived in a medieval Christian milieu where this assumption was never questioned.

The Christian parallels to Rashbam cited above are not necessarily intended to suggest influence; they merely illuminate the conceptual hierarchy implicit in his exegetical practice. In fact, there is no real need to seek any external influence for Rashbam's privileging of *derash* over *peshat*—a hierarchy well established in Jewish tradition. The overturning of this hierarchy as manifested in Maimonides, on the other hand, was revolutionary, and does require explanation—which can be furnished by consideration of his Muslim intellectual milieu, especially the conceptions that he had appropriated from *uṣūl al-fiqh*, as discussed above. But the truth is that a gradual shift away from the ancient Jewish conception of interpretation was already well under way in the Judaeo-Arabic tradition of learning that Maimonides had inherited—quite clearly as a result of exposure to Muslim conceptions of scriptural interpretation.

Indeed, Sa'adyah had drawn upon quranic hermeneutics to begin a new

[97] Compare Weiss Halivni's argument that, for Rashbam, the study of *peshuto shel mikra* represents a special fulfilment of 'the mitsvah of *talmud torah* [Torah study] . . . *lishmah* . . . [i.e.] for its own sake' (*Midrash, Mishnah, and Gemara*, 110–11). This comports with the expanded conception of Torah study in medieval Ashkenaz in general noted in Kanarfogel, *The Intellectual History and Rabbinic Culture of Medieval Ashkenaz*, 31.

chapter in Jewish Bible exegesis.[98] In contrast to the assumptions of ancient Jewish and Christian interpreters regarding the cryptic nature of the Bible, a plethora of quranic statements attest that it conveys God's will in clear, plain language, and Quran 3. 7, as understood by Muslim interpreters, states that 'the clear verses [*muḥkamāt*; sing. *muḥkam*] . . . are the essence of the Book'.[99] This led to the default presumption that any given quranic verse is *muḥkam* and must be understood in its 'apparent' or literal sense (*ẓāhir*). Sa'adyah embraces this presumption in his oft-repeated hermeneutical axiom that one must always posit initially that the language of the Hebrew Bible is *muḥkam* and should be interpreted 'according to its apparent sense [*ẓāhir*] . . . unless that would contradict sense perception . . . rational knowledge . . . another verse . . . or a tradition [of the rabbis] . . . [in which case] the verse is not meant literally, but contains non-literal language'. These exceptions parallel ones discussed among Muslim interpreters of the Quran.[100] To be sure, Sa'adyah was quite adept at engaging in non-literal interpretation—often to reconcile the biblical text and rabbinic traditions, especially in the realm of halakhah.[101] But, at least conceptually, those cases were exceptions to the rule that made the surface layer of the biblical text the focus of exegesis.

Sa'adyah's perspective prompted the development, in Judaeo-Arabic lands, of a robust tradition of philological Bible interpretation, best represented by the eleventh-century Andalusian authors Jonah Ibn Janāḥ, Moses Ibn Chiquitilla, and Judah Ibn Balam.[102] It was primarily the exegetical

[98] See Ben-Shammai, 'The Tension between Literal Interpretation and Exegetical Freedom'; id., *A Leader's Project* (Heb.), 12–13, 276–88. It is beyond the scope of this study to discuss whether primacy should be given to the Karaites in this regard, a matter debated in modern scholarship. See Ben-Shammai, 'The Doctrines of Religious Thought of Abū Yūsuf Ya'aqūb al-Qirqisānī and Yefet ben Eli' (Heb.); Drory, *The Emergence of Jewish–Arabic Literary Contacts* (Heb.), 156–78; Zucker, *Rav Saadya Gaon's Translation of the Torah* (Heb.). For our purposes it is sufficient to note that Sa'adyah was the first major Rabbanite exegete to shift away from the traditional rabbinic exegetical orientation. It is entirely apt that Ibn Ezra refers to Sa'adyah as 'the first speaker in all areas' (*Sefer moznayim*, 1*b*).

[99] See Kinberg, 'Muḥkamāt and Mutashābihāt'.

[100] *Commentary on Genesis*, ed. and trans. Zucker, 17–18 (Arab.), 190–1 (Heb.). Sa'adyah repeats this axiom elsewhere in his writings; see Ben-Shammai, 'The Tension between Literal Interpretation and Exegetical Freedom', 34–6. It is important to emphasize that Sa'adyah did not use the term *peshat* in this context. The term he uses for the literal sense is *ẓāhir*, which cannot be equated with *peshat* automatically; nor is his non-literal interpretation necessarily midrashic. See Cohen, *Opening the Gates of Interpretation*, 35–44.

[101] See Ben-Shammai, *A Leader's Project*, 336–73; Cohen, *Opening the Gates of Interpretation*, 42; Zucker, *Rav Sa'adyah Gaon's Translation of the Torah* (Heb.), 319–441.

[102] See Maman, 'The Linguistic School'.

method that these authors developed that Ibn Ezra termed 'the way of *peshat*', which was thus privileged, as a rule, over midrashic interpretation.[103] Maimonides took the next logical step of granting unique halakhic authority to *peshuto shel mikra*. Within his hermeneutical system *peshuto shel mikra* conveys, in the words of Sara Japhet, 'the original meaning of the Torah, and has the full authority of the original statement', whereas *derash* is '"hinted at" in the biblical text, but its authority and binding power derive from later exegesis, that of the rabbis'.

[103] See Simon, *The Ear Discerns Words* (Heb.). As discussed above, Ibn Ezra will at times allow halakhic traditions to override his own philological analysis (which, we now see, follows a precedent established by Sa'adyah), but in such cases he argues that the halakhic tradition itself serves as a factor in determining *peshuto shel mikra*. See Cohen, *Opening the Gates of Interpretation*, 74–82.

Bibliography

BEN-SHAMMAI, HAGGAI, 'The Doctrines of Religious Thought of Abū Yūsuf Yaʿaqūb al-Qirqisānī and Yefet ben Eli' [Shitot hamaḥshavah hadatit shel abu yosef ya'akov alkirkisani veyefet ben eli], Ph.D. diss. (Hebrew University of Jerusalem, 1977).

——*A Leader's Project: Studies in the Philosophical and Exegetical Works of Sa'adyah Gaon* [Mifalo shel manhig: iyunim bemishnato hahagutit vehaparshanit shel rasag] (Jerusalem, 2015).

——'The Tension between Literal Interpretation and Exegetical Freedom', in Jane D. McAuliffe, Barry D. Walfish, and Joseph W. Goering (eds.), *With Reverence for the Word: Scriptural Exegesis in Judaism, Christianity, and Islam* (New York, 2003), 33–50.

BRODY, ROBERT, *The Textual History of the She'iltot* [Letoledot nusaḥ hashe'iltot] (New York, 1991).

COHEN, MORDECHAI Z., 'Emergence of the Rule of *Peshat* in Jewish Bible Exegesis', in Mordechai Z. Cohen and Adele Berlin (eds.), *Interpreting Scriptures in Judaism, Christianity and Islam: Overlapping Inquiries* (Cambridge, 2016), 204–23.

——*Opening the Gates of Interpretation: Maimonides' Biblical Hermeneutics in Light of His Geonic-Andalusian Heritage and Muslim Milieu* (Leiden, 2011).

COULTER, DALE, '*Historia* and *Sensus Litteralis*: An Investigation into the Approach to Literal Interpretation at the Twelfth-Century School of St Victor', in Franklin T. Harkins (ed.), *Transforming Relations: Essays on Jews and Christians throughout History in Honor of Michael A. Signer* (Notre Dame, Ind., 2010), 101–24.

DE VISSCHER, EVA, *Reading the Rabbis: Christian Hebraism in the Works of Herbert of Bosham* (Boston, 2014).

DRORY, RINA, *The Emergence of Jewish–Arabic Literary Contacts at the Beginning of the Tenth Century* [Reshit hamaga'im shel hasifrut hayehudit im hasifrut ha'aravit bame ah ha'asirit] (Tel Aviv, 1988).

ELON, MENACHEM (ed.), *The Principles of Jewish Law* (Jerusalem, 1975).

ENELOW, HYMAN GERSON, 'The Midrash of Thirty-Two Rules of Interpretation', *Jewish Quarterly Review*, 23 (1933), 357–67.

EVANS, G. R., *The Language and Logic of the Bible: The Earlier Middle Ages* (Cambridge, 1984).

FREDRIKSEN, PAULA, 'Allegory and Reading God's Book: Paul and Augustine on the Destiny of Israel', in Jon Whitman (ed.), *Interpretation and Allegory* (Leiden, 2000), 125–49.

GARFINKEL, STEPHEN, 'Clearing *Peshat* and *Derash*', in Magne Sæbø, Menahem Haran, and Chris Brekelmans (eds.), *Hebrew Bible/Old Testament: The History of Its Interpretation. I: From the Beginnings to the Middle Ages* (Göttingen, 2000), 129–34.

GERSONIDES, LEVI BEN GERSHOM, *Perushei hatorah lerabenu levi ben gershom* [Pentateuch commentary], ed. Y. Levy (Jerusalem, 1992).

HAAS, JAIR, 'Rashi's Criticism of Mahberet Menahem' (Heb.), in Michael Avioz, Elie Assis, and Yael Shemesh (eds.), *Zer rimonim: Studies in Biblical Literature and Jewish Exegesis Presented to Professor Rimon Kasher* [Zer rimonim: meḥkarim bamikra uvefarshanuto mukdashim liprofesor rimon kasher] (Atlanta, 2013), 449–61.

HALBERTAL, MOSHE, *People of the Book: Canon, Meaning and Authority* (Cambridge, Mass., 1997).

HALLAQ, WAEL, *The Origins and Evolution of Islamic Law* (New York, 2005).

HARRIS, JAY M., *How Do We Know This? Midrash and the Fragmentation of Modern Judaism* (Albany, NY, 1995).

HARRIS, ROBERT, 'The Literary Hermeneutic of R. Eliezer of Beaugency', Ph.D. diss. (Jewish Theological Seminary, 1997).

HENSHKE, DAVID, 'The Basis of Maimonides' Concept of Halakhah' (Heb.), *Shenaton hamishpat ha'ivri*, 20 (1995–7), 103–49.

HUGH OF SAINT-VICTOR, *Didascalicon*, ed. Charles Henry Buttimer (Washington, DC, 1939). English edn.: *The Didascalicon of Hugh of St. Victor: A Medieval Guide to the Arts*, trans. Jerome Taylor (New York, 1991).

IBN EZRA, ABRAHAM, *Perush hatorah lerabenu avraham ibn ezra* [Pentateuch commentary], ed. Asher Weiser, 3 vols. (Jerusalem, 1977).

—— *Yesod mora vesod torah*, ed. J. Cohen and U. Simon, 2nd edn. (Ramat Gan, 2007).

JAPHET, SARA, 'The Tension between Rabbinic Legal Midrash and the "Plain Meaning" (Peshat) of the Biblical Text—an Unresolved Problem? In the Wake of Rashbam's Commentary on the Pentateuch', in Chaim Cohen, Avi Hurvitz, and Shalom M. Paul (eds.), *Sefer Moshe: The Moshe Weinfeld Jubilee Volume* (Winona Lake, Ind., 2004), 403–25.

KAHANA, MENAHEM, 'The Halakhic Midrashim', in Shmuel Safrai et al. (eds.), *The Literature of the Sages, Second Part: Midrash and Targum, Liturgy, Poetry, Mysticism, Contracts, Inscriptions, Ancient Science and the Languages of Rabbinic Literature* (Assen, 2006), 3–106.

KAMIN, SARAH, *Rashi's Exegetical Categorization in Respect to the Distinction between Peshat and Derash* [Rashi: peshuto shel mikra umidrasho shel mikra] (Jerusalem, 1986).

KANARFOGEL, EPHRAIM, *The Intellectual History and Rabbinic Culture of Medieval Ashkenaz* (Detroit, 2013).

KINBERG, LEAH, 'Muḥkamāt and Mutashābihāt (Koran 3/7): Implication of a Koranic Pair of Terms in Medieval Exegesis', *Arabica*, 35 (1988), 143–72.

KLEPPER, DEANNA, *The Insight of Unbelievers: Nicholas of Lyra and Christian Readings of Jewish Texts in the Later Middle Ages* (Philadelphia, 2007).

KRAEMER, JOEL, 'Naturalism and Universalism in Maimonides' Thought', in Ezra Fleischer et al. (eds.), *Me'ah She'arim: Studies in Medieval Jewish Spiritual Life in Memory of Isadore Twersky* [Me'ah she'arim: sefer hazikaron liprof. yitsḥak twersky] (Jerusalem, 2001), 47–81.

KUGEL, JAMES, *The Bible As It Was* (Cambridge, Mass., 1997).

LOCKSHIN, MARTIN, 'Tradition or Context: Two Exegetes Struggle with Peshat', in Jacob Neusner et al. (eds.), *From Ancient Israel to Modern Judaism: Intellect in Quest of Understanding: Essays in Honor of Marvin Fox* (Atlanta, 1989), ii. 173–86.

LUBAC, HENRI DE, *Exegese medievale: Les Quatre Sens de l'Écriture*, 4 vols. (Paris, 1961).

MAIMONIDES, MOSES, *Hakdamot harambam lamishnah* [introductions to sections of the Mishnah], ed. and trans. Isaac Shailat (Ma'aleh Adumim, 1992).

—— *Mishnah im perush r. mosheh ben maimon* [Mishnah commentary], ed. and trans. Yosef Kafih, 6 vols. (Jerusalem, 1963–8).

—— *Mishneh torah* [standard printed version with traditional commentaries] (Vilna, 1900).

—— *Sefer hamitsvot*, ed. and trans. Yosef Kafih (Jerusalem, 1971).

—— *Teshuvot harambam*, ed. Joshua Blau, 3 vols. (Jerusalem, 1958).

MAMAN, AHARON, 'The Linguistic School', in Magne Sæbø, Menahem Haran, and Chris Brekelmans (eds.), *Hebrew Bible/Old Testament: The History of Its Interpretation. I: From the Beginnings to the Middle Ages* (Göttingen, 2000), 261–81.

MENAHEM BEN SARUK, *Maḥberet*, ed. and Spanish trans. Angel Saenz-Badillos (Granada, 1986).

MINNIS, ALASTAIR, *Medieval Theory of Authorship: Scholastic Literary Attitudes* (Philadelphia, 2008).

—— and A. B. SCOTT, with DAVID WALLACE (eds.), *Medieval Literary Theory and Criticism c.1100–c.1375: The Commentary Tradition*, 2nd edn. (Oxford, 1991; repr. 2001).

MONDSCHEIN, AHARON, 'Concerning the Relationship of the Commentaries of R. Abraham Ibn Ezra and R. Samuel ben Meir to the Pentateuch: A New Appraisal' (Heb.), in Yair Hoffman (ed.), *Studies in Judaica*, Te'udah 16–17 (Tel Aviv, 2001), 15–46.

—— '"Only One in a Thousand of his Comments may be Called *Peshat*": Towards Ibn Ezra's View of Rashi's Commentary to the Torah' (Heb.), in Moshe Garsiel et al. (eds.), *Studies in Bible and Exegesis 5, Presented to Uriel Simon* [Iyunei mikra ufarshanut 5: minḥat yedidut vehukrah le'uriel simon] (Ramat Gan, 2000), 221–48.

NAHMANIDES, MOSES, *Perush haramban al hatorah* [Pentateuch commentary], ed. H. D. Chavel, 2 vols. (Jerusalem, 1976).

—— *Sefer hamitsvot im hasagot haramban* [critique of Maimonides' *Sefer hamitsvot*], ed. H. D. Chavel (Jerusalem, 1981).

NEUBAUER, YEKUTIEL Y., *Maimonides on the 'Words of the Scribes'* [Harambam al divrei soferim] (Jerusalem, 1957).

RAVITSKY, AVIRAM, 'Maimonides and Alfarabi on the Development of the Halakhah' (Heb.), in Aviezer Ravitzky and Avinoam Rosenak (eds.), *New Streams in Philosophy of Halakhah* [Iyunim ḥadashim befilosofyah shel halakhah] (Jerusalem, 2008), 211–30.

SA'ADYAH GAON, *Sa'adyah's Commentary on Genesis* [Perushei rav sa'adyah gaon livereshit], ed. and trans. M. Zucker (New York, 1984).

—— *Tafsīr* [Pentateuch translation], in *Œuvres complètes de R. Saadia ben Iosef al-Fayyoûmî*, ed. J. Derenbourg (Paris, 1893).

SAMUEL BEN MEIR (RASHBAM), *Perush hatorah asher katav rashbam* [Pentateuch commentary], ed. David Rosin (Breslau, 1881).

SCHACHT, JOSEPH, *An Introduction to Islamic Law* (Oxford, 1964).

SIMON, URIEL, *The Ear Discerns Words: Studies in Ibn Ezra's Exegetical Methodology* [Ozen milin tivḥan: meḥkarim bedarko haparshanit shel r. avraham ibn ezra] (Ramat Gan, 2013).

SKLARE, DAVID, *Samuel ben Hofni Gaon and His Cultural World* (Leiden, 1996).

SMALLEY, BERYL, *The Study of the Bible in the Middle Ages*, 3rd edn. (Notre Dame, 1983).

SOLOMON BEN ISAAC (RASHI), *Raschi: der Kommentar des Salomo B. Isak über den Pentateuch*, ed. A. Berliner, 2nd edn. (Frankfurt am Main, 1905).

TOUITOU, ELEAZAR, *Exegesis in Perpetual Motion: Studies in the Pentateuchal Commentary of Rabbi Samuel ben Meir* ('Hapeshatot hamitḥadshim bekhol yom': iyunim beferusho shel rashbam latorah] (Ramat Gan, 2003).

TWERSKY, ISADORE, *Introduction to the Code of Maimonides* (New Haven, 1980).

VAN LIERE, FRANS, 'Andrew of St. Victor, Jerome, and the Jews: Biblical Scholarship in the Twelfth-Century Renaissance', in Thomas J. Heffernan and Thomas E. Burman (eds.), *Scripture and Pluralism: Reading the Bible in the Religiously Plural Worlds of the Middle Ages and Renaissance* (Leiden, 2005), 59–75.

VAN 'T SPIJKER, INEKE, 'The Literal and the Spiritual: Richard of Saint-Victor and the Multiple Meaning of Scripture', in Ineke van 't Spijker (ed.), *The Multiple Meaning of Scripture: The Role of Exegesis in Early-Christian and Medieval Culture* (Leiden, 2009), 225–47.

VAN ZWIETEN, J. W. M., 'The Place and Significance of Literal Exegesis in Hugh of St. Victor', Ph.D. diss. (Universiteit van Amsterdam, 1992).

WEISS, BERNARD G., *The Search for God's Law: Islamic Jurisprudence in the Writings of Sayf al-Din al-Amidi* (Salt Lake City, 1992).

—— *The Spirit of Islamic Law* (Athens, Ga., 1998).

WEISS HALIVNI, DAVID, *Midrash, Mishnah, and Gemara: The Jewish Predilection for Justified Law* (Cambridge, Mass., 1986).

—— *Peshat and Derash: Plain and Applied Meaning in Rabbinic Exegesis* (New York, 1991).

WHITMAN, JON, 'Antique Interpretation of Formative Texts', in id. (ed.), *Interpretation and Allegory: Antiquity to the Modern Period* (Leiden, 2000), 34–45.

—— (ed.), *Interpretation and Allegory: Antiquity to the Modern Period* (Leiden, 2000).

ZUCKER, MOSHE, *Rav Sa'adyah Gaon's Translation of the Torah* [Al targum rasag latorah] (New York, 1959).

—— 'Studies and Notes' (Heb.), *Proceedings of the American Academy for Jewish Research*, 49 (1982), 97–104.

CHAPTER SIX

The 'Our Talmud' Tradition and the Predilection for Works of Applied Law in Early Sephardi Rabbinic Culture

TALYA FISHMAN

PRIOR TO THE THIRTEENTH CENTURY, the text of the Babylonian Talmud played significantly different roles in the Jewish communities of Ashkenaz and Sepharad, the most visible and enduring of the rabbinic subcultures that emerged in the Middle Ages. Ashkenazi scholars of northern Europe placed the study of the Talmud at the centre of the rabbinic curriculum, while their counterparts in North Africa and al-Andalus studied eleventh-century talmudic commentaries produced in the region by R. Nisim, R. Hananel, and R. Isaac Alfasi, and, later, the *Mishneh torah*, Maimonides' twelfth-century legal code. Unlike the Talmud, each of these works relayed applied legal decisions (*halakhah lema'aseh*). Approaches to decision-making were also different. Engaging the Talmud directly, Ashkenazi adjudicators negotiated its relationship to other sources of legal authority, custom prominent among them. By contrast, Sephardim relied less on Talmud than on works of decided law, whether these were expressed in commentaries, geonic responsa, or legal digests. Sephardim also appear to have paid little attention to the legal weight of custom. Scholars have noted each of these differences, but the reasons for the regional variations are not well understood.[1]

This study builds on an earlier effort to understand distinctive features of the rabbinic subcultures of Ashkenaz and Sepharad by situating them

[1] Surveys of halakhic literature in medieval Ashkenaz and medieval Sepharad occur in two encyclopedic compilations written by Israel Ta-Shma. The two volumes of *Commentarial Literature on the Talmud* (Heb.) are organized chronologically, with the first volume covering 1000–1200, and the second, 1200–1400. The first two of his three-volume *Collected Studies* (Heb.) are devoted, respectively, to 'Ashkenaz' and 'Sepharad'. The disparate weight accorded to custom (*minhag*) in the legal culture of different medieval Jewish communities is noted by Jacob Katz in 'Evening Prayer in Its Prescribed Time' (Heb.).

within their broader historical and regional contexts.[2] The present undertaking explores a poorly understood teaching transmitted by medieval Andalusian rabbinic scholars, the 'our Talmud' tradition.[3] It sets forth a speculative hypothesis about its origins, traces the changing meaning of the tradition for different generations of Andalusian Jews, and considers its relationship to the noted Sephardi predilection for rabbinic works of applied law.[4]

Two preliminary remarks are in order regarding terminology and chronology. In cautioning against the tendency to 'essentialize' Sephardiness, a recent study has compellingly argued that an actual Sephardi identity did not emerge until the sixteenth century. It was only generations after 1492 that the descendants of expelled Jews, now living in the Ottoman empire and other lands, came to regard the finer calibrations of their former regional identities—their ancestral residence in specific Iberian towns or kingdoms—as being of negligible significance.[5] Jonathan Ray's claim that, between the thirteenth century and the Expulsion, Spanish Jews 'represented little more than a loose association of social networks based on family, city, profession and intellectual bloc' is well supported by the array of archival sources that he adduces.[6] Yet, as he acknowledges, members of the early modern Sephardi diaspora shared a 'religio-legal constitution in the Talmud and its voluminous interpretations and commentaries'.[7] The present study considers elements of this common legacy, what Ray calls 'raw material',[8] and it assumes that there

[2] Fishman, *Becoming the People of the Talmud*, esp. ch. 3.

[3] Reference is made to the 'our Talmud' tradition ibid. 12, 72, 74–5, 88, 122, 128, 142–3, 176, 257, 269, and in the accompanying notes.

[4] Though Shraga Abramson challenged Mordecai Margalioth's claim that 11th-century Andalusian Jews composed, or aspired to compose, comprehensive codes of Jewish law, it is hard to ignore the fact that the programmatic guidelines spelled out in Samuel Hanagid's oath poem of 1049 correspond to features of the *Mishneh torah* that Maimonides took pains to emphasize 130 years later in his introduction to that work: omission of legal dispute, use of clear and accessible language, inclusion of the latest opinions, comprehensiveness of scope, and preemption of the need for any other legal work. As Margalioth noted, the celebrated codes of Jewish law—Maimonides' 12th-century *Mishneh torah*, R. Jacob ben Asher's 14th-century *Arba'ah turim*, and R. Joseph Karo's 16th-century *Shulḥan arukh*—were all produced by scholars in the Andalusian orbit. See Abramson, 'From the Legal Teachings of R. Samuel Hanagid' (Heb.), 13. Margalioth, *The Laws of the Nagid* (Heb.), 37, 52. And see Fishman, *Becoming the People of the Talmud*, 82–4.

[5] Ray, *After 1492: The Expulsion from Spain*, 9.

[6] Ibid. 12. Ray accepts Shlomo Dov Goitein's characterization of the earlier Iberian Jewish communities as participants in a shared society of Mediterranean Jews, and he roots this in 'the absorption of Jews in the *Pax Islamica* of the ninth century' (ibid. 2–3).

[7] Ibid. 13, 14.

[8] Ibid. 7–8.

was a shared understanding of a distinctly Sephardi approach among rabbinic scholars.

The chronological endpoint of this enquiry is the start of the thirteenth century, when a confluence of factors led to a narrowing of the gap between the subcultures of Ashkenaz and Sepharad.[9] It was then that the towering Catalan scholar Nahmanides (1194–1270) encountered the talmudic glosses composed by north European Tosafists and introduced changes in the region's approach to halakhic study. This led to something of a rapprochement between subsequent Sephardi rabbinic culture and that of Ashkenaz, for Nahmanides taught the foremost rabbis of Spain's next generation, who followed him in composing *ḥidushim* (novellae) on the Talmud.[10] Developments in northern Europe also diminished the cultural gap between Ashkenaz and Sepharad in the same period. The burning of the Talmud in the 1240s led the Jews of France to rely on what they dubbed the *Talmud katan*, the talmudic commentary-code of R. Isaac Alfasi (1013–1103).[11]

*

Alfasi wrote the *Sefer hahalakhot* in Qal'at Hammad, before moving, in his eighties, to al-Andalus, where he assumed leadership of the yeshiva in Lucena. His hand-picked Andalusian successor, Rabbi Joseph Ibn Migash (1077–1141), observed that the Babylonian Talmud's use of the term *talmud* must refer to something other than the written corpus of that name.[12] Sherira Gaon had implicitly made this distinction in his *Epistle* (*Igeret rav sherira ga'on*) composed in 987, where he defined *talmud* as the body of teachings derived, inferentially, from the Mishnah.[13] But Ibn Migash's late eleventh- or early twelfth-century commentary explicitly distinguished between *talmud*

[9] Ephraim Kanarfogel discusses other literary manifestations of growing familiarity with the rabbinic writings of the other subculture in the 13th century, and emphasizes the place of the Maimonidean controversy in bringing the scholars of Sepharad and Ashkenaz into closer contact; Kanarfogel, 'Between Ashkenaz and Sefarad', 239–43. See too Grossman, 'Connections between Sephardi and Ashkenazi Jews in the Middle Ages' (Heb.).

[10] On the shift initiated by Nahmanides see Ta-Shma, *Commentarial Literature on the Talmud* (Heb.), ii. 35–7.

[11] On the reference to Alfasi's *Sefer hahalakhot* as 'Talmud katan' see Ibn Daud, *Sefer ha-Qabbalah*, 84.

[12] See Fishman, *Becoming the People of the Talmud*, 72–5 and 175–6. On *talmud* as an approach and not a literary corpus see Goldin, 'Freedom and Restraint of Haggadah', 253–5.

[13] On Sherira Gaon's use of the term *talmud* in his *Epistle* see Fishman, *Becoming the People of the Talmud*, 26–7, 30.

and Talmud.[14] Commenting on the tannaitic passage 'one does not learn halakhah from *talmud*',[15] he noted that the sages who had formulated this dictum could not possibly have been referring to the written composition of that name, since it did not yet exist. Thus, he reasoned, *talmud* for the ancient rabbis evidently denoted something quite different from what he called 'our Talmud' (*hatalmud shelanu*). Elaborating on this point, he wrote,

> this Talmud of ours [*hatalmud shelanu*] is [a corpus of] applied law [*halakhah lema'aseh*], for it was not consigned to writing [*ki lo nikhtav*] until after several generations of investigation and scrutiny, and after several redactions. And it is as if that which they told us in it is applied law. After all, they wrote it down for the explicit purpose of [guiding] practice [*sheharei la'asot bo ma'aseh ketavuhu*].[16]

According to Ibn Migash, 'our Talmud' differs from the earlier *talmud* in two ways: unlike unwritten *talmud*, 'our Talmud' was transmitted in writing. But the two are also distinct in content, for when 'our Talmud' was written, its language was purposefully shaped to meet a practical end: the giving of applied legal guidance. The teachings in 'our Talmud' are thus doubly vetted; they bear the imprimatur of received legal tradition, halakhah, along with that of attested practice, *ma'aseh*. From Ibn Migash's perspective the consignment of the Babylonian Talmud to writing entailed more than a change of medium; it marked the occasion when the included traditions were consciously shaped for readers.

The 'our Talmud' tradition also finds expression in a (non-legal) reference by R. Judah al-Barceloni to the 'Talmud transmitted to us, which is *halakhah lema'aseh*',[17] in the late eleventh or early twelfth century, and in the more elaborate remarks of a contemporaneous Toledan scholar. Commenting on the above-mentioned tannaitic dictum, 'one does not learn halakhah from *talmud*', R. Meir Halevi Abulafia (1170–1244) sharpened the contrast between the use of the term *talmud* in that statement and the body of writing known

[14] See Ta-Shma, 'The Literary Oeuvre of R. Joseph Ibn Migash' (Heb.), 138–42, and id., *Commentarial Literature on the Talmud* (Heb.), i. 175–84. Ibn Migash received accolades from, among others, Maimonides (whose father had been a student of his), Menahem Hame'iri, and Abraham Ibn Daud.

[15] BT *BB* 130*b*. On a variant manuscript tradition, *ein lomedin halakhah mipi talmid* (one does not derive halakhah from a student) and its meaning for Ibn Migash, see Abramson, 'Clarifications' (Heb.), 183–5, and Urbach, *The Halakhah* (Heb.), 229–30.

[16] Ibn Migash, *Ḥidushin* on *BB* 130*b*, from a manuscript cited in Danzig, *Introduction to Sefer halakhot pesukot* (Heb.), 134, 138–9; emphasis is mine. It seems that what has been transcribed in Danzig's text as *halakhah lemosheh misinai* is actually supposed to be *halakhah lema'aseh*. Cf. Y. Sussman, 'Once Again on JT *Nezikin*' (Heb.), 105 n. 196.

[17] *Perush sefer yetsirah*, 186–8.

as 'our Talmud':

For this [ancient rabbinic prohibition against deriving applied law from *talmud*] applies to *their talmud*, which they recited orally. But *our* Talmud, once it was/which is written, was written for purposes of applied law [*halakhah lema'aseh*] . . . For when it was written, it was written in order that applied law might be derived from it.[18]

Though medieval Sephardim possessed a tradition that portrayed their ancestors as very early recipients of the written Babylonian Talmud,[19] none of their etiological narratives about the Talmud's arrival in Iberia pertains to the 'our Talmud' tradition. Missing from each is the claim of a causal nexus between the consignment of this work to writing and the transmission of applied law. By contrast, both Ibn Migash and Meir Halevi Abulafia asserted that 'our Talmud', a compendium of applied law, was produced *because* and *when* formerly oral traditions were consigned to writing.

One clue to this enigmatic claim may lie in a particular cultural assumption that prevailed in the heartland of the former Roman empire, but not in its borderlands. This was the assumption that writings became 'official', that is, bearers of cultural weight, when they were 'published', that is, made public. This perspective and its corollary practices were rooted in the Hellenistic distinction between the *syngrama*, an authorized inscription accorded official status, and the *hypomnema*, written notes designed for private use (known in rabbinic culture as *megilot setarim*).[20] As residents of lands in which Roman legal culture persisted long after the empire's collapse,[21] the Jews of North Africa and al-Andalus would have assumed that the consignment of the Talmud to writing, described in the above-mentioned narratives, signalled the transformation of this formerly oral corpus into a text of applied, decided law.

The regionally specific assumption about the nexus between 'publication'

[18] Abulafia, *Sefer yad ramah* on BT *BB* 130, and cf. Abramson, 'Clarifications' (Heb.), 185. In 184 n. 2 Abramson noted that a citation from JT *Pe'ah*, preserved in a *Yad ramah* recension in *Shitah mekubetset*, says *ela min hatalmud*, not *velo min hatalmud*.

[19] On the Sephardi tradition that their ancestors had acquired the written Talmud quite early, see Fishman, *Becoming the People of the Talmud*, 72–5, and 267 nn. 63–6; Danzig, 'From Oral Talmud to Written Talmud' (Heb.), 62.

[20] Lieberman, *Hellenism in Jewish Palestine*, 87 f., 204 f.; id., *The Greeks and Hellenism in the Land of Israel* (Heb.), 213–24; Gerhardsson, *Memory and Manuscript*, 159 ff. Rina Drory made a significant contribution to our understanding of this distinction in *The First Encounters between Jewish and Arabic Literature* (Heb.)

[21] On the persistence of Roman law in Spain and North Africa see Riché, *Education and Culture in the Barbarian West*; Collins, 'Visigothic Law and Regional Custom', 85–104.

and the promulgation of applied law may also shed light on specific differences between the two versions of Sherira Gaon's *Epistle*. According to the family of manuscripts found in French-speaking lands, which scholars have labelled 'French', Rabbi Judah Hanasi had 'arranged' the Mishnah. But according to the 'Spanish' manuscripts of the *Epistle*, Rabbi Judah had actually 'written' the Mishnah.[22] Living in a region saturated with the legal assumptions and practices of earlier Roman culture, it would have been natural for Andalusian Jews to presume that 'official' laws (as opposed to customs, for example) were those that took written form.

*

Jews in Muslim lands made pioneering strides in biblical exegesis by applying the insights of Arabic poetics and grammar to their reading of Scripture. Among the concepts they introduced was that of the *mudawwin*, the recorder-narrator-editor figure who fashioned and controlled the discourse in a written text.[23] According to Haggai Ben Shammai, the Arabic term *tadwīn* can refer to the ordering of the traditions received, or to the act of consigning the traditions to writing.[24] The distinct parallels noted between the text-centred operations ascribed to the *mudawwin* by Jewish scholars in Muslim lands on the one hand, and the operations ascribed to the *sadran* (lit. 'orderer') by Jewish Bible exegetes in medieval Byzantium on the other,[25] have given rise to scholarly conjectures about the pathway of the transmission of the concept.[26] Though Muslim scholars never referred to a *mudawwin* in their exegesis of the Quran,[27] Jewish Bible exegetes, both Rabbanite and Karaite, did so from the early tenth century onwards. Just as Sa'adyah Gaon[28] and

[22] Both recensions appear in *Igeret rav sherira gaon*, ed. Levin. On the identification of the 'French' recension as the version more compatible with geonic cultural assumptions, see e.g. Beer, 'Studies on the Epistle of Sherira Gaon' (Heb.); Friedman, 'On the Contribution of the Genizah to Halakhic Research' (Heb.). The claim that all 'Spanish' manuscripts of Sherira's *Epistle* are late and were subject to 'heavy-handed reworking' in order to bring them into accord with the writings of Maimonides appears in Sussman, 'Oral Torah' (Heb.), 234 n. 26. Contemporary geonic scholars regard the 'French' recension as the version that most accurately reflects geonic perspectives.

[23] Polliack, 'Karaite Conception of the Biblical Narrator', 357, column B; ead., 'The Karaite Inversion of Written and Oral Torah', 288.

[24] Ben Shammai, '*Al Mudawwin*' (Heb.), 76–7.

[25] Steiner, 'A Jewish Theory of Biblical Redaction'. Steiner mentions the parallel on p. 134.

[26] Ben Shammai ('*Al Mudawwin*' (Heb.), 76) thinks that the concept travelled from the Arabic to the Byzantine world through Karaite mediators.

[27] Polliack, 'Karaite Conception of the Biblical Narrator', 353, column A.

[28] On Sa'adyah's references to Moses as *mudawwin* see Ben Shammai, '*Al Mudawwin*' (Heb.), 106–10. The biblical passages that trigger these reflections are Exod. 11: 4 and 16: 23. See

Ya'qub al-Qirqisānī[29] drew attention to the role of the *mudawwin* in their writings on scriptural passages, later Rabbanites and Karaites also discerned stylistic interventions in Tanakh.[30]

All Jewish exegetes acknowledged God as the source of the Torah's teachings, but in Muslim lands some identified the hand of the *mudawwin* in a range of intellectual and literary mediations that resulted in the written text of Scripture. In 937–8 al-Qirqisānī set forth thirty-seven propositions of interpretation in the introduction to his Bible commentary;[31] the first of these established that Moses was the *mudawwin* who had arranged or written the Torah.[32] Other activities ascribed by Jewish biblical exegetes to the *mudawwin* (who, in some cases, was Moses, but where other parts of the Tanakh were concerned, a different redactor) included the collation of passages, their internal sequencing and arrangement,[33] and the use of particular rhetorical techniques in mediating the narrative content, for example delay in imparting information.[34] God determined what would go into the Torah, but the *mudawwin* could decide where to place it and how it would be told.[35] The *mudawwin* was responsible for the arrangement of words, and, when necessary, even for their translation. Noting that some of the figures mentioned in the Bible did not speak Hebrew, al-Qirqisānī explained that it was the *mudawwin* who formulated their utterances in Scripture.[36] The same was true

also Sa'adyah's commentary on Prov. 25: 11 in *Sefer mishle*, and his introduction to *Perush sefer yetsirah*.

[29] Even before al-Qirqisānī there were Torah interpreters who noted that some words in Scripture were not those of God but of Moses, the arranger. See Ben Shammai, '*Al Mudawwin*' (Heb.), 92.

[30] Eli ben Yisra'el, a Rabbanite exegete of the first half of the 11th century who was familiar with Karaite exegesis, cited it, appreciated it—and used the concept of *mudawwin* in his commentary on the book of Samuel; Ben Shammai, '*Al Mudawwin*' (Heb.), 100. Ben Shammai identifies a number of Karaite authors on pp. 99–100. Discussions of *tadwīn* are prominent in the writings of other 10th- and 11th-century Karaites; see e.g. Polliack, 'The Karaite Inversion of Written and Oral Torah'; Polliack and Schlossberg, 'Historical, Literary and Rhetorical and Redactional Methods of Interpretation'; Polliack, 'The "Voice" of the Narrator and the "Voice" of the Characters'; Goldstein, *Karaite Exegesis in Medieval Jerusalem*.

[31] His propositions are published in Arabic, with an English introduction (pp. 1–38), in Hirschfeld, *Qirqisani Studies*, and are discussed in Ben Shammai, '*Al Mudawwin*' (Heb.).

[32] Qirqisānī asserted that Moses was responsible for every word in the Torah, even the things said after his death. See his references to 'the Torah of Moses' in Josh. 8: 31 and Mal. 3: 22. See Hirschfeld, *Qirqisani Studies*.

[33] Ibid. 77–8; Polliack, 'Karaite Conception of the Biblical Narrator', 356, column B.

[34] Polliack, 'Karaite Conception of the Biblical Narrator', 362–8.

[35] Ben Shammai, '*Al Mudawwin*' (Heb.), 106–10.

[36] Ibid. 77.

of place names, he observed; this could be seen in biblical passages that named a location for events that had taken place far earlier.[37]

Identification of the *mudawwin*'s interventions enabled Jewish biblical exegetes to account for logical and chronological inconsistencies in Scripture. But within the predominantly Muslim environment, insights of this nature were a double-edged sword.[38] On the one hand, Jews could account for incongruities in the text. On the other, their acknowledgement of Scripture's 'contrived nature . . . as a literary work'[39] made it vulnerable to the Muslim polemical charge of *taḥrīf*,[40] the claim that the Jews had falsified the original Torah which God had revealed to Moses. Some elliptical comments in the Bible commentary of Abraham Ibn Ezra (1089–1167) evince anxiety about the sharing of observations of a historicist nature, though he wrote them after he had left Muslim Spain.[41] Where he hints at the chronological implications of a given scriptural passage, Ibn Ezra characteristically concludes on an evocative note: *vehamaskil yavin* ('a word to the wise is sufficient').[42]

Building on the insights of their predecessors, later Jewish exegetes of Christian Spain uncovered other structural features of the biblical text—without any evident anxiety.[43] Nahmanides pointed out many recurring narrative

[37] Ben Shammai, '*Al Mudawwin*' (Heb.), 78.

[38] Polliack, 'The Karaite Inversion of Written and Oral Torah', 291.

[39] Polliack, 'Karaite Conception of the Biblical Narrator', 355, column A.

[40] See e.g. Quran 2. 75; Perlmann, 'The Medieval Polemics between Islam and Judaism'; Jacobs, 'Interrreligious Polemics in Medieval Spain'.

[41] See e.g. Ibn Ezra's Bible commentary on Gen. 12: 6 and Deut. 1: 2. On his sensitivity to poetic ornamentation and his use of the term *tsaḥot* to indicate poetic playfulness, see Simon, 'Abraham Ibn Ezra', i. 385–6. Reflections on the relationship between Ibn Ezra's historicist observations and the eighth principle of the Jewish creed formulated by Maimonides appear in Shapiro, *The Limits of Orthodox Theology*, 91–121. Additional bibliography on the biblical criticism produced by premodern Jews appears in Fishman, *Becoming the People of the Talmud*, 247 n. 117.

[42] Readers encountering Ibn Ezra's allusive asides may have (wrongly) assumed that his guardedness was due to the fact that his historicist insights flouted the eighth principle of Maimonides' formulation of the Jewish creed. It is unlikely, however, that Ibn Ezra (1089–1167) was familiar with any of the writings of Maimonides (1135–1204). Rather, his fear was that his insights might be used as ammunition by Muslim polemicists, who claimed that Jews had falsified the original Torah revealed by God. The possibility that Maimonides was familiar with Ibn Ezra's writings is considered in Twersky, 'Did R. Abraham Ibn Ezra Influence Maimonides?' (Heb.).

[43] It is also the case that Karaite anxiety about *tadwīn*-related insights diminished over time. In explaining why Yefet ben Eli, rather than his Karaite predecessors al-Qirqisānī and Salmon ben Yeroham, was in a position to articulate a *mudawwin* hermeneutical theory, Meira Polliack

and linguistic patterns in his thirteenth-century Bible commentary,[44] and Abarbanel's fifteenth-century commentaries married the literary sensibilities fostered in Muslim al-Andalus with the rhetorical concepts and terminology of Christian scholasticism.[45] Living outside a Muslim environment, these later Spanish commentators were insulated from the accusation of *taḥrīf*; they also made no references to a *mudawwin*-like figure when identifying occasions of intentional literary crafting in the scriptural text.

*

Along with geonic and Kairouanese teachings, Rabbi Isaac Alfasi brought the Jews of al-Andalus a practical orientation to Jewish law. This was reflected in his decision to omit from *Sefer hahalakhot* the Talmud's dialectical deliberations regarding matters he saw as impractical and those tractates whose Temple-related legal content could not be applied in his time. In adopting this approach, Alfasi was following in the footsteps of the rabbinic scholars of eleventh-century Kairouan, Rabbenu Nissim and Rabbenu Hananel, as well as geonim.[46] Yet there was an essential difference between his approach and that of his predecessors when it came to discerning the law to be applied, *halakhah lema'aseh*, from the welter of unresolved talmudic disputes.

Alfasi's predecessors, the geonim, had drawn conclusions from the Talmud by applying principles of adjudication (*kelalei pesikah*) that they developed through their analysis of tannaitic and amoraic discourse; some of these rules were specific to disputes involving particular tradents.[47] In so doing, they added to the principles of adjudication articulated by amoraim. Alfasi relied on these principles as well, but, unlike his predecessors, he assigned greater weight to the Talmud's late, anonymous stratum (known to modern scholars as the *setam*) in drawing legal conclusions.[48] According

observes that the passage of time made it easier for Karaites (as well) to 'lower . . . defenses with regard to its [the Torah's] oral past': 'The Karaite Inversion of Written and Oral Torah', 299.

[44] See Elman, 'Moses ben Nahman'.

[45] See Lawee, 'Isaac Abarbanel'.

[46] Ta-Shma, 'Did Maimonides Have a Revolutionary Approach to Talmud Study?' (Heb.), 111–17.

[47] See Levy, 'Alfasi, *Sugyan* and the Authority of the *Stam*', 162. Levy explains that Hai Gaon regarded 'specific phenomena in the editorial presentation of the tannaitic and amoraic opinions to be overriding indicators of a legal decision'.

[48] The Kairouanese scholar Rabbenu Hananel (990–1053) also paid close attention to the Talmud's anonymous stratum, but did not ascribe to it the authority that Alfasi later did. R. Hananel also recognized the *setam* as a unitary editor, but he nonetheless followed the conclusions of the geonim, trusting their logic. See Levy, 'Alfasi, *Sugyan* and the Authority of the *Stam*', 156, 161–2.

to Alfasi, the precise manner in which the anonymous stratum framed any legal debate subtly guided the discerning reader to the legal conclusions that were to be drawn.[49]

In his important study of *Sefer hahalakhot*, Leonard Levy has explained that the Talmud's anonymous stratum was authoritative for Alfasi because he regarded the *setam* as the work of 'a unitary, consistent editor who deliberately used a number of methods to signal the legal sources that were authoritative, and those that were not'.[50] Where the geonim were comfortable transmitting more than one version of a tradition, Alfasi was not. In *Sefer hahalakhot* Alfasi referred to this anonymous editor as 'Gemara',[51] and in his Arabic writings as 'al-Talmūd'.[52]

I suggest that Alfasi construed the Talmud's anonymous stratum as the voice of a purposeful redactor because he regarded it as the Talmud's *mudawwin*. It is noteworthy that Muslim scholars engaged in the science of hadith used the term *tadwīn al-ḥadīth* to indicate 'the collecting of traditions in writing in order to derive legal precepts from them and not as a mere memory aid'.[53] According to G. H. A. Juynboll, the collection of oral traditions for mnemonic (and presumably non-official) purposes was designated by a different term, *kitābat al-ḥadīth*. Whether or not Alfasi used the term *tadwīn* to describe the redactional activities of 'al-Talmūd', he would certainly have known that scholars of the majority culture were scrutinizing and shaping their own oral traditions in order to render applied law. Learned Jews in the book-centred Arab world were no less concerned than Muslims to

[49] Levy, 'Rabbi Yitzhaq Alfasi's Application of Principles of Adjudication', 178–9.

[50] Ibid. Levy notes the disparate views of an unnamed gaon (perhaps Hai) and Alfasi regarding divergent talmudic narratives of allocations of property by Rami bar Hama's mother. While the gaon had claimed that the passages in *Ket.* 94*b* and *BB* 151*a* referred to one and the same event, in his Judaeo-Arabic commentary Alfasi claimed that they were two separate cases. He asserted that the editor, 'al-Talmūd', 'must be presumed not to contradict himself', except in those places where he acknowledges doing so.

[51] Identifying the passages in *Sefer hahalakhot* where Alfasi uses the term *gemara* to refer to the *setam*, Levy cites *BB* 133*a*, *Ket.* 96*a*, *Pes.* 36*a*, and *Pes.* 119*b*; see 'Alfasi, *Sugyan* and the Authority of the *Stam*', 160 n. 64, with cross-references.

[52] Levy, 'The Decisive Shift', 117. According to Boaz Cohen, when Alfasi needed to discuss certain legal points in greater detail, he did so in Judaeo-Arabic and appended the discussions at the end of the tractate. See Cohen, 'Three Arabic Halakhic Discussions of Alfasi', 356, 360–1 and n. 12. R. Solomon ben Joseph of Saragossa offered an overview of geonic, Andalusian, and Maghribi scholars who wrote halakhic works in Arabic. Use of this language, he noted, made it easier 'for the questioners and the students'; see Sklare, 'R. David ben Sa'adyah al-Ger' (Heb.), 103. Cf. Ta-Shma, 'R. Isaac Ibn Ghiyyat's Commentary on Tractate *Bava Metsia*' (Heb.), ii. 6.

[53] Juynboll, 'Tadwīn'.

demonstrate that their foundational texts displayed the internal logic, consistency, and elegance that the category 'book' demanded.[54] Whereas the analytical efforts of Karaite scholars served to showcase that these were the characteristics of Written Torah,[55] Alfasi's sensitive reading of rhetorical cues in Oral Torah—now available as a written text—demonstrated that the Talmud, or Gemara, redacted by 'al-Talmūd', was itself a 'book', that is, a carefully crafted composition whose legal prescriptions could be systematically retrieved.

The revolutionary import of Alfasi's perspective has been well explained by Levy. Babylonian geonim tolerated the existence of variant traditions, and transmitted them—without granting exclusive authority to any single one. Moreover, in drawing conclusions about applied law, geonim relied heavily on guidance from extra-talmudic traditions—all of which were part of geonic institutional memory. Among these traditions were customs long practised in the community and the practice of masters—themselves living links in the chain of transmission—which the geonim themselves had witnessed. By contrast, Alfasi relied largely on the talmudic text itself, and especially its latest stratum, that of the anonymous *setam*, in establishing applied Jewish law. In Levy's words, Alfasi's preference for the authority of the talmudic text over and above that of traditions received from the geonic yeshivas 'cut the final umbilical ties between the Talmud and the traditions of the academies which produced it'.[56]

Alfasi's students left Lucena for many other places in Spain, displacing local traditions and introducing a uniformity of practice that came from their observations of the master and from shared pedagogical experience.[57] Indeed, *Sefer hahalakhot* was seminal to all subsequent Sephardi halakhic compositions.[58] But it may also be the case that Alfasi's designation of applied law as Gemara and as 'al-Talmūd' had an important, if hitherto undetected, afterlife. His anomalous use of these terms may shed light on the enigmatic Sephardi tradition of 'our Talmud'. Beginning with Alfasi's students, medieval Sephardim may have come to assume that 'their' Talmud was designed to serve as a

[54] See Frenkel, 'The Literary Canon as a Tool' (Heb.); Polliack, 'The Karaite Inversion of Written and Oral Torah', 255, 277–8.

[55] Polliack, 'The Karaite Inversion of Written and Oral Torah', 243–61.

[56] Levy, 'Alfasi, *Sugyan* and the Authority of the *Stam*', 163.

[57] See Ta-Shma, *Commentarial Literature on the Talmud* (Heb.), i. 154; cf. Fishman, *Becoming the People of the Talmud*, 84.

[58] The status of Alfasi's work in Joseph Karo's 16th-century *Shulḥan arukh* is discussed in Elon, *Jewish Law* (Heb.), iii. 968–9.

guide to applied Jewish law, precisely because it had been transformed through the redactional, ordering, and transcriptive activities of a *mudawwin*. The 'our Talmud' tradition certified that the text on which Sephardim relied was one that imparted the practical legal guidance they needed[59]—if only in theory.

*

The very Ibn Migash who transmitted the 'our Talmud' tradition also wrote a responsum in which he exhorted judges tasked with rendering legal decisions to bypass the Babylonian Talmud and rely instead on geonic responsa or on legal digests that were designed as reference works. At first blush, this might seem decidedly odd. If the written Talmud had been produced as a work of applied law (as the 'our Talmud' tradition asserts), why would Ibn Migash have warned Jewish judges to steer clear of that text, and to base their rulings, instead, on extra-talmudic formulations of decided law? This seeming incongruity will be discussed below.

> [Question:] What would our master say about this man, who never in his life read a *halakhah* with a master, who knows neither the way of halakhah nor its interpretation, nor even how to read it—though he has seen many of the geonic responsa and books of *dinim* [regulations] . . . [Answer:] One who instructs on the basis of geonic responsa and relies upon them—even if he cannot understand Talmud—is more proper and praiseworthy than a man who thinks that he knows Talmud and relies upon himself... It is better to permit him to give instruction than many other people who have established themselves as teachers in our time.[60]

Though this responsum singled out the judge who was untrained in Talmud study, adjudication from the talmudic text alone was not an option, even for the learned Ibn Migash himself. He was willing to diverge from the legacy of his teacher where talmudic exegesis was concerned, but did not deviate from Alfasi's rulings in matters of law.[61] Were it not for Ibn Migash's own behav-

[59] Compare the conception of the 'self-sufficiency of the talmudic text', embraced by Rabbenu Meshulam, adversary of Rabbenu Tam, in a late 12th-century vitriolic exchange. (See Reiner, 'Rabbenu Tam and His Contemporaries' (Heb.), 313.) As Rabbenu Meshulam hailed from Narbonne, I have suggested elsewhere that his perspective, so different from that of the scholars of northern France, may reflect regional differences. In this matter, as in others, the Jews of medieval Provence may have absorbed outlooks prevalent among the Jews of Spain. (See Fishman, *Becoming the People of the Talmud*, 142–6.)

[60] Ibn Migash, responsum no. 114, cited in Goitein, *Study Arrangements in the Geonic Era* (Heb.), 167; Twersky, 'Maimonides' *Mishneh torah*' (Heb.), 3–4 n. 12; Ta-Shma, 'The Literary Oeuvre of R. Joseph Ibn Migash' (Heb.), 136–46, 541–53.

[61] Ta-Shma, 'The Literary Oeuvre of R. Joseph Ibn Migash' (Heb.), 143–6; Kanarfogel, 'Between Ashkenaz and Sefarad', 298.

iour, his cautionary message might be interpreted as reflecting the inferior education of the *dayanim* in Andalusian Jewish society. Like *qādīs*, their Muslim counterparts, Jewish judges were tasked with the administration of Jewish law and may not have had much exposure to the study of Talmud.[62] But as Ibn Migash (the teacher of Maimonides' father) was, by all accounts, a formidable talmudic scholar,[63] his own abstention from revisiting adjudicated matters suggests that his attitude was shaped by something other than misgivings about the mediocrity of Andalusian rabbinic learning.

*

Important scholarly headway has been made in situating both the geonic project[64] and Maimonides' oeuvre[65] within the broader contexts of the Islamicate legal cultures of their respective times and places. No comparable research has been undertaken as yet for the halakhic writings of scholars in Kairouan and al-Andalus. The following preliminary observations may open a small window onto a rich area of research that remains to be explored by scholars equipped with the necessary languages and bodies of erudition.

From the ninth century onwards, the Mālikī school of law held a monopoly in both Kairouan and al-Andalus, homes to some of the earliest post-talmudic rabbinic communities outside the domains of the geonic yeshivas of Babylonia and the Land of Israel.[66] In composing the *Kitāb al-Muwwaṭṭa* ('Writing of the Smoothed Path'), the school's founder Mālik ibn Anas (d.796) attempted to create a practical guide that would resolve disputed mat-

[62] As is clear from the introduction to a six-volume Arabic halakhic compilation designed for *dayanim* [judges] in Spain in the second quarter of the 11th century, the author did not presuppose a readership learned in Talmud; his aim was to 'establish basic concepts of law and clear exposition of all the ordinances from the sources of halakhah', and to present readers with 'whatever *dayanim* need of the science of legislated law for purposes of judging' (in Sklare, 'R. David ben Sa'adyah al-Ger' (Heb.), 104). On the very divergent assessments of R. David ben Sa'adyah's *Kitab al-Hawi* by Samuel Hanagid and Isaac Alfasi, and their implications for the rise in the calibre of rabbinic learning after the latter's arrival in al-Andalus, see Fishman, *Becoming the People of the Talmud*, 81–2, and notes.

[63] Even Maimonides, who was generally sparing in praise, complimented this work in the introduction to his *Commentary on the Mishnah*.

[64] See Libson, 'Halakha and Reality in the Geonic Period'; id., *Jewish and Islamic Law*; Sklare, *Samuel ben Hofni Gaon*; id., 'R. David ben Sa'adyah al-Ger' (Heb.), 103–23; Stampfer, 'Jewish Law in Eleventh-Century Spain' (Heb.).

[65] See Stroumsa, *Maimonides in His World*, esp. 53–69.

[66] On the 'domains' (*reshuyot*) of the geonim see Brody, *The Geonim of Babylonia*, 58–9. On the relationships between the Kairouanese Jewish community and those of Italy see Ben-Sasson, 'Italy and Ifriqiyya from the Ninth to the Eleventh Centuries'; id., *The Jews of Sicily, 825–1068* (Heb.).

ters of law and justice. In fact, the success of the *Muwwaṭṭa*—the earliest extant work of Muslim law—has been attributed to its stance of compromise. Mālik presented the practices of Medina, where the foundations of Muslim law were established, and generally recorded the consensus of opinion (*ijmā*) that prevailed in that town. Though he carefully scrutinized hadiths before selecting them for the *Muwwaṭṭa* (thereby earning the praise of his student, al-Shāfiʿī), he did not regard hadith traditions as the ultimate arbiter of law. Where they were in conflict with *ʿamal*, the actual practice in Medina, he ascribed greatest legal weight to the latter. And in unresolved legal cases, where there was no clear practice or consensus in Medina, Mālik exercised personal effort (*ijtihād*) and used his own judgement (*raʾy*, a 'seeing' of the heart) in order to render decisions.[67]

The successor code to the *Muwwaṭṭa*, and the most influential Mālikī work of law, *Al-Mudawwana al-Kubrā*, was written in early ninth-century Kairouan by Saḥnūn ibn Saʿīd ibn Ḥabīb at-Tanūkhī (*c.*777–855).[68] A collection of Mālikī *fiqh* containing responses to questions and corrections made by eighth-century scholars of tradition,[69] the *Mudawwana* spread widely, spawning commentaries and summaries. Under Saḥnūn's guidance, Kairouan became an important centre of Muslim law, and the diffusion of his code is credited with having brought al-Andalus into the orbit of Mālikism.[70]

Like Mālik, Saḥnūn exercised personal effort and considered opinion or judgement in formulating the legal decisions included in his code. These two jurists were the first and last Mālikīs to do so, however. All other Muslims in Mālikī lands were expected to demonstrate *taqlīd*, submission to religious experts. Not only was personal effort abandoned, the study of Quran and hadith was replaced in these regions by reliance on manuals of applied *fiqh*, called *furūʿ*.[71] Dependence on *furūʿ* increased in the late eleventh and early

[67] These very preliminary remarks draw upon Wymann-Landgraf, *Malik and Medina*; Carmona, 'The Introduction of Malik's Teachings in Al-Andalus', 41–56 and notes; Fierro, 'Proto-Malikis, Malikis and Reformed Malikis in Al-Andalus', 57–77 and notes; Urvoy, 'The Ulama of Al-Andalus', and several essays in Bearman et al. (eds.), *Encyclopaedia of Islam, Second Edition*, accessed online through the University of Pennsylvania. Entries consulted include: E. J. Schacht, 'Mālik b. Anas'; J. Wakin and A. Zysow, 'Ra'y'; M. Talbi, 'Saḥnūn'; N. Calder, 'Taḳlīd'.

[68] Sahnun's teacher, the Tunisian ʿAlī b. Ziyād (d.799), was the first to introduce the *Muwaṭṭa'* of Mālik into Kairouan; N. Cottert, 'Malikiyya', in Bearman et al. (eds.), *Encyclopaedia of Islam, Second Edition*, accessed online through the University of Pennsylvania.

[69] Ibid. Foremost among these was the Egyptian Ibn al-Qāsim al-ʿAtakī (d.[191]/807, Saḥnūn's teacher and a disciple of Mālik himself, who relayed the opinions of his master.

[70] Ibid. Of Saḥnūn's 700 disciples, fifty-seven lived in Muslim Spain.

[71] Cottert, 'Malikiyya'; Urvoy, 'The Ulama of Al-Andalus', 850–1, 853. Students with the

twelfth centuries, with the conquest of Spain's Muslim *ṭā'ifa* kingdoms by Berber Almoravids.[72]

*

This intervening excursus on developments in Mālikī Islamic jurisprudence of al-Andalus, Rabbi Ibn Migash's determining cultural environment, may shed light on the discrepancy between his seemingly dissonant perspectives, set forth above. Both his exhortation of Jewish judges to steer clear of the Talmud and base their rulings on extra-talmudic formulations of decided law, and his own reliance on the decisions of Alfasi, his master, suggest to me that the Jews of his time and place shared the ethos of *taqlīd* that permeated the broader legal culture. Whether or not there was a formal articulation of submission to the authority of the rabbinic master, students in Spain were quite different from their counterparts in medieval northern Europe. There, students were eager to challenge their teachers;[73] indeed, their novel insights and perspectives added to their prestige.[74]

The tension between the two teachings of Ibn Migash may be resolved by regarding the 'our Talmud' tradition as one whose meaning changed over time in order to address the disparate cultural needs of different generations of Andalusian Jews. Through intimate familiarity with the talmudic text (which he had studied in Kairouan), the long-lived R. Alfasi determined that the consistent and singular voice of the anonymous *setam* (which he called 'al-Talmūd') subtly guided the attuned reader to the legal decision as it was to be

requisite philological expertise may wish to consider whether there are structural similarities between al-Ghazālī's denunciation of the Mālikīs for marginalization of the *sunna* and critiques levelled against Maimonides for bypassing the Talmud.

[72] Ibid.

[73] Writing in early 15th-century Spain, R. Joseph Ibn Habiba contrasted the pedagogical etiquette in his own land with that of the Jewish communities of northern Europe: 'Today in the Kingdom[s] of Ashkenaz and France . . . there are students who know as much halakhah as the rabbi . . . they at times best him in debate . . . But in our regions, the Kingdom of Aragon and Spain, where the rabbi is very accomplished and much more erudite than the students, where the students at times don't understand the language, and the rabbi teaches them, it would not be appropriate for them to enter into this' (*Ḥidush lemasekhet berakhot*, cited in Breuer, 'The Typology of Western Yeshivas' (Heb.), 45 n. 1). See Fishman, *Becoming the People of the Talmud*, 89–90.

[74] In the words of the 13th-century Shneur brothers of Evreux, 'one can no longer say to a student that he must not give halakhic instruction [in the presence of his teacher, or without the latter's permission], and a student, through powers of casuistry, can contradict the words of his teacher' (Moses and Samuel Shneur, *Orḥot ḥayim*, i: *Hilkhot talmud torah*, *halakhah* 800, no. 21, 64*b*, cited in Urbach, *The Tosafists* (Heb.), i. 479). See Fishman, *Becoming the People of the Talmud*, 136, 166–7.

applied, *halakhah lema'aseh*. It may be presumed that Ibn Migash understood his master's method, but his own formulation of the 'our Talmud' tradition was precipitated by the need to resolve a terminological problem posed by the tannaitic passage mentioned at the outset: 'one does not learn halakhah from *talmud*'. In this exegetical context (and in that addressed later by Meir Halevi Abulafia) the 'our Talmud' tradition offered a—needed—catechistic distinction.

Ibn Migash's two positions are consistent and synergistic in their privileging of *halakhah lema'aseh*. Together they reassured Sephardi Jews that the very purpose of rabbinic learning was the transmission of the dos and don'ts of Jewish practice. After all, the paragon of rabbinic texts, the Babylonian Talmud, had been consigned to writing for this very purpose, and the early Talmud commentaries of Kairouan, which offered shortcuts to applied law, followed suit.[75] When considering the Sephardi preference for abridgements of applied law, it is worth remembering that, because of the 'our Talmud' tradition, Jews of al-Andalus did not share the assumption (so foundational in Ashkenazi culture) that the commandment of *talmud torah* was best fulfilled through primary, and even exclusive, engagement with the Babylonian Talmud and its commentaries.[76]

*

Andalusian rabbinic scholars were never isolated from Muslim contemporaries or from the broader legal culture—where submission to religious authority was emphasized, the exercise of independent legal reasoning was eschewed, and law was transmitted in the form of manuals. The predilection of the Mālikī environment for digests of applied law constitutes an important context for considering the compilations of applied Jewish law composed by the Andalusians, Daniel ben Sa'adyah,[77] Isaac Ibn Ghiyyat,[78] Judah al-Barceloni,[79] and the erstwhile Andalusian, Moses Maimonides. It supplies an

[75] On the presentation of decided law in rabbinic writings of Kairouan, see Ta-Shma, 'Did Maimonides Have a Revolutionary Approach to Talmud Study?' (Heb.), and Fishman, *Becoming the People of the Talmud*, 67–71. On the close ties between the Jews of Kairouan and al-Andalus see Fishman, 71–2.

[76] Cf. S. Friedman, 'Maimonides and the Talmud' (Heb.), 222.

[77] On this figure and his composition see Sklare, 'R. David ben Sa'adyah al-Ger' (Heb.), 103–23; Stampfer, 'Jewish Law in Eleventh-Century Spain' (Heb.), 217–36.

[78] On Ibn Ghiyyat's 'encyclopedic' Aramaic collection of legal rulings, *Halakhot kelulot*, see Abramson, 'From the Legal Teachings of R. Samuel Hanagid of Spain' (Heb.), 16–17, 19, 23; Sklare, 'R. David ben Sa'adyah al-Ger' (Heb.), 122 n. 56.

[79] Though large parts have not been found, it has been suggested that three treatises by Judah al-Barceloni—*Sefer ha'itim*, on the sabbath and festivals in the Jewish calendar;

additional lens through which to assess Maimonides' perturbing claims about the place of Talmud study in the Jewish curriculum. His recurring references to the time-saving nature of his law code, the *Mishneh torah*, and his explicit devaluation of the place of the Talmud in pedagogy in the introduction to this code and elsewhere,[80] caused consternation both in his own lifetime and in ours.[81] When seen as a product of his own rabbinic legal culture—and not through the anachronistic lens of later historical developments, among them Nahmanides' pedagogical revisions and the triumph of Tosafism in yeshiva culture—the attitude towards the study of Talmud and its commentaries that Maimonides expresses (more than once) in his Judaeo-Arabic letters to his student R. Joseph bar Judah may be seen as accurately reflecting his own pedagogical assumptions and ideals. Like other medieval Jewish scholars both before and after him, Maimonides painted an unflattering portrait of the talmudist as one who cultivates expertise in dialectical give and take for purposes of self-aggrandizement.[82] Like earlier geonim, and later Andalusians, he expressed concern about the effect of far-fetched talmudic *agadot* on the credulous.[83] And he insisted that that which is important in Talmud is not its disputatious style, but its mediation of that which is utilitarian in Oral Torah, *halakhah lema'aseh*. In a letter fragment to his student, he writes that the Babylonian Talmud may once have had other cultural functions, but he asserts that these are no longer understood:

Yiḥus she'er basar, on marriage and personal law [*hilkhot ishut*]; and *Sefer hadin*, on civil law—comprised a comprehensive legal compendium.

[80] Maimonides' remarks on the utility of his code appear in his introduction to the *Mishneh torah*, in his introduction to *Sefer hamitsvot*, and in several letters to his student R. Joseph bar Judah. Shamma Friedman discusses these passages in 'Maimonides and the Talmud' (Heb.), 222–8. See also Halkin, 'In Defence of the *Mishneh torah*' (Heb.).

[81] The earliest figure to perceive this as a challenge was R. Pinhas Hadayan, who had moved to Alexandria from Provence. See *Igerot harambam*, ed. Shailat, ii. 433–54. Cf. Twersky, 'The Beginnings of *Mishneh Torah* Criticism'. Surveying some of the modern scholars who have grappled with these claims, Shamma Friedman has observed that Twersky appears to have revised this position over time ('Maimonides and the Talmud' (Heb.), 230–6). See Twersky, 'Some Non-Halakhic Aspects of the *Mishneh Torah*', 106–11; id., *Introduction to the Code of Maimonides*, 489–93; Fishman, *Becoming the People of the Talmud*, 159–60.

[82] In *Igerot harambam*, ed. Shailat, i. 256 (Judaeo-Arabic), i. 258–9 (Heb. translation). The recurring criticism of the self-aggrandizing motives of talmudists levelled by medieval Jewish writers is discussed in Twersky, 'Religion and Law', 81 n. 27; id., *Introduction to the Code of Maimonides*, 199 nn. 26–7; Fishman, *Becoming the People of the Talmud*, 161–4.

[83] An analysis of Maimonides' attitude towards aggadah appears in Lorberbaum, 'Changes in Maimonides' Attitude to Midrash' (Heb.). The challenge that aggadah posed for medieval Jewish rationalists is discussed in Saperstein, *Decoding the Rabbis*, 1–20.

For the intended goal of all that is collected in the Talmud and [in] other [writings] has already been extinguished and lost. And the goal of pedantic scholars [*ḥalamdanim*] is the waste of time in the Talmud's give and take—as if the intention and goal were training in disputation, and nothing more. And this was not the primary intention; rather, the give and take and the disputation came about by accident . . . But, in fact, the primary intention was the knowledge of what one must do [and] that of which one should be wary . . . For this reason, we have mobilized ourselves towards the primary intention, that it might be more easily remembered, and even more, to make it known, for this has already been lost in all the give and take.[84]

In a longer letter to this same student, Maimonides indicates that the need for Talmud study was characteristic of an earlier time: 'And should you squander your time in interpretations, and in the explanations of the Gemara's disputes and in those matters of drudgery that we have relinquished, this is a big waste of time and of little utility.'[85]

Maimonides' assessment of the Talmud was directly related to his understanding of the cultural function of that text. Since he, like other medieval Sephardim, assumed that it had been consigned to writing with the express purpose of relaying applied law, he judged it a rather inefficient vehicle. He therefore undertook to replace the Talmud with a halakhic code (*ḥibur*)—one written in clear mishnaic Hebrew, with a systematic, topical arrangement of decided law—and divested of those elements that he regarded as extraneous to *halakhah lema'aseh*, law as it was to be practised.[86]

[84] *Igerot harambam*, ed. Shailat, i. 258–9.

[85] Ibid. 312–13. Where Shailat's Hebrew translation reads *ve'otam hadevarim asher henaḥnu me'amalam*, Kafih translates *ve'otam hadevarim asher patarnu mehem*, suggesting that there was some liberation from the Talmud's give and take. *Igerot harambam*, ed. Kafih, 134.

[86] See the analysis of Maimonides' reasons for composing the *Mishneh torah* in Twersky, *Introduction to the Code of Maimonides*, 61–81.

Bibliography

ABRAHAM IBN DAUD, *Sefer ha-Qabbalah: The Book of Tradition*, trans. Gerson D. Cohen (Philadelphia, 1967).

ABRAMSON, SHRAGA, 'Clarifications' (Heb.), *Sinai*, 58 (1966), 181–92.

—— 'From the Teachings of R. Samuel Hanagid of Spain' (Heb.), *Sinai*, 100 (1987), 7–73.

ABULAFIA, MEIR HALEVI, *Sefer yad ramah: shitah lemahadurah batra* (Salonica, 1790–1; Tel Aviv, 1962).

BEARMAN, P., et al. (eds.), *Encyclopaedia of Islam, Second Edition* (Leiden, 2012), accessed online.

BEER, MOSHE, 'Studies on the Epistle of Sherira Gaon' (Heb.), *Shenaton bar ilan*, 4–5 (1967), 181–95.

BEN-SASSON, MENAHEM, 'Italy and Ifriqiyya from the Ninth to the Eleventh Centuries', in J. L. Miege (ed.), *Les Relations intercommunautaires juives en Mediterrannée et en Europe occidentale* (Paris, 1984), 34–50.

—— *The Jews of Sicily, 825–1068: Documents and Sources* [Yehudei sitsilyah, 825–1068: te'udot umekorot] (Jerusalem, 1991).

BEN SHAMMAI, HAGGAI, '*Al Mudawwin*: The Arranger of Biblical Books in Judaeo-Arabic Bible Exegesis' (Heb.), in J. Hacker, B. Z. Kedar, and Y. Kaplan (eds.), *From Sages to Savants: Studies Presented to Avraham Grossman* [Rishonim va'aḥaronim: meḥkarim betoledot yisra'el mugashim le'avraham grosman] (Jerusalem, 2010), 73–110.

BREUER, MORDECAI, 'Research on the Typology of Western Yeshivas in the Middle Ages' (Heb.), in I. Etkes and Y. Salmon (eds.), *Studies in Jewish Society in the Medieval and Early Modern Periods* [Perakim betoledot haḥevrah hayehudit biyemei habeinayim uva'et haḥadashah] (Jerusalem, 1980), 45–55.

BRODY, ROBERT, *The Geonim of Babylonia and the Shaping of Medieval Jewish Culture* (New Haven, 1998).

CARMONA, ALFONSO, 'The Introduction of Malik's Teachings in Al-Andalus', in P. Bearman, R. Peters, and F. Vogel (eds.), *The Islamic School of Law: Evolution, Devolution and Progress* (Cambridge, Mass., 2005), 41–56.

COHEN, BOAZ, 'Three Arabic Halakhic Discussions of Alfasi', *JQR*, NS 19 (1928–9), 355–410.

COLLINS, ROGER, 'Visigothic Law and Regional Custom in Disputes in Early Medieval Spain', in W. Davies and P. Fouracre (eds.), *The Settlement of Disputes in Early Medieval Europe* (Cambridge, 1986), 85–104.

DANZIG, NAHMAN, 'From Oral Talmud to Written Talmud' (Heb.), *Sefer hashanah bar ilan*, 30–31 (2006), 49–112.

—— *Introduction to Sefer halakhot pesukot* [Mavo lesefer halakhot pesukot] (New York, 1993).

DRORY, RINA, *The First Encounters between Jewish and Arabic Literature in the Tenth Century* [Reshit hamaga'im shel hasifrut hayehudit im hasifrut ha'aravit bame'ah ha'asirit] (Tel Aviv, 1988).

ELMAN, YAAKOV, 'Moses ben Nahman/Nahmanides (Ramban)', in Magne Sæbø, Menahem Haran, and Chris Brekelmans (eds.), *Hebrew Bible / Old Testament: The History of Its Interpretation. I: From the Beginnings to the Middle Ages* (Göttingen, 2000), 420–30.

ELON, MENAHEM, *Jewish Law: History, Sources, Principles* [Hamishpat ha'ivri: toledotav, mekorotav, ekronotav] (Jerusalem, 1973).

FIERRO, MARIBEL, 'Proto-Malikis, Malikis and Reformed Malikis in Al-Andalus', in P. Bearman, R. Peters, and F. Vogel (eds.), *The Islamic School of Law: Evolution, Devolution and Progress* (Cambridge, Mass., 2005), 57–77.

FISHMAN, TALYA, *Becoming the People of the Talmud: Oral Torah as Written Tradition in Medieval Jewish Cultures* (Philadelphia, 2011).

FRENKEL, MIRIAM, 'The Literary Canon as a Tool for the Consolidation of the Social Elite in the Society of the Genizah' (Heb.), in A. Lieblich et al. (eds.), *Uncovering the Canon: Studies in Canonicity and Genizah* [Hakanon hasamui min ha'ayin: ḥikrei kanon ugenizah] (Jerusalem, 2010), 88–110.

FRIEDMAN, MORDECAI AKIVA, 'On the Genizah's Contribution to Halakhic Research' (Heb.), *Mada'ei hayahadut*, 38 (1993), 277–94.

FRIEDMAN, SHAMMA, 'Maimonides and the Talmud' (Heb.), *Diné Israel*, 26–7 (2009), 221–39.

GERHARDSSON, BIRGER, *Memory and Manuscript: Oral Tradition and Written Transmission in Rabbinic Judaism and Early Christianity* (Copenhagen, 1961).

GOITEIN, SHELOMO DOV, *Study Arrangements in the Geonic Era and in the Maimonidean Orbit* [Sidrei ḥinukh biyemei hage'onim uveit harambam] (Jerusalem, 1962).

GOLDIN, JUDAH, 'Freedom and Restraint of Haggadah', in Judah Goldin, Barry L. Eichler, and Jeffrey H. Tigay (eds.), *Studies in Midrash and Related Literature* (Philadelphia, 1988), 253–70.

GOLDSTEIN, MIRIAM, *Karaite Exegesis in Medieval Jerusalem: Judeo-Arabic Pentateuch Commentary of Yusuf ibn Nuh and Abu al-Faraj Harun* (Tübingen, 2011).

GROSSMAN, AVRAHAM, 'Connections between Sephardi and Ashkenazi Jewries in the Middle Ages' (Heb.), in H. Beinart (ed.), *The Legacy of Sepharad* [Moreshet sefarad] (Jerusalem, 1992), 174–89.

HALKIN, ABRAHAM, 'Defence of the Mishneh Torah' (Heb.), *Tarbiz*, 25 (1956), 414–28.

HIRSCHFELD, HARTWIG, *Qirqisani Studies* (London, 1918).

Igeret rav sherira gaon mesuderet bishenei nusḥaot: nusaḥ sefarad venusaḥ tsarefat im ḥilufei girsa'ot, ed. B. M. Levin (Haifa, 1921).

Igerot harambam, ed. Yosef Kafih (Jerusalem, 1972).

Igerot harambam, ed. Isaac Shailat, 2 vols. (Jerusalem, 1995).

JACOBS, MARTIN, 'Interreligious Polemics in Medieval Spain: Biblical Interpretation between Ibn Hazm, Ibn Adret and Shimon ben Zemah Duran', *Jerusalem Studies in Jewish Thought*, 27 (2007), 36*–57*.

JUDAH AL-BARCELONI, *Perush sefer yetsirah*, ed. S. J. Halberstam (Berlin, 1885).

JUYNBOLL, G. H. A., 'Tadwīn', in P. Bearman et al. (eds.), *Encyclopaedia of Islam, Second Edition* (Leiden, 2012), accessed online.

KANARFOGEL, EPHRAIM, 'Between Ashkenaz and Sefarad: Tosafist Teachings in the Talmud Commentaries of Ritva', in E. Kanarfogel and M. Sokolow (eds.), *Between Rashi and Maimonides* (New York, 2010), 237–73.

KATZ, JACOB, 'Evening Prayer in Its Prescribed Time or Not: An Example of the Relationship between *Minhag*, Halakhah, and Society' (Heb.), in id. (ed.), *Halakhah and Kabbalah* [Halakhah vekabalah] (Jerusalem, 1984), 175–200.

LAWEE, ERIC, 'Isaac Abarbanel: From Medieval to Renaissance Jewish Biblical Scholarship', in Magne Sæbø, Menahem Haran, and Chris Brekelmans (eds.), *Hebrew Bible / Old Testament: The History of Its Interpretation. II: The Middle Ages* (Göttingen, 2007), 190–214.

LEVY, LEONARD, 'Alfasi, *Sugyan* and the Authority of the *Stam*', *Jewish Law Association Studies*, 16 (2007), 136–65.

——'The Decisive Shift: From the Geonim to Rabbi Yizhaq Alfasi', in *Tiferet Le-Yisrael: Jubilee Volume in Honor of Israel Francus* (New York, 2010), 93–130.

——'Rabbi Yitzhaq Alfasi's Application of Principles of Adjudication in *Halakhot Rabbati*', Ph.D. diss. (Jewish Theological Seminary, 2002).

LIBSON, GIDEON, 'Halakha and Reality in the Geonic Period: *Taqqanah, Minhag*, Tradition and Consensus', in Daniel Frank (ed.), *The Jews of Medieval Islam: Community, Society and Identity* (Leiden, 1995), 67–100.

——*Jewish and Islamic Law: A Comparative Study of Custom during the Geonic Period* (Cambridge, Mass., 2003).

LIEBERMAN, SAUL, *Greek and Hellenism in the Land of Israel* [Yevanim viyevanut be'erets yisra'el] (Jerusalem, 1962).

——*Hellenism in Jewish Palestine: Studies in the Literary Transmission, Beliefs and Manners of Palestine in the I Century B.C.E.–IV Century C.E.* (New York, 1950).

LORBERBAUM, YAIR, 'Changes in Maimonides' Attitude to Rabbinic Midrash' (Heb.), *Tarbiz*, 78 (2009), 81–122.

MARGALIOTH, MORDECAI, *The Laws of the Nagid* [Hilkhot hanagid] (Jerusalem, 1962).

PERLMANN, MOSHE, 'The Medieval Polemics between Islam and Judaism', in S. D. Goitein (ed.), *Religion in a Religious Age* (Cambridge, Mass., 1974), 103–20.

POLLIACK, MEIRA, 'Karaite Conception of the Biblical Narrator (*Mudawwin*)', in J. Neusner and A. J. Peck (eds.), *Encyclopedia of Midrash: Biblical Interpretation in Formative Judaism* (Leiden, 2005), ii. 350–72.

——'The Karaite Inversion of Written and Oral Torah in Relation to the Islamic Arch-Models of Quran and Hadith', *JSQ*, 22 (2015), 243–302.

——'The "Voice" of the Narrator and the "Voice" of the Characters in the Biblical Commentaries of Yefet Ben 'Eli', in C. Cohen et al. (eds.), *Birkat Shalom, Presented to Shalom Paul* (Winona Lake, 2008), 891–915.

——and ELIEZER SCHLOSSBERG, 'Historical, Literary and Rhetorical and Redactional Methods of Interpretation in Yefet ben 'Eli's Introduction to the Minor Prophets', in G. Khan (ed.), *Exegesis and Grammar in Medieval Karaite Texts* (Oxford, 2001), 1–39.

RAY, JONATHAN, *After 1492: The Expulsion from Spain and the Making of Sephardic Identity* (New York, 2013).

REINER, AVRAHAM, 'Rabbenu Tam and His Contemporaries: Connections, Influences, and His Methods of Talmud Study' [Rabenu tam uvenei doro: kesharim, hashpa'ot, vedarkei limudo batalmud], Ph.D. diss. (Hebrew University of Jerusalem, 2002).

RICHÉ, PIERRE, *Education and Culture in the Barbarian West, Sixth through Eighth Centuries* (Columbia, SC, 1976).

SA'ADYAH GAON, *Perush sefer yetsirah*, ed. Yosef Kafih (Jerusalem, 1972).

—— *Sefer mishle 'im: tirgum uferush rabenu sa'adyah gaon*, ed. Yosef Kafih (Jerusalem, 1975–6).

SAPERSTEIN, MARC, *Decoding the Rabbis: A Thirteenth-Century Commentary on the Aggadah* (Cambridge, Mass., 1980).

SHAPIRO, MARC, *The Limits of Orthodox Theology: Maimonides' Thirteen Principles Reappraised* (Oxford, 2004).

SHNEUR, MOSES, and SAMUEL SHNEUR, *Orḥot ḥayim*, i: *Hilkhot talmud torah* (Jerusalem, 1957).

SIMON, URIEL, 'Abraham Ibn Ezra', in Magne Sæbø, Menahem Haran, and Chris Brekelmans (eds.), *Hebrew Bible / Old Testament: The History of Its Interpretation. I: From the Beginnings to the Middle Ages* (Göttingen, 2000), 377–87.

SKLARE, DAVID, 'R. David ben Sa'adyah al-Ger and His Work *Kitab al-Hawi*' (Heb.), *Te'udah*, 14 (1998), 103–23.

—— *Samuel ben Hofni Gaon and His Cultural World* (Leiden, 1996).

STAMPFER, YEHUDA ZVI, 'Jewish Law in Eleventh-Century Spain: From the Geonim to the Rishonim (on the Basis of R. David ben Sa'adyah's *Kitab al-Hawi*)' (Heb.), *Shenaton hamishpat ha'ivri*, 38 (2008), 217–36.

STEINER, RICHARD, 'A Jewish Theory of Biblical Redaction from Byzantium: Its Rabbinic Roots, Its Diffusion and Its Encounter with the Muslim Doctrine of Falsification', *Jewish Studies Internet Journal*, 2 (2003), 123–67.

STROUMSA, SARAH, *Maimonides in His World: Portrait of a Mediterranean Thinker* (Princeton, 2009).

SUSSMAN, YA'AKOV, 'Once Again on Jerusalem Talmud *Nezikin*' (Heb.), *Meḥkerei talmud*, 1 (1990), 55–133.

—— 'Oral Torah—Understand It as It Sounds' (Heb.), *Meḥkerei talmud*, 3 (2005), 209–384.

TA-SHMA, ISRAEL, *Collected Studies in Medieval Rabbinic Literature* [Keneset meḥkarim: iyunim besifrut harabanim biyemei habeinayim], 3 vols. (Jerusalem, 2004).

—— *Commentarial Literature on the Talmud* [Hasifrut haparshanit latalmud], 2 vols. (Jerusalem, 2000).

—— 'Did Maimonides Take a Revolutionary Approach to Talmud Study?' (Heb.), in A. Ravitzky (ed.), *The Rambam: Conservatism, Originality, Radicalism* [Harambam: shamranut, mekoriut, mahapkhanut] (Jerusalem, 2008), 111–17.

—— 'The Literary Oeuvre of R. Joseph Ibn Migash' (Heb.), *Kiryat sefer*, 46 (1971), 136–46, 541–53; repr. in id., *Collected Studies in Medieval Rabbinic Literature*

[Keneset meḥkarim: iyunim besifrut harabanim biyemei habeinayim] (Jerusalem, 2004), ii. 15–69.

——'R. Isaac Ibn Ghiyyat's Commentary on Tractate *Bava metsia*' (Heb.), in id., *Collected Studies in Medieval Rabbinic Literature* [Keneset meḥkarim: iyunim besifrut harabanim biyemei habeinayim] (Jerusalem, 2004), ii. 3–14.

TWERSKY, ISADORE, 'The Beginnings of *Mishneh Torah* Criticism', in A. Altmann (ed.), *Biblical and Other Studies* (Cambridge, Mass., 1963), 161–82.

——'Did R. Abraham Ibn Ezra Influence Maimonides?' (Heb.), in I. Twersky and J. Harris (eds.), *Abraham Ibn Ezra: Studies in the Writings of a Twelfth Century Polymath* (Cambridge, Mass., 1993), 21–48.

——*Introduction to the Code of Maimonides* (New Haven, 1980).

——'Maimonides' *Mishneh torah*: Its Purpose and Role' (Heb.), *Proceedings of the Israel Academy of Sciences and Humanities*, 5 (1972), 1–22.

——'Religion and Law', in S. D. Goitein (ed.), *Religion in a Religious Age* (Cambridge, Mass., 1974), 69–82.

——'Some Non-Halakhic Aspects of the *Mishneh Torah*', in A. Altmann (ed.), *Jewish Medieval and Renaissance Studies* (Cambridge, Mass., 1967), 95–119.

URBACH, EPHRAIM ELIMELEKH, *The Halakhah: Its Sources and Development* [Hahalakhah: mekoroteiha vehitpatḥutah] (Jerusalem, 1984).

——*The Tosafists: Their History, Writings, and Method* [Ba'alei hatosafot: toledoteihem, ḥibureihem, shitatam], 2 vols. (Jerusalem, 1980).

URVOY, DOMINIQUE, 'The Ulama of Al-Andalus', in Salma Khadra Jayyusi (ed.), *The Legacy of Muslim Spain* (Leiden, 1992), 849–77.

WYMANN-LANDGRAF, UMAR F. ABD-ALLAH, *Malik and Medina: Islamic Legal Reasoning in the Formative Period* (Leiden, 2013).

PART III

Geopolitical Boundaries and Their Impact on Jewish Regional Identities

CHAPTER SEVEN

From Germany to Northern France and Back Again: A Tale of Two Tosafist Centres

EPHRAIM KANARFOGEL

SIMCHA EMANUEL has recently pointed to a lacuna in the rabbinic leadership of German Jewry during the second quarter of the thirteenth century. Following the passing of several distinguished Tosafists and halakhic authorities who had been active throughout the first two decades of that century (including Barukh ben Samuel of Mainz, d.1221; Eliezer ben Joel Halevi (Ravyah) of Cologne, d. *c.*1225; Simhah ben Samuel of Speyer, d. *c.* 1230; and Eleazar ben Judah of Worms, d. *c.*1230), not a single outstanding rabbinic figure flourished in Germany for nearly a generation. This crisis of leadership lasted until Meir ben Barukh (Maharam) of Rothenburg (d.1293) succeeded in re-establishing the highest levels of Torah scholarship and teaching in Germany during the second half of the thirteenth century.[1]

Emanuel indicates that he is unable to explain why this cohort of leading rabbinic scholars did not cultivate any students who could serve as their successors in Germany. The absence was particularly noteworthy in Mainz, which had an otherwise unbroken record of productive scholarship and teachers since the early eleventh century. Emanuel suggests that looking at northern France might prove helpful.

Twenty-five years ago, Ya'akov Sussman showed that the connections between the Tosafist study halls in northern France and in Germany were severed during the last quarter of the twelfth century and the beginning of the thirteenth.[2] German students (and those from points further east) stopped travelling to northern France to study, as they had done during the days of the

[1] Emanuel, 'The Rabbis of Germany in the Thirteenth Century' (Heb.).

[2] Sussman, 'The Scholarly Oeuvre of Professor Ephraim Elimelekh Urbach' (Heb.), 39–40 (n. 63), 48–54. See also Soloveitchik, *Halakhah, Economy, and Self-Image* (Heb.), 82–5, 97–100.

towering Tosafist figure, Rabbenu Tam (1100–71). Emanuel theorizes that the return of German students to French study halls around the period of weakness in German rabbinic leadership cannot be coincidental. This return was epitomized by Isaac ben Moses Or Zarua's participation in the *beit midrash* of Judah ben Isaac Sirleon in Paris just after 1215, and he was followed by others including Meir of Rothenburg, who studied with Yehiel ben Joseph of Paris in the early 1240s. Indeed, rabbinic scholarship in Germany during the 1240s had none of the vibrancy of the study halls of Yehiel and other French Tosafists at that time (such as the brothers of Evreux, Moses, Samuel, and Isaac ben Shneur), which attracted students from outside northern France as well.

In my view, the gap in rabbinic leadership in thirteenth-century Germany, the cessation of contact between German and northern French *batei midrash* noted by Sussman, and an earlier shift in northern France during the days of Isaac ben Samuel (Ri) of Dampierre (d.1189)—to be discussed below—are all related. They reflect the presence (or absence) of teachers who were engaged in teaching and developing the dialectical method in the manner of Rabbenu Tam in Germany during the Tosafist period, from the mid-twelfth century onwards. A larger discussion of the differences between the German and northern French Tosafist centres is necessary to properly contextualize this proposed solution.

The *Tosafot* glosses to the standard edition of the Babylonian Talmud reflect an overwhelmingly northern French orientation and milieu.[3] The chapter headings of E. E. Urbach's seminal study on the Tosafists and their writings indicate that there were distinctions between the two regions within northern Europe (Ashkenaz) in which these rabbinic figures flourished,[4] and subsequent scholarship has identified an array of trenchant analytical and doctrinal differences between Tosafists in northern France and Germany. For example, I have demonstrated that rabbinic attitudes towards *aliyah* to the Land of Israel developed primarily along either northern French or German lines, a claim that has been ratified and further refined.[5] Israel Ta-Shma has shown that the Jews of northern France and Germany held different halakhic

[3] See Urbach, *The Tosafists* (Heb.), ii. 600–75; Soloveitchik, 'The Printed Page of the Talmud'; Kanarfogel, *The Intellectual History and Rabbinic Culture of Medieval Ashkenaz*, 1–9.

[4] See Sussman, 'The Scholarly Oeuvre of Professor Ephraim Elimelekh Urbach' (Heb.), 38–9.

[5] Kanarfogel, 'The *Aliyyah* of "Three Hundred Rabbis" in 1211'; E. Reiner, '*Aliyah* and Pilgrimage to the Land of Israel' (Heb.), 39–40, 59–66; Ta-Shma, *Collected Studies* (Heb.), i. 254–60; Emanuel, 'The Origins and Career of R. Barukh b. Isaac' (Heb.), 431 (n. 37), 439–40; A. Reiner, 'Rabbenu Tam and His Contemporaries' (Heb.), 88–90.

opinions about whether a non-Jewish servant was permitted to raise the heat in a Jewish home on the sabbath,[6] and Emanuel has noted regional differences regarding the cancellation of marriage commitments (*bitul shidukhin*).[7] This bifurcation of views is also evident in mourning practices,[8] the halakhic status of a woman experiencing post-partum bleeding,[9] the structuring of the *tefilin* placed on the arm (*tefilin shel yad*), and other matters.[10]

Divergences are also present in more theoretical discussions, such as whether drinking the Kiddush wine at the arrival of the sabbath is mandated by Torah law or by rabbinic law. According to the northern French rabbis, only the recitation of the text of Kiddush is required according to Torah law; this position was associated initially with Rabbenu Tam, and then supported by Elhanan, son of Ri of Dampierre, Judah Sirleon, Moses of Coucy, and other French Tosafists. The German view, that drinking the wine is also required according to Torah law, is found in the pseudo-Rashi commentary on tractate *Nazir* composed in the Rhineland, and in Eliezer of Mainz's *Sefer ravan* (which also cites Moses ben Joel of Regensburg). It is further presented by Joseph Kara in the name of Kalonymos (ben Shabetai) of Rome, whom Kara had encountered at the academy in Worms.[11]

However, given the many similarities between the dialectical methods of

[6] See Ta-Shma, *Ritual, Custom and Reality in Franco-Germany* (Heb.), 149–67. This may also reflect differences in climate and housing structures. Cf. Katz, *The Shabbes Goy* (Heb.), 40, 43–57.

[7] See Emanuel, 'Invalidating a Marriage Agreement' (Heb.).

[8] See Zimmer, *Society and Its Customs* (Heb.), 193–6, 206.

[9] See ibid. 228–35, 296–7. Distinctions between regions within Germany were also a factor here.

[10] Ibid. 263–7; see also 281–6 (on baking matzah); Strauss, '*Pat 'Akkum* in Medieval France and Germany', 17–38; and Eleazar of Worms, *Sha'arei sheḥitah uterefah*, 37–9 (based on MS JTS Rabb. 1923 = MS Bodl. 696, fos. 40^r–41^v), regarding lung adhesions in slaughtered animals. See also *Sefer ravyah*, ed. Aptowitzer, ii. 142–3 (*Pesaḥim*), sec. 514: 'There are those who assume that once someone drinks from a cup of wine used for a ritual purpose such as the recitation of Kiddush, any wine that remains must be poured out and other wine must be used if another person wishes to recite Kiddush over that cup . . . This is the custom in northern France, and I also observed that this was the custom of my teacher the rabbi [Eliezer] of Metz . . . However, in my father's home, I saw that they did not pour out the wine but merely added some wine or water to the cup. And this is the custom in Germany, which seems to me to be correct.'

[11] See Urbach, *The Tosafists* (Heb.), i. 41–5; Grossman, *The Early Sages of France* (Heb.), 216 (n. 275), 255; *Sefer ravan*, 'Even ha'ezer', ed. Ehrenreich, fo. 288*a*. See also *Sefer hayashar lerabenu tam*, ed. Schlesinger, 55 (sec. 62); *Tosafot r. yehudah sirleon al masekhet berakhot*, ed. Zaks, i. 246 (on *Ber.* 20*b*, and esp. n. 448); Eleazar of Worms, *Sefer roke'aḥ*, sec. 52; *Tosafot rid* (Isaiah di Trani) on *Pes.* 106*a* (*mahadurah telita'ah*); Isaiah's *Sefer hamakhria*, ed. Wertheimer, 441–56 (sec. 71; and cf. Ta-Shma, *Collected Studies*, iii. 40–3); Isaac ben Moses, *Sefer or zarua*, pt. II, 'Hilkhot erev shabat', sec. 25 (fo. 6*b*); and *Tosafot*, *Shevu.* 20*b*, s.v. *nashim*.

French and German Tosafists as well as between their overall halakhic outlooks,[12] systematic attempts to find essential patterns of difference between the Tosafists of northern France and Germany along regional lines may be misguided. It is unclear, for example, to what extent the two regions approached biblical interpretation differently.[13] Moreover, even during the forty-year period between the death of Rabbenu Tam and the first decade of the thirteenth century, the interval when talmudic students did not move between the regions, a number of texts and ideas did.[14]

On the whole, French Tosafists were largely unaware of the work of their German counterparts during this interval, as can be seen from the dearth of references to German scholars in the *Tosafot* in the standard edition of the Talmud.[15] Still, formulations by Ri of Dampierre, Rabbenu Tam's successor, did reach German Tosafists, as can be seen especially in the writings of Ravyah.[16] Moreover, Ri corresponded with Joel ben Isaac Halevi of Bonn,

[12] See e.g. Kanarfogel, 'Returning to the Jewish Community in Medieval Ashkenaz'. See also Ta-Shma, *Ritual, Custom and Reality in Franco-Germany* (Heb.), 201–15 regarding *kedushat bekhor behemah* (the sanctity of a firstborn animal); 228–40 on tax exemptions for Torah scholars; 241–60 regarding prohibitions associated with *yemei eideihem* (festivals of non-Jews); Zimmer, *Society and Its Customs* (Heb.), 23–4 on head-covering for men; 48–50 on sidelocks; 100–1 regarding physical movements during prayer; 163–6 regarding the *sukah* on Shemini Atseret; 243–5 regarding the seven-day *nidah* period; 253–7 on the permissibility of the fat that surrounds an animal's stomach; 288–9 on wearing a *talit* on the night of Yom Kippur; Kanarfogel, 'Medieval Rabbinic Conceptions of the Messianic Age'; id., 'Ashkenazi Messianic Calculations' (Heb.); id., 'Unanimity, Majority and Communal Government in Ashkenaz'; id., 'The Development and Diffusion of Unanimous Agreement in Medieval Ashkenaz'; id., 'Halakhah and *Mezi'ut* (Realia) in Medieval Ashkenaz'. This last study suggests that while Tosafists from both northern France and Germany proposed readings and rulings to address and alleviate situations in which widespread Ashkenazi practice appears to conflict with talmudic and rabbinic law, the French Tosafists were somewhat more innovative in this endeavour.

[13] See e.g. Kanarfogel, 'Midrashic Texts and Methods'.

[14] Eleazar of Worms, who studied with two of Rabbenu Tam's students, frequently cites Rashbam's commentary on *Avodah zarah* (and on the last chapter of *Pesaḥim*), as well as Rabbenu Tam's *Sefer hayashar*, but he barely cites anything in these areas from Ri. See *R. Eleazar mivermaiza*, ed. Emanuel, editor's introduction, 22–3, 50. At the same time, however, Eleazar composed *Tosafot* based directly on those of Ri on *Bava kama* (as edited by Ri's student, Judah Sirleon). Urbach (*The Tosafists* (Heb.), i. 403–5, ii. 660) notes that Eleazar of Worms is cited only once in the *Tosafot* in the standard edition of the Talmud.

[15] Sussman, 'The Scholarly Oeuvre of Professor Ephraim Elimelekh Urbach' (Heb.) and Soloveitchik, 'The Printed Page of the Talmud'; id., 'The Halakhic Isolation of the Ashkenazic Community', 45; Emanuel, 'The Origins and Career of R. Barukh b. Isaac' (Heb.), 438–9; Kanarfogel, *The Intellectual History and Rabbinic Culture of Medieval Ashkenaz*, 4–5 (n. 9).

[16] See e.g. Aptowitzer, *Mavo lesefer ravyah*, 261–2, 379–80. To be sure, Ravyah cites Rabbenu Tam's *Sefer hayashar* much more extensively than he does Ri. See A. Reiner, 'From Rabbenu

Ravyah's father, and with Barukh ben Isaac of Regensburg, while Simhah of Speyer sent a question to Ri's successor in Dampierre, Isaac ben Abraham (Ritsba, d.1209).[17] In addition, questions regarding Jewish law and custom from Ashkenazi lands were posed simultaneously to both French and German Tosafists.[18] All these findings suggest a somewhat porous situation. Moreover, shifts over time in the patterns of scholarly migration, and the emergence of new regional variations and perspectives,[19] tended, on the whole, to narrow the differences between the centres of rabbinic scholarship in Ashkenaz in both interpretation and practice.[20]

In the absence of temporal factors such as royal, church, feudal, or other restrictions that might have inhibited the movement of German students to northern France following the death of Rabbenu Tam,[21] this general cessation of contact may best be explained by considering the manner in which Tosafist teachings and methods were transmitted. Unlike his uncle and teacher Rabbenu Tam, who had attracted a noticeable number of German and east

Tam to R. Isaac of Vienna', 273–82. Note also that Barukh ben Samuel of Mainz, who cites both Rashi and Rabbenu Tam, does not mention Ri (or any of his French students) at all in his *Sefer haḥokhmah*, although he did perhaps send a responsum to one of Ri's students, Solomon of Dreux. See Emanuel, *Shivrei luḥot*, 108–9, 115, 134 (n. 138); *Sefer mordekhai lemasekhet yevamot*, sec. 21.

[17] See Aptowitzer, *Mavo lesefer ravyah*, 367; Urbach, *The Tosafists* (Heb.), ii. 637–8; Emanuel, 'The Origins and Career of R. Barukh b. Isaac' (Heb.), 438 (n. 68).

[18] See e.g. *Sefer or zarua*, pt. III, 'Piskei bava kama', sec. 457 (fos. 36*d*–37*a*), for rulings issued by both Samson of Sens and Simhah of Speyer regarding proper payment for a matchmaker (*shadkhan*) in the same specific case.

[19] For contacts between the two centres during the pre-Crusade period and beyond, see Grossman, *The Early Sages of France* (Heb.), 542–5, 572–86. Cf. A. Reiner, 'The Acceptance of *Halakhot Gedolot* in Ashkenaz' (Heb.); Kanarfogel, *Jewish Education and Society*, 68–9.

[20] See e.g. Emanuel, '"When the Master of the Universe Went Down to Egypt"' (Heb.). The key difference here is liturgical, a fairly common occurrence even between various regions within Germany. See e.g. *Maḥzor sukot, shemini atseret vesimḥat torah*, ed. Goldschmidt and Fraenkel, editors' introduction, 9–48; Zimmer, *Society and Its Customs* (Heb.), 114–18; 125–8, 268–72; Sussman, 'The Scholarly Oeuvre of Professor Ephraim Elimelekh Urbach' (Heb.), 58–61. As Emanuel shows, these textual differences diminished after 1220, by which time the Tosafist centres in northern France and Germany had become 'reacquainted', and they disappeared altogether by the end of the 13th century. There could also sometimes be mixed results within the same larger issue. See Kanarfogel, 'Changing Attitudes toward Apostates'.

[21] See Emanuel, 'The Rabbis of Germany in the Thirteenth Century' (Heb.), 561–2. Cf. Thomson, 'Richard Southern and the Twelfth-Century Intellectual World'; id., 'The Place of Germany in the Twelfth-Century Renaissance'; Mews, 'Scholastic Theology in a Monastic Milieu'; Jaeger, 'Pessimism in the Twelfth-Century Renaissance'; Sheffler, *Schools and Schooling in Late Medieval Germany*, 15–40.

European students (together with those who hailed from northern France),[22] virtually all of Ri of Dampierre's many students (whose total matched the number of those who had come to study with Rabbenu Tam) came from within northern France.[23] This striking difference, along with the broader absence of contact between the Tosafist centres in northern France and Germany following the death of Rabbenu Tam, may be explained by the following development: a few of Rabbenu Tam's German students later established teaching presences in locales in or near Germany. Students from central (and eastern) Europe who wished to be exposed to the methods of close reading and enlightening source comparison and dialectic, first developed and taught by Rabbenu Tam, could more easily reach teachers such as Moses ben Solomon Hakohen of Mainz[24] and Eliezer ben Samuel of Metz

[22] Urbach (*The Tosafists* (Heb.), i. 114–64) identifies more than fifteen outstanding students of Rabbenu Tam from northern France (not including Isaac of Dampierre), as well as several others who were not as prominent. Rami Reiner, in 'Rabbenu Tam: His (French) Teachers and Ashkenazi Disciples' (Heb.), discusses nearly fifteen students of Rabbenu Tam who hailed from the Rhineland and central Germany, as well as from eastern Europe.

[23] See Urbach, *The Tosafists* (Heb.), i. 235–344, for more than ten important French students of Ri. Although Urbach asserts (i. 345) that 'a large number of German students reached the study hall of Ri and those of his students', the only German students that he identifies explicitly are Eliezer of Toul (and Boppard) and his brother Abraham (ibid. i. 335–6). Cf. *Sefer arugat habosem*, ed. Urbach, iv. 117; Sussman, 'The Scholarly Oeuvre of Professor Ephraim Elimelekh Urbach' (Heb.), 50 n. 83; Emanuel, 'The Origins and Career of R. Barukh b. Isaac' (Heb.), 439 (n. 68). Urbach includes a treatment of Ri's dedicated student, Barukh ben Isaac, author of *Sefer haterumah* (identified as Barukh of Worms) at the beginning of a chapter on German Tosafists (i. 345–61). However, his hesitation about Barukh's association with Worms has been shown to be fully justified by Simcha Emanuel, who has demonstrated that Barukh had no connection to Germany ('The Origins and Career of R. Barukh b. Isaac' (Heb.), 423–36). On the size of the study halls of Rabbenu Tam and Ri, see Breuer, 'Towards A Typology of Western Yeshivas in the Middle Ages' (Heb.) and Kanarfogel, *Jewish Education and Society*, 66–7, 164–6.

[24] See Aptowitzer, *Mavo lesefer ravyah*, 385–6; Urbach, *The Tosafists* (Heb.), i. 184–6 (and n. 10, for the citation of the no longer extant *Sefer hadinim sheyasad rabenu mosheh hakohen*, *Piskei harosh lemasekhet kidushin*, 1: 20; A. Reiner, 'Rabbenu Tam: His (French) Teachers and Ashkenazi Disciples' (Heb.), 103–5. Moses of Mainz's literary output does not appear to have been heavy and he is cited only infrequently in Tosafist texts, yet he was a major conduit for Rabbenu Tam's material in the Rhineland. He composed *Tosafot* on *Pesaḥim* and *Yevamot*, and his rulings are cited in 13th-century halakhic compendia such as *Sefer or zarua* and *Shibolei haleket*. See also Emanuel, *Shivrei luḥot*, 108–9; *Sidur rabenu shelomoh migermaiza*, ed. Hershler, 200: 'That the blessing [on a fast day] is concluded with both the phrases *ha'oneh be'et tsarah* and *shome'a tefilah* is a mistake on their part. I found this in the composition [*biyesod*] of R. Moses Hakohen' = MS Verona (Municipal Library) 100 (85.2) [IMHM #32667; Ashkenaz, 14th century], fo. 63[r]; MS Modena (Archive) [ph #6886], 101.4 (at the last line: *vekhen horeh lanu beshem rabenu mosheh hakohen*); and the literature cited in Urbach, *The Tosafists* (Heb.), i. 186 (n. 19). The Ashkenazi

(d.1198).[25] Metz and its environs are located approximately 120 miles from the Rhineland, less than half the distance to Dampierre.[26] In addition, Eliezer of Metz taught for a period in the Rhineland city of Mainz.[27]

Ephraim ben Isaac of Regensburg (d.1175) was part of a group of students who initially studied with Isaac ben Asher (Riva) Halevi of Speyer (d.1133), and then with Rabbenu Tam, before Ephraim returned to Regensburg to teach.[28] Noteworthy and prolific students of Moses Hakohen of Mainz, Eliezer of Metz (and Mainz), and Ephraim of Regensburg included Joel Halevi of Bonn (who composed *Tosafot* that are no longer extant, as well as numerous responsa and *pesakim* preserved by Ravyah and others) and the group of German rabbinic figures highlighted by Emanuel: Barukh of Mainz (to be discussed below), Ravyah, Simhah of Speyer (author of the no longer extant halakhic compendium *Seder olam*), and Eleazar of Worms (author of *Sefer roke'aḥ* and other halakhic treatises).[29]

rabbinic chain of tradition recorded in *Teshuvot maharshal*, no. 29, lists Moses Hakohen of Mainz as a student of both Rabbenu Tam and Ri. The parallel passage in MS Bodl. 847 (fos. 36[r–v]) lists Moses as Ri's student—and not as the student of Rabbenu Tam—although Moses' linkage to Ri is otherwise unattested. See Emanuel, 'The Origins and Career of R. Barukh b. Isaac' (Heb.), 433 n. 44. This chain of tradition has been attributed to a student of Meir of Rothenburg, perhaps Asher ben Yehiel. See Epstein, 'Likutim' (Heb.), 129–30. MS Bodl. 847 focuses more on teachers in northern France and less on those in Germany. See Kanarfogel, *The Intellectual History and Rabbinic Culture of Medieval Ashkenaz*, 81 (n. 162), and below.

[25] See Urbach, *The Tosafists* (Heb.), i. 154–64, and Emanuel, *Shivrei luḥot*, 293–7.

[26] See Mendel, 'Les Juifs à Metz avant 1552'; id., 'Les Juifs à Metz'; and Gross, *Gallia Judaica*, 346–50. Metz, near the eastern border of France in the Lorraine region, was considered to be a part of the Holy Roman Empire and an independent imperial town until the mid-16th century. On Jewish settlement in and around Metz during the medieval period see Soloveitchik, *Wine in Ashkenaz in the Middle Ages* (Heb.), 23, 190.

[27] See Reiner, 'Rabbenu Tam: His (French) Teachers and Ashkenazi Disciples' (Heb.), 105–12. According to the chain of tradition in *Teshuvot maharshal*, no. 29, Eliezer taught Ravyah, Barukh of Mainz, and Simhah of Speyer in Mainz; none of these (German) figures are mentioned in MS Bodl. 847.

[28] See Urbach, *The Tosafists* (Heb.), i. 199–207; Reiner, 'Rabbenu Tam: His (French) Teachers and Ashkenazi Disciples' (Heb.), 68, 79–102; Ta-Shma, *Early Franco-German Ritual and Custom* (Heb.), 95–8. Members of this student group continued to correspond with Rabbenu Tam even after they returned to the east, although they often ruled in matters of law and custom according to German traditions.

[29] Joel Halevi studied with Ephraim of Regensburg and Rivam (see Aptowitzer, *Mavo lesefer ravyah*, 39–40; Urbach, *The Tosafists* (Heb.), i. 202, 210; and Emanuel, *Shivrei luḥot*, 81–6, regarding his *Tosafot*). Barukh of Mainz studied with Ephraim, Moses Hakohen of Mainz, and Eliezer of Metz (see Urbach, *The Tosafists* (Heb.), i. 425–9; Emanuel, *Shivrei luḥot*, 105–9). Ravyah studied with Eliezer and Moses Hakohen (see Aptowitzer, *Mavo lesefer ravyah*, 22–3, 312–14; Urbach, *The Tosafists* (Heb.), i. 378–9; Reiner, 'Rabbenu Tam: His (French) Teachers and

Additional channels through which Rabbenu Tam's teachings reached German Tosafists who did not study directly with him can be glimpsed in the work of Judah ben Kalonymos (Rivak) of Speyer (d.1199). Rivak mentions what he heard from (or in the name of) Ephraim of Regensburg, and there is evidence that he and Ephraim exchanged halakhic queries, but Rivak had received most of his training from Shemaryah ben Mordecai and Abraham ben Samuel Hehasid in Speyer. The only northern French Tosafists named in Rivak's *Sefer yiḥusei tana'im ve'amora'im* are Rabbenu Tam and his student Hayim ben Hananel Hakohen, who also spent some time in the Rhineland. Shemaryah ben Mordekhai of Speyer, a student of Riva, also interacted with Rabbenu Tam and even appeared for a brief period in northern France. Thus Rivak's awareness of Rabbenu Tam's teachings could have come from Shemaryah of Speyer, Ephraim of Regensburg, or Hayim Hakohen,[30] all of whom had direct contact with Rabbenu Tam.[31]

Whereas German scholars who had studied directly with Rabbenu Tam, such as Moses Hakohen of Mainz, Eliezer of Metz, and Ephraim of Regensburg, produced their own distinguished German Tosafist students—including Barukh of Mainz, Ravyah, and Eleazar of Worms—this subsequent

Ashkenazi Disciples' (Heb.), 111 n. 382), as did Simhah of Speyer (see Apowitzer, *Mavo lesefer ravyah*, 412–14; Urbach, *The Tosafists* (Heb.), i. 411–13; Emanuel, *Shivrei luḥot*, 154–5; Reiner, 'Rabbenu Tam: His (French) Teachers and Ashkenazi Disciples' (Heb.)). Eleazar of Worms, who hailed from Mainz, also studied with these teachers (see Urbach, *The Tosafists* (Heb.), i. 389–90; Reiner, 'Rabbenu Tam: His (French) Teachers and Ashkenazi Disciples' (Heb.); and see *Teshuvot maharshal*, no. 29). Samson of Sens mentions three of Rabbenu Tam's German students (Ephraim of Regensburg, Moses Hakohen of Mainz, and Rivam) in his *Tosafot* on *Pesaḥim*. See Urbach, *The Tosafists* (Heb.), i. 283–4 and 350 n. 40 for references to Rabbenu Tam's German students in *Sefer haterumah* by Barukh ben Isaac.

[30] See Aptowitzer, *Mavo lesefer ravyah*, 417; Urbach, *The Tosafists* (Heb.), i. 362–4, 372–3; Sussman, 'The Scholarly Oeuvre of Professor Ephraim Elimelekh Urbach' (Heb.), 39 n. 63; A. Reiner, 'Rabbenu Tam: His (French) Teachers and Ashkenazi Disciples' (Heb.), 99–103; Emanuel, *Shivrei luḥot*, 287–8, 307–8. Urbach shows that Judah was aware of the *Tosafot* of Ri, although he does not cite any names in this connection. For Hayim Hakohen's presence in Germany see A. Reiner, 'Rabbenu Tam and His Contemporaries' (Heb.).

[31] A seeming exception to this pattern is found in a German commentary on *Tamid* (the so-called pseudo-Rabad commentary), which identifies Ephraim of Regensburg as the author's teacher. A passage in this commentary criticizes the aggressive dialectical methods of the French *Tosafot*. See Urbach, *The Tosafists* (Heb.), i. 355; Kanarfogel, 'Study of the Order of *Kodashim*' (Heb.), 73 n. 19. To be sure, unrestrained or otherwise erroneous dialectic was denigrated by Tosafists in all regions, from Rabbenu Tam and his students Ri and Eliezer of Metz to Moses Taku of Regensburg (d. *c*.1235); see Urbach, *The Tosafists* (Heb.), i. 26–7 and Kanarfogel, 'Study of the Order of *Kodashim*' (Heb.), 82–5.

generation did not, as Emanuel has carefully documented.[32] Neither did their older contemporary Joel ben Isaac Halevi, for while he taught Talmud (as he occasionally notes) and composed *Tosafot*, he produced no students of renown with the exception of his son, Ravyah.[33] Simhah of Speyer was a bit more successful in this regard; one of his students was Isaac ben Moses Or Zarua of Vienna (who lived in Simhah's home for a time and also studied with Ravyah). However, Emanuel also notes that, like Isaac of Vienna, other important students of Simhah, such as Avigdor ben Elijah Katz of Vienna, did not hail from Germany and did not remain there to teach.[34]

The exciting and far-reaching possibilities generated by the emerging method of dialectic were what drew students to Rabbenu Tam, and earlier (though in smaller numbers) to Riva Halevi of Speyer.[35] From the patterns of

[32] See Emanuel, 'The Rabbis of Germany in the Thirteenth Century' (Heb.), 551–6. Emanuel suggests that a passage associated with Eleazar of Worms, in which the author laments the lack of suitable students in esoteric studies, refers to talmudic and halakhic studies as well. In fact, however, Eleazar had several capable students in esoteric studies, which suggests that this lament should be understood in a more nuanced way. See Abrams, 'The Literary Emergence of Esotericism'; Kanarfogel, *'Peering through the Lattices'*, 25; Ta-Shma, *Collected Studies* (Heb.), i. 273–81; Ben-Shalom, 'Kabbalistic Circles Active in the South of France' (Heb.), 581–3. Only Isaac Or Zarua and Abraham ben Azriel of Bohemia refer to Eleazar as their rabbinic teacher. However, Isaac cites what he heard directly from Eleazar only five times, mainly in pietistic contexts, while three other citations are from Eleazar's writings alone. See Fuchs, 'Studies in the *Sefer or zarua*' (Heb.), 19 (n. 43). On Abraham ben Azriel see below, n. 34.

[33] See Aptowitzer, *Mavo lesefer ravyah*, 44. Ravyah writes that 'I presented an argument before my father and the whole yeshiva and they agreed with my position' (see *Sefer ravyah*, i. 360, sec. 289). In another instance Joel Halevi responds that he would look carefully at a point made by Ravyah 'when I have a chance, because I am in the midst of teaching my students tractate *Gitin*' (see *Teshuvot ravyah*, ed. Deblitzky, i, sec. 922). However, none of these students are identified. Indeed, while the second citation clearly indicates that Joel taught Talmud to students, the first can also refer to an assembly that had gathered at the circumcision ceremony. See also the reports in *Sefer ravyah* and *Sefer or zarua* of an interaction between Joel Halevi and yeshiva students in Bonn (*talmidim sheba'ir*), noted in Urbach, *The Tosafists* (Heb.), i. 211 n. 23. Here, too, none of the students are identified by name, and it is not clear from these reports that they were necessarily Joel's students.

[34] On Avigdor Katz of Vienna see Emanuel, *Shivrei luḥot*, 154–66, 175–84; Kanarfogel, *The Intellectual History and Rabbinic Culture of Medieval Ashkenaz*, 4 n. 9; 238–40; 428–9; 469–77. Another of Simhah's students, Abraham ben Azriel of Bohemia, compiled the extensive *piyut* commentary *Sefer arugat habosem*. Abraham is characterized by Urbach as a *rosh yeshivah*; he was in contact with several German Tosafists, but there is no firm evidence that he was a Tosafist. See *Sefer arugat habosem*, ed. Urbach, iv. 112–27; Ta-Shma, *Commentarial Literature on the Talmud* (Heb.), ii. 118–19; Kanarfogel, *The Intellectual History and Rabbinic Culture of Medieval Ashkenaz*, 23–5; and below, at n. 57.

[35] See Kanarfogel, *The Intellectual History and Rabbinic Culture of Medieval Ashkenaz*, 5 n. 11,

study that have been presented to this point, however, it would seem that the ability to teach and transmit the methods of Rabbenu Tam and Riva of Speyer was largely absent among those German scholars who had not directly studied with these great teachers. This phenomenon may be explained by focusing on an aspect of rabbinic scholarship and culture that was unique to Germany.

In his treatment and thematic reconstruction of Barukh of Mainz's no longer extant *Sefer haḥokhmah*, a voluminous compilation devoted in large measure to marital and monetary law, Simcha Emanuel concludes that Barukh did not have any students (except perhaps his son, Samuel Bamberg). Emanuel cogently suggests that Barukh served only as a rabbinic court judge and was not an academy head at all, for while *Sefer haḥokhmah* contains Barukh's *Tosafot* on *Megilah* (among other tractates), along with other forms of talmudic interpretation, it also includes a wide selection of the judicial decisions and cases of the Mainz court.[36]

In fact, whether or not they composed *Tosafot*, the leading communal judges in Germany who were contemporaries of Joel Halevi and Barukh did not produce any well-known figures in talmudic interpretation or halakhah. This is true for Menahem ben Jacob (d.1203), a leading judge in Worms who taught halakhah (though there are few literary remains of these teachings),[37]

41 n. 18, 80 n. 160, 102–3, and the literature cited. Recent scholarship has debated whether Riva had studied in northern France, as well as the nature of his dialectic. Ta-Shma suggests that Riva wielded his dialectic, as a jurist might, to limit the various possibilities that emerged, while Rabbenu Tam's approach was more lawyer-like, to generate a range of possibilities; see Ta-Shma, *Commentarial Literature on the Talmud* (Heb.), i. 70; ii. 116–17. Eliezer ben Nathan (Ravan) of Mainz—who was younger than Riva and a bit older than Rabbenu Tam—does not seem to have had students outside his immediate family (see Aptowitzer, *Mavo lesefer ravyah*, 52; Urbach, *The Tosafists* (Heb.), i. 184). Although Ravan corresponded with Rashbam and Rabbenu Tam (and their father, Meir), and appears to have reached northern France at least once, it is unclear with whom he studied (see Urbach, *The Tosafists* (Heb.), i. 174–5). Shalom Albeck (cited in Aptowitzer, p. 52) hypothesizes that Riva was one of his teachers, among other rabbinic scholars in Mainz and Speyer at that time (including his father-in-law Elyakim ben Joseph, and Jacob ben Isaac). There is evidence for personal contact and correspondence between Ravan and Riva; see Ghedalia, 'The Historical Background to the Writing of *Sefer even ha'ezer*' (Heb.), 45–50.

[36] See Emanuel, *Shivrei luḥot*, 109, 146. On the court proceedings and decisions found in *Sefer haḥokhmah* see ibid. 127–35, and Kanarfogel, 'The Development and Diffusion of Unanimous Agreement', 26–8; 39–40. On Samuel Bamberg see Urbach, *The Tosafists* (Heb.), i. 430, and Emanuel, *Shivrei luḥot*, 106–7.

[37] See Urbach, *The Tosafists* (Heb.), i. 370, 406; Aptowitzer, *Mavo lesefer ravyah*, 382–4; Kanarfogel, *The Intellectual History and Rabbinic Culture of Medieval Ashkenaz*, 25, 462–3, especially the passages from *Sefer ha'asufot*.

and of Ephraim of Regensburg's colleagues on the *beit din* in Regensburg —Isaac ben Mordecai and Moses ben Joel—both of whom composed and circulated *Tosafot* texts.[38] Indeed, Simhah of Speyer remains the lone exception to this rule.

In short, the Tosafists in Germany and northern France appear to have been similarly regarded and equally matched as religious leaders, but their professional responsibilities and proclivities differed considerably. Unlike their French counterparts, German Tosafists and rabbinic scholars typically served as heads and judges of established local rabbinic courts. As I have demonstrated elsewhere, these scholars adjudicated actual cases and communicated with other courts as needed—at times compiling records of these exchanges and interactions. They also dealt with appeals from individual scholars and from other court jurisdictions. Not surprisingly, they saw (and conducted) themselves as jurists rather than as academy heads whose primary role was the teaching of students. There are specific references to the judicial activities of virtually every one of the German Tosafists mentioned thus far.[39] Ravyah, who served as the leading judge in Cologne, describes an argument he presented before the Mainz rabbinic court, seeking its approval. While sitting in the study hall or *scriptorium* (*beit hasefer*) with Barukh ben Samuel, who had advocated on behalf of several orphans, and other judicial colleagues—including Moses Hakohen of Mainz—Ravyah presented his argument that the orphans should not prevail in this case. His formulation suggests that the Mainz court was, in some way, connected to a study hall, with the rabbinic court appearing to be the more prominent institution of the two.[40]

It is true that Rabbenu Tam himself had also served as the head of an active court, and that he was involved in the training of judges.[41] Yet his major

[38] For the *Tosafot* of Rivam and Moses ben Joel see Urbach, *The Tosafists* (Heb.), i. 196–9, 207–8; Emanuel, *Shivrei luḥot*, 82–6, and above, n. 29. Like Rivam, Moses ben Joel studied with Riva Halevi, although his contact with Rabbenu Tam was more limited. Isaac (Ri) Halavan of Bohemia studied briefly with Riva and more extensively with Rabbenu Tam. He composed *Tosafot* and sat on the Regensburg court but he, too, does not seem to have had any students. See Urbach, *The Tosafists* (Heb.), i. 218–21; Kanarfogel, 'R. Judah *he-Hasid*', 22–6.

[39] See Kanarfogel, *The Intellectual History and Rabbinic Culture of Medieval Ashkenaz*, 38–53.

[40] See *Teshuvot ravyah*, ed. Deblitzky, i. 54–6 (sec. 925: 'and [R. Barukh] was then sitting with me in the *scriptorium* [*beit hasefer*] and I made my argument before him and before the other masters, R. Judah and my teacher R. Moses'). Cf. *Sefer mordekhai al masekhet ḥulin*, sec. 684.

[41] See e.g. *Tosafot*, *Ket.* 69*a*, s.v. *ve'ishtik*, and cf. *Tosafot harosh* and *Ḥidushei haritva* ad loc. See also *Sefer or zarua*, pt. III, 'Piskei bava metsia', sec. 202 (fo. 29*b*); *Tosafot*, *BK* 118*a*, s.v. *rav*

role—and the way that he was perceived, especially by later generations—was as an academy head and teacher. And it was in this role that he attracted students from throughout Europe. Moreover, Rabbenu Tam's successor, Ri of Dampierre, and Ri's leading student, Samson ben Abraham of Sens, do not appear to have served as judges on permanently constituted, ongoing courts, though they did receive appeals from various rabbinic courts and litigants. Although they may have served occasionally as judges on temporary or *ad hoc* (*zabla*) courts, they, too, saw themselves primarily as *rashei yeshivah*.[42] This was also true for Judah ben Isaac Sirleon of Paris (d.1224), another student of Ri, who opened his study hall when Jews were allowed to return to the royal realm in 1198. He, too, continued the teaching and interpretational programme of his northern French predecessors.[43]

The only exception to this pattern in northern France involved the rabbinic courts that were convened to supervise the writing and granting of bills of divorce; many of the most important French Tosafists participated in these courts and often presided over them. The halakhic requirements in divorce procedures were so complex—and the consequences of bills of divorce that were not properly executed were so grave—that the participation of all leading rabbinic scholars was necessary. Thus even those rabbinic figures in northern France who were not regularly involved in local judicial institutions or processes lent their expertise and support to this endeavour. Leaving aside this exception, however, it was several decades after the death of Rabbenu Tam before northern French Tosafists began, again, to sit with regularity on rabbinic courts for deciding monetary and ritual matters, as Rabbenu Tam and others in his day had done. By the second quarter of the thirteenth century, in the days of Judah Sirleon's successor, Yehiel ben Joseph of Paris, and his

naḥman; *Tosafot*, *Ket.* 105*b*, s.v. *mai*, and *Tosafot harosh* ad loc.; *Sefer yere'im hashalem*, i. 22 (sec. 7); *Tosafot*, *Kid.* 52*a*, s.v. *vehilkheta*; *Ḥidushei harashba lekidushin* 51*b*; MS JTS Rab. 673, fo. 363r; and Urbach, *The Tosafists* (Heb.), i. 148.

[42] See Kanarfogel, *The Intellectual History and Rabbinic Culture of Medieval Ashkenaz*, 41–2, 57–64. Thus, for example, Samson of Sens notes that Ri had *heard* that Rabbenu Tam accepted written testimony, while Joel Halevi accepted such testimony himself as a judge. See Fuss, 'Written Testimony in Financial Legal Cases' (Heb.), 331–7. Rabbenu Tam's German students, Ephraim of Regensburg and Moses Hakohen of Mainz, served as ongoing or permanent rabbinic court judges, even as Eliezer of Metz did not. (Metz was perhaps more 'French' in this respect; see above, n. 26.) Among Rabbenu Tam's French students only Joseph ben Isaac of Orleans served as a judge. See A. Reiner, 'Rabbinical Courts in France', and below, n. 53.

[43] See Kanarfogel, *The Intellectual History and Rabbinic Culture of Medieval Ashkenaz*, 60–1; and cf. Urbach, *The Tosafists* (Heb.), i. 323–34.

contemporary Tosafist colleague Samuel ben Solomon of Falaise, German rabbinic scholars had begun to consult with these rabbinic courts as well.[44]

Another difference between the rabbinic scholars of the two regions concerns their treatment of responsa. Rabbis in both northern France and Germany composed responsa, but only the latter systematically collected and preserved theirs, along with those of others. And just as most leading French scholars did not preserve their responsa in a significant or systematic way, they did not feel the need to record any judicial decisions that they may have rendered. Evidence for any such decisions is extremely hard to come by, despite the vastness of their talmudic and rabbinic writings.[45] By contrast, the responsa produced by leading German Tosafists and halakhists constitute important sources for judicial activity.[46] It would seem that, in Germany, leading scholars felt that they could best serve the community and exert the greatest influence as masters of the rabbinic courts.

In addition, German scholars retained the convention, prevalent in the Rhineland during the pre-Crusade period, of identifying institutions of learning by their community or locale and its traditions, rather than by the important figures who taught in them. In northern France, on the other hand, the *rosh yeshivah* was seen as the most important identifier of an academy. Students followed leading scholars as they changed locales, and they saw themselves as students of the *rosh yeshivah*, rather than identifying themselves with the locale of the academy or its practices. This is reflected in differences in compositional nomenclature: the pre-Crusade Mainz commentaries on various talmudic tractates can be called *Perushei magentsa*, but the glosses of northern France are called *Tosafot hari* or *Tosafot r. yehudah sirleon*, and so on.[47]

[44] See Kanarfogel, *The Intellectual History and Rabbinic Culture of Medieval Ashkenaz*, 64–9, and below, n. 56.

[45] See ibid. 70–1.

[46] See e.g. Soloveitchik, *Halakhah, Economy, and Self-Image* (Heb.); and id., 'Catastrophe and Halakhic Creativity', 76–8. Cf. Ta-Shma's introduction to *Mafte'aḥ hashe'elot vehateshuvot*, ed. Lifshitz and Shochetman, 11–13 (= *Collected Studies* (Heb.), i. 117–25); ibid., ii. 73–4; Emanuel, 'The Origins and Career of R. Barukh b. Isaac' (Heb.), 439–40. The relatively recent publication of *Teshuvot ravyah* serves as a stark reminder of this. German Tosafists tended to preserve citations of earlier material (including their own) to a much greater extent than their French counterparts did. See Soloveitchik, 'The Halakhic Isolation of the Ashkenazic Community', 43–5; Emanuel, *Shivrei luḥot*, 29.

[47] See Grossman, *The Early Sages of Ashkenaz* (Heb.), 165–74; and Ta-Shma, *Commentarial Literature on the Talmud* (Heb.), i. 35–40. See also *Teshuvot rabenu gershom me'or hagolah*, ed. Eidelberg, 98–100, no. 32; Grossman, *The Early Sages of Ashkenaz* (Heb.), 120. See *Sefer or zarua*, pt. IV ('Piskei avodah zarah', sec. 262, fo. 35*a*) for a parallel situation in Paris, around 1220. For a fuller discussion of these distinctions and sources—including parallels to educational

Moreover, there is a series of French rabbinic texts that describe how students sought to challenge the *rosh yeshivah* on the basis of their own understanding of underlying texts. Scholarly reputations in this region were made on the basis of intellectual and exegetical abilities. Ri of Dampierre asserts that the availability of talmudic commentaries and post-talmudic halakhic texts in his day meant that a student could more easily develop the ability to rule in matters of Jewish law.[48] He notes that this situation differed considerably from that which had prevailed during the talmudic period, when the teacher had access to bodies of knowledge and analyses that were not easily available to students. In the words of Samson of Sens, 'that which was hidden to earlier scholars is sometimes revealed to later scholars . . . for a student can sometimes see what his teacher cannot from [the Talmud's] words. He can "outsmart" his teacher and sharpen the [teacher's] interpretation.'[49] The heads of the Tosafist academy at Evreux, Moses and Samuel ben Shneur (d. *c*.1250), wrote that

talmudic texts, commentaries, novellae, and [halakhic] compositions are the teachers of men; all is determined by one's perspicacity. Thus, it was usual in their locale that a student opened his own study hall without concern for the talmudic dictum that 'one who decides a matter of law in his teacher's presence is punishable by death'. Similarly, a student can contradict his teacher on the basis of superior reasoning.[50]

The prerogative was predicated on the student's ability to demonstrate convincingly his interpretations and positions with respect to talmudic literature and law. The centrality of the academy head in the Jewish intellectual and halakhic community was linked to the virtuosity of the aspiring scholar.[51]

These differences between Germany and northern France centred around the following question: Is rabbinic leadership or power primarily derived from, and expressed through, an ability to discover new talmudic interpreta-

conventions in medieval Christian society—see Kanarfogel, *Jewish Education and Society*, 70–2. The so-called *Tosafot shants* are not the collective product of the study hall in Sens, but rather the *Tosafot* composed there by Samson ben Abraham. See Kanarfogel, *The Intellectual History and Rabbinic Culture of Medieval Ashkenaz*, 84–110.

[48] See *Sefer semak mizurich*, ed. Har-Shoshanim, i. 27; Kanarfogel, 'Rabbinic Authority', 242.

[49] See Abulafia (Ramah), *Kit'āb al Rasā'il*, ed. Brill, 131–2.

[50] For the formulation by the brothers of Evreux see *Sefer orḥot ḥayim*, 'Hilkhot talmud torah', sec. 21 (fos. 29*a*–*b*), cited with slight variation in *Teshuvot maharashdam*, 'Ḥoshen mishpat', no. 1. See also Urbach, *The Tosafists* (Heb.), i. 479–80; and Elon, 'The Law, Books and Libraries', 16–18.

[51] For a fuller discussion of these French formulations and their implications see Kanarfogel, 'Rabbinic Authority', 233–50; id., 'Progress and Tradition in Medieval Ashkenaz'.

tions and correlations (*ḥidushim*)? Or is it embodied in *dayanim* (and in their associates) who render Jewish law, and are thus viewed as its authoritative spokesmen? The former was the model in northern France, and the latter was the approach favoured in Germany.[52] During the pre-Crusade period differences between northern France and Germany in these matters were less pronounced,[53] and this was also the case from the second half of the thirteenth century, once significant contact between the two centres had resumed.

The continued presence of strong Tosafist teachers in northern France throughout the first half of the thirteenth century, and their absence in Germany during this time, accounts for the gap in German Tosafist leadership between the period of Barukh of Mainz, Ravyah, Simhah of Speyer, and Eleazar of Worms on the one hand, and the days when Maharam of Rothenburg was active. Overall, German Tosafists did not have nearly as many students and successors as their counterparts in northern France, owing in large measure to their preoccupation with judicial functions and activities. Although several of the German scholars discussed here also headed study halls, the largest Tosafist academy consisted of no more than twenty-five students, and the average size was more likely in the mid-teens or even less.[54] Nothing was faulty with the Germans' methods of study or analysis; they were simply not as committed to teaching those methods, certainly not out-

[52] Discussion of judicial matters here has been limited to communal courts, and has not taken into account *takanot hakahal* (communal ordinances) or the functioning of the *kehilah* (community) itself as a *beit din* (court) with respect to setting communal policy. Similarly, there has been no discussion of the role of rabbinic scholars in super-communal government (and the promulgation of *takanot*), where it may be assumed, of necessity, that leading figures would have greater authority. Prominent Tosafists and local communal judges figured among the signatories on the various super-communal *takanot* promulgated during the 12th and 13th centuries. See e.g. Finkelstein, *Jewish Self-Government in the Middle Ages*, 42 (Ravan of Mainz, Eliezer ben Samson of Cologne), 62–3 (Eleazar of Worms, Ravyah, Simhah of Speyer, Barukh of Mainz), 155 (Rabbenu Tam, Rashbam, Ravan), 165 (Rabbenu Tam), 198 (Yehiel of Paris), 223 (David ben Kalonymos of Münzberg). Note also the roles played by a number of these rabbinic scholars in applying *takanot rabenu tam* and *takanot kehilot shum* (of the 1220s), which stipulated that the wife's family was entitled to retrieve her dowry if she died within the first year of marriage. See Cohen, 'Communal Ordinances' (Heb.), 148–50.

[53] While a full analysis of pre-Crusade judicial antecedents cannot be presented here, Rashi appears to have served on a court in Troyes. See *Teshuvot rashi*, ed. Elfenbein, 74, and Grossman, *The Early Sages of France* (Heb.), 131 n. 33. Cf. Breuer, 'Towards A Typology of Western Yeshivas in the Middle Ages' (Heb.), 46. *Sefer or zarua* (pt. III, 'Piskei bava kama', sec. 85, fo. 5*b*) records a responsum by Rashi to three judges (*sheloshet hanedivim*) regarding the *ketubah* of a woman who had developed certain blemishes. See also Soloveitchik, 'Pawnbroking', 205–8.

[54] See Kanarfogel, *Jewish Education and Society*, 66–7. As noted above (n. 46), the study hall in Mainz appears to have been somewhat secondary to the rabbinic court there.

side the judicial realm. In the absence of committed teachers of Rabbenu Tam's dialectic in Germany at the turn of the thirteenth century, German students once again began to travel to northern France to find this dimension.

When Isaac ben Moses Or Zarua travelled to Paris to study with Judah Sirleon in order to connect more directly with the teachings and methods of Rabbenu Tam, the forty years of separation between the northern French and German talmudic centres was effectively ended.[55] Even after he left northern France, Isaac Or Zarua consulted with the French Tosafists Yehiel of Paris and Samuel of Falaise,[56] and this pattern, in which students from Germany and points east once again came to northern France to study, continued beyond Isaac's day as well.

Isaac studied with several leading Tosafists, although the precise trajectory of his educational career is somewhat difficult to pinpoint. He appears to have hailed from a Slavic land (perhaps Bohemia) or from Hungary, where he probably studied first, before moving to Germany. He refers to two Bohemian scholars as his teachers, Jacob ben Isaac Halavan (a student of Rabbenu Tam) and Abraham ben Azriel (a student of Simhah of Speyer). His German teachers included Abraham ben Moses of Regensburg, Judah Hehasid, and Jonathan ben Isaac of Würzburg, but his main teachers in Germany were Simhah of Speyer and Ravyah of Cologne. It appears that Isaac Or Zarua then completed his student days in northern France, during the second decade of the thirteenth century. In addition to studying with Judah Sirleon, who is considered to be his third major teacher, Isaac studied with another of Ri's students, Samson of Coucy (d.1221), and he also refers to Jacob of Provins as his teacher.[57] During his sojourn in northern France, he wrote about a sign that the Jews were required to wear, even on the sabbath; this may be the earliest Jewish source to confirm the wearing of the badge mandated in 1215 by the Fourth Lateran Council.[58]

[55] Cf. A. Reiner, 'From Rabbenu Tam to R. Isaac of Vienna'.

[56] See e.g. *Sefer or zarua*, pt. I, 'Hilkhot ḥalitsah', sec. 773; pt. III, 'Piskei bava metsia', sec. 180, fo. 26*a*; Urbach, *The Tosafists* (Heb.), i. 438–9; Emanuel, *Shivrei luḥot*, 189 nn. 18–19. For questions sent to these French rabbinic figures by Hezekiah of Magdeburg (who may also have studied with Samson of Coucy) and Yakar of Cologne, see Urbach, *The Tosafists* (Heb.), ii. 565; and cf. Ta-Shma, *Collected Studies* (Heb.), i. 169–71, 233–4, 239.

[57] See Fuchs, 'Studies in the *Sefer or zarua*' (Heb.), 11–20; Kanarfogel, *The Intellectual History and Rabbinic Culture of Medieval Ashkenaz*, 469–72. On Jacob of Provins, who is also mentioned in MS Bodl. 847 (fo. 36^{v}), see Kanarfogel, *'Peering through the Lattices'*, 98, 207.

[58] See *Sefer or zarua*, pt. II, 'Hilkhot shabat', sec. 84, fo. 20*a*, and Urbach, *The Tosafists* (Heb.), i. 343, 438. Since, as Urbach notes, Isaac also mentions rulings that he had heard from Samson of

Following the path of his father, Moses Hakohen of Mainz, who had travelled to northern France to study with Rabbenu Tam, Judah Hakohen of Würzburg went to Paris (along with Aaron of Regensburg) to study with Judah Sirleon. Indeed, he may have slightly preceded Isaac Or Zarua in this endeavour.[59] Meir (Maharam) of Rothenburg, who had studied in Isaac ben Moses of Vienna's *beit midrash* at a young age,[60] and with Judah Hakohen in Würzburg,[61] spent most of his student years in northern France with Yehiel of Paris (who succeeded Judah Sirleon) and other French Tosafists, including Ezra of Moncontour (a student of Ri's), Samuel of Falaise, and Samuel of Evreux, before returning to Germany.[62]

A younger contemporary of Maharam, Yedidyah ben Israel of Nuremberg, also studied with Yehiel of Paris and Samuel of Evreux. Maharam cites material that Yedidyah had sent from northern France in the name of Yehiel, and Yedidyah, while still in northern France, turned to Maharam with a question.[63] Tuvyah ben Elijah of Vienne, a colleague of the brothers of Evreux and Yehiel of Paris, apparently had quite a few (largely unidentified) German

Sens (who departed for the Land of Israel *c.*1210), he may well have arrived in northern France before 1215.

59 See Urbach, *The Tosafists* (Heb.), ii. 526 (including references to Judah Hakohen in the standard *Tosafot*). The chain of tradition in *Teshuvot maharshal*, no. 29, lists both Judah and Aaron of Regensburg (who led the rabbinic court there from 1225 to 1260) as students of Isaac ben Abraham (Ritsba), the successor of Ri in Dampierre and a senior colleague of Judah Sirleon. The version of this chronology in MS Bodl. 847 (fos. 36^{r-v}) omits these German students of Ritsba. See Kanarfogel, *The Intellectual History and Rabbinic Culture of Medieval Ashkenaz*, 45, 48–9, and above, n. 24. For Judah Hakohen's interaction with French rabbinic scholars see Emanuel, *Shivrei luḥot*, 254 n. 143. For a responsum by Judah and others regarding effects of the persecutions in Frankfurt during 1241, see Kanarfogel, *The Intellectual History and Rabbinic Culture of Medieval Ashkenaz*, 52 (and 429–30 for his related *piyutim*). On Judah's locale see A. Reiner, 'Rabbenu Tam: His (French) Teachers and Ashkenazi Disciples' (Heb.), 127–8; and Emanuel, 'The Rabbis of Germany in the Thirteenth Century' (Heb.), 563–4. On his relationship with Isaac Or Zarua see Ta-Shma, *Collected Studies* (Heb.), i. 161.

60 See Urbach, *The Tosafists* (Heb.), ii. 523–5, and Kanarfogel, *Jewish Education and Society*, 18, 121–2 n. 14.

61 See Urbach, *The Tosafists* (Heb.), ii. 526–7. Maharam also studied in Würzburg with Samuel ben Menahem; see Emanuel, 'The Rabbis of Germany in the Thirteenth Century' (Heb.), 565.

62 See Urbach, *The Tosafists* (Heb.), ii. 522–8; Kupfer, *Teshuvot ufesakim*, 324; and see also Agus, *Rabbi Meir of Rothenburg*, i. 7–11.

63 See Urbach, *The Tosafists* (Heb.), ii. 566–70; *Teshuvot ba'alei hatosafot*, ed. Agus, 233–48; and Kanarfogel, 'Between Ashkenaz and Sefarad', 254–6. After Maharam's death his German student, R. Mordecai ben Hillel, studied in northern France with R. Perets ben Elijah of Corbeil; see Urbach, *The Tosafists* (Heb.), ii. 579.

students,[64] although the proximity of Vienne (in central eastern France) to Germany may at least partially account for this fact. Eliezer of Tuchheim (Tukh), the German compiler of a series of *Tosafot* collections, also studied in northern France. His French teachers, Yehiel of Paris and Tuvyah of Vienne, were more accomplished Tosafists than most of his German teachers and colleagues.[65]

Meir of Rothenburg does not appear to have served as a sitting judge who presided over the first hearings of cases, but he did respond to the plethora of appeals sent by various rabbinic courts. Remarkably, he managed to do so while composing *Tosafot* and training students and successors in Germany.[66] Maharam's experiences with an array of Tosafist teachers in northern France undoubtedly shaped his perception of the importance of raising students. As noted, two of his German teachers, Isaac Or Zarua of Vienna and Judah Hakohen of Mainz, had also studied in northern France.

A final observation: it is no coincidence that the Tosafist study halls developed in northern France during the twelfth and thirteenth centuries in the very areas which saw the rise of the cathedral schools and the formation of the university at Paris. These Christian institutions and their masters were at the centre of the intellectual world in northern Europe, and great prestige was associated with those who studied there. German schools, on the other hand, were not as dynamic at this time, and did not enjoy the same lofty reputation on the whole. The discrete patterns of rabbinic leadership in northern France and Germany presented here—the ability of Rabbenu Tam and his students, both French and German, to teach cutting-edge Tosafist dialectic to attract capable students, and to perpetuate this pursuit in northern France—may perhaps be further understood by exploring the roles played by the most capable and energetic Christian teachers in these regions.[67]

[64] See Urbach, *The Tosafists* (Heb.), ii. 487; Sussman, 'The Scholarly Oeuvre of Professor Ephraim Elimelekh Urbach' (Heb.), 51; Kanarfogel, 'Midrashic Texts and Methods', 269–70.

[65] See Ta-Shma, *Collected Studies* (Heb.), i. 235 n. 31; id., *Commentarial Literature on the Talmud* (Heb.), ii. 101, 111, 119–20; Emanuel, *Teshuvot maharam mirothenburg veḥaverav*, ed. Emanuel (Jerusalem, 2012), 52–3; and Leibowitz, 'Tosafot *Tukh* on the Talmud', 29–32, 47–9, 205–20, 243–51.

[66] See Urbach, *The Tosafists* (Heb.), ii. 529, 538–9, 563–4; Kanarfogel, *The Intellectual History and Rabbinic Culture of Medieval Ashkenaz*, 51–2; Emanuel, 'The Rabbis of Germany in the Thirteenth Century' (Heb.), 561; id., *Teshuvot maharam mirothenburg*, 181–2.

[67] See Kanarfogel, *The Intellectual History and Rabbinic Culture of Medieval Ashkenaz*, 84–110; and Smith, 'The Theological Framework'. On the penetration of Tosafist teachings into southern France see A. Reiner, 'From France to Provence'.

Bibliography

ABRAMS, DANIEL, 'The Literary Emergence of Esotericism in German Pietism', *Shofar*, 12 (1994), 67–85.

ABULAFIA, MEIR BEN TODROS HALEVI (RAMAH), *Kit'b al Ras'il*, ed. J. Brill (Paris, 1871).

AGUS, I. A., *Rabbi Meir of Rothenburg*, 2 vols. (Philadelphia, 1947).

APTOWITZER, AVIGDOR, *Mavo lesefer ravyah* (Jerusalem, 1938).

BEN-SHALOM, RAM, 'Kabbalistic Circles Active in the South of France in the Thirteenth Century' (Heb.), *Tarbiz*, 82 (2014), 569–605.

BREUER, MORDECHAI, 'Towards a Typology of Western Yeshivas in the Middle Ages' (Heb.), in I. Etkes and Y. Salmon (eds.), *Studies in Jewish Society in the Medieval and Early Modern Periods* [Perakim betoledot haḥevrah hayehudit biyemei habeinayim uva'et haḥadashah] (Jerusalem, 1980), 48–55.

COHEN, YEDIDYAH, 'Communal Ordinances Regarding a Husband Inheriting from His Wife' (Heb.), *Shenaton hamishpat ha'ivri*, 6–7 (1979/80), 133–76.

ELEAZAR OF WORMS, *Sefer roke'aḥ* (Jerusalem, 1968).

—— *Sha'arei sheḥitah uterefah*, ed. E. Kozme (Jerusalem, 2010).

ELON, MENAHEM, 'The Law, Books and Libraries', *National Jewish Law Review*, 2 (1987), 1–29.

EMANUEL, SIMCHA, 'Invalidating a Marriage Agreement' (Heb.), in G. Bacon et al. (eds.), *Studies on the History of the Jews in Ashkenaz, Presented to Eric Zimmer* [Meḥkarim betoledot yehudei ashkenaz: sefer yovel likhvod yitsḥak (erik) tsimer (Ramat Gan, 2008), 157–71.

——'The Origins and Career of R. Barukh b. Isaac' (Heb.), *Tarbiz*, 69 (2000), 423–40.

——'The Rabbis of Germany in the Thirteenth Century: Continuity or Crisis?' (Heb.), *Tarbiz*, 82 (2014), 549–67 (= id., 'German Sages in the Thirteenth Century: Continuity or Crisis?', *Frankfurter Judaistische Beitrage*, 39 (2014), 1–19).

—— *Shivrei luḥot* (Jerusalem, 2006).

——'"When the Master of the Universe Went Down to Egypt": On the History of a Paragraph in the Pesach Haggadah' (Heb.), *Tarbiz*, 77 (2008), 109–28.

EPSTEIN, Y. N., 'Likutim', *Hakedem*, 1 (1907/8), 129–30 (= id., *Studies in Talmudic Literature and in Semitic Languages* [Meḥkarim besifrut hatalmud uvilshonot shemiyot] (Jerusalem, 1984–91), ii. 771–2).

FINKELSTEIN, L., *Jewish Self-Government in the Middle Ages* (New York, 1969).

FUCHS, UZIEL, 'Studies in the *Sefer or zarua* by R. Isaac ben Moses of Vienna' [Iyunim besefer or zarua lerabi yitsḥak ben mosheh mivina], MA thesis (Hebrew University of Jerusalem, 1993).

FUSS, ABRAHAM, 'Written Testimony in Financial Legal Cases' (Heb.), *Shenaton hamishpat ha'ivri*, 3–4 (1975/6), 327–39.

GHEDALIA, MATANIAH, 'The Historical Background to the Writing of *Sefer even ha'ezer*' [Hareka hahistori likhetivat sefer even ha'ezer], MA thesis (Touro College Israel, 2012).

GROSS, HENRI, *Gallia Judaica* (Paris, 1897).

GROSSMAN, AVRAHAM, *The Early Sages of Ashkenaz: Their Lives, Leadership and Works (900–1096)* [Ḥakhmei ashkenaz harishonim: koroteihem, darkam behanhagat hatsibur, yetsiratam haruḥanit mereshit yeshivatam ve'ad ligezerat tatnu (1096)] (Jerusalem, 1981).

—— *The Early Sages of France: Their Lives, Leadership and Works* [Ḥakhmei tsarfat harishonim: koroteihem, darkam behanhagat hatsibur, yetsiratam haruḥanit] (Jerusalem, 1995).

Index to the Responsa of the Rabbinic Scholars in Germany, France and Italy [Mafte'aḥ hashe'elot vehateshuvot shel ḥakhmei ashkenaz, tsarfat ve'italyah], ed. B. Lifshitz and E. Shochetman (Jerusalem, 1977).

ISAAC BEN MOSES, *Sefer or zarua*, pts. 1–2 (Zhitomir, 1862); pts. 3–4 (Frankfurt, 1887).

ISAIAH DI TRANI, *Sefer hamakhria*, ed. S. A. Wertheimer (Jerusalem, 1998).

JAEGER, C. S., 'Pessimism in the Twelfth-Century Renaissance', *Speculum*, 78 (2003), 1151–83.

KANARFOGEL, EPHRAIM, 'The *'Aliyyah* of "Three Hundred Rabbis" in 1211: Tosafist Attitudes toward Settling in the Land of Israel', *Jewish Quarterly Review*, 76 (1986), 191–215.

——'Ashkenazi Messianic Calculations: From Rashi and His Contemporaries through the Period of the Tosafists' (Heb.), in A. Grossman and S. Japhet (eds.), *Rashi: His Image and His Works* [Rashi, demuto veyetsirato] (Jerusalem, 2008), 381–400.

——'Between Ashkenaz and Sefarad: Tosafist Teachings in the Talmudic Commentaries of Ritva', in E. Kanarfogel and M. Sokolow (eds.), *Between Rashi and Maimonides* (New York, 2010).

——'Changing Attitudes toward Apostates in Tosafist Literature', in E. Carlebach and J. J. Schacter (eds.), *New Perspectives on Jewish–Christian Relations* (Leiden, 2012), 297–327.

——'The Development and Diffusion of Unanimous Agreement in Medieval Ashkenaz', in I. Twersky and J. Harris (eds.), *Studies in Medieval Jewish History and Literature* (Cambridge, Mass., 2001), iii. 21–44.

——'Halakhah and *Mezi'ut* (Realia) in Medieval Ashkenaz: Surveying the Parameters and Defining the Limits', *Jewish Law Annual*, 14 (2003), 193–224.

—— *The Intellectual History and Rabbinic Culture of Medieval Ashkenaz* (Detroit, 2013).

—— *Jewish Education and Society in the High Middle Ages* (Detroit, 1992).

——'Medieval Rabbinic Conceptions of the Messianic Age: The View of the Tosafists', in E. Fleischer et al. (eds.), *Me'ah She'arim: Studies in Medieval Jewish Spiritual Life in Memory of Isadore Twersky* [Me'ah she'arim: sefer hazikaron leprofesor yitsḥak twersky] (Jerusalem, 2001), 147–70.

——'Midrashic Texts and Methods in Tosafist Torah Commentaries', in M. Fishbane and J. Weinberg (eds.), *Midrash Unbound: Transformations and Innovations* (Oxford, 2013), 267–319.

——*'Peering through the Lattices': Mystical, Magical and Pietistic Dimensions in the Tosafist Period* (Detroit, 2000).

——'Progress and Tradition in Medieval Ashkenaz', *Jewish History*, 14 (2000), 287–315.

——'R. Judah *he-Hasid* and the Rabbinic Scholars of Regensburg', *Jewish Quarterly Review*, 96 (2006), 17–37.

——'Rabbinic Authority and the Right to Open an Academy in Medieval Ashkenaz', *Michael*, 12 (1991), 233–50.

——'Returning to the Jewish Community in Medieval Ashkenaz: History and Halakhah', in M. A. Shmidman (ed.), *Turim: Studies in Jewish History and Literature Presented to Dr. Bernard Lander* (New York, 2007), 69–97.

——'Study of the Order of *Kodashim* and the Academic Aims and Self-Image of Rabbinic Scholars in Medieval Europe' (Heb.), in Yaron Ben-Naeh et al. (eds.), *Studies in Jewish History Presented to Joseph Hacker* [Asufah leyosef] (Jerusalem, 2014), 68–91.

——'Unanimity, Majority and Communal Government in Ashkenaz during the High Middle Ages: A Reassessment', *PAAJR*, 58 (1992), 79–106.

KATZ, JACOB, *The Shabbes Goy* [Goy shel shabat] (Jerusalem, 1984).

KUPFER, EPHRAIM, *Teshuvot ufesakim* (Jerusalem, 1973).

LEIBOWITZ, ARYEH, '*Tosafot Tukh* on the Talmud', Ph.D. diss. (Yeshiva University, 2012).

Maḥzor sukot, shemini atseret, vesimḥat torah, ed. D. Goldschmidt and Y. Fraenkel (Jerusalem, 1981).

MENDEL, PIERRE, 'Les Juifs à Metz', *Annales de l'est*, 31 (1979), 239–57.

——'Les Juifs à Metz avant 1552', *Mémoires de l'Académie nationale de Metz*, 15 (1971–2), 77–93.

MEWS, C.J., 'Scholastic Theology in a Monastic Milieu in the Twelfth Century: The Case of Admont', *Speculum*, 77 (2002), 217–39.

Rabi elazar mivermaiza—derashah lepesaḥ, ed. S. Emanuel (Jerusalem, 2006).

REINER, AVRAHAM (RAMI), 'The Acceptance of *Halakhot Gedolot* in Ashkenaz' (Heb.), in H. Kreisel (ed.), *Study and Knowledge in Jewish Thought*, 2 vols. (Heb. and Eng.) (Beer Sheva, 2006), ii. 95–121.

——'From France to Provence: The Assimilation of the Tosafists' Innovations in the Provencal Talmudic Tradition', *Journal of Jewish Studies*, 65 (2014), 77–87.

REINER, AVRAHAM (RAMI), 'From Rabbenu Tam to R. Isaac of Vienna: The Hegemony of the French Talmudic School in the Twelfth Century', in C. Cluse (ed.), *The Jews of Europe in the Middle Ages* (Turnhout, 2004), 273–82.

——'Rabbenu Tam and His Contemporaries: Connections, Influences, and His Methods of Talmud Study' [Rabenu tam uvenei doro: kesharim, hashpa'ot vedarkhei limudo batalmud], Ph.D. diss. (Hebrew University of Jerusalem, 2002).

——'Rabbenu Tam: His (French) Teachers and Ashkenazi Disciples' [Rabenu tam: rabotav (hatsarfatim) vetalmidav benei ashkenaz], MA thesis (Hebrew University of Jerusalem, 1997).

——'Rabbinical Courts in France in the Twelfth Century: Centralization and Dispersion', *Journal of Jewish Studies*, 60 (2009), 298–318.

—— 'The Titles of the Deceased on the Tombstones in the Wurzburg Cemetery, 1146–1346', *Tarbiz*, 78 (2008), 123–52.

REINER, ELHANAN, '*Aliyah* and Pilgrimage to the Land of Israel' [Aliyah ve'aliyah laregel le'erets yisra'el, 1099–1517], Ph.D. diss. (Hebrew University of Jerusalem, 1988).

Sefer arugat habosem lerabi avraham ben azri'el, ed. E. E. Urbach, 4 vols. (Jerusalem, 1963).

Sefer hayashar lerabenu tam (ḥelek haḥidushim), ed. Schlesinger (Jerusalem, 1974).

Sefer orḥot ḥayim lerabi aharon hakohen milunel (repr. Jerusalem, 1986).

Sefer ravan, ed. S. Z. Ehrenreich (Jerusalem, 1975).

Sefer ravyah, ed. A. Aptowitzer, 3 vols. (New York, 1983).

Sefer semak mizurich, ed. Y. Har-Shoshanim, 3 vols. (Jerusalem, 1973).

Sefer yere'im hashalem lerabi eliezer mimetz (Vilna, 1901).

SHEFFLER, D. L., *Schools and Schooling in Late Medieval Germany* (Leiden, 2008).

Sidur rabenu shelomoh migermaiza, ed. M. Hershler (Jerusalem, 1972).

SMITH, LESLIE, 'The Theological Framework', in M. Rubin and W. Simons (eds.), *The Cambridge History of Christianity in Western Europe, 1100–1500* (Cambridge, 2009), 75–88.

SOLOVEITCHIK, HAYM, 'Catastrophe and Halakhic Creativity: Ashkenaz—1096, 1242, 1306 and 1298', *Jewish History*, 12 (1998), 71–85.

——*Halakhah, Economy, and Self-Image* [Halakhah, kalkalah vedimui atsmi] (Jerusalem, 1985).

——'The Halakhic Isolation of the Ashkenazic Community', *Simon Dubnow Institute Yearbook*, 8 (2009), 41–7.

——'Pawnbroking: A Study in *Ribbit* and of the Halakhah in Exile', *Proceedings of the American Academy for Jewish Research*, 38–9 (1972), 203–68.

——'The Printed Page of the Talmud: The Commentaries and their Authors', in S. M. Mintz and G. G. Goldstein (eds.), *Printing the Talmud* (New York, 2005), 37–42.

——*Wine in Ashkenaz in the Middle Ages: Yeyn Nesekh—A Study in the History of Halakhah* [Hayayin biyemei habeinayim—yein nesekh: perek betoledot hahalakhah be'ashkenaz] (Jerusalem, 2008).

STRAUSS, DAVID, '*Pat 'Akkum* in Medieval France and Germany', MA thesis (Yeshiva University, 1979).

SUSSMAN, YA'AKOV, 'The Scholarly Oeuvre of Professor Ephraim Elimelekh Urbach' (Heb.), in D. Assaf (ed.), *Musaf mada'ei hayahadut*, 1 (Jerusalem, 1993), 7–116.

TA-SHMA, ISRAEL M., *Collected Studies in Medieval Rabbinic Literature* [Keneset meḥkarim: iyunim besifrut harabanim biyemei habeinayim], 3 vols. (Jerusalem, 2004–5).

——*Commentarial Literature on the Talmud* [Hasifrut haparshanit latalmud], 2 vols. (Jerusalem, 2000).

——*Early Franco-German Ritual and Custom* [Minhag ashkenaz hakadmon] (Jerusalem, 1992).

——*Ritual, Custom and Reality in Franco-Germany, 1000–1350* [Halakhah, minhag umetsi'ut be'ashkenaz, 1000–1350] (Jerusalem, 1996).

Teshuvot ba'alei hatosafot, ed. I. A. Agus (New York, 1954).

Teshuvot maharam mirothenburg veḥaverav, ed. Simcha Emanuel (Jerusalem, 2012).

Teshuvot maharshal (Jerusalem, 1969).

Teshuvot rabenu gershom me'or hagolah, ed. S. Eidelberg (New York, 1955).

Teshuvot rashi, ed. I. Elfenbein (New York, 1943).

Teshuvot ravyah, ed. D. Deblitzky (Benei Berak, 1989).

THOMSON, R. M., 'The Place of Germany in the Twelfth-Century Renaissance', in A. I. Beach (ed.), *Manuscripts and Monastic Culture* (Turnhout, 2007), 19–41.

——'Richard Southern and the Twelfth-Century Intellectual World', *Journal of Religious History*, 26 (2002), 264–73.

Tosafot rabi yehudah sirleon al masekhet berakhot, ed. N. Zaks, 2 vols. (Jerusalem, 1969).

Tosafot rid (Jerusalem, 1968).

URBACH, EPHRAIM ELIMELEKH, *The Tosafists: Their History, Writings, and Method* [Ba'alei hatosafot: toledoteihem, ḥibureihem, shitatam], 2 vols. (Jerusalem, 1980).

ZIMMER, ERIC, *Society and Its Customs: Studies in the History and Metamorphosis of Jewish Customs* [Olam keminhago noheg] (Ramat Gan, 1996).

CHAPTER EIGHT

Rabbinic Politics, Royal Conquest, and the Creation of a Halakhic Tradition in Medieval Provence

PINCHAS ROTH

THE JEWISH CULTURE of early medieval Europe is largely hidden by the mists of time, emerging into the light of surviving literary evidence only in the eleventh century. Figures such as R. Isaac ben Jacob of Fez (Alfasi) and R. Gershom ben Judah of Mainz provide a starting point for solid information about what rabbinic Judaism looked like in Spain and Germany. Although they were clearly not the first talmudic scholars to appear in those communities, it is very difficult to say anything with certainty about those who came before them. By the beginning of the twelfth century the talmudic academies of Spain and Germany were fully evolved, with a literary output that survives to this day and that allows historians to draw a fairly well-documented sketch of their culture.[1] In the second half of the eleventh century R. Solomon ben Isaac (Rashi) travelled from his home in northern France to the academies of the Rhineland, and on his return home inaugurated what would quickly become the most creative Talmud centre in medieval Europe.[2]

In southern France, however, the curtain did not rise until the mid-twelfth century, leaving historians to theorize about what was going on in the Midi while the Spanish and German academies were putting down roots.[3] Scholarly consensus detects an early Ashkenazi orientation in southern France; this corresponds to the area's subservience to the Carolingian empire

This study was written while I was a Scholar at the NYU Tikvah Center for Law and Jewish Civilization, and I am profoundly grateful to the Tikvah Center for the optimal conditions it afforded me in 2012–13.

[1] Grossman, *The Early Sages of Ashkenaz* (Heb.); id., 'Characteristics of the Yeshivas in Islamic Spain' (Heb.).

[2] Grossman, *The Early Sages of France* (Heb.).

[3] Benedikt, *The Torah Centre in Provence* (Heb.), 1–17; Ta-Shma, *Rabbi Zerahiah Halevi* (Heb.), 32–8; Mack, *The Mystery of Rabbi Moses Hadarshan* (Heb.).

and its successors.[4] During the first half of the twelfth century, however, contact with the Andalusian south began to increase, and it grew much more intense with the arrival in the southern French academies of Andalusian Jewish intellectuals who had fled the Almohad invasion.[5] This contact set the stage for one of the most dramatic cultural encounters of the Jewish Middle Ages—the correspondence between the sages of Montpellier and Moses Maimonides of Egypt.[6] Southern France became Maimonides' first and most stable foothold in Europe: his philosophical, scientific, and legal heritage was revered there for generations.[7]

An additional cultural influence arrived in southern France in the second half of the twelfth century.[8] The talmudic methodology of Rashi's grandsons, Samuel ben Meir (Rashbam) and Jacob ben Meir (Rabbenu Tam), moved southwards during their lifetime. Rashbam's commentary on the talmudic tractate of *Bava batra* was quoted in the 1130s by R. Abraham ben Isaac of Narbonne. R. Abraham's disciple, Isaac ben Abba Mari of Marseilles, sent legal questions to Rabbenu Tam that found their way into the writings of the great R. Abraham ben David (Rabad) of Posquières. Rabad's sparring partner, Zerahyah Halevi, became notorious for his near-slavish adoption of Rabbenu Tam's innovative talmudic explanations.

It fell to subsequent generations to make sense of these encounters and to forge them into a coherent halakhic tradition. Their attempt is the focus of the present essay. I have drawn my case studies from the responsa literature of the late thirteenth and early fourteenth centuries,[9] preserved primarily in two manuscripts. The first was published in 1967 by Abraham Sofer under the title *Teshuvot ḥakhmei provintsyah* (translated on the English title page as *Responsae of the Sages of Provence*).[10] The second manuscript has not been published in its entirety, but extensive selections were included in Israel Lévi's study of the manuscript published in serial form from 1899 to 1902.[11] These publica-

[4] Sussman, 'Rabad on *Shekalim*?' (Heb.); Zimmerman, 'Western Francia: The Southern Principalities'.

[5] Freudenthal, 'Arabic into Hebrew: The Emergence of the Translation Movement'.

[6] Sela, 'Queries on Astrology'; Kraemer, *Maimonides*, 426–43.

[7] Robinson, 'We Drink Only from the Master's Water'.

[8] Reiner, 'From France to Provence'.

[9] See more extensively Roth, 'Later Provençal Sages' (Heb.).

[10] *Teshuvot ḥakhmei provintsyah*, ed. Schreiber (Sofer). The manuscript now exists in two parts: MS Oxford, Bodleian, Neubauer cat. no. 2550; and MS London, British Library, Margoliouth cat. no. 572.

[11] MS Paris, Bibliothèque Nationale de France héb. 1391; Lévi, 'Un recueil de consultations inédites'.

tions notwithstanding, the responsa of late medieval southern France have received scant attention in the historical and rabbinic scholarship of the past century.

FROM TOULOUSE TO CORBEIL: CASES OF FRIVOLOUS MARRIAGE

The first major case discussed in *Teshuvot ḥakhmei provintsyah* relates to an act of marriage that probably took place in Toulouse around 1270.[12] Three men were eating together in a tavern, where they were joined by a woman named Hannah. They ate until there was no food left, and Hannah asked one of the men, whose name was Solomon, to give her a penny to buy pears. Reaching into his pocket, he pulled out a silver coin, more than enough to pay for the fruit. Hannah asked to see the coin, and when he passed it to her, the young man made the declaration, 'This coin is given to you for the purpose of *kidushin* [marriage].' Then he turned to his friends and said, 'You are my witnesses.'[13] On this basis Solomon claimed that Hannah was now his wife. Hannah did not dispute the facts of the case, but she claimed to have been totally unaware that Solomon was proposing marriage to her, or that her acceptance of the coin from him could have had any legal ramifications.

The case came before Nathan ben Moses, a respected rabbi in Toulouse.[14] He ruled that the marriage was not binding, but his ruling was apparently disputed; he therefore penned a responsum defending his position and distributed it to his rabbinic colleagues.[15] The manuscript collection contains responses he received from three areas—Narbonne, Chinon, and a rabbinic court in the area of Paris.[16] Three rabbis of northern France, including R. Isaac ben Joseph of Corbeil, author of the extremely popular legal work *Amudei hagolah* (also known as *Sefer mitsvot katan*, or *Semak*), expressed strong and fundamental disagreement with R. Nathan's position. Isaac of Corbeil declared the woman to be legally married and forbidden to marry anyone else without first receiving a divorce from Solomon.[17] R. Isaac ben Isaac of Chinon, described as 'head of the academies in France', addressed himself to Isaac of Corbeil and concurred with his position.[18] By contrast, Mordecai

[12] *Teshuvot ḥakhmei provintsyah*, 1–54.

[13] Ibid. 1–2.

[14] For his location in Toulouse see ibid. 86.

[15] Ibid. 2–17.

[16] Historians have suggested that Paris ceased to play a role in rabbinic history in the late 13th century. See Chazan, *Medieval Jewry in Northern France*, 188; Jordan, 'Archbishop Eudes Rigaud and the Jews of Normandy', 44 n. 26.

[17] *Teshuvot ḥakhmei provintsyah*, 17–24, 29–35.

[18] Ibid. 25–9. On Isaac ben Isaac of Chinon see Sirat, 'Un rituel juif de France', 30–3.

Kimhi and David ben Levi, rabbis and judges in Narbonne, expressed their unequivocal support for their counterpart in Toulouse.[19]

Within this debate, which split neatly between rabbis of northern and southern France, two legal issues were at stake. The first was whether the formal requirements of marriage had been met, and, specifically, whether the language used by Solomon when giving the coin to Hannah contained all the requisite components. The second was whether it was possible to take the context into account, and to conclude—from the tavern setting and the negotiations over dessert—that this act of marriage was never meant seriously, or at least that Hannah did not take it as a serious marriage offer. The bulk of the discussion among the various rabbis in this case was devoted to the first question, but it was on the second that they were most sharply divided. In his original responsum, Nathan ben Moses invoked Rabad of Posquières, the great twelfth-century sage of southern France; the latter provided a major precedent for the position that the marriage was invalid, inasmuch as the context of the marriage was not serious enough to assume that the woman had given real consent.[20] It was this position that provoked the most violent response from the northern court and led Isaac of Corbeil to accuse R. Nathan himself, or some earlier copyist, of having invented Rabad's ruling out of whole cloth.[21]

The question whether the circumstances under which a marriage act was performed can be used to disqualify the marriage and to sidestep more formal legal considerations has deep roots. It was debated by Christian canon lawyers, whose tradition emphasized the need for consent in order to contract the marriage.[22] In fact, law professors at the university of Toulouse in the late thirteenth century discussed a scenario very similar to the one described above: a girl of 13 named Berta became drunk at a party. She was cornered by some older boys, who pressured her to marry one of them, telling her that it was just a joke. After analysing the intent of the boy and Berta's mental and emotional state at the time, the professors concluded that the marriage was invalid—without ever considering the language that had been used to contract it.[23] Other canonists, however, attributed great significance to the language and paid less attention to the context. Peter Lombard wrote, 'if they express in words what they do not will in their hearts, then, if there is no

[19] *Teshuvot ḥakhmei provintsyah*, 35–46, 47–54. [20] Ibid. 13–14. [21] Ibid. 17.

[22] Donahue, *Law, Marriage, and Society*, 16–18 (with references to his earlier studies); Duggan, 'The Effect of Alexander III's "Rules on the Formation of Marriage"'; Reynolds, 'The Regional Origins of Theories about Marital Consent'.

[23] Meijers, *Responsa Doctorum Tholosanorum*, quaestio LV, pp. 133–6; Hine Mundy, *Men and Women at Toulouse*, 80.

coercion or fraud, that obligation of words by which they consent, saying "I take you as my husband, and I you as my wife", makes a marriage'.[24]

As R. Nathan of Toulouse pointed out, Rabad had privileged the element of consent in twelfth-century Languedoc. In his responsum, R. Mordecai Kimhi of Narbonne pointed to an earlier rabbinic precedent—Hai Gaon, the last great Babylonian decisor, who had died in Baghdad in 1038. Hai Gaon had encouraged communities to follow the example of his own grandfather, Hananyah Gaon, who had instituted a rule that automatically disqualified any marriage made without a proper ceremony or signing a *ketubah* (marriage contract).[25] In later generations this privileging of social context and bridal consent over the formalities of marriage terminology became a hallmark of Sephardi jurisprudence. By contrast, Ashkenazi rabbis tended to emphasize and investigate formal issues—for example the words used in proposing the marriage or the ownership and value of the object given to the woman.[26]

It is, therefore, worthwhile to regard R. Nathan's responsum as an exercise in rabbinic diplomacy. Nathan had already made his own decision as rabbi and judge in Toulouse. He probably chose to justify his decision in a letter sent to other rabbis because of opposition to his position—perhaps from within his community. His clear aim in composing the letter was to evoke support from his correspondents. Judging by the outcome, we can guess that the support from Narbonne was expected. But R. Nathan probably knew it would be more difficult to sell his position to the rabbis of the north, and he did what he could to improve his chances. First, he devoted almost the entire responsum to the formal question of the wording of the marriage proposal, and buried Rabad's controversial position regarding social context in the midst of his linguistic analysis. Second, he mentioned the names of many rabbis from Rashi's prominent northern French family, who were founding fathers and major figures of the Tosafist movement. In the space of just a few pages he quoted

[24] Lombard, *The Sentences—Book 4: On the Doctrine of Signs*, distinction 27: 3, p. 161. See also Donahue, *Law, Marriage, and Society*, 22.

[25] *Teshuvot ḥakhmei provintsyah*, 42. This concern with the formal setting of the wedding as not simply an indication of the participants' intentions but as a condition for the legitimacy of the ceremony is analogous to the problem in canon law of 'clandestine marriage', i.e. a marriage conducted without the presence of a priest or other ceremonial components. See Donahue, *Law, Marriage, and Society*, 4–6, 612–13; McSheffrey, *Marriage, Sex, and Civic Culture*, 28–32.

[26] For a striking example see Ouziel, *Mishpetei uzi'el*, v: *Even ha'ezer*, 169–75, 188–95. In the 1930s this question became coloured by political considerations as well. See Eliash, 'The Relations between the Chief Rabbinate and the Mandatory Government in Palestine' (Heb.), 393–5; ead., 'The Chief Rabbinate in Palestine and Fictitious Marriages during the 1930s' (Heb.), 87–90.

Rashi, his son-in-law R. Meir, three of Meir's sons—Rashbam, Rabbenu Tam, and their much less prominent brother Isaac—and Meir's great-grandson Elhanan ben Isaac.[27] Meir and Isaac ben Meir appear very rarely in halakhic discussions, and their comments on this topic, along with Nathan's quotations from Rashbam and R. Elhanan, are not known from any other source. Assuming that R. Nathan did not concoct these sources, he evidently went to great lengths to locate them. They were patently calculated to impress upon the readers of his responsum—and specifically those from northern France—that his own argument was well supported by the northern French Tosafist position.

This strategy failed to sway R. Isaac of Corbeil and his colleagues. Their response was negative and antagonistic, laced with insults and a lightly veiled threat of excommunication, and it emphasized the superiority of their own tradition and community.[28] The respondents from the south did not ignore the northerners' attitude. Mordecai Kimhi, in his closing lines, emphasized that Solomon, the young man from the tavern, should be punished 'by the elders of his people who are close to the gate of his town'.[29] R. Isaac of Chinon expressed his agreement with the stringent position of the northern rabbis, then begged R. Isaac of Corbeil to treat Nathan of Toulouse with respect.[30] It would have been unseemly, he claimed, for one with R. Isaac of Corbeil's reputation for saintliness to foment a fight.[31] Having made a passing reference to Isaac of Corbeil's own illustrious lineage, Isaac of Chinon then noted that Nathan of Toulouse was descended from R. Meshulam and was related to R. Yakar and R. Solomon the Pious. It seems likely that this Meshulam was R. Meshulam ben Nathan of Melun, a twelfth-century Provençal sage who travelled north, engaging in an intense series of arguments with Rabbenu Tam.[32] R. Yakar of Chinon was a contemporary of Yehiel of Paris—Isaac of Corbeil's father-in-law.[33] Through invoking these names, Isaac of Chinon

[27] Rashi—*Teshuvot ḥakhmei provintsyah*, 4; Rabbenu Tam—p. 7; R. Meir and R. Isaac ben Meir—p. 10; Rashbam—p. 11; R. Elhanan—p. 16.

[28] Isaac ben Joseph: 'For it is well known in Israel and Judah' (ibid. 17); 'who are they who dare to do thus, and who brought them this far?' (p. 20); Moses: 'These judges [*morim*] should not be ashamed to recant, for we see in regard to oil [JT *Shab.* 1: 3*d*] that [Rav was forced] to permit it or be declared a rebellious elder—all the more so for judges [*morim*] who issued an erroneously permissive ruling!' (p. 33). The term *morim*, which Moses used consistently to refer to Rabbi Nathan, can also be translated as 'rebels' (see Num. 20: 10).

[29] *Teshuvot ḥakhmei provintsyah*, 46.

[30] Ibid. 28–9.

[31] Kanarfogel, 'German Pietism in Northern France'.

[32] Reiner, 'Exegesis and Halakhah' (Heb.).

[33] Urbach, *The Tosafists* (Heb.), 578.

hoped to diminish any antagonism on the part of Isaac of Corbeil by convincing him that he and the rabbi of Toulouse belonged to the same rabbinic elite.

Isaac of Chinon also wrote to the rabbis of the south, addressing his letter to Nathan of Toulouse and the judges of Narbonne.[34] He conceded that he had erred in his earlier stringent ruling; it seemed quite possible that the marriage was invalid. However, he was not willing to release the woman on these grounds. Isaac tried to persuade the southern French rabbis to accept his position in the face of the fierce opposition from within the community and from the northern rabbis. His self-appointed role as intermediary between the sparring rabbis flowed from his personal connections with both sides, including family ties with R. Nathan himself.[35]

Despite the withering opposition of R. Isaac of Corbeil and the entreaties of R. Isaac of Chinon, the rabbis of southern France did not change their position. Decades later, sometime after 1306, a similar (if more extreme) case unfolded in Carpentras.[36] A group of friends was dining in a brothel.[37] One of the men gave his servant a *clement* to go out and buy wine.[38] When the servant came back after failing to find wine for sale, he returned the coin to his master, who then handed it to one of the prostitutes, saying that it was for the purpose of *kidushin*. The judges of Carpentras, who were notified of the occurrence, asked two prominent rabbis to express their opinion on the question of whether the prostitute was now considered married. R. Abba Mari ben Moses of Arles and R. Isaac Kimhi both responded that there were no grounds for considering the woman married, since the context made it amply clear that the marriage act was no more than a joke.[39] Kimhi made reference to the Toulouse case, in which his father, Mordecai Kimhi, had been a participant. The son chose to remember Isaac of Chinon's second letter as having totally capitulated to the position of the southern rabbis, rather than having issued a limited correction. And he even turned the staunch opposition of R. Isaac of Corbeil into a statement of support:[40]

[34] *Teshuvot ḥakhmei provintsyah*, 46–7.

[35] The family tree in Sirat, 'Un rituel juif de France', 32, is based on a misunderstanding of this source.

[36] *Teshuvot ḥakhmei provintsyah*, 108–23.

[37] On legal prostitution in southern France see Otis, *Prostitution in Medieval Society*; Rollo-Koster, 'From Prostitutes to Brides of Christ'. On Jewish prostitutes in medieval Spain see Assis, 'Sexual Behaviour in Mediaeval Hispano-Jewish Society', 44–5.

[38] On this coin, named after Pope Clement V, see Spufford, *Handbook of Medieval Exchange*, 123.

[39] On Abba Mari ben Moses see G. Stern, *Philosophy and Rabbinic Culture*, 115–28, 222–3.

[40] *Teshuvot ḥakhmei provintsyah*, 117–18.

A number of years ago a ruling was issued by Rabbi [David ben Levi], our relative, author of the *Mikhtam*, and by my father, may his memory be a blessing. The French rabbis, who were then of a venerable age and renowned, agreed with them and permitted her to marry without [first] receiving a divorce. And one rabbi, who was the greatest of the generation in France and had originally tried to be stringent, retracted his decision, saying, 'The things I said before you were mistaken.'

In the historical memory of the Kimhi family, and of Provençal rabbis more generally, the Toulouse case was one in which representatives of the southern French rabbinic tradition stood up to the Tosafists of northern France, and emerged victorious.

In fact, however, the Tosafists had not conceded defeat, nor did their successors in northern France show more respect for southern French rabbis in the years that followed. What did change in the intervening decades, from the case in Toulouse to the incident in Carpentras, was the political and demographic reality. The expanding presence of the French kingdom in the south, together with the escalating pressure exerted on Jews that culminated in the 1306 expulsion, led to an increase in the population of French Jews in the County of Provence, just beyond the borders of France.[41]

This commingling of Jewish groups almost inevitably resulted in social tension.[42] The southern French halakhic tradition was particularly vulnerable to attack.[43] Perhaps this was due to the late emergence of the southern French rabbinic tradition, a good century or more after the rabbis of Andalusia and Ashkenaz had established their authority. It can be argued that the Tosafist tradition included a strain of intolerance and an elitist ethos.[44] But it may also have been a reflection of a much larger process, whereby local civil authorities attempted to assert their own, palpably dwindling, authority in the face of Languedoc's ongoing assimilation into the kingdom of France, and the imposition of French law on the newly acquired territories.[45]

[41] Shatzmiller, *Recherches sur la communauté juive de Manosque*, 11–28. On the French presence in the south and its ramifications for the Jews see Jordan, *The French Monarchy and the Jews*, 105–27, 194–9. The growing pressure of the French monarchy on the Jews over the course of the 13th century is a central theme of Jordan's book, and of Chazan's *Medieval Jewry in Northern France*. The movement of Jews in the south from royal cities to other dominions is discussed in Jordan, *The French Monarchy and the Jews*, 165–8.

[42] Shatzmiller, 'Counterfeit of Coinage in England'.

[43] As illustrated by the bickering in Perpignan between adherents to the southern French customs and more recent arrivals from Catalonia that led to Menahem Hameiri's book *Magen avot*. Assis, '"Sefarad": A Definition', 29–37.

[44] Soloveitchik, 'Three Themes in the Sefer Hasidim'; id., 'The Halakhic Isolation of the Ashkenazic Community'.

[45] On this process and its southern malcontents see Given, *State and Society in Medieval*

THE POLITICS OF LITURGY: KOL NIDREI AS A FRENCH MISADVENTURE

In the years following the expulsion of the Jews from France, R. Isaac Kimhi emerged as the foremost halakhic respondent in Provence and the Dauphiné. He was asked to express his opinion on a component of liturgy, the famous and controversial Kol Nidrei:[46]

> You asked me, exalted officer—may God increase your honour and raise your station—about the version of Kol Nidrei which is written in some of the prayer books, whether it is proper to recite it on the eve of Yom Kippur or not. And to explain whether it is an absolution of vows made 'from the previous Yom Kippur to this Yom Kippur' or a condition absolving any vows made in the future, 'from this Yom Kippur to the next Yom Kippur'.

As a liturgical solution to the legal problem of binding vows, Kol Nidrei had aroused the opposition of rabbis since it first appeared in the tenth century. According to biblical and talmudic law, the absolution of a vow required a thorough investigation by a sage, who would ascertain whether the vow contained formal flaws or whether it had been made on the basis of erroneous assumptions. The Kol Nidrei prayer rendered this procedure obsolete by giving laypeople the power to cancel their own vows once a year. Hence the harsh words of Amram Gaon in his prayer book: 'It is a foolish custom and one is forbidden to do so.'[47] European communities with a strong allegiance to the Babylonian geonim, such as Andalusia and southern France, continued to resist the incorporation of Kol Nidrei into their liturgy, but in northern France it became an integral component of the Yom Kippur service.[48] R. Meir, Rashi's son-in-law, proposed a textual solution: instead of cancelling vows made in the previous year, the prayer would focus on the future; it could pre-empt the effectiveness of any vows that the congregant might make over the course of the coming year. This solution proved popular, but was often simply grafted onto the old, retrospectively focused version instead of replac-

Europe; Gardner, 'Practice and Rhetoric: Some Thirteenth-Century Perspectives'; Turning, *Municipal Officials, Their Public, and the Negotiation of Justice*, 17–41.

[46] MS Paris BnF 1391, fos. 48^{v}–49^{r} (Lévi, 'Un recueil de consultations inédites', 76–84; S. E. Stern, *Me'orot harishonim*, 118–22). For a responsum by Gersonides written in response to the same question see Touati, 'Le Problème du Kol Nidrey'.

[47] *Seder rav amram gaon*, ed. Goldschmidt, 163.

[48] Deshen, 'The Enigma of Kol Nidre' (Heb.).

ing it as R. Meir had intended.[49] It was also often identified with R. Meir's son, Rabbenu Tam.[50]

In his response, R. Kimhi presented the entire saga as a French liturgical misadventure that had been initiated by 'some of the Frenchmen' and then unsuccessfully emended by Rabbenu Tam:

> This custom, whichever version is chosen, is not a custom but an error, according to the straightforward tradition of the geonim of Babylonia and Sepharad, whose words guide us and whose practices we follow. That is why this custom was not mentioned by the Fathers of the World, Alfasi and Maimonides, in their works—because it goes against the roots of tradition. Today this custom has been eradicated in most places where there are great and learned sages . . . In the days of my late father [R. Mordecai Kimhi] I never saw anyone who even thought of saying Kol Nidrei in his presence, either in Narbonne or in any other place. And so we have done in his wake.

Kimhi made his allegiances perfectly clear. The historical foundations of his halakhic tradition—that of Narbonne, greatest of the pre-expulsion Provençal communities—lay in Andalusia and were expressed in the legal codes of Alfasi and Maimonides. Despite his bravado, though, Kimhi's response and the question itself make it clear that the French prayer was making major inroads in Provence. In fact, other sources confirm that the practice of reciting Kol Nidrei was already well established in Languedoc and Provence by the end of the twelfth century. Additionally, as mentioned above, the prayer did not originate in France, although the textual emendation on which Kimhi focused did.

BUTCHERS AND BAKERS AND COMMUNITY MAKERS

In other cases R. Isaac Kimhi expressed a surprisingly high degree of tolerance towards divergent customs within the Provençal community, especially in regard to French Jews who refused to accept indigenous Jewish practices. One of the best known of these was the custom of Narbonne regarding the lungs of a slaughtered animal.[51] According to the Talmud, an animal is deemed non-kosher if the lobes of its lungs have membranes, causing the lobes to adhere to each other.[52] Rashi explained that the adhesion was a sign of a hole in the lung, which excreted the liquid that stuck the lobes together.[53]

[49] Wieder, *The Formation of Jewish Liturgy* (Heb.), 372–81.

[50] Many medieval sources regard Rabbenu Tam as the author of this change. See Wieder, *The Formation of Jewish Liturgy* (Heb.), 368.

[51] Amar, 'The Laws of "Sirkhot hare'a"' (Heb.), 148–71.

[52] BT *Ḥul.* 46*b*.

[53] Rashi, *Ḥul.* 46*b*, s.v. *leit lehu bedikuta*.

According to the custom of Narbonne's Jews, however, if these membranes were short, wide, or numerous enough to ensure that the lobes would not separate—a situation described as *devek* (adhesion)—the animal could be eaten, possibly because the wound was then considered closed.[54] The custom came under harsh criticism even within the Narbonne community from the twelfth century onwards, but it had a venerable history and was followed by some well into the fourteenth century.[55]

R. Kimhi was asked about such a case: a kosher butcher had slaughtered an animal and, before flaying the skin, discovered that its lungs contained *devek*.[56] The butcher himself considered such meat to be non-kosher, but wondered whether he was permitted to continue preparing the meat for sale. He knew that if the meat was deemed non-kosher (*terefah*) he would be forbidden any monetary benefit from it. Basing himself on the position of Alfasi in another context, R. Kimhi claimed that, because there were some Jews in the community for whom the meat was permitted, it was to be considered 'for the purpose of food'.[57] He expressed no opinion about the relative worth of either position—the lenient Narbonnaise view held by part of the community, or the more stringent opinion of the butcher. Instead, he took for granted the fact that such differences existed within the community, and allowed the butcher to accept the other opinion as a legitimate one.

This tolerant attitude towards divergent and contradictory customs within the community emerges even more strikingly from another question Kimhi received from the same person:[58]

You wrote to me, my brother, about a certain French rabbi who did not want to eat the bread of Jews and instructed [his followers?] to purchase from the [non-Jewish] baker. You begged me to explain the matter to you, if I could. You should know, my brother, that this ruling was made some years ago by a few French rabbis . . . For it is the habit of the women of this land that when they put aside part of the dough in order to make sourdough, they take it out after removing the priestly portion [*ḥalah*] from the dough. Therefore it is now exempt from the priestly portion, and when it is used as sourdough for a fresh batch of dough, there are exempt and liable parts mixed

[54] Amar, 'The Laws of "Sirkhot hare'a"' (Heb.), 151–6; Meir ben Simeon Hame'ili, *Sefer hame'orot*, ed. Blau, 153. Rav Nahman (BT *Ḥul.* 58*a*) considered the possibility of the wound being stopped up.

[55] Amar, 'The Laws of "Sirkhot hare'a"' (Heb.), 164.

[56] MS Paris fo. 83v.

[57] Alfasi (BT *Pes.* 14*b* in the Alfasi foliation) allowed lay, i.e. non-priestly, Jews in the diaspora to bake bread on a festival (*yom tov*) without removing the priestly portion of *ḥalah* since a priest who was a minor could consume it, even though neither lay Jews nor adult priests could do so.

[58] MS Paris fos. 84v–85r.

together. The liable part is the fresh dough, provided it is large enough to be liable for *ḥalah*, and the exempt part is the sourdough added into it, which comes from dough that has already had *ḥalah* taken from it . . . Another reason is that the women nowadays are not careful to make the oven kosher. Thus, they consider every place to be one where there is no [Jewish] baker since in their opinion the Jewish bread is not baked properly and they buy from a non-Jewish baker.

The French rabbi's ruling, as described by the questioner, was extremely provocative. Although the prohibition against bread baked by non-Jews was often overlooked, even in talmudic times, it gave clear expression to the distinction between Jews and others.[59] Invocation of the halakhic category of 'a place where there is no Jewish baker'—and legitimation of the consumption of bread baked by non-Jews[60]—effectively rendered the local Jews invisible.

R. Kimhi's second explanation for the French rabbi's permission of the non-Jews' bread—the claim that the ovens used by the local Jewish women had not been made kosher—probably means that Jewish women in southern France did not practise a particular custom. In order to render the communal oven acceptable for their use, Jews participated in stoking the fire by throwing a twig into the bread-oven.[61] This custom became all the more important in the twelfth century, as bread-ovens in France and elsewhere increasingly became a feudal monopoly; this forced Jews to use the same ovens as all the other inhabitants of their towns.[62] However, the leading halakhists of southern France believed that tossing a twig into the oven was insufficient to revoke the status of non-Jewish bread; the dough itself had to be prepared by a Jew.[63] Kimhi could have framed the question of the twig as another difference of

[59] Freidenreich, *Foreigners and Their Food*, 76–83; id., 'Contextualizing Bread: An Analysis of Talmudic Discourse'.

[60] BT *AZ* 35*b*; Maimonides, *Mishneh torah*, 'Laws of Forbidden Foods', 17: 12. It must be borne in mind that northern French halakhah was traditionally extremely permissive of bread baked by non-Jews. See Strauss, 'Pat Akum in Medieval France and Germany', 17–26.

[61] In the context of bread-baking, this refers to a Jew throwing a twig into the bread-oven, which is considered Jewish participation in the baking process. On this custom, which was especially widespread in northern France, see Strauss, 'Pat Akum in Medieval France and Germany', 24–5, 38–41 (and see 53 n. 79 on the term 'making the oven kosher'). One of the French Jews of Manosque found himself on trial for attempted poisoning after he was caught tossing a twig into the town oven. See Shatzmiller, *Recherches sur la communauté juive de Manosque*, 131–3; Stouff, 'Les Juifs et l'alimentation en Provence', 142.

[62] See Shatzmiller, *Recherches sur la communauté juive de Manosque*, 132; Zimmer, 'Baking Practices and Bakeries in Medieval Ashkenaz' (Heb.); Stouff, *La Table Provençale*, 11–18.

[63] Abraham ben Isaac of Narbonne, *She'elot uteshuvot*, ed. Kafih, no. 216; Abraham ben David of Posquières, *Perush harabad al masekhet avodah zarah*, ed. Schreiber, 81–2; Menahem Hame'iri, *Beit habeḥirah al avodah zarah*, ed. Schreiber, 130. Nevertheless there were Jews in

custom between north and south, but instead he presented it only from the northern French perspective, thus implying that the southern custom was deficient in the eyes of French Jews.

French Jews and their rabbinic leadership preferred to imagine that, in moving southwards, they had reached a land with no pre-existing Jewish presence. They continued to follow their time-honoured customs and practices unselfconsciously, and without wondering how they might be seen by others. They continued to revere and follow their own religious leadership though those leaders might live far away. And they navigated their interactions with their non-Jewish surroundings oblivious to pre-existing local arrangements between Jews and non-Jews. Some further evidence suggests that this was in fact their policy. For example, in seeking to enforce his excommunication (*nidui*) of a defiant student, R. Barukh of Digne—a French rabbi living in Provence—turned to the rabbis of his home community in northern France for support.[64] His excommunicated disciple, Isaac Hakohen, who went on to become the rabbi of Manosque, was also from northern France, but he broke with the cultural conventions of his place of origin by enlisting the support of local southern rabbis from Avignon, Carpentras, and Arles (or Aix).[65] Upon hearing the news of excommunication, the rabbis of Avignon were indignant; they found the intervention of northern French rabbis in a local affair presumptuous:[66]

> Even if [Isaac of Manosque] should be considered worthy of *nidui*, and if the court or other sages are obliged to place him under ban, in our opinion this is purely the responsibility of the court in his own town or the one closest to him . . . Therefore I am baffled by the sages of France who declared a *nidui* in this matter. Even if their court should be considered a *beit va'ad* [superior court], they should have sent [a request] to the court in our land to summon him before them.

The Talmud allowed a *beit va'ad* to supersede the jurisdiction of local courts under certain circumstances.[67] Medieval commentators were divided over whether a superior court such as this could, or did, exist in their own times.

southern France who did follow this custom, which led their Christian neighbours to ask them about it (Talmage, *Apples of Gold in Settings of Silver*, 242).

[64] On the medieval Jewish community in Digne see Iancu-Agou, *Provincia Judaica*, 49–52.

[65] Shatzmiller, 'Rabbi Isaac ha-Cohen of Manosque and His Son', 73–5. The responses of the Provençal rabbis are found in de Lattes, *She'elot uteshuvot*, ed. Friedländer, 33–45.

[66] De Lattes, *She'elot uteshuvot*, ed. Friedländer, 40. The phenomenon of rabbis excommunicating each other became an acute problem in 15h-century Germany, a period that similarly saw major dislocations of Jewish communities and leadership; Yuval, *Scholars in Their Time* (Heb.), 404–23.

[67] Shochetman, *Civil Procedure in Jewish Law* (Heb.), 89–91, 445–7.

Maimonides and the French R. Samson of Sens believed that it could; it existed, they claimed, in any place where great rabbinic scholars were to be found.[68] The Jews of Avignon were prepared to recognize the French rabbis as superior to them in rabbinic learning and juristic expertise, and they offered this status as a charitable explanation for their behaviour. Even according to this explanation, however, the behaviour of the northern French rabbis was inexcusable, for they simply ignored the existence of local Provençal courts and their claim to jurisdiction over all Jews living in Provence, including those from the north.

For the Provençal rabbis, being a cultural minority within Judaism was not a new experience. For generations they had been dominated by larger and more vocal Jewish centres and they were under no illusion that theirs was the only extant rabbinic tradition.[69] Their goal was to follow their own path, faithful to local practices while cognizant of nearby developments.[70] It was unthinkable for Isaac Kimhi and his colleagues to change the traditional liturgy because of French influence, but they thought it unremarkable that French Jews followed a divergent ruling on the baking of bread in the ovens of non-Jews. Nevertheless the onslaught of northern French rabbinic culture was as instrumental in the formation of a Provençal Jewish identity as it was in the emergence of an Occitan Christian one.[71]

[68] Fuchs, 'Three New Responsa of R. Isaac of Vienna' (Heb.), 127–31; Ta-Shma, 'What is the Significance of *Bet-Din Hashuv*?' (Heb.), 335–45.

[69] On the influences from Andalusia and northern France see above.

[70] On their complex relationship with Hispanic halakhists see Emanuel, 'La Lutte pour l'indépendance halakhique de la Provence', 45–55.

[71] Cheyette, *Ermengard of Narbonne and the World of the Troubadours*, 41; Paterson, *Culture and Society in Medieval Occitania*, ch. 1.

Bibliography

ABRAHAM BEN DAVID OF POSQUIÈRES, *Perush hara'abad al masekhet avodah zarah*, ed. Abraham Schreiber (Sofer) (New York, 1960).

ABRAHAM BEN ISAAC OF NARBONNE, *She'elot uteshuvot*, ed. Yosef Kafih (Jerusalem, 1962).

AMAR, MOSHE, 'The Laws of "Sirkhot hare'a" (Lung Adhesions): Their Origins and Evolution in Jewish Practice' [Dinei sirkhot hare'ah: mekoram vehitpatḥutam], Ph.D. diss. (Bar Ilan University, 1997).

ASSIS, YOM TOV, '"Sefarad": A Definition in the Context of a Cultural Encounter', in Carlos Carrete Parrondo et al. (eds.), *Encuentros and Desencuentros: Spanish Jewish Cultural Interaction throughout History* (Tel Aviv, 2000), 29–37.

——'Sexual Beḥaviour in Mediaeval Hispano-Jewish Society', in Ada Rapoport-Albert and Steven J. Zipperstein (eds.), *Jewish History: Essays in Honour of Chimen Abramsky* (London, 1988), 25–59.

BENEDIKT, B. Z., *The Torah Centre in Provence* [Merkaz hatorah beprovans] (Jerusalem, 1985).

CHAZAN, ROBERT, *Medieval Jewry in Northern France: A Political and Social History* (Baltimore, 1973).

CHEYETTE, FREDRIC L., *Ermengard of Narbonne and the World of the Troubadours* (Ithaca, NY, 2001).

DE LATTES, ISAAC BEN IMMANUEL, *She'elot uteshuvot*, ed. Markus Hirsch Friedländer (Vienna, 1860).

DESHEN, SHLOMO, 'The Enigma of Kol Nidre: An Anthropological and Historical Investigation' (Heb.), in Immanuel Etkes and Yosef Salmon (eds.), *Studies in the History of Jewish Society in the Middle Ages and in the Modern Period* (Jerusalem, 1980), 136–53.

DONAHUE, CHARLES, *Law, Marriage, and Society in the Later Middle Ages* (Cambridge, 2007).

DUGGAN, ANNE J., 'The Effect of Alexander III's "Rules on the Formation of Marriage" in Angevin England', *Anglo-Norman Studies*, 33 (2010), 1–22.

ELIASH, SHULAMIT, 'The Chief Rabbinate in Palestine and Fictitious Marriages during the 1930s' (Heb.), *Sinai*, 91 (1984), 86–90.

——'The Relations between the Chief Rabbinate and the Mandatory Government in Palestine (1936–1945)' [Hayaḥasim bein harabanut harashit le'erets yisra'el vehashilton hamandatori, 1936–1945], Ph.D. diss. (Bar Ilan University, 1979).

EMANUEL, SIMCHA, 'La Lutte pour l'indépendance halakhique de la Provence au XIIIe siècle', in Danièle Iancu-Agou (ed.), *Philippe le Bel et les Juifs du royaume de France (1306)* (Paris, 2012), 45–55.

FREIDENREICH, DAVID, 'Contextualizing Bread: An Analysis of Talmudic Discourse in Light of Christian and Islamic Counterparts', *Journal of the American Academy of Religion*, 80 (2012), 411–33.

——*Foreigners and Their Food: Constructing Otherness in Jewish, Christian, and Islamic Law* (Berkeley, Calif., 2011).

FREUDENTHAL, GAD, 'Arabic into Hebrew: The Emergence of the Translation Movement in Twelfth-Century Provence and Jewish–Christian Polemic', in David M. Freidenreich and Miriam Goldstein (eds.), *Beyond Religious Borders: Interaction and Intellectual Exchange in the Medieval Islamic World* (Philadelphia, 2012), 124–43.

FUCHS, UZIEL, 'Three New Responsa of R. Isaac of Vienna' (Heb.), *Tarbiz*, 70 (2000), 109–132.

GARDNER, CHRISTOPHER K., 'Practice and Rhetoric: Some Thirteenth-Century Perspectives on the Legal Frontier Between "France" and Toulouse', in

O. Merisalo (ed.), *Frontiers in the Middle Ages: Proceedings of the Third European Congress of Medieval Studies* (Louvain-la-Neuve, 2006), 223–35.

GIVEN, JAMES B., *State and Society in Medieval Europe: Gwynedd and Languedoc under Outside Rule* (Ithaca, NY, 1990).

GROSSMAN, AVRAHAM, 'Characteristics of the Yeshivas in Islamic Spain' (Heb.), in Immanuel Etkes (ed.), *Yeshivas and Batei Midrash* [Yeshivot uvatei midrashot] (Jerusalem, 2006), 57–73.

—— *The Early Sages of Ashkenaz: Their Lives, Leadership and Works (900–1096)* [Ḥakhmei ashkenaz harishonim: koroteihem, darkam behanhagat hatsibur, yetsiratam haruḥanit mereshit yeshivatam ve'ad ligezerat tatnu (1096)] (Jerusalem, 1981).

—— *The Early Sages of France: Their Lives, Leadership and Works* [Ḥakhmei tsarfat harishonim: koroteihem, darkam behanhagat hatsibur, yetsiratam haruḥanit] (Jerusalem, 1995).

HINE MUNDY, JOHN, *Men and Women at Toulouse in the Age of the Cathars* (Toronto, 1990).

IANCU-AGOU, DANIELE, *Provincia Judaica: Dictionnaire de géographie historique des Juifs en Provence médiévale* (Paris, 2010).

JORDAN, WILLIAM CHESTER, 'Archbishop Eudes Rigaud and the Jews of Normandy, 1248–1275', in Steven J. McMichael and Susan E. Meyers (eds.), *Friars and Jews in the Middle Ages and Renaissance* (Leiden, 2004), 39–52.

—— *The French Monarchy and the Jews: From Philip Augustus to the Last Capetians* (Philadelphia, 1989).

KANARFOGEL, EPHRAIM, 'German Pietism in Northern France: The Case of R. Isaac of Corbeil', in Yaakov Elman and Jeffrey S. Gurock (eds.), *Hazon Nahum: Studies in Jewish Law, Thought and History Presented to Dr. Norman Lamm* (New York, 1997), 207–27.

KRAEMER, JOEL L., *Maimonides: The Life and World of One of Civilization's Greatest Minds* (New York, 2008).

LEVI, ISRAEL, 'Un recueil de consultations inédites de rabbins de la France méridionale', *REJ*, 38 (1899), 103–22; 39 (1899), 76–84, 226–41; 43 (1901), 237–58; 44 (1902), 73–86.

LOMBARD, PETER, *The Sentences—Book 4: On the Doctrine of Signs*, trans. Giulio Silano (Toronto, 2010).

MACK, HANANEL, *The Mystery of Rabbi Moses Hadarshan* [Misodo shel rabi mosheh hadarshan] (Jerusalem, 2010).

MCSHEFFREY, SHANNON, *Marriage, Sex, and Civic Culture in Late Medieval London* (Philadelphia, 2006).

MEIJERS, E. M., *Responsa Doctorum Tholosanorum* (Haarlem, 1938).

MEIR BEN SIMEON HAME'ILI, *Sefer hame'orot vesefer hahashlamah al masekhtot mo'ed katan veḥulin*, ed. M. Y. Blau (Brooklyn, 1964).

MENAHEM HAME'IRI, *Beit habeḥirah al masekhet avodah zarah*, ed. Abraham Schreiber (Sofer) (Jerusalem, 1965).

OTIS, LEAH LYDIA, *Prostitution in Medieval Society: The History of an Urban Institution in Languedoc* (Chicago, 1985).

OUZIEL, BEN-ZION MEIR HAI, *Mishpetei uzi'el*, v: *Even ha'ezer* (Jerusalem, 2002).

PATERSON, LINDA M., *Culture and Society in Medieval Occitania* (Ashgate, 2011).

REINER, AVRAHAM (RAMI), 'Exegesis and Halakhah: A Return to the Study of the Polemic between Rabbenu Tam and Rabbenu Meshulam' (Heb.), *Annual of the Institute for Research in Jewish Law*, 21 (2000), 207–39.

—— 'From France to Provence: The Assimilation of the Tosafists' Innovations in the Provençal Talmudic Tradition', *Journal of Jewish Studies*, 65 (2014), 77–87.

REYNOLDS, PHILIP L., 'The Regional Origins of Theories about Marital Consent and Consummation during the Twelfth Century', in Mia Korpiola (ed.), *Regional Variations in Matrimonial Law and Custom in Europe, 1150–1600* (Boston, 2011), 43–75.

ROBINSON, JAMES T., 'We Drink Only from the Master's Water: Maimonides and Maimonideanism in Southern France, 1200–1306', *Studia Rosenthaliana*, 40 (2007–8), 27–60.

ROLLO-KOSTER, JOËLLE, 'From Prostitutes to Brides of Christ: The Avignonese *Repenties* in the Late Middle Ages', *Journal of Medieval and Early Modern Studies*, 32 (2002), 109–44.

ROTH, PINCHAS, 'Later Provençal Sages: Jewish Law (Halakhah) and Rabbis in Southern France, 1215–1348' [Hakhmei provans hame'uḥarim: halakhah ufoskei halakhah bidrom tsarfat, 1215–1348], Ph.D. diss. (Hebrew University of Jerusalem, 2012).

Seder rav amram gaon, ed. Daniel Goldschmidt (Jerusalem, 1971).

SELA, SHLOMO, 'Queries on Astrology Sent from Southern France to Maimonides: Critical Edition of the Hebrew Text, Translation, and Commentary', *Aleph*, 4 (2004), 89–190.

SHATZMILLER, JOSEPH, 'Counterfeit of Coinage in England of the Thirteenth Century and the Way It Was Remembered in Medieval Provence', *Moneda y Monedas en la Europa Medieval* (= *Actas de la XXVI Semana de Estudios Medievales de Estella*) (Pamplona, 2000), 387–97.

—— 'Rabbi Isaac ha-Cohen of Manosque and His Son Rabbi Peretz: The Rabbinate and Its Professionalization in the Fourteenth Century', in Ada Rapoport-Albert and Steven J. Zipperstein (eds.), *Jewish History: Essays in Honour of Chimen Abramsky* (London, 1988), 61–83.

—— *Recherches sur la communauté juive de Manosque au Moyen Âge, 1241–1329* (Paris, 1972).

SHOCHETMAN, ELIAV, *Civil Procedure in Jewish Law* [Seder hadin le'or mekorot hamishpat ha'ivri] (Jerusalem, 1988).

SIRAT, COLETTE, 'Un rituel juif de France: Le Manuscrit hébreu 633 de la Bibliothèque nationale de Paris', *REJ*, 119 (1961), 7–40.

SOLOVEITCHIK, HAYM, 'The Halakhic Isolation of the Ashkenazic Community', *Simon Dubnow Institute Yearbook*, 8 (2009), 41–7.

—— 'Three Themes in the *Sefer Ḥasidim*', *AJS Review*, 1 (1976), 339–54.

SPUFFORD, PETER, *Handbook of Medieval Exchange* (London, 1986).

STERN, GREGG, *Philosophy and Rabbinic Culture: Jewish Interpretation and Controversy in Medieval Languedoc* (London, 2009).

STERN, SHEMUEL ELIEZER, *Me'orot harishonim* (Bene Berak, 2002).

STOUFF, LOUIS, 'Les Juifs et l'alimentation en Provence à la fin de la période médiévale', in Carol Iancu (ed.), *Armand Lunel et les Juifs du Midi* (Montpellier, 1986), 141–53.

—— *La Table Provençale: Boire et manger en Provence à la fin du Moyen Age* (Avignon, 1996).

STRAUSS, DAVID L., 'Pat Akum in Medieval France and Germany', MA thesis (Yeshiva University, 1979).

SUSSMAN, YA'AKOV, 'Rabad on *Shekalim*? A Bibliographical and Historical Riddle' (Heb.), in Ezra Fleischer et al. (eds.), *Me'ah She'arim: Studies in Medieval Jewish Spiritual Life in Memory of Isadore Twersky* [Me'ah she'arim: sefer hazikaron liprof. yitsḥak twersky] (Jerusalem, 2001), 150–61.

TALMAGE, FRANK, *Apples of Gold in Settings of Silver: Studies in Medieval Jewish Exegesis and Polemics* (Toronto, 1999).

TA-SHMA, ISRAEL M., *Rabbi Zerahiah ha-Levi, the Author of Ha-Maor, and His Circle* [Rabi zeraḥiah halevi: ba'al hama'or uvenei ḥugo] (Jerusalem, 1992).

—— 'What Is the Significance of *Bet-Din Hashuv*?' (Heb.), in Ya'akov Habba and Amihai Radzyner (eds.), *Studies in Jewish Law: Judge and Judging* [Iyunim bemishpat ivri uvehalakhah: dayan vediyun] (Ramat Gan, 2007), 335–45.

Teshuvot ḥakhmei provintsyah, ed. Abraham Schreiber (Sofer) (Jerusalem, 1967).

TOUATI, CHARLES, 'Le Problème du Kol Nidrey et le responsum inédit de Gersonide (Lévi ben Gershom)', *REJ*, 154 (1995), 327–42.

TURNING, PATRICIA, *Municipal Officials, Their Public, and the Negotiation of Justice in Medieval Languedoc: Fear Not the Madness of the Raging Mob* (Leiden, 2013).

URBACH, EPHRAIM ELIMELEKH, *The Tosafists: Their History, Writings, and Method* [Ba'alei hatosafot: toledoteihem, ḥibureihem, shitatam], 2 vols. (Jerusalem, 1980).

WIEDER, NAPHTALI, *The Formation of Jewish Liturgy in the East and the West: A Collection of Essays* [Hitgabshut nusaḥ hatefilah bamizraḥ uvama'arav] (Jerusalem, 1998).

YUVAL, ISRAEL JACOB, *Scholars in Their Time: The Religious Leadership of German Jewry in the Late Middle Ages* [Ḥakhamim bedoram: hamanhigut haruḥanit shel yehudei germanyah beshilhei yemei habeinayim] (Jerusalem, 1988).

ZIMMER, ERIC, 'Baking Practices and Bakeries in Medieval Ashkenaz' (Heb.), *Zion*, 65 (2000), 141–62.

ZIMMERMAN, MICHEL, 'Western Francia: The Southern Principalities', in Timothy Reuter (ed.), *The New Cambridge Medieval History*, iii: *c.900–c.1024* (Cambridge, 1999), 420–55.

CHAPTER NINE

Mediterranean Regionalism in Hebrew Panegyric Poetry

JONATHAN DECTER

ONE RECOGNIZED yet under-appreciated resource for studying Jewish culture in the medieval Mediterranean is the Hebrew panegyric corpus. Anathema to the tastes of scholars of Jewish literature and a frustratingly ungenerous source for scholars of Jewish history, Hebrew panegyrics have largely been discounted as mere sycophantic dedications, often composed for pay, that occasionally yield titbits of factual data. It is true that, for the most part, panegyrics offer typology, not biography. However, properly read, the several hundred surviving Hebrew panegyrics illuminate medieval Mediterranean Jews' most essential notions of group cohesion, human virtue, leadership, and politics.

In the Islamic Mediterranean, Hebrew panegyrics were composed in all major centres, most often for figures proximate to their authors but often across distances. They were composed for men who held transregional positions of power (such as geonim and exilarchs), for their appointees and supporters in satellite communities, and for the local leadership (including *negidim*, heads of the Jews, judges, and cantors). They were also exchanged among other types of intellectuals (poets, grammarians, etc.) as well as among merchants (the categories could overlap). The practice of panegyric writing similarly became widespread among Jews in Christian Mediterranean centres as these developed significant concentrations of Jewish population. The panegyric corpus thus offers a series of cross-sections of Jewish society in the medieval Mediterranean—from the macrostructures of transregional leadership down to circles of intellectuals and merchants, and even individual friendships. Further, they elucidate how given individuals were ensconced within multiple networks simultaneously. Judah Halevi wrote panegyrics for

I wish to thank Arnold Franklin and Raymond Scheindlin for reading an earlier draft of this essay.

Jewish dignitaries in Egypt, for travelling merchants, countless poets, grammarians, and rabbinic scholars in al-Andalus, as well as for Jewish leaders in Christian Castile. Eleazar ben Jacob Habavli wrote for men of rank in Baghdad who bore political sobriquets such as *najm al-dawla* (Star of the State) and *amīn al-dawla* (Security of the State), for Abraham son of Moses Maimonides in Egypt, and for a certain Joseph concerning the mundane subject of 'settling accounts' between author and addressee.[1]

In the discussion below I offer a few general comments about the nature of Jewish panegyric and the language of Jewish political legitimacy that was common throughout the Mediterranean, and then turn to the particular subject of regional variation.[2]

THE POETICS OF JEWISH LEGITIMACY

As stated, panegyrics are a relatively poor source for biographical reconstruction. It seems that addressees did not desire personalized representations of themselves so much as portrayals of ideal social types that they were said to embody. Yet it is precisely this point that makes panegyrics a valuable source for the study of notions of leadership. Panegyric has been utilized to study idealized representations of political legitimacy with respect to emperors in late antiquity, caliphs, English monarchs, and others.[3] Literary representations of leaders tend to pass over individual characteristics in favour of fairly stable and conventional images. They change slowly, are culturally determined, and are contingent upon historical circumstances. Like visual portraits, panegyrics operate according to a code of cultural norms that tell us at

[1] Van Bekkum, *The Secular Poetry of El'azar Ben Ya'aqov ha-Bavli*; for these specific poems see 79, 119, 158. Panegyrics also deepen our knowledge about subjects such as Rabbanite–Karaite relations; even Judah al-Harizi, who fictionalized a vigorous debate wherein a Rabbanite trounces a Karaite interlocutor, composed panegyrics for flesh-and-blood Karaites in Syria. See Beeri, 'Eli ben Amram' (Heb.); Yeshaya, *Medieval Hebrew Poetry in Muslim Egypt*, e.g. 54–6; Fleischer, 'Collections of Paronomastic Poems by Judah al-Harizi' (Heb.), iii. 1077–1173. Some other panegyrics are treated in Rustow, *Heresy and the Politics of Community*.

[2] My forthcoming book on the subject of Jewish panegyric from social, ethical, literary, political, and theological perspectives is entitled *Dominion Built of Praise: Panegyric and Legitimacy among Jews in the Medieval Mediterranean*.

[3] Relevant examples of other panegyric studies include: Whitby (ed.), *The Propaganda of Power*; Rees, *Layers of Loyalty in Latin Panegyric*; Roche, *Pliny's Praise*; Hägg, Rousseau, and Høgel (eds.), *Greek Biography and Panegyric*; Gruendler, *Medieval Arabic Praise Poetry*; Stetkevych, *The Mantle Odes: Arabic Praise Poems to the Prophet Muhammad*; ead., *The Poetics of Islamic Legitimacy*; Safran, 'The Command of the Faithful in al-Andalus'; Hackett, 'Dreams or Designs, Cults or Constructions?'

least as much, or usually more, about the society that produced them as about the individuals they portray. For these reasons seemingly minor shifts within a highly conventional corpus of praise literature can be of great value—both to literary scholars and to historians—not because they reveal much about the biographies of the leaders in question, but because they represent shifting ideals of leadership itself.

The most immediate context for the practice of medieval Hebrew panegyric was panegyric in the classical Islamic world, where it played an essential role in state propaganda and in the promotion of the caliphal image. Apart from general praiseworthy characteristics such as generosity and valour, caliphs and governors were praised for the nobility and purity of their lineage, their suppression of religious dissidents, their power to thwart enemies, and the eloquence of their tongues and pens in classical Arabic. Poets often concluded panegyrics with hopes for the addressee's long life, for it was through him that the best of all political circumstances were sustained.[4]

A systematic study of Jewish panegyric, at least with respect to figures who, in some sense, held power, reveals a language of political legitimacy that combines elements of the 'Jewish political tradition' with the contemporary idiom of Islamic power. Qualities such as modesty, wisdom, and generosity are mediated through archetypal figures of Israel's ancient past and are combined with images of eloquence, ascension over enemies, and the suppression of heretics. A seemingly universal characteristic such as humility, for example, can be shown to reverberate against highly specific diachronic and synchronic images of legitimacy. Thus, humility is the noted character trait of Israel's archetypal leader, Moses (Exod. 12: 3), and several passages in Proverbs extol this virtue (for example 22: 4). It is highlighted in Judaeo-Arabic ethical treatises,[5] and has a prominent place in Jewish political writing in particular; Maimonides stresses the trait among the requisite qualities of Israelite kings.[6]

Similarly, humility is strongly associated with Muhammad and the early caliphs, and is frequently emphasized in Islamic political writing as a requisite quality of the ruler. The great literary anthology known as *al-ʿiqd al-farīd* (The Unique Necklace) by the Andalusian poet and anthologist Ibn ʿAbd Rabbih (860–940) opens with a book on the ruler that contains a chapter on humility, with sayings on this theme by the Prophet, the caliphs, and various

[4] See Gruendler, *Medieval Arabic Praise Poetry*, and Stetkevych, *The Mantle Odes: Arabic Praise Poems to the Prophet Muhammad.*

[5] See e.g. Ibn Gabirol, *The Improvement of the Moral Qualities*, 63–5.

[6] Maimonides, *Mishneh torah*, 'Laws of Kings and Their Wars', 2: 6–11.

poets. Typical are the statements of ʿAbd al-Malik b. Marwān—'The greatest of men is he who has humility concerning high rank, who swears off of dominion, and who apportions power'; Ibn al-Sammāk—'Your humility concerning your nobility is [even] greater than your nobility!'—and the verses by Ibn al-ʿAtāhiyya:

> If you wish to see the most honoured among all men,
> look at a king in the garb of a beggar.
> This is the one for whom God magnified His favour;
> this one is fitting for the world and religion [*al-dunyā wa-al-dīn*].[7]

It is thus not surprising that we find a Hebrew formulary preserved in the Cairo Genizah that presents the following suggested introduction for addressing a gaon:

> To the lord of Israel, their leader and prince, their pride, wonder, and crown, their judge, light, and flame: To whom can I liken and compare his copious [knowledge of] Torah, his dear wisdom, his sought-out intelligence, his known humility and famed modesty, his known honesty, his faith, his righteousness?

Isaac Ibn Khalfun praised Ibrāhīm ibn ʿAtā' of Kairouan as wise, courageous, generous, and humble: 'he is superior like the palm, but humble like the hyssop'.[8] To Abū Isḥaq Ibn Māṭir, Moses Ibn Ezra wrote, 'He walks with men and God in humility; wisdom is with the modest' (cf. Prov. 11: 2).[9] Ibn Ezra praised another figure with the following words: 'He is pure; his Torah grows by the day but so does his humility! How he fled from dominion but it pursued him.'[10] The humility of Moses was so paradigmatic that it could be exploited with only the slightest allusion: '[He has] the countenance of a lion yet his humility is like *his* humility. Never has there been one like him in Israel!'[11]

It is clear, then, that humility, more than a general character trait that should be cultivated by all, was linked specifically with the legitimation of leadership. Conversely, a lack of humility was enough to declare a person an illegitimate leader and to disqualify him from office. Ephraim ben Shemaryah, a representative of the Jerusalem academy in Fustat, was sometimes accused of being haughty and, perhaps as (over)compensation, he referred to himself as 'the meek and poor'.[12] A Rabbanite heresiography recounts that Anan ben David, the figure associated with the founding of Karaism, was not

[7] All of these are contained in Ibn ʿAbd Rabbih, *Al-ʿiqd al-farīd*, i. 35–6. See also ii. 201.

[8] See Brener, *Isaac Ibn Khalfun*, 116–17.

[9] Ibn Ezra, *Shirei haḥol*, i. 170–1 [172], l. 24.

[10] Ibid. 191 [192], ll. 3–4.

[11] Ibid. 315 [*Sefer ha'anak*, 1: 71].

[12] Bareket, *Fustat on the Nile*, 133.

selected for the exilarchate despite his impressive learning and Davidic lineage because of his 'lawlessness and lack of piety'; instead, his younger brother Hananyah was chosen, due to his 'great modesty'.[13] A letter sent on behalf of the community of Alexandria to Judah Halevi, then residing in Fustat, complains of a leader 'who loves dominance and strife'. As Miriam Frenkel points out, love of rule is often cited as a trait that makes one wicked; humility is the ideal.[14] In the late twelfth century Abraham Ibn Daud identified modesty as the one character trait that Joseph, son of Samuel Hanagid, did not inherit from his father; this deficiency caused his downfall and precipitated the massacre of the Jews of Granada in 1066.[15] We will probably never know exactly which leaders of the medieval Jewish world were truly modest and which were haughty; what is clear is that humility was a central aspect of political legitimacy that resonated with contemporary Islamic and Jewish discourses of power and, as such, was emphasized in Hebrew panegyric throughout the Mediterranean.

REGIONALISM

Despite their highly conventional character, panegyrics can also shed light on the subject of regionalism. First, they often elucidate the dynamics between the great academies of Iraq and Palestine and their respective satellite communities. A fascinating case in this regard is al-Andalus, which has commonly been viewed as the prime example of a local leadership that broke away from Iraqi moorings. *Sefer hakabalah* (The Book of Tradition) by Abraham Ibn Daud, the proud Andalusian chronicler who wrote from Castile in 1161, after the fall of Andalusian Jewry during the Almohad revolution, portrays the decline of the great academies of Baghdad in the tenth century and the 'divinely ordained' rise of an independent Andalusian academy just before that. As he relates it, 'the King [the Andalusian Caliph ʿAbd al-Raḥmān III] . . . was delighted by the fact that the Jews of his domain no longer had need of the people of Babylonia'.[16] Although Ibn Daud's representation has held powerful sway over the reconstruction of events, his portrayal of Baghdad's

[13] Nemoy, *Karaite Anthology*, 4.

[14] Frenkel, *The Compassionate and the Benevolent* (Heb.), 200. See also the invective by Ibn Ezra in *Shirei haḥol*, i. 221–2 [218], ll. 14–15: 'You have been prideful! You dwell apart like a watering garden but our souls are dry. With the act of your hand you have acted haughtily like a ruler [*moshel*], such that you have become a byword [*mashal*] [of cruelty] in the mouth of every man and woman!' See also Ben-Shammai, 'The Judeo-Arabic Vocabulary of Sa'adia's Bible Translation'.

[15] Ibn Daud, *Sefer ha-Qabbalah*, 75–6 (Eng. section).

[16] Ibid. 66 (Eng. section).

decline, and of the severance of Andalusian Jewry from eastern authority by the mid-tenth century, is far too neat.[17] Ongoing relations between East and West, and the fidelity of the latter to the former, are apparent in numerous panegyrics produced in al-Andalus. Writing in the tenth century, Menahem ben Saruk praises Hasdai Ibn Shaprut (*c.*915–*c.*970) as a *rosh kalah* (Head of the Assembly). This title, which would have been bestowed upon him by a Baghdadi gaon, testifies to the Andalusian Jewish courtier's fealty to the centre in Iraq during the reign of ʿAbd al-Raḥmān III. Dunash ben Labrat likewise praised Ibn Shaprut: 'Every year he sends an offering to the judges [in Babylonia]'.[18] Famed for his panegyrics honouring Ibn Shaprut, Ben Labrat is less well known for a poem that he wrote for Shemaryah ben Elhanan, a leader of the Babylonian community in Fustat.[19] Samuel Ibn Naghrila (993–*c.*1055) also viewed himself as part of a broader Mediterranean network; he authored a panegyric in honour of Sahlan ben Abraham of Fustat, another for the Palestinian gaon Daniel ben Azaryah, and composed a lament upon the death of Hai Gaon of Baghdad.[20] A generation later Solomon Ibn Gabirol (*c.*1020–*c.*1057) composed a panegyric for two emissaries of the Sura academy who had arrived in al-Andalus.[21] At least until the first half of the eleventh century, al-Andalus thus appears to have been a satellite community like any other that exhibited strong local networks and ties to distant centres simultaneously.[22] Inasmuch as a panegyric demonstrates a link (though sometimes an aspirational one) between two men, a full map of panegyric exchanges allows for a kind of representation, however partial, of Jewish social relations in the medieval Mediterranean, both spatially and across ranks. As seen, panegyrics contribute to our knowledge concerning the interplay between local and central Jewish authority as well as between hierarchical

[17] See e.g. Ashtor, *The Jews of Moslem Spain*, i. 230–41.

[18] See Elizur, 'Secular Hebrew Poetry in Spain' (Heb.), 204.

[19] Mann, *The Jews in Egypt and in Palestine*, ii. 21–3, discussed by Mann in i. 27.

[20] For Sahlan see Samuel Hanagid, *Dīwān shemuel hanagid*, 200 [62] (ENA 2917.13–14); 139 [40]; 231–6 [85]. Sahlan had received honorific titles from academies in both Palestine and Babylonia; he ultimately rejected the Palestinian appellation in favour of the Babylonian. See Gil, *A History of Palestine*, 592–4. Although Daniel ben Azaryah became gaon in Palestine, he hailed from a powerful Babylonian family. See Gil, *A History of Palestine*, 719–36. Also within the western Mediterranean, the Nagid wrote a letter of condolence and a lament (both in Aramaic) for Hananel ben Hushiel upon the latter's death in Kairouan, 256–60 [107].

[21] Ibn Gabirol, *Shirei haḥol*, i. 76–8 [42].

[22] Most often, panegyrics were sent from peripheral communities to the major centres, which makes sense given the general upward, hierarchic flow of panegyric from those less powerful to those more powerful. However, see the interesting case of Hai Gaon's panegyrics for affiliates of the academy below.

and horizontal structures, and thus constitute an important source for charting what Marina Rustow has recently called the 'jagged shape' of the Jewish community.[23]

Another way in which panegyric allows us to approach the subject of regionalism is to consider minor fluctuations in representations of leadership across the different micro-regions of the Mediterranean. When Hai ben Sherira, gaon of the Sura academy in Baghdad, dedicated a nearly 200-line panegyric to Judah Rosh Haseder (Head of the Order) of Kairouan on the occasion of the wedding of the latter's son, the gaon included an extensive section wherein he imagined the luxurious setting of the wedding celebration and how he would 'dwell there for the days of the feast among friends'. An earlier section of the same poem describes extensively the patron's material possessions. Hai was familiar with the cultural style of Jewish leadership in the Islamic West and undoubtedly tailored his portrait of Judah accordingly.[24] Interestingly, the gaon, who outranked Judah in the spiritual and intellectual hierarchy, assumed the posture of a poet before a patron; this is a telling aspect about the negotiation of power in the practice of Jewish 'statecraft' in the Islamic Mediterranean. Even the most hierarchically ordered relationships were of a reciprocal and interdependent nature.

THREE PANEGYRICS BY JUDAH HALEVI

In what follows I present three political poems from major phases of the life of Judah Halevi, a consummate 'Mediterranean' figure in that he moved between Muslim and Christian territories in Iberia and then journeyed to the Islamic East (Egypt and possibly Palestine).[25] All three poems are in the strophic *muwashshaḥ* form,[26] all are dedicated to figures attributed with 'dominion' (*misrah*), and all make allusions to rituals of power acclamation. The poems also relate to geography in different ways.

[23] 'The Genizah and Jewish Communal History'. Rustow seeks to go beyond geonic or Mediterranean models to integrate mercantile, religious, and political authority and the multiple allegiances they involved.

[24] The fullest version of the poem is published in Fleischer, 'R. Hai Gaon's Poem to R. Judah Rosh Haseder' (Heb.), iii. 1295–1327; see especially ll. 128–33. Fleischer also believes that Hai adjusted his poem to the addressee's tastes and goes so far as to suggest that Hai might not have introduced his letter with a panegyric at all had it not been for Judah's 'Sephardi' predilections. However, the gaon also wrote other panegyrics, including one for an exilarch in Baghdad (though only the very beginning of that poem survives).

[25] See also Stroumsa, *Maimonides in His World*.

[26] On the *muwashshaḥ* form see Rosen, 'The Muwashshaḥ'.

'Clear a road and pay honour to our king!'

The first poem, which is likely to be the earliest, is dedicated to Abū al-Ḥasan Meir Ibn Kamniel, a *wazīr* whom Halevi encountered during his early career in Seville. This is actually one of several poems he dedicated to Ibn Kamniel; taken together, they reveal a good deal about the development and vicissitudes of the poet–patron relationship. In what is probably the first of the series, Halevi rebuked all the residents of Seville with the exception of Ibn Kamniel, who is praised for his kindness, generosity, eloquence, and intelligence.[27] In another, he refers to having fallen out of favour with his patron; the poem, which praises Ibn Kamniel as the 'light of Torah', is a gesture of reconciliation.[28] Yet another poem, written after the relationship between poet and patron had grown quite intimate, was composed when Ibn Kamniel departed for the East and Halevi awaited his return. The separation led him to apostrophize the four winds:

> The day the friend left me for a distant land,
> Troubles waged against me an intense war and
> sent a burning fire in my body[29] so that I cried aloud . . .
>
> O North Wind, rouse for me a scent that captures souls!
> O South Wind, return to me the one who has fled on wings of dreams!
> O East Wind, bring him greetings until the moon will be no more!
>
> O West Wind that wafts and fans the flame [of my heart],
> blow and answer me, is there any distress like mine? . . .
>
> We shall ascend and cross the sea from Sepharad for a cherub,
> Meir, who is flowing myrrh, unique in dominion.[30]

Although the poet never names a specific place apart from Sepharad (al-Andalus), physical distance inspires his geographical imagination to think beyond the boundaries of his locale. In many ways, the device in this poem prefigures the wind imagery in Halevi's famous poems for Zion.[31]

'Clear a road and pay honour to our king!' is the most political of Halevi's poems for Ibn Kamniel and may have been written for the day the latter ascended to office.[32] The poem includes a play on Ibn Kamniel's name Meir, meaning 'he who illumines', and concludes with a *kharja* in Hispano-

27 Halevi, *Dīwān*, i. 127–8 [88]. 28 *Dīwān*, i. 57 [42]. 29 Lit. 'loins'.
30 *Dīwān*, i. 186–7 [126]. 31 See Scheindlin, *The Song of the Distant Dove*, 226–9.
32 *Dīwān*, i. 176–7 [118]. Another poem for Ibn Kamniel, praised together with Solomon Ibn al-Muʿallim, can be found in *Dīwān*, i. 42 [33].

Romance,[33] one of the vernacular languages of Jews in the peninsula:

> Clear a road[34] and pay honour to our king!
> The heralding voice runs upon the earth like the running of lightning.
> The hearts of those who wait for the repairer of the breach[35] rejoice as though they were drinking a goblet [of wine],
> When his form emits a scent,[36] it is healing for all the maimed.
> His memory is honeycomb to our mouths; he is our hopes' very desire. 5
> His parents called him Meir and ever since then they could not conceal him,
> for they found him to be a luminary of Truth; his name is like his essence.
> They raised him at their bosom yet hewed his habitation[37] above the heavenly abode!
> He peered from behind a lattice[38] and illumined our darkness.
> At your heels, Israel's straight path is revealed, for your thoughts are [only of] wisdom, generosity, and fear of God. 10
> Strengthen the cords and draw the hearts of those who say, 'Be willing!'[39]
> And speak to those who draw after you, speak in order to bless us.
> The men of our age see your myriads, the host of heaven,
> each calling before you and your chariots, 'I kneel!'[40] 15
> saying in your ears, 'Deck yourself with majesty[41] for so were your fathers,
> They were our princes! You are the *nasi* of God in our midst.'
> O you raised in the bosom of Dominion, drink and delight in her love.
> Since the day he was created, her [i.e. Dominion's] necklace was fitting for his neck.
> She plays a lovely song and so brings relief to her friends: 20
> *Son of foreign lands, you have drunk, now sleep upon my breast!*[42]

[33] *Kharja* refers to the concluding verses of a *muwashshaḥ* and it often involves a shift from one language to another (e.g. Hebrew to Arabic or Romance). Further on this see Rosen, 'The Muwashshaḥ'.

[34] Isa. 57: 14.

[35] Isa. 58: 12.

[36] Lit. 'is spat from his form'.

[37] Lit. 'nest'.

[38] The wording is drawn from Song of Songs 2: 9, but see below regarding the political significance of the practice.

[39] i.e. 'be willing to accept this office'.

[40] Heb. *avrekh*; cf. Gen. 41: 43. Commentators differ significantly on this word. My translation follows Abraham Ibn Ezra. Ibn Janāḥ takes it as an imperative of the same root, 'Kneel!' Sa'adyah Gaon translates it as the sobriquet by which people refer to Joseph *al-ẓarīf*, 'the Elegant'. What matters for our purposes is that it refers to the moment at which Joseph was given power, and pertains to one of the rituals of empowerment.

[41] Cf. Job 40: 10.

[42] This is Benabu's translation in '"Rivers of Oil Inundated the Valley of Stones"', 25. His essay offers valuable instructions for the philologist trying to reconstruct the Romance *kharjas*. This translation is an improvement over Samuel Miklos Stern's ('Son of a stranger, remain in my bosom!') in his pioneering study *Hispano-Arabic Strophic Poetry*, 138. Sola-Solé, in *Corpus de Poesia Mozarabe*, 243, translates it thus into modern Spanish: 'Hijo ajeno siempre te duermes en mi seno' ('Foreign son, may you always sleep in my bosom').

It is likely that 'Clear a road' mentions no place name and offers no representation of geography because Ibn Kamniel held claim to local authority only and because poet and addressee were then of the same place. This point is striking in comparison with Halevi's poem to Ibn Kamniel written during their separation, in which a geographical expanse comes into view. The specificity of an Andalusian style and an intended local audience are apparent in the Hispano-Romance *kharja*, which would not have been intelligible in the rest of the Arabic-speaking Mediterranean. The language was quite possibly selected over Arabic, in this case, because the speaker, Dominion, is gendered feminine. In love poems of the *muwashshaḥ* form, words placed in the mouth of the female beloved are often rendered in the Romance vernacular, quite possibly pointing to the gendered nature of language distribution in al-Andalus (men were more likely than women to know Arabic, the language of learning, government, and commerce).[43]

In several respects the political rituals suggested by the poem elicit comparison with the Islamic ceremony of swearing loyalty (*bayʿa*): the heralding voice, the acclamations of allegiance, and perhaps also Ibn Kamniel's peering from 'behind a lattice', for men of power were often shut off from public view.[44] The incipit 'Clear a road' is based on Isaiah 57: 14, famously evoked in the New Testament as John the Baptist's herald for Christ (Matt. 3: 3); here the verse is directed towards a far more mundane 'ruler'. Yet allegiance is professed also in the celestial realm, for the hosts of heaven call out *avrekh* (translated here as 'I kneel!'), the word the Egyptians exclaimed before Joseph at the moment of his ascension to power, when he was given Pharaoh's signet ring and the chariot of the second in command (Gen. 41: 43). As stated, the occasion of the poem may well have been Ibn Kamniel's ascension to power, though we do not know whether such a poem would have been recited as part of a ceremony. Professions of allegiance and boisterous singing recur in other poems suggestive of similar occasions.[45]

[43] López-Morillas, 'Language', esp. 45–50.

[44] See e.g. Marsham, *Rituals of Islamic Monarchy*. In Abraham Ibn Daud's depiction of Ibn Jau's appointment, the people sign a document 'certifying his position as *nasi*, which stated, "Rule thou over us, both thou, and thy son, and thy son's son also"'; *Sefer ha-Qabbalah*, 69 (Eng. section).

[45] Moses Ibn Ezra composed a poem (*Shirei haḥol*, i. 249–51 [240]) that bears the superscription 'To a friend who has been appointed to the position of judge [*tawallā al-quḍā*]' and contains, 'lift up the wonder of Dominion for it is your hands' possession and an inheritance from your fathers. They say to you, "you have the right of succession, rise up and redeem your inheritance, rise and become a judge for us, for we have not found a healer like you".' Another poem in Ibn Ezra's *dīwān* (*Shirei haḥol*, i. 272–3 [257]) includes the following verses: 'How comely on the

Ibn Kamniel is portrayed in 'Clear a road' as Israel's salvation and healing; the incipit phrase from Isaiah evokes the image of deliverer. His merits include wisdom, generosity, and fear of God. These traits are often at the centre of Arabic panegyric poetry as well. The other focal point is Ibn Kamniel's lineage; the poem mentions his parents, 'who raised him at their bosom', and his forebears: 'they were our princes'.

Ibn Kamniel is called *nasi*, a term often reserved for one who traces his descent from King David.[46] In a recent book Arnold Franklin demonstrates that Jews in the Islamic East were preoccupied with claims of Davidic descent, which emerged or intensified as a form of political capital that paralleled Muslim claims of descent from Muhammad's noble family, the *ahl al-bayt*.[47] While there was certainly no guarantee that a *nasi* would rise to power, members of this family line held a claim that others did not. Franklin also calls attention to regional variation in the use or emphasis of the term *nasi*. In Christian Europe 'the functional aspect of the title, signifying succession to a recognized office of authority, was brought to the foreground and transferred to new types of communal leadership, while the implied genealogical ties to David, which became so important in the East, tended to recede into the background'.[48] Franklin also points out that Abraham Ibn Daud, the proud Andalusian native who fled to Castile during the late twelfth century, gives a 'muted role to the scions of the royal line' when recounting the Andalusian myth of origins.[49]

What can we say about the term *nasi* in al-Andalus during the late eleventh and early twelfth centuries, and about Halevi's use of it in this poem?

mountain are the footsteps of the herald announcing [Isa. 52: 7] | that a shepherd has come to bring comfort to the flock wandering in the forest. | Behold, the sound of the people in its boisterousness [Exod. 32: 17] is heard calling him in song: | "Our rejoicing before you is like the joy of a multitude on their holiday. | May you reign over us! You and your son and your son's son!'" See Pagis's comments about Moses Ibn Chiqitilla's possible authorship of this poem; for our purposes, precise authorship is not as important as Andalusian origin. Also, Ibn Daud specifies that certain people (Joseph Ibn Sahl, Joseph Ibn Tsadik) were appointed judges (*nismakh badayanut*), it seems by the laying on of hands, in particular years. *Sefer ha-Qabbalah*, 61 (Heb. section), ll. 236, 239.

[46] The specific formulation '*nasi* of God' (which appears also in the poem below for Samuel ben Hananyah of Egypt), although predicated of Abraham in Gen 22: 6, seems particularly redolent with the Islamic formulation *khalīfat Allāh*, 'caliph of God'. On the controversial meaning of the latter see Crone and Hinds, *God's Caliph*, and critiques thereof.

[47] Franklin, *This Noble House: Jewish Descendants of King David*.

[48] He also points out that for Abraham Ibn Daud '*nasi* signified above all else someone who was entrusted with communal authority'. See ibid. 45–7. See also n. 49 below.

[49] Ibid. 226 n. 69; see also Franklin's comments on p. 45 concerning Ibn Jau.

First, it is possible that he did not intend any association with the Davidic family. In the Bible *nasi* can refer to a leader in the general sense before the rise of David; for example, 'And the leader of the leaders [*nesi nesi'ei*] of the Levites was Eleazar son of Aaron the priest' (Num. 3: 32); this *nasi* thus enjoyed claims of prestigious lineage, but to Aaron and Levi, not to David.[50] Before Halevi, Solomon Ibn Gabirol praised Yekutiel Ibn Hasn with the terms *nasi* and *nagid* interchangeably, and there is no evidence corroborating Yekutiel's descent from the Davidic line.[51] Moses Ibn Ezra used *nesi arav* to refer to a Muslim leader, obviously preserving the non-Davidic sense.[52] Further, among Jews in Christian Iberia, *nasi* seems to be the Hebrew appellation given to the figure called *wazīr* in Arabic (irrespective of Davidic claims); this practice may have been carried over from al-Andalus.[53]

Abraham Ibn Ezra, writing in the twelfth century, identifies the 'House of David' as a 'great and powerful family in Baghdad'; hence David's descendants do not seem particularly prominent in the Islamic West, and the term *nasi* was at least sometimes divorced from the sense of 'Davidic dynast'.[54] However, Franklin and others have pointed out that members of the Davidic family had moved westwards, even to al-Andalus, by the tenth century.[55] A number of Andalusian poems from the eleventh century are dedicated to figures addressed as *nasi*, including two by Moses Ibn Ezra that bear the title 'the lofty *nasi*' (*al-nasi al-ajall*) in the superscription.[56] A panegyric by Halevi for the Andalusian Isaac Ibn Barukh on the occasion of his grandson's circumcision calls Isaac 'the *nasi* of all princes', and the grandson 'A boy who is called "son of God" on high and on earth is called "son of kings"'.[57] Halevi undoubtedly intended 'son of God' in the political sense, for this appellation is associ-

[50] See also Num. 16: 2.

[51] He is praised as the 'one who arose in the place of the three shepherds' (Moses, Aaron, and Miriam), but not as a replacement, let alone a descendant, of David. See Schirmann, *The History of Jewish Poetry in Muslim Spain* (Heb.), 274–5, esp. nn. 105, 106, and 109.

[52] 'The Christian general, the Muslim leader [*nesi arav*], and the Greek sage are all silenced from speaking before him' (*Shirei haḥol*, i. 195–8 [195], l. 33).

[53] Fleischer believes that *wazīr* was a title bestowed upon those who already held the title *nasi* among Jews. See his comment in Schirmann, *The History of Jewish Poetry in Muslim Spain* (Heb.), 287–8 n. 38. It seems more likely to me that the opposite was the case: the title *nasi* would have been bestowed upon someone considered a *wazīr*. In any case, there is no indication that such *nesi'im* were necessarily Davidic. See below regarding Abraham Ibn al-Muhājir, who is called a *nasi* in a poem and a *wazīr* in a superscription.

[54] See his commentary on Zech. 12: 7; also Franklin, *This Noble House*, 52.

[55] Franklin, *This Noble House*, 53–5.

[56] *Shirei haḥol*, i. 62 [64]; i. 113–14 [112].

[57] *Dīwān*, i. 120 [84], ll. 1, 5–6.

ated with biblical kings, especially Solomon.[58] The poem may well have been for a family that claimed descent from David.

Moses Ibn Ezra praised the *wazīr* Abraham Ibn al-Muhājir as the '*nasi* of God':

> Kings' perfume derives from the powder of his feet and *nesi'im* [pl. of *nasi*] wrap their heads with the strap of his sandal [as a turban].
> Ministers halt their words before him, and to him all leaders bow their heads like bulrush . . .
> The sons of Time do not go hastily to fight him, they do not battle with him lest they be struck down,
> for the merit of the fathers is a shield for the son, and the riches he bestows are better than drawn swords.

The poem includes a dedication that begins, 'Take, O anointed of God, a necklace of speech', and concludes,

> May you be exalted, O *nasi* of God, as long as men like jackals breathe in the wind of your generosity!
> May your throne be established as long as [men's] mouths chirp like birds for your goodness and kindness.[59]

Did Ibn al-Muhājir lay claim to Davidic descent? Given that the poem uses '*nasi* of God' together with 'God's anointed', and that it stresses the 'merit of the fathers' as well as hope for continued dominion, it is tempting to attribute Davidic status to this recipient.[60] Further, Ibn Daud mentions a late eleventh-century figure, R. Joseph Hanasi bar R. Meir ben Muhājir, and so it seems that the family name was more broadly associated with the title *nasi*.[61] I would guess that Ibn Ezra's addressee was associated with the Davidic line. Still, the two other panegyrics by Ibn Ezra for Abraham Ibn al-Muhājir make no mention of his being a *nasi*, which suggests that this was not the foremost aspect of his legitimacy in the poet's view.[62] Even if Ibn al-Muhājir were a

[58] See e.g. 1 Chron. 17: 13. Jews were more than happy to remind Christians of this point in polemical writings.

[59] *Shirei haḥol*, i. 182–5 [183], ll. 27–8, 37–8, 41, 49–50. Brody suggests that the poem served as a second dedication for *Sefer ha'anak*. See his comments in *Shirei haḥol*, ii. 344.

[60] Note also that an anonymous poet praises Judah Rosh Haseder of Kairouan as a '*nasi* of God'; see Fleischer, 'R. Hai Gaon's Poem to R. Judah Rosh Haseder' (Heb.), 1311, l. 9.

[61] Ibn Daud, *Sefer ha-Qabbalah*, 62 (Heb.), 84 (Eng.). On the family see also Schirmann, 'Poets in the Generation of Moses Ibn Ezra and Judah Halevi' (Heb.), 344.

[62] The two other panegyrics are *Shirei haḥol*, i. 279–81 [261] and the introduction to *Sefer ha'anak*, 300–1.

member of the Davidic dynasty, such descent is not cited as the basis of his legitimacy.

To know with certainty when *nasi* is used in the general sense of 'leader' and when in the specific sense of 'Davidic dynast' is admittedly difficult.[63] The ambiguity of the term obtains in the case of Ibn Kamniel. Lineage is certainly a recurring motif in Halevi's panegyrics for him; regarding those who were astounded at his wisdom despite his youth, Halevi wrote, 'Had they known his fathers, they would say that [wisdom] is a quality that passes from father to son. The honour of his fathers is a fitting crown for him, just as the headdress was fitting for Aaron's head.'[64] Still, the type of lineage that is emphasized here is of a rather general variety and does not stress a progenitor from a distant past. By way of contrast, an unpublished, beautifully calligraphed panegyric preserved in the Cairo Genizah, dated 1146 (a few years after Halevi's death), praises Abū Saʿīd al-Dāʾūdī, whose relational name (*nisba*) clearly attests to a Davidic claim:

> . . . of the nation and crown of the *nesi'im*, majesty of all the fearing,
> associated by lineage to the father of the house of kingship and the dynasty of those selected as *negidim* [pl. of *nagid*].
> He is distinguished among the most eminent, for he is a lion while they are wild beasts.
> He is beautiful among the children of Adam and Eve, and one who fears the Creator of created things, anointed in the oils of wisdom like the Messiah, whom the prophets anointed.[65]

Further, Halevi's inclusion of Davidic descent as a quality worth praising does not necessarily mean that he viewed such status as a unique or ultimate claim to authority. This is suggested by a panegyric for the well-known rabbinic scholar Joseph Ibn Migash; the poet stresses the addressee's lineage, describing him as the 'seed of Moses and Aaron', and concludes, 'through him

[63] For example in *Dīwān*, i. 23 [17], Halevi calls Abū Sāʿīd Halfon Halevi of Damietta *nasi levi*, i.e. a Levite *nasi*; perhaps he simply meant a Levite leader, or perhaps one who claimed descent from David and also belonged to a Levite family. To an unidentified leader from the East who had come to reside in al-Andalus, Halevi concluded a poem, 'Sepharad [al-Andalus] boasts over Shinar [Iraq] because of you, and through your name *nesi'im* are blessed.' This, I assume, was dedicated to an Eastern figure who claimed Davidic descent. *Dīwān*, i. 65–7 [49], ll. 52–3.

[64] *Dīwān*, i. 127 [88], ll. 38–40.

[65] TS 10 J 22 3*v*. Gil believes (*A History of Palestine*, 595 n. 81) that it is written in the handwriting of Sahlan ben Abraham. Mentioned also in Franklin, *This Noble House*, appendix B, 7. Goitein left a transcription, which is available through the Princeton Geniza Project (l. 1 should read *al-ra'īs al-jalīl*, not *al-ḥalīl*).

nesi'im are blessed and seek the status of lineage by associating with his family'.[66] The poem thus gives weight to lineage of noble stock, yet gives no particular precedence to descent through David.

The movement of *nesi'im* from the Islamic East to the Islamic West may well have challenged existing power structures in al-Andalus, where those who claimed authority usually bore names such as Hakohen (the priest) or Halevi (the Levite).[67] This is not to say that Andalusians did not respect lineage, including lineage from David, or that they valued individual merit over bloodlines. It seems that the status of *nasi* was given weight, but no greater weight than other claims of legitimacy. Panegyrists generally worked with the material they had; if an addressee claimed status as a Davidic dynast, the poet would praise him as such, just as he might praise the Levite descent of one who bore the family name Halevi. The 'muted role given to scions of the royal line'[68] that becomes apparent in Christian Europe in the late twelfth century may already be present earlier in the Islamic West. It is possible that the multivalent usage of the term *nasi* in al-Andalus is indicative of this neutralized status.

'When the people's chiefs assemble'

Sometime after 1090 Halevi moved to Christian Iberia, to the kingdom of Castile, and there he praised Jewish figures associated with the court of Toledo, among them Alfonso VI's doctor, Joseph Ibn Ferrizuel, nicknamed Cidellus. (Like the name of the famous El Cid, this name is derived from the Arabic *sayyid*, here with a Romance diminutive, hence 'little lord'.)[69] Apparently the Jewish courtier had appeared in Wādī al-Ḥijāra (Guadalajara, lit. the Valley of Stones), which had come under Christian control in the late eleventh century, for the place name is mentioned explicitly in the concluding Hispano-Romance verses to the poem.

> When the people's chiefs assemble, kings in their counsel,
> they all praise Joseph for he is the source of their honour.
> He strives to rule by the hand of God and so he rules over men.
> That which men desire, which all declare to be unique and pure,

[66] *Dīwān*, i. 173 [114].

[67] This is apparent from simply perusing names in the index to Ibn Daud's *Sefer ha-Qabbalah*. Further, Andalusian identity was often seen as a matter of descent from the 'Jerusalemite community that resided in Sepharad' (Obad. 1: 20).

[68] Franklin, *This Noble House*, 226 n. 69.

[69] On this figure see Baer, *A History of the Jews in Christian Spain*, i. 50–1 (the poem is mentioned in i. 68–9), and Schirmann, *The History of Jewish Poetry in Muslim Spain* (Heb.), 437.

is the dominion prepared for a *nagid*, a glorious crown.[70] 5
If [some claim that] the most precious desire of man is the world and
everything in it,
I say,[71] [The world] has said that its very purpose[72] is this leader,[73]
Joseph! God[74] created [the world] as a habitation for him, not for waste
did He create it.[75]
Through him thick clay[76] is lifted for he has grown powerful and ruled.
Upon the tower of might he established his standard with [a troop] of ten.[77] 10
You are a fruitful vine with a taut bow,[78] all your works are skilful.
The good of days comes from you, and for you [the days] renew song!
You are the sun and rain pouring down but your value is even greater!
Through you the eternal luminaries rise and daylight shines
upon the world. [The world] too testifies that it was aided by you. 15
Why does this degraded people that blames Time for its wrongs grumble
when every briar will be removed and burned in a fire of brushwood
with[79] the advance of [the man] full of God's glory, who stands among
the myrtles?
For his roar terrifies princes; he can sling [a stone] at a hair [and not miss],[80]
His God made him alone a fortress of might in a time of distress. 20

[70] Cf. Isa. 28: 5.

[71] Brody takes the speaker here to be 'Dominion', which is also possible. If so, then line 8 should read 'God created [Dominion] as a habitation for him.' The verse is admittedly difficult and either reading seems possible.

[72] Heb. *inyan*, lit. 'matter'. Like the Arabic *maʿnā*, this word carries a range of meanings, perhaps approaching here the English 'quintessence'.

[73] Brody's edition here reads 'I said, "it said" etc.' However, on the basis of one manuscript that has a *heh* instead of a *yod*, Brody suggests the vocalization *imratah*, which seems right to me.

[74] Lit. 'Rock'.

[75] Cf. Isa. 45: 18.

[76] Heb. *avtit*, a hapax legomenon in Hab. 2: 6. While the modern Jewish Publication Society Bible translates it as 'heavy debts' (according to the root *ayin-beit-tav*), the medieval Jewish commentators generally understand it as a composite of the two words *av* (cloud, something thick) and *tit* (clay). This corresponds to the King James translation 'thick clay'. Perhaps here it refers to the suffering of Israel (Baer's translation reads 'oppressive burden'). The conclusion of the verse in Baer's translation reads, 'like a tower of might he stayed the people fleeing in ten directions', which is also possible but awkward. If so, the poem may refer most specifically to his aiding refugees in the vicinity, but this is not conclusive.

[77] I am emending the text to read *niso* instead of *nuso*. Establishing a standard, sometimes for the 'nations', is a typical political image; see e.g. Isa. 11: 12. For the meaning 'to establish a military force' see Dan. 11: 11, 13. For 'ten' standing for ten men see Gen. 18: 32. 'Ten' could conceivably refer to the height of the tower, 'ten cubits'.

[78] Reference to the biblical Joseph, from Jacob's blessings in Gen. 49: 22, 24. The verse is chosen here because the addressee is also named Joseph.

[79] Lit. 'before', in the spatial sense.

[80] 'Sling a stone at a hair'; cf. Judg. 20: 16.

Rivers of oil flood the *wādī* of stones[81]
when the lord who nurses God's people with delights is heralded:
'May the prince live! And say "Amen!"' And they broke out in song:
'Whence does my master come? Such glad tidings!
It is as if a ray of sunlight appears in Wādī al-Ḥijāra.'[82] 25

Like the poem for Ibn Kamniel, this piece evokes a ritual of allegiance and probably refers to an actual event during which the Toledan courtier appeared in Guadalajara. Cidellus is presented as an amalgam of archetypal biblical leaders who embodies their diverse qualities: prowess, reverence for the Divine, and close tending of the people. The poem is exceptionally dense with evocations of political figures from Israel's past. The addressee is associated with his namesake, the biblical Joseph who 'ruled over all of Egypt' (Gen. 41: 41) through the language of Jacob's blessing (line 11; cf. Gen. 49: 22). The opening verse evokes Moses' final address (Deut. 33: 5), when he 'became a king in Jeshurun', and Moses returns in line 22 with reference to the archetypal leader's own words to God, 'Did I conceive all this people, did I bear them, that You should say to me, "Carry them in your bosom as a nurse carries an infant"?' (Num. 20: 11). Yet the most central political figure is King David, who 'ruled men with justice, ruled with the fear of God' (2 Sam. 23: 3; cf. line 3). The '*wādī* of stones' (line 21) works brilliantly on multiple levels. It is a Hebraization of the place name given in the concluding verse, Wādī al-Ḥijāra; a new 'king' is anointed in Guadalajara. Yet the verse also deepens the association with David, for it was at a river that David took 'five smooth stones' to fight Goliath (1 Sam. 17: 40); the idea is reinforced in line 19 with the precision of Cidellus' shot.[83] Line 21 thus brings together two stages of David's life: the brave boy who slew the Philistine and the mature, anointed king.

Joseph is the epitome of generosity, one who instils dread and is the source of eternal light that brings benefit to the 'world', a term whose Arabic equivalent is *dunyā*. Many caliphs are described as fit for the paired realms of *al-dīn wa-al-dunyā*, 'religion and the world' (see the verses by Ibn al-ʿAtāhiyya above), and the motif echoes in other Hebrew panegyrics as well.[84] The

[81] Heb. *naḥal*, 'river', but this can be in the sense of a dry river bed, a *wadi*.

[82] *Dīwān*, i. 157–8 [102]. The *kharja*, in Hispano-Romance (including the Arabic word *bishāra* and the Arabic place name for Guadalajara), like other *kharja*s, has been the subject of significant philological research. I am using the version in Benabu and Yahalom, 'The Importance of the Genizah Manuscripts for the Hispano-Romance *Kharjas*', 153. See Rosen, 'The Muwashshaḥ' on *kharja*s more generally.

[83] In point of fact, the reference in Judg. 20: 16 is not to David.

[84] See the poem above by Ibn al-ʿAtāhiyya.

addressee as a source of light is also a common motif in Arabic, especially Ismāʿīlī, panegyric, as is the addressee's association with the otherworldly, 'the hand of God', which entitles him to 'rule over men'.[85]

Further, Joseph is the one who 'stands among the myrtles', an image drawn from an angelic being that appears to the prophet Zechariah (Zech. 1: 8). Here, however, 'myrtles' is probably code for the Andalusian-style elite, since other poets use the word as a metaphor for that group. A fixture of the Andalusian garden, the myrtle had come, in Christian Iberia, to symbolize Andalusian culture itself, as well as the transplanted remnant that embodied its values. Following his move to Christian Iberia, for example, Moses Ibn Ezra referred to his circle as estranged among the less cultured Jews of the Christian north: 'among them we are like myrtles among the trees of the forest, our leaves withering'.[86] This is one way in which Halevi's poem sheds light on the particularity of the political moment and the particularity of the region.

The description of Joseph as a 'fortress in a time of distress' probably refers to his activity in resettling Andalusian Jewish refugees in Castile during the Almoravid period.[87] The specificity of the region is also evident in that the concluding song (the *kharja*) is recorded in Hispano-Romance—though, as seen, this language was also used by Jews in Islamic territories of al-Andalus.[88] Finally, the poem is rare in that it refers to an Iberian place name in transliterated form (though notably in the *kharja* rather than in the Hebrew section).[89]

[85] The 'eternal light' may refer to the light that existed on the first day of Creation, before the creation of the sun and the moon on the fourth day. On light imagery in Arabic, especially Ismāʿīlī, panegyric, see al-Azmeh, *Muslim Kingship*, 162.

[86] The angel reference suggests that the addressee of the panegyric is marked by sacrality. See Alfonso, 'The Body, Its Organs and Senses'. On referring to 'cultured' men of al-Andalus as myrtles, see my *Iberian Jewish Literature*, ch. 1.

[87] On these activities see Baer, *A History of the Jews in Christian Spain*, i. 50–1, 68–9. This reading is augmented if one accepts Baer's reading of line 10 (following Brody's interpretation), 'like a tower of might he stayed the people fleeing in ten directions', i.e. he took in refugees.

[88] A *muwashshaḥ* composed by Halevi for Moses Ibn Ezra of Granada, in contrast, presents its concluding verses in Arabic (the last two lines, in italics): 'When company assembled and princes counselled together | Dominion desired that he would be the leader of their intimate circle | And also the Torah spoke in the language of men: | *O chiefs of Knowledge, Augustness and Nobility* | *Back away for Moses is in your midst!*' (Brody, 122 [86], ll. 18–22). The phrase 'The Torah spoke in the language of men', which derives from BT *Ber.* 31*b*, was quite famous in the medieval period, largely in connection with explicating the allegorical form of the Bible. See e.g. Klein-Braslavy, 'Bible Commentary', esp. 249. I believe that the use of the expression here to refer to Arabic is unique.

[89] Calling it the '*wadi* of stones' in Hebrew is similar to referring to Granada as *beit rimon*, 'house of the pomegranate'.

The emphasis on place may be explained by the fact that Guadalajara was home neither to the poet nor his addressee; it came into view with Cidellus' arrival. While this is no grand representation of geography, the poem does demonstrate how locale becomes important when one is writing about a place other than 'home'.

In this poem Ibn Ferrizuel is called *nagid*, a title that was used throughout the Islamic Mediterranean to refer to a locally appointed communal leader; its use here might point to the transference of that office with its attending communal structure to Christian soil. Interestingly, Halevi does not refer to him, as Ibn Daud later would, as a *nasi*, though he does use this title in connection with Solomon Ibn Ferrizuel, Cidellus' nephew and also a courtier in Castile: 'Return, Solomon, my *nasi* . . . Time has donned the robe of a *nasi*'s majesty; they are but the robe's hem while you alone are its ornamented collar.'[90] If Halevi used this term to denote Davidic ancestry, Solomon may have been among the last such dynasts to hold power in Spain, since Ibn Daud describes Hiya ben al-Dā'ūdī, who died in Castile in 1154, as 'the last renowned person of the house of David' in Sepharad.[91] In any case, Halevi's depiction of Cidellus focuses on communal authority rather than descent and likewise supports the thesis that royal lineage did not carry the weight it did, at this time, in the Islamic East.

'"Grace, grace!" unto him'

Famously, Halevi departed the Iberian peninsula in 1140 to make pilgrimage to Palestine, disembarking at Alexandria en route, and residing in Cairo for a period. He wrote panegyrics for several Egyptian dignitaries, the most illustrious of whom was Samuel ben Hananyah, who held the title of *nagid*. Among Halevi's four surviving panegyrics dedicated to this figure is the following one:[92]

[90] For the title *nasi* for Cidellus see Ibn Daud, *Sefer ha-Qabbalah*, 95 (Eng. section). For the panegyric to Solomon see Schirmann, *Hebrew Poetry in Spain and Provence* (Heb.), ii. 457–9 [184], ll. 37–40.

[91] Ibn Daud, *Sefer ha-Qabbalah*, 45 (Heb. section): 've'aḥarav lo nishar be'erets sefarad adam mefursam shehu mibeit david'. Cohen's translation on p. 62 (Eng. section) reads, 'After him there did not remain in Spain a single person known to be of the house of David.' The point is not that Davidic scions did not exist but rather that they had diminished recognition and authority. In any case, Ibn Daud does not describe him as a *nasi*, which suggests that his use of *nasi* elsewhere may have been in the broader sense. Ibn Daud also describes Judah the Nasi, who was appointed ruler of Calatrava under Alfonso VI, and some of his relatives as being 'of royal seed from the nobility' (cf. Dan. 1: 3, where the 'royal seed' is Davidic); see p. 98 (Eng.), 71 (Heb.).

[92] *Dīwān*, i. 76–7 [57].

[Shouts of] 'Grace, grace!' unto him who tends his vineyard, who fences in its vine at the time of planting.[93]
His name is Samuel, for God appointed him to bear the shield of His salvation.[94]
They sounded[95] loud cymbals for his name, his reputation was heard throughout the world.
A *nagid* who seeks his people's welfare and pronounces peace for all his seed,[96]
A righteous man who rules over men, who rules with the fear of God.[97] 5
He came to strengthen himself through God and so he was taken aloft,
The holy [angels] brought him into their inner circle, and so he stood in the counsel of the shining ones.
Then his enemies were weakened and prophets and seers counselled together.
The Lord his God is with him, He is his fortress and rock.[98]
The day he arose as the prince of princes, people from afar set their faces [on him].[99] 10
They did not believe what was said until they beheld with their own eyes,
They reaped a hundredfold[100] because of what their ears heard.
They all appointed him prince[101] to rule over them and their children.
May God prolong dominion upon his shoulder[102] and choose rulers from among his seed.
Canaan envies Mitsrayim because it is illumined by the light of his face; 15
Shinar studies his ways and beseeches Majestic Full of Light
to behold the king who stands above the waters of the Nile.
Sepharad joins them to measure the extent [of his greatness].[103]
Perhaps [Spain] will be a treading ground for his footsteps, a treading ground for Pharaoh's chariots.
Ariel proclaimed, 'This is my king whom I have awaited like dew! 20
I have accepted him as chieftain and prince to teach justice to Israel!'[104]
He called his name Samuel, because I asked the Lord for him.[105]
He has not withheld from me a redeemer so that my enemy cannot say, 'I have overcome him.'
May He make peace above and grant kindness to David and his seed.

[93] References to Zech. 4: 7; S. of S. 1: 16; Isa. 17: 11.
[94] See 2 Sam. 22: 36, of David.
[95] Lit. 'set, established'.
[96] Esther 10: 3, of Mordecai.
[97] Again, 2 Sam. 23: 3, of David (David's final words).
[98] See 2 Sam. 22: 2.
[99] See 1 Kgs 2: 15.
[100] i.e. they prospered; cf. Gen. 26: 12.
[101] Heb. *ma'amirim*; cf. Deut. 26: 17–18. As Brody points out, Sa'adyah Gaon reads the word as though derived from the Arabic *emir* (prince).
[102] Cf. Isa. 9: 5.
[103] *Dīwān*, i. 76–7 [57]. 'To measure out his boundary', i.e. to measure his greatness. 'Majestic Full of Light' is a reference to God. Mann thinks the figure might be identifiable with the court physician Abū Manṣūr, who served the caliph al-Ḥāfiẓ; see Mann, *The Jews in Egypt and in Palestine*, i. 229–30.
[104] Exod. 2: 14, of Moses.
[105] Cf. 1 Sam. 1: 20.

The imagined geography presented in lines 15–18 is both expansive and ordered; Iraq (Shinar), Palestine (Canaan), and al-Andalus (Sepharad) all focus their gaze upon Egypt (Mitsrayim) because of the 'king who stands above the waters of the Nile'. By comparison, the previous panegyric, 'The people's chiefs', only mentions, first by allusion and then by name, Wādī al-Ḥijāra, the city where Cidellus had risen to power, while the first, 'Clear a road', for Ibn Kamniel, makes no reference to place at all. The broad expanse sketched out in 'Grace, grace' is possibly a function of the magnitude of its addressee and of the fact that the poem was composed by an Andalusian for an Egyptian. The geographical representation includes the Islamic East (*al-mashriq*) and the Islamic West (*al-maghrib*) and betrays a spatial ordering that is largely the opposite of what had traditionally been the intellectual and legal hierarchy of the Jewish world. Iraq and Palestine were generally understood to be the main 'centres' upon which those in Egypt and al-Andalus both gazed. The relatively minor status of al-Andalus is preserved in that it 'joins' the great centres of Iraq and Palestine and is mentioned only after them, while the status of Egypt is greatly augmented. However, this does not signify a reversal in power relations in the twelfth century so much as a hyperbolic representation of the *nagid*'s status.[106]

Spatial representation is common in the panegyric corpus and conveys something about how authors and audiences conceptualized geography. Hai Gaon of Baghdad commands that his (nearly 200-line) panegyric for Judah Rosh Haseder (Head of the Order) of Kairouan be recited 'in all of Babylonia . . . unto Assyria and Syria . . . unto Elam and Persia'; with such an instruction the Baghdadi gaon was essentially claiming his jurisdiction over these multiple regions. A funerary elegy (similar to a panegyric in many respects) by Moses Ibn Ezra for a certain Barukh in al-Andalus maintains that lamentation shall not cease in 'Bat Bavel, Admat Edom, Mitsrayim, and Em Sefarad' (Iraq, Christian Iberia, Egypt, and Cordoba, lit. the 'mother of Sepharad').[107] Taken together, the literary corpus reveals something of the imagined geographies of Arabic-speaking Jews and justifies the 'Mediterranean' as a unit of study even as it presents multiple ways of conceptualizing the interrelation among regions.

[106] On the idea of 'imagined geography' see also Goldberg, *Trade and Institutions in the Medieval Mediterranean*.

[107] *Shirei hahol*, i. 92–4 [93], ll. 19–20. It is conceivable that by Admat Edom the poet means the Levant, the area where the biblical Esau actually settled, rather than the territory of the Christian Roman empire that was ultimately associated with Edom. It is not uncommon in Arabic to call the capital of a region the 'mother' of that region.

Similarly to the previous poems, 'Grace, grace' evokes rituals of empowerment, and it is conceivable that it was written for Ben Hananyah's initiation to the office of *nagid* (probably around 1140).[108] The poem refers to the 'day he arose as prince', when 'they all appointed him prince to rule over them'. Line 10 also refers to a gesture of loyalty, and invokes 1 Kings 2: 15, 'all Israel set their faces on me, that I should reign'.[109] The ritual is further dramatized with a personified Israel (and specifically Ariel, that is, Jerusalem[110]) taking an oath of allegiance: 'I have accepted him as chieftain and prince'. As with the other poems, these elements are highly reminiscent of the *bayʿa* ceremony of caliphal acclamation.[111]

Although Ben Hananyah is not explicitly called a *nasi* in this poem (he is called *sar hasarim* and, of course, *nagid*), Brody and Mann have rightly pointed out that the emphasis on David's seed in the concluding verse suggests that Ben Hananyah emanated from a Davidic family. Here the poet looks not only backwards, towards Davidic origins, but forwards, towards future leaders from the same line and possibly even towards the Davidic messiah (further below). Unsurprisingly, lineage also recurs as a central motif throughout Halevi's panegyrics for Ben Hananyah, sometimes centring on the expression *noḥel umanḥil*, 'one who inherits and passes on an inheritance'.[112] The phrase itself derives from rabbinic literature (e.g. BT *BB* 142*a*), where it applies to the inheritance of property, but it was employed in panegyric writing to describe the rightful transfer of power from father to son.[113] Although the interest in lineage is, as we have seen, not exclusive to Davidic scions, it seems to amplify the claims of rightful 'rule' in the case of Ben Hananyah.

[108] According to Mark Cohen, the earliest reference to Samuel ben Hananyah as *nagid* is from 1140, just before Halevi's departure from al-Andalus; *Jewish Self-Government in Medieval Egypt*, 35.

[109] The words are Adoniyah's; however, I do not think that the verse is meant to elicit Adoniyah specifically since he was the 'illegitimate' contender with Solomon for the throne after David.

[110] Cf. Isa. 29: 1.

[111] Marsham, *Rituals of Islamic Monarchy*.

[112] *Dīwān*, i. 110 [76], ll. 6, 8 ('Whom does majesty await? Only one who inherits greatness and passes it on as an inheritance . . . from generation to generation their crown will stand'). See also 111 [77], l. 7.

[113] However, the same phrase appears in connection with the inheritance of authority among those lacking ties with archetypal figures such as David, e.g. Aaron Ibn al-Amānī as well as others. See *Dīwān*, i. 93 [67], l. 14, and Brody's comment, p. 159, notes. It occurs most often in connection with figures in the East, though Moses Ibn Ezra uses it in a poem of comfort for Abū Umar Ibn Kamniel upon the death of his brother: 'He should not reject the garment of his majesty, for it is the majesty that he inherited and will pass on [*naḥal veyanḥil*] to his offspring and descendants after his death.' See *Shirei haḥol*, i. 37 [39], ll. 21–2.

Like Cidellus, Ben Hananyah has a place among the host of heaven. And just as Cidellus 'strives to rule by the hand of God and so he rules over men', Ben Hananyah is a 'righteous man who rules over men, who rules with the fear of God'. In this case, the allusion is specifically to King David (2 Sam. 23: 3). As with the other panegyrics, David is only one political figure of Israel's past to be evoked; the poem also links the addressee with the biblical Samuel, the last chieftain (*shofet*), Mordecai, the archetypal *nagid*, and Moses (lines 4, 21, 22). Yet David occupies a place in this poem that he does not occupy in the others; he is evoked further in lines 2 and 9, and, in line 14, through a well-known reference to Isaiah 9: 5, the poet entwines the Davidic imagery with messianic expectation. Halevi hopes that God will 'choose rulers from among his seed' and concludes with blessings for 'David and his seed'. Although David serves as an archetypal ruler in Halevi's panegyrics for Ibn Kamniel and Cidellus, this poem stresses Davidic descent as a matter of political capital in the present.

Messianism, with specific reference to the Davidic line, is explicit in other panegyrics by Halevi for Ben Hananyah. In the conclusion to one, Halevi addresses Israel with the words, 'Samuel has arisen and David comes after him![114] You will be tranquil as you were in days of old.'[115] By 'David' he probably intended a messiah of Davidic stock. Another panegyric concludes,

> And so the nations shall praise him, from the desert to the islands of the sea,
> For he is a banner and *nagid* over all nations, and the birthright is his.
> May the name of God be magnified and sanctified in their days, may kingship be renewed,
> and may Israel[116] return in song to the sanctuary of her Lord.[117]

'Banner over nations' is a reference to Isaiah 11: 10, a well-known messianic passage (which begins, 'And there shall come forth a shoot out of the stock of Jesse'); the 'birthright' is that of the Davidic line. Franklin also sees a messianic overtone in one of Halevi's letters to the *nagid*.[118]

Should the absence of the messianic motif in Halevi's panegyrics for Iberian figures—yet its inclusion in the panegyrics for an Eastern figure—be viewed as a function of the poet's age? Was it possible that redemption became more pressing for him as his life progressed? Was messianic expecta-

[114] Lit. 'came', possibly referring to David arising as king in the days of the biblical Samuel. However, I agree with Brody here, who interprets, 'Samuel has already come and soon David [the messiah son of David] will come after him.'

[115] *Dīwān*, i. 144 [97], ll. 91–2.

[116] Lit. 'the dark and comely one'; cf. the traditional interpretation of S. of S. 1: 5.

[117] *Dīwān*, i. 110–11 [76], ll. 14–17.

[118] *This Noble House*, 133.

tion emphasized in the panegyrics for Ben Hananyah because of the Davidic claims of the addressee? Or does the distinction reflect different conventions between Andalusian and Egyptian audiences? In general, the inclusion of messianic expectation within panegyric seems more a fixture of Hebrew panegyric from the Islamic East than from the Islamic West.[119] It strikingly inverts the insistence, in Islamic panegyric, that a caliph's reign was a manifestation of the best of political circumstances.[120] It seems that Halevi accommodated his praise in order to fit the expectations of addressees and audiences within the micro-regions of the medieval Mediterranean.

[119] Other panegyrics for figures in the Islamic East that have messianic conclusions appear in Mann, *The Jews in Egypt and in Palestine*, ii. 21–3; Beeri, 'Eli ben Amram' [11]; TS 8 J 13, ll. 1–5, published in Schechter, *Saadyana*, 71; TS 10 J 22 3*v*. This is not to say that Andalusian Jews did not write messianic poems or entertain messianic expectations; the theme was simply not included in panegyric with any frequency. One might also compare the conclusions to Dunash ben Labrat's panegyrics for Shemaryah ben Elhanan and Hasdai Ibn Shaprut cited above, nn. 18 and 19.

[120] Stetkevych, *The Poetics of Islamic Legitimacy*.

Bibliography

AL-AZMEH, AZIZ, *Muslim Kingship: Power and the Sacred in Muslim, Christian, and Pagan Polities* (London, 1997).

ALFONSO, ESPERANZA, 'The Body, Its Organs and Senses: A Study of Metaphor in Medieval Hebrew Poetry of Praise', *Middle Eastern Literatures*, 9 (2006), 1–22.

ASHTOR, ELIYAHU, *The Jews of Moslem Spain*, 3 vols. (Philadelphia, 1973).

BAER, YITZHAK, *A History of the Jews in Christian Spain*, 2 vols. (Philadelphia, 1992).

BAREKET, ELINOAR, *Fustat on the Nile: The Jewish Elite in Medieval Egypt* (Leiden, 1999).

BEERI, TOVA, 'Eli ben Amram: An Eleventh-Century Hebrew Poet in Egypt' (Heb.), *Sefunot*, 8 [23] (2003), 279–345.

BENABU, ISAAC, '"Rivers of Oil Inundated the Valley of Stones": Towards a Methodology for Reading the Hispano-Romance *Kharja*s in Hebrew Characters', in Alan Jones and Richard Hitchcock (eds.), *Studies in the Muwashshah and the Kharja* (Oxford, 1991), 16–28.

—— and YOSEF YAHALOM, 'The Importance of the Genizah Manuscripts for the Hispano-Romance *Kharjas*', *Romance Philology*, 40 (1986), 139–58.

BEN-SHAMMAI, HAGGAI, 'The Judeo-Arabic Vocabulary of Sa'adia's Bible Translation as a Vehicle for Eschatological Messages: The Case of Sa'adya's Usage of the 8th Form of Arabic *QDR*', in Benjamin H. Hary and Haggai Ben-Shammai (eds.), *Esoteric and Exoteric Aspects in Judeo-Arabic Culture* (Leiden, 2006), 191–225.

BRENER, ANN, *Isaac Ibn Khalfun: A Wandering Hebrew Poet of the Eleventh Century* (Leiden, 2003).

COHEN, MARK, *Jewish Self-Government in Medieval Egypt* (Princeton, NJ, 1981).

CRONE, PATRICIA, and MARTIN HINDS, *God's Caliph: Religious Authority in the First Centuries of Islam* (Cambridge, 1986).

DECTER, JONATHAN, *Iberian Jewish Literature: Between al-Andalus and Christian Europe* (Bloomington, Ind., 2007).

ELIZUR, SHULAMIT, 'Secular Hebrew Poetry in Spain: Towards the Version and Genre of Dunash ben Labrat's Poem "Someone said, Awake!"' (Heb.), in David Rosenthal (ed.), *The Cairo Genizah Collection in Geneva: Catalogue and Studies* [Osef hagenizah hakahirit bigenevah] (Jerusalem, 2010), 200–7.

FLEISCHER, EZRA, 'Collections of Paronomastic Poems by Judah al-Harizi', in Ezra Fleischer, *Hebrew Poetry in Spain and Communities Under Its Influence* [Hashirah ha'ivrit bisefarad uvisheluḥoteiha], ed. Shulamit Elizur and Tova Beeri (Jerusalem, 2010), iii. 1077–1173.

——'R. Hai Gaon's Poem to R. Judah Rosh Haseder of Kairouan: Circumstances and Environment' (Heb.), in Ezra Fleischer, *Hebrew Poetry in Spain and Communities Under Its Influence* [Hashirah ha'ivrit bisefarad uvisheluḥoteiha], ed. Shulamit Elizur and Tova Beeri (Jerusalem, 2010), iii. 1295–1327.

FRANKLIN, ARNOLD, *This Noble House: Jewish Descendants of King David in the Medieval Islamic East* (Philadelphia, 2013).

FRENKEL, MIRIAM, *'The Compassionate and Benevolent': The Leading Elite in the Jewish Community of Alexandria in the Middle Ages* ['Ha'ohavim vehanedivim': ilit manhigah bekerev yehudei aleksandriyah biyemei habeinayim] (Jerusalem, 2006).

GIL, MOSHE, *A History of Palestine, 634–1099* (Cambridge, 1992).

GOLDBERG, JESSICA L., *Trade and Institutions in the Medieval Mediterranean: The Geniza Merchants and Their Business World* (Cambridge, 2013).

GRUENDLER, BEATRICE, *Medieval Arabic Praise Poetry: Ibn al-Rūmī and the Patron's Redemption* (London, 2003).

HACKETT, HELEN, 'Dreams or Designs, Cults or Constructions? The Study of the Images of Monarchs', *The Historical Journal*, 44 (2001), 811–23.

HÄGG, TOMAS, PHILIP ROUSSEAU, and CHRISTIAN HØGEL (eds.), *Greek Biography and Panegyric in Late Antiquity* (Berkeley, Calif., 2000).

HALEVI, JUDAH, *Dīwān des Abū-l-Ḥasan Jehuda ha-Levi*, ed. Heinrich Brody, 4 vols. (Berlin, 1901–30).

HANAGID, SAMUEL, *Dīwān shemuel hanagid*, ed. Dov Jarden (Jerusalem, 1966).

IBN 'ABD RABBIH, AḤMAD, *Al-'iqd al-farīd*, ed. Mufīd Qamīḥa, 2 vols. (Beirut, 2006).

IBN DAUD, ABRAHAM, *Sefer ha-Qabbalah: The Book of Tradition*, trans. Gerson D. Cohen (Philadelphia, 1967).

IBN EZRA, MOSES, *Shirei haḥol*, ed. Heinrich Brody, 2 vols. (vol. i, Berlin, 1935; vol. ii, Jerusalem, 1941).

IBN GABIROL, SOLOMON, *The Improvement of the Moral Qualities*, ed. and trans. Stephen S. Wise (New York, 1952).

—— *Shirei haḥol lerabi shelomoh ibn gabirol*, ed. Dov Jarden (Jerusalem, 1975).

KLEIN-BRASLAVY, SARA, 'Bible Commentary', in Kenneth Seeskin (ed.), *The Cambridge Companion to Maimonides* (Cambridge, 2005), 245–72.

LÓPEZ-MORILLAS, CONSUELO, 'Language', in María Rosa Menocal, Raymond P. Scheindlin, and Michael Sells (eds.), *The Literature of al-Andalus* (Cambridge, 2000), 33–59.

MANN, JACOB, *The Jews in Egypt and in Palestine under the Fatimid Caliphs*, 2 vols. (London, 1920, 1922).

MARSHAM, ANDREW, *Rituals of Islamic Monarchy: Accession and Succession in the First Muslim Empire* (Edinburgh, 2009).

NEMOY, LEON, *Karaite Anthology: Excerpts from the Early Literature* (New Haven, 1952).

REES, ROGER, *Layers of Loyalty in Latin Panegyric* (Oxford, 2002).

ROCHE, PAUL, *Pliny's Praise: The Panegyricus in the Roman World* (Cambridge, 2011).

ROSEN, TOVA, 'The Muwashshaḥ', in María Rosa Menocal, Raymond P. Scheindlin, and Michael Sells (eds.), *The Literature of al-Andalus* (Cambridge, 2000), 165–89.

RUSTOW, MARINA, 'The Genizah and Jewish Communal History', in Ben Outhweite and Siam Bhayro (eds.), *From a Sacred Source: Genizah Studies in Honor of Stefan C. Reif* (Leiden, 2014), 289–317.

—— *Heresy and the Politics of Community: The Jews of the Fatimid Caliphate* (Ithaca, NY, 2008).

SAFRAN, JANINA, 'The Command of the Faithful in al-Andalus: A Study in the Articulation of Caliphal Legitimacy', *International Journal of Middle East Studies*, 30/2 (1998), 183–98.

SCHECHTER, SOLOMON, *Saadyana: Geniza Fragments of R. Saadya Gaon and Others* (Cambridge, 1903).

SCHEINDLIN, RAYMOND P., *The Song of the Distant Dove: Judah Halevi's Pilgrimage* (Oxford, 2008).

SCHIRMANN, HAYIM, *Hebrew Poetry in Spain and Provence* [Hashirah ha'ivrit bisefarad uveprovans] (Tel Aviv, 1954–60).

—— *The History of Hebrew Poetry in Muslim Spain* [Toledot hashirah ha'ivrit bisefarad hamuslemit], ed. Ezra Fleischer (Jerusalem, 1995).

—— 'Poets in the Generation of Moses Ibn Ezra and Judah Halevi' (Heb.), *Yedi'ot hamakhon leḥeker hashirah ha'ivrit*, 2 (1936), 117–94.

SOLA-SOLE, J. M., *Corpus de Poesia Mozarabe* (Barcelona, 1973).

STERN, SAMUEL MIKLOS, *Hispano-Arabic Strophic Poetry*, ed. L. P. Harvey (Oxford, 1974).

STETKEVYCH, SUZANNE PINCKNEY, *The Mantle Odes: Arabic Praise Poems to the Prophet Muhammad* (Bloomington, Ind., 2010).

—— *The Poetics of Islamic Legitimacy* (Bloomington, Ind., 2002).

STROUMSA, SARAH, *Maimonides in His World: Portrait of a Mediterranean Thinker* (Princeton, NJ, 2009).

VAN BEKKUM, WOUT, *The Secular Poetry of El'azar Ben Ya'aqov ha-Bavli* (Leiden, 2006).

WHITBY, MARY (ed.), *The Propaganda of Power: The Role of Panegyric in Late Antiquity* (Leiden, 1998).

YESHAYA, JOACHIM, *Medieval Hebrew Poetry in Muslim Egypt: The Secular Poetry of the Karaite Poet Moses ben Abraham Dar'i* (Leiden, 2011).

CHAPTER TEN

Attraction and Attribution: Framings of Sephardi Identity in Ashkenazi Prayer Books

ELISABETH HOLLENDER

WHEN *maskilim* and early representatives of Wissenschaft des Judentums—following their assumptions about the cultural gap between the most prominent medieval Jewish subcultures—divided the shares of Jewish culture between Ashkenaz (Talmud study, piety, martyrdom) and Sepharad (rationalism, sciences, philosophy, aesthetics), they did so in order to address questions of Jewish identity that arose in eighteenth- and nineteenth-century Germany.[1] Their perceptions of medieval Jewish culture affected the views of their contemporaries, along with those of later generations, who accepted both this division of cultural goods between the Jewish communities of Ashkenaz and Sepharad and the notion of the divide itself.[2]

More recent scholarship has tried to show that these medieval communities were actually in constant contact with one another, although they had different traditions and lived in different environments, embedded in disparate non-Jewish cultures. Recent studies show how texts and ideas were transmitted between the different communities, and were adapted and incorporated into the regional Jewish cultures. Collective cultural identities and their dynamism can be studied in a nuanced way through examination of the transfer of cultural objects from one region to another. The constant interaction between collectives prevented the emergence of clear or static borders. In order to map shifting collective identities it is necessary to consider the self-conscious claims that groups made about themselves over time, and the claims (even if reductive or disdainful) made about them by others.[3]

[1] Schorsch, *From Text to Context*, 71–92.

[2] A rather polemical sketch of the historiography of Sepharad versus Ashkenaz can be found in Malkiel, *Reconstructing Ashkenaz*, 3–33.

[3] Emcke, *Kollektive Identitäten*, 19–20.

Though medieval Ashkenazi Jews received and adapted cultural products from elsewhere, they rarely reflected on matters of 'otherness' or consciously documented these acts of appropriation. Medieval Ashkenazi self-consciousness can only be reconstructed from a very few sources, which require careful interpretation in order to yield any understanding of the self and of the other. This is fairly easy in the case of the Christian other, who is often polemically addressed or described, but interactions between Ashkenazi and other contemporary Jewish communities have left fewer explicit traces. There is clear evidence of Ashkenazi opposition to the halakhic rulings of other Jewish communities, but other types of inner Jewish cultural transfer appear to have elicited little comment or explicit rejection on the part of Ashkenazi authors. Among the few medieval sources that provide insight into the Ashkenazi understanding of other Jewish subcultures of the time are meta-texts on authorship (rubrics) that introduce the Sephardi texts that were incorporated into Ashkenazi liturgical manuscripts.

Liturgy is one of the fields in which differences between Jewish communities are apparent to travellers attending prayer services in a Jewish community that follows another rite. In some cases the exact wording of a prayer may be different, but it is in the field of liturgical poetry (*piyut*) that the differences between communities become most evident. The Sephardi and Ashkenazi traditions differed regarding the fixed liturgical texts to which *piyutim* were attached, and were distinguished by many features of the *piyutim* themselves, such as their subject, structural pattern, style, and linguistic elements. Nevertheless, during the late twelfth and early thirteenth centuries some Sephardi texts were incorporated into the Ashkenazi prayer collections. Some of these importations occurred in places within parts of the liturgy that had received less attention from the early Ashkenazi poets; they also occurred where multiple texts could be recited, as in the case of the *kinot* (laments) for the fast day of Tishah Be'av. To the modern reader these Sephardi texts stand out within the Ashkenazi liturgy because they mirror the Andalusian tradition of Hebrew poetry; they are linked to distinct passages in the fixed liturgy and generally employ aesthetic and poetic techniques that are typical of their cultural sphere of origin. Interestingly, these Sephardi *piyutim* also served as models for Ashkenazi writers of the late twelfth and thirteenth centuries. They composed their own poetic creations for the same liturgical passages and adopted formal elements of the Sephardi poems, such as stanza forms, biblical language, and quantitative metre. Thus, by the time that the majority of liturgical manuscripts were copied, that is, from the late thirteenth to the fifteenth centuries, Ashkenazi prayer books contained a multitude of poems for prayers such as 'Barkhu', Kaddish, and Yizkor; these *piyutim* could be recited whenever the community wished.[4] A comparable development can be seen in manuscripts for Tishah Be'av. Ashkenazi liturgy for that day had long contained both classical *kinot*, composed mainly by Eleazar birabbi Kalir, and Ashkenazi *kinot* from the twelfth to thirteenth centuries. The former lamented the destruction of Jerusalem and the Temple and the latter linked laments over the past destruction with mourning for the victims of contemporary persecutions.[5] Now, however, a new component was added: Sephardi strophic *kinot* on the destruction of Jerusalem. Some newer manuscripts also contain Ashkenazi *kinot* that imitate Sephardi ones. Several—derivative—Ashkenazi compositions were modelled on Judah Halevi's lament 'Zion, will you not enquire after the welfare of your prisoners?'[6] The mixture of classical Ashkenazi, Sephardi, and Sephardi-style *kinot* offers an exemplary corpus for examining the ways that different texts were treated, even if the study sample is rather small.

The Ashkenazi scholars and poets did not express their relation to the Sephardi *piyutim* in the Ashkenazi *maḥzor* (festival prayer book) in any conscious or reflective manner. Even in *piyut* commentary, a genre that allowed for discussions of authorship and style, there are no comments about the 'otherness' of these Sephardi *piyutim*, or reflections on the ways that they are different from classical or Ashkenazi *piyutim*.[7] Only in the rubrics to specific compositions, the meta-texts that frame certain *piyutim*, can one find discussions of authorship or comments on aspects of performance that highlight the

[4] Such collections occur in many French and Ashkenazi *sidur* manuscripts. An initial study will be part of a projected monograph on Sepharad in *Maḥzor ashkenaz*.

[5] In several Ashkenazi *kinot* the description of the destruction of Jerusalem is very similar to that of contemporary persecutions, partly because the Ashkenazi *paytanim* saw the world through the lens of biblical expressions and experience, and partly because the genre dictated strict rules of content. The influence of the rabbinic notion that 'the death of righteous people is equivalent to the burning of the Temple of the Almighty' (BT *RH* 17*a*) may also have been a factor.

[6] A full study of the Ashkenazi derivatives of 'Zion, will you not enquire?' will be part of the aforementioned projected monograph on Sepharad in *Maḥzor ashkenaz*. For a first study of one of the Ashkenazi derivatives see Hollender, '"Tsion She'arit Bne Ya'aqov": An Ashkenazic *Qina* in Sephardic Garb'. Other Zionides are discussed in Hollender, '"Zion, Will You not Inquire After the Well-Being of Your Miserable Ones?"'

[7] Several commentaries on Sephardi *piyutim* have been transmitted in Abraham ben Azriel's *Sefer arugat habosem*, ed. Urbach. Further commentaries have been identified in Hollender, *Clavis Commentariorum of Hebrew Liturgical Poetry*.

differences between traditional Ashkenazi *piyutim* and those imported from the Sephardi cultural arena. In general, rubrics to *piyutim* identify the relevant 'anchor' in the fixed liturgy (e.g. 'for the Shema prayer on the sabbath of *ḥol hamo'ed* Sukkot') and offer 'stage directions' (e.g. 'After this, [the liturgy continues] as on the previous day'). This general type of rubric should be differentiated from shorter rubrics on specific *piyutim*, which contain limited information about the type of *piyut*, its author, or the melody (*nigun*) associated with it. On rare occasions a rubric may contain information about the circumstances of the text's composition.[8]

In general, rubrics were written by the scribe who penned the manuscript, but in some manuscripts they were added by later hands. Scribes who crafted the rubrics culled their information from the liturgical manuscripts they copied, from name acrostics in the *piyutim* themselves, and probably from *piyut* commentaries. Additional sources of knowledge cannot be identified at present.[9]

In most Ashkenazi liturgical manuscripts there was no systematic use of rubrics for *piyutim*. They were at times inserted before a series of *piyutim* which the scribe presumed were by the same author, or which he saw as a grouping. Sometimes the rubric relays information which the scribe considered important enough to pass on. This usually pertained to the authorship of the *piyut*,[10] and, more rarely, the occasion for which it was written or the event that it memorialized. The rubric might also list the model which a certain *piyut* followed, or the melody with which it was associated. Even though Ashkenazi authors later copied the style of Sephardi *piyutim* that had been included in the Ashkenazi liturgy of the thirteenth century, the 'originals' remained stylistically distinct. In such cases, rubrics could have both identified the Sephardi poetry as imported from another Jewish subculture and served to incorporate the foreign texts into their new Ashkenazi environment.

[8] One unique manuscript, MS British Library 659 (copied in 1349 in Jerusalem and later brought to Europe, where it was used by Ashkenazi communities), labels *piyutim* according to the local rite in which they used to be recited; see E. Fleischer, 'Prayer and Liturgical Poetry in the Great Amsterdam Mahzor', 41.

[9] For examples of rubrics and their various sources see e.g. E. Fleischer, 'Prayer and Piyyut in the Worms Maḥzor', 55–7.

[10] This would have been the case for the Ashkenazi authors who constituted part of the known intellectual society. Some manuscripts display an interest in the Ashkenazi *paytanim* that could be construed as an effort to record a kind of intellectual history or *Gelehrtengeschichte* of medieval Ashkenaz.

For this initial study of rubrics containing attributions and descriptions, forty-four Ashkenazi liturgical manuscripts from the thirteenth to fifteenth centuries were analysed. Collectively they contain more than 1,400 *kinot*. The collections include both prayer books for the whole year and specialized collections of *kinot*. Only a minority of the *kinot* in these manuscripts carry meaningful rubrics, that is, ones that contain more than the word *aḥeret* ('another one') or the phrase *kinah aḥeret* ('another *kinah*') to indicate the beginning of the next *piyut*. This study examines only the meaningful rubrics of *kinot* that were either composed by Sephardi authors or that follow Sephardi style; the data consists of eighty-three rubrics for twenty-two different *kinot*. Only seven of these *kinot*, resulting in thirty-three related rubrics, were composed by Sephardi *paytanim*. Twelve *kinot* were most probably composed in Ashkenaz; three that have Sephardi-related rubrics and which also show Sephardi influence are anonymous and might therefore be attributed to Sephardi or non-Sephardi authors.

The difference in quantity and quality between the rubrics for Sephardi and Ashkenazi *piyutim* suggests that external sources of information about Sephardi *piyutim* were less readily available.[11] However, at least with regard to the name acrostics that were used to sign the pieces (usually in the first letters of stanzas) as a source of information on their authors, the availability of information may be attributed to regional customs: while Ashkenazi *paytanim* signed with their name plus their patronym, Sephardi authors would typically incorporate only their given names, and the rare exceptions might add further identifying descriptors.[12]

Interestingly, the term 'Sephardi' occurs in this corpus only in connection

[11] The material transmission of Sephardi poetry into Ashkenaz has not yet been researched. It can be assumed that transmission occurred via France, but since we do not know much about the collections in which the texts appeared, nothing can be said about the transmission of meta-knowledge together with the texts. Like their Ashkenazi counterparts, Sephardi copyists sometimes inserted rubrics with attributions in liturgical manuscripts. It is unclear whether the manuscript versions of the best-known Sephardi *piyut* commentary—that of David ben Joseph Abudraham—transmit all of the rubrics that appear in the printed edition (*Sefer tashlum abudraham. Vehu seder avodat yom hakipurim hameyuḥas leyosi ben yosi vegam piyutim shonim shel paytanim hagedolim im perush gadol hamefarshim rabenu david bar yosef bar david abudraham*, ed. Prins). Many of the rubrics in this commentary are based on the acrostics, although in some cases the full name of the author is provided—even though the acrostic does not present it in this form. This evidence proves that some information about Andalusian authors reached Christian Spain, from where this knowledge could have been transmitted to Ashkenaz.

[12] On the introduction of long patronyms and other names into acrostics in *piyutim*, see E. Fleischer, 'Issues Regarding the Poetry of the First Italian *Paytanim*' (Heb.), 139–40.

with three *kinot*, two of them composed in Ashkenaz. The third one is 'Esh tukad bekirbi be'aloti al libi' (א 7736, 'Fire burns inside me'[13]), an anonymous text with alphabetical acrostic but without indication of its author or country of origin. Among all the *kinot* in the Ashkenazi liturgy that employ Sephardi style, this is the hardest to identify either as an originally Sephardi piece or as an Ashkenazi one employing Sephardi style, since it is highly structured in both form and content. The only clue to Sephardi authorship is the fact that it was used not only in Ashkenaz, but also in Sepharad, Rome, and Yemen. The *kinah* was incorporated early on into the Ashkenazi liturgy, but was rarely transmitted with a rubric. The three meaningful rubrics are identical, naming it *kinah sefaradit*, without identifying any particular author.[14] This presumably reflects the absence of additional information. By contrast, the rubrics to similarly structured *kinot* in the same section of the liturgy identify their Ashkenazi authors; only 'Me'onei shamayim sheḥakim' (מ 1987; 'Palaces of heaven') by Menahem ben Jacob of Worms (d.1204), which precisely replicates the strophic and poetic structures of 'Fire burns inside me', is described as Sephardi in two rubrics.

It is possible that its own similarities to the Sephardi 'Fire burns inside me' influenced the rubrics written for 'Palaces of heaven'. Two rubrics on this *kinah* contain the instruction '[to be sung] using a [the?] Sephardi melody [*nigun*]'.[15] Still, while the reference to the Sephardi melody is transmitted in two rubrics, the *kinah* itself is attributed to its well-known Ashkenazi author in all of the thirteen meaningful rubrics in the corpus studied; the city of Worms is mentioned in seven of them.[16] It was clearly easier for the Ashkenazi scribes who composed the rubrics to identify the Ashkenazi author and his home town—and it may also have been more important than referring to the Sephardi style of the *kinah*. By differentiating between the Sephardi

[13] *Piyutim* are referred to by their initial words and number in Davidson, *Thesaurus* (Heb.).

[14] See MS Arras, Bibliothèque Municipale MS 560; MS Prague, Národní Knihovna v Praze VI Ea 2; MS Vatican, Biblioteca Apostolica ebr. 312.

[15] MS Arras, Bibliothèque Municipale MS 560; MS Oxford Bodleian Library Can Or 139 (Neubauer 1027). MS Parma, Biblioteca Palatina, Cod. Parm 3005 also contains 'on the melody', but then ends without identifying the melody. This is most probably a mistake of the copyist. The Hebrew texts use the preposition *b*-, but since they are not vocalized, the question of determination cannot be answered. It is possible that the first author of the rubric referred to the melody of the only *kinah* termed Sephardi in all its meaningful rubrics, 'Fire burns inside me', which belongs to the same group of *kinot* and is recited in close proximity to it, in which case one might want to read a determination with the preposition.

[16] MS Parma, Biblioteca Palatina Cod. Parm. 3005 attributes it to 'the same author' as the previous *kinah* and thereby correctly identifies the author.

piyut and the Ashkenazi one, to be performed using a Sephardi tune, the Ashkenazi rubricators firmly anchored 'Palaces of heaven' within the sphere of Ashkenaz.

The third text which rubrics explicitly identify as 'Sephardi' is the anonymous Zionide,[17] 'Tsiyon keḥi kol tsari gilad' (צ 318; 'Zion, take all the balm of Gilead'). Eight meaningful rubrics for this poem exist in the corpus studied. Three describe the *kinah* as Sephardi,[18] and one identifies it as derived, in construction and melody, from Judah Halevi's 'Tsiyon halo tishali lishlom asirayikh?' (צ 292; 'Zion, will you not enquire after the well-being of your imprisoned ones?').[19] The difference in terminology in these rubrics suggests that their authors had no uniform and authoritative information on the origin of the *piyut*; this situation is also mirrored in the ascription of the *kinah* to other authors (see below). Out of the ten Ashkenazi Zionides modelled on Judah Halevi's lament and which possess meaningful rubrics, this is the only one that is described as 'Sephardi', though each appears with a rubric that identifies its author.[20] The authorship and provenance—Sephardi or Ashkenazi—of this *kinah* was debated by both medieval rubricators and modern scholars.[21] This may be due to the fact that 'Zion, take all the balm of Gilead' was introduced into the Ashkenazi liturgy before other anonymous Zionides, which are transmitted in far fewer manuscripts. Moreover, the latter piece usually appears right after Judah Halevi's famous poem.

The term 'Sephardi' is thus explicitly used only in connection with a lone

[17] The term 'Zionide' describes both Judah Halevi's 'Zion, will you not enquire?' and the *kinot* composed on that model, for the same term is the opening word in each of the compositions. In Ashkenazi liturgy Zionides form a subgenre of *kinot* recited on the afternoon of Tishah Be'av.

[18] Cremona, Archiva Municipale, fragment 34; Erlangen, Universitätsbibliothek MS 2601; Vatican, Biblioteca Apostolica MS ebr. 312.

[19] Leiden, Universiteitsbibliotheek Acad. 214.

[20] Of these ten Ashkenazi Zionides, six have only one meaningful rubric, two have two meaningful rubrics, one has three meaningful rubrics, and the Zionide by Eleazar ben Judah of Worms has six meaningful rubrics. Additionally the anonymous 'Zion, take all the balm of Gilead' has eight meaningful rubrics. Only the latter *kinah* and Eleazar ben Judah's Zionide have rubrics that mention style and melody. On these two *kinot* see also Hollender, 'Adoption and Adaptation'.

[21] In the corpus studied none of the other Ashkenazi Zionides without a name acrostic has a meaningful rubric. Confusion as to which *paytan* named Meir was also called Meir Lombard is mirrored by the attribution to Meir Lombard of two different Zionides (one by Meir ben Eleazar and the other by Meir ben Judah), albeit in different manuscripts. Similarity of name also led to the erroneous attribution of Eleazar ben Judah's Zionide to Eleazar Hadarshan of Würzburg, in MS Dresden, Sächsische Landesbibliothek Eb A. In all cases, these errors concern Ashkenazi *paytanim*.

anonymous Sephardi *kinah*, which entered the Ashkenazi liturgy in the twelfth century at the latest, and in connection with two Ashkenazi *kinot* that closely follow a Sephardi model. It is tempting to assume that the main feature the rubricators identified as 'Sephardi' was the quantitative metre—which would certainly have influenced the choice of melodies for synagogue performance, since in all three cases some rubrics specify the melody as a special feature of the *kinah*. But most *kinot* that employ quantitative metre (even the aforementioned Ashkenazi 'derivatives', labelled 'Sephardi' in the rubrics) are not singled out as Sephardi.

What features of an anonymous *kinah* led Ashkenazi scribes to label it 'Sephardi' in the rubrics they composed? The example of Menahem ben Jacob's 'Palaces of heaven'—whose author is named and whose melody is labelled 'Sephardi'—suggests that the only criteria shared by the texts labelled 'Sephardi' are their anonymity and certain structural features, such as the monorhyme of verses with *caesura* in the case of the Zionide. However, these criteria are not sufficient to necessitate the description of a text as Sephardi in the rubrics, since another anonymous Sephardi *kinah* with these same features, 'Baleil hazeh yivkheyun viyelilu banai' (ב 721; 'In this night my sons will cry and wail'), is never explicitly labelled Sephardi. This *kinah* appears in numerous Ashkenazi manuscripts, usually with rubrics indicating recitation on the eve of Tishah Be'av (and in some communities, only when that coincides with the end of sabbath). In one instance it is introduced with the melody to be used[22]—the one associated with Eleazar birabbi Kalir's 'Ad anah bekhiyah tsiyon' (א 2104; 'How long must Zion cry', also known as 'Az beḥata'einu ḥarav mikdash'). Yet the structural differences between the Kalirian *kinah* and its Sephardi counterpart would seem to preclude parallels in their performance; and it is possible that an inaccurate rubric had been copied by an inattentive scribe. In short, the term 'Sephardi' was not used consistently for Sephardi *kinot* or for ones inspired by Sephardi models. The label did not function as a marker to differentiate between *kinot* that originated in different Jewish cultures.

The most important information transmitted in rubrics was generally about the author of the *piyut*. Almost all meaningful rubrics on Ashkenazi *kinot* contain such attributions; these were copied into printed *maḥzorim* and have informed modern readers. The three main Sephardi poets who contributed to the Ashkenazi liturgy are present in the corpus studied: Judah Halevi, Solomon Ibn Gabirol, and Abraham Ibn Ezra.

[22] See MS Paris, Musée de Cluny 12290.

Judah Halevi was undeniably the best-known Sephardi poet in medieval Ashkenaz. In addition to numerous short pieces of his that are included among miscellaneous *piyutim* at the end of many Ashkenazi *sidur* manuscripts, two of his *kinot* appear in the Ashkenazi liturgy for Tishah Be'av. Both were transmitted in Ashkenazi manuscripts with meaningful rubrics containing correct ascriptions: 'Yom akhpai hikhbadtiv yikhpelu avonai' (י 1605; 'The day of my oppression weighed heavily upon me') is attributed to 'Rabbenu Judah' once (Oxford, Bodleian Library MS Opp. 12) and to 'Rabbenu Judah Castilian' in five other manuscripts.[23] The famous Zionide 'Tsiyon halo tishali lishlom asirayikh?' (צ 292; 'Zion, will you not enquire after the wellbeing of your imprisoned ones?') is introduced with attributions to 'Rabbenu Judah (the) Castilian' in seventeen manuscripts. Even though the poem does not contain a name acrostic, in Ashkenazi manuscripts it is attributed only to Judah Halevi, and not to any other *paytan*. We can thus conclude that the lament was imported to Ashkenaz together with meta-information about the author. Eight of the manuscripts also include the information that Judah Halevi composed or recited this *kinah* when standing at Mount Zion. Perhaps this meta-information was also transferred to Ashkenaz along with the lament.[24] The identification of Judah Halevi as 'Castilian' and not 'Sephardi' correctly reflects both geopolitical realities and Andalusian traditions. Judah Halevi's Andalusian contemporaries knew him as 'the Castilian', for he had come to Andalusia from Christian-ruled territories. He is also commonly referred to as 'Castilian' in the liturgical manuscripts from Ashkenaz and northern France that contain his *piyutim*; it is noteworthy that these sources never use the same label for any other poet. While Judah Halevi's *piyutim* are not always explicitly attributed to him, and while it cannot be ruled out that some *piyutim* were inaccurately attributed to him—beyond the corpus studied here—the number of correct attributions is indicative of the exceptional status afforded to this Sephardi poet in Ashkenaz. Apparently his

[23] Hamburg, Staats- und Universitätsbibliothek Cod. hebr. 37, fo. 168^v; Jerusalem, The National Library of Israel MS Heb. 4° 6724, fo. 34^r; Oxford , Bodleian Library, MS Mich 571 (Neubauer 1097), 130^r; Paris, Musée de Cluny 12290, fo. 351^v; Prague, Jewish Museum of Prague (Židovské muzeum), MS 120, fo. 135^r.

[24] For a discussion of this early nucleus of the legend about Judah Halevi's death as a martyr in Jerusalem that was then formulated by Gedalyah Ibn Yahya, see Fraenkel, 'An Ashkenazi Tradition on the Arrival of R. Judah Halevi in Jerusalem' (Heb.), 5–14. Fraenkel's assumption that the narrative was transmitted to Ashkenaz twice—once with the story about the 'king of Sepharad', whom Judah Halevi is said to have accompanied, and once without reference to the king—cannot be substantiated. Neither can his assumption that the personal lament was turned into a *kinah* in Sepharad and subsequently imported into Ashkenaz.

unusual moniker 'the Castilian', whose use was limited to rubrics in liturgical manuscripts, was part of the meta-knowledge transmitted together with his *piyutim* when they were transferred from Sepharad to Ashkenaz.[25] Most rubrics retain this information; it is missing in only two out of the twenty-three rubrics on the two *kinot* by Judah Halevi. On the other hand only four rubrics, all of them for 'Zion, will you not enquire?', contain the identifier 'Halevi'. Moreover, the rubrics concerning him do not follow the standard syntax of attributions employed in Ashkenazi liturgical manuscripts. These generally identify the author and, if they mention his place of origin or residence, they introduce that information with the preposition *mi-* (from), for example *elazar mivormaiza*.

Did the Ashkenazi scribes and their audiences understand the label 'Castilian' as a reference to an identifiable Jewish community located outside Sepharad, namely the Jewish community in Christian Spain—as the Andalusian authors of the twelfth century would have argued?[26] Frequent travel—and its corollary, cultural transfer—between Jewish communities could have made contemporaneous Jews conscious of the differences between Andalusia under Islamic rule and the two most important Christian kingdoms, Castile and Aragon, at least with respect to the dissimilar legal status of Jews and their (limited) cultural differences. This might have resulted in the choice of terminology that distinguishes between the two realms. However, the term Kastilya (קשטליא) and its grammatical derivations are not common in medieval Ashkenazi writings.[27] Similarly, contemporary High Middle German does not differentiate between the parts of the Iberian peninsula, using *spanje* (which only later turned into the plural Spanien) indiscriminately when it comes to this region.

Use of the label 'Castilian' for Judah Halevi, together with the absence of the term *hasefaradi*—even for Abraham Ibn Ezra and Solomon Ibn Gabirol

[25] Obviously Judah Halevi had been recognized as a renowned poet in Andalusia. That position would have prompted Sephardi scribes to include attributions in the manuscripts that ultimately would have served as sources for the copies that came to Ashkenaz.

[26] In the 12th century a major political (and to some extent cultural) border divided the Iberian peninsula, demarcating the Muslim kingdoms in Andalusia and the Christian kingdoms of Castilia and Aragon. Judah Halevi had come to Granada from Christian Spain. On his contemporaries' assessment of the significance of his migration see Brener, *Judah Halevi and His Circle*, 55–6, 64–9.

[27] Asher ben Yehiel used the term Kastilya (קשטיליא) in one of his responsa, though only after he had emigrated to the Iberian peninsula; see Bar Ilan Responsa Project, *She'elot uteshuvot harosh*, ch. 17, §6: ומיום בואי לארץ זאת מנעתי בכל ארץ קשטיליא שלא לכוף ('and from the day of my arrival in this country I prohibited in the whole land of Kastilya to bow').

when their *piyutim* were transmitted in Ashkenaz—raises the possibility that the Ashkenazi scribes, who listed the towns of origin of many Ashkenazi *paytanim*, were not interested in identifying poets who belonged to Jewish communities outside Ashkenaz. If the geographical information provided for Ashkenazi *paytanim* was usually their town of origin, the sparse information about Sephardi authors in rubrics to their *piyutim* may also point to a lack of detailed knowledge, particularly if we assume that liturgical manuscripts were often copied by professional scribes and not by scholars.[28] As *Sefer ḥasidim* noted, professional scribes were often less educated than scholars and teachers. When faced with the meta-information transmitted together with Judah Halevi's poems, a poorly educated scribe might easily have assumed the foreign-looking word קשטלין to be a personal name, not a geographical term, especially when prefixed by the definite article rather than the standard preposition.

This apparently happened in later manuscripts. By the end of the thirteenth century the spelling of 'Castilian' had changed to קעשטלין, that is [kɛstliːn], in a number of manuscripts. Not coincidentally, this was a period in which the transcription of German into Hebrew letters changed: the *ayin* came into use for the sounds [eː] and [e].[29] Also, a few vocalized manuscripts present the pronunciation [kɛstlin], vocalizing the *kof* with *tsere*. This strengthens the impression that the Ashkenazi scribes were looking for a German name rather than for a geographical identifier, and accordingly reinterpreted the string of consonants along patterns that were familiar to them. The syllable *-lin* was a known German diminutive and, following German morphology, a *Kasten* (box) could be turned into a small *Kästlin*. Alternatively, this word could have been derived from *Kestene* (chestnuts). The unfamiliar 'Castilian' was thus easily mistaken for a personal name, one that accorded with familiar morphology.[30] These attributions could be seen as evidence

[28] On the role of scholars in the production of Hebrew manuscripts see Beit-Arié, 'Transmission of Texts by Scribes and Copyists'.

[29] On the use of *ayin* as a grapheme for the Middle High German vowels [eː] and [e], see Timm, *Graphische und phonetische Struktur des Westjiddischen*, 122–31.

[30] On the other hand, there was the partial visual parallel between קשטלין and קליר, especially since both were often prefixed with the definite article, creating the often quoted form *hakalir* and a hypothetical *hakastlin*. This would, however, have produced a doubly closed syllable, *kastl*, which cannot exist in Hebrew and would have had to be split into *kas-te-lin* with three syllables, partly destroying the parallel. This form is attested in several liturgical manuscripts, both from France and from Ashkenaz, in rubrics for *piyutim* by Judah Halevi that were appended to the *sidur*. However, in the selected corpus of rubrics on *kinot* under consideration here, the determined form without the proper name is not attested. Only two out of sixteen meaningful

of a (possibly unwitting) masking of Judah Halevi's foreign origins, which facilitated his assimilation into the Ashkenazi cultural sphere.

The corpus studied also includes an erroneous attribution to Judah Halevi. The only manuscript that contains a meaningful rubric for the Ashkenazi *kinah* 'Sarfu habirah lehakhis el hanora' (ש 2203; 'They burned the capital to infuriate the awesome God'), ascribes it to Judah Halevi (אחרת מרבינו יהודה קשטלין, another [one] by R. Judah Kastelin/Kestlin).[31] This *kinah* is parallel in form to Baruch ben Samuel's 'Etsba'otai shaflu' (א 7244; 'My fingers are lowered'), with regard to the quantitative metre and the *caesura* in each stich, and to the laments that conclude each stich. It lacks the name acrostic that would otherwise ease identification. It seems that the attribution of this anonymous *kinah* to Judah Halevi was initiated by a scribe who recognized that Sephardi poetic techniques were employed in the *kinah*, and thus assumed that it belonged to the most famous Sephardi poet. However, false attributions, even for Ashkenazi compositions, are common in rubrics of *piyutim* that have no name acrostic.[32] They are more common in the case of Sephardi *piyutim* and of those that employ Sephardi poetic techniques (such as quantitative metre) than in the case of 'standard' Ashkenazi *piyutim*. Not only was it more difficult to obtain information on Sephardi authors; once a text was identified as Sephardi, the choice of known authors to whom it could be attributed was rather limited.

Information about *paytanim* was transmitted in different literary environments in Ashkenaz and Sepharad. In the former, *piyutim* were usually signed with extended name acrostics. Rubricators distilled this information and, on rare occasions, mention the events lamented in the *piyutim*. *Piyut* commentaries also transmit some information on famous *paytanim* and on the way they composed their works.[33] When Sephardi *piyutim* contain name acrostics, these are short. The most important Sephardi work containing detailed information on Hebrew poets, Moses Ibn Ezra's treatise on rhetoric and poetry,

rubrics on the great Zionide combine the name Judah with the determined form *hakestlin* (assuming that the vocalization from Oxford, Bodleian Library, MS Mich 571 (Neubauer 1097) can be transferred to the non-vocalized occurrence in Dresden, Sächsische Landesbibliothek Eb A).

[31] Hamburg, Staats- und Universitätsbibliothek Cod. hebr. 37.

[32] The most interesting cases of fictitious attribution in the Ashkenazi *maḥzor* are probably those of 'Unetaneh tokef', attributed to R. Amnon, and of 'Asher heni', attributed to R. Asher Halevi, whose role as assumed founder of the Jewish community in Worms is tied to this *piyut*. See Raspe, 'Ascher ha-lewi und die Gründung des jüdischen Worms'.

[33] Hollender, *Piyyut Commentary in Medieval Ashkenaz*, 147–70.

Kitāb al-Muḥāḍara wa-al-Mudhākara, is not a liturgical composition. Written in Arabic, it was not accessible to Ashkenazi scholars and scribes.[34]

In the case of Solomon Ibn Gabirol, the rubrics show that his name and his identity as a poet were both known in Ashkenaz, but little more. Only one *kinah* of his is included among the Ashkenazi *kinot* for Tishah Be'av: 'Shomron kol titen' (ש 686; 'Shomron proclaimed') is written in *muwashshaḥ* style and bears the name acrostic 'Solomon'. The *kinah* is introduced in one rubric with the melody to be used, that of 'Me'onei shamayim sheḥakim' ('Palaces of heaven'), a *kinah* in Sephardi style by Menahem ben Jacob (mentioned above). Since the same manuscript (Erlangen Universitätsbibliothek 2601) describes that *kinah* as 'Sephardi', Ibn Gabirol's *kinah* is, at least implicitly, placed in the relevant cultural sphere. In the second meaningful rubric (Oxford, Bodleian Library MS Opp. 12), however, the *kinah* is ascribed to the tenth-century Italian *paytan* Solomon Habavli, whose *piyutim* share only one essential element with many of Solomon Ibn Gabirol's poems: the name acrostic 'Solomon' that is sometimes extended to 'Solomon Hakatan' (Solomon the Young One). Yet Solomon Habavli never employed quantitative metre or *muwashshaḥ*-type stanzas. The misattribution was clearly based on the acrostic; and it shows that Solomon Ibn Gabirol was less known in Ashkenaz than the earlier Italian *paytan*.

Two *kinot* in the corpus studied are erroneously attributed to Solomon Ibn Gabirol. 'Shekurat lo miyayin hashlikhi tupyakh' (ש 1158; 'You who are drunk but not with wine, cast away your timbrels'), by Solomon ben Isaac Gerondi, is attributed to different authors in three different manuscripts: to 'Rabbenu Solomon' (Oxford, Bodleian Library MS Opp. 12), to 'R. Solomon Gabirol, may the memory of this righteous one be blessed' (Paris, Musée Cluny 12290), and to the above-mentioned Solomon Habavli (Vatican, Biblioteca Apostolica ebr. 312). Once again, the name acrostic 'Solomon' triggered all of these attributions. Since the *kinah* is Sephardi in style, the attribution to Solomon Ibn Gabirol may have been inspired by the knowledge that he was a Sephardi poet who had contributed some *piyutim* to the Ashkenazi liturgy. The other erroneous attribution concerns the Ashkenazi Zionide 'Zion, take all the balm of Gilead' discussed above, which does not have a name acrostic.[35]

The situation is similar with regard to Abraham Ibn Ezra. Unlike the other Sephardi poets discussed up to this point, he was known in Ashkenaz mainly for his Bible commentaries, which were quoted in the circles of the

[34] Halkin, ed., *Moses Ibn Ezra* (Heb.).

[35] On the different attributions of this *kinah* see below.

German Pietists from the early thirteenth century (if not earlier) and in thirteenth-century compilations of Tosafist Torah commentaries.[36] Although his correspondence with Rabbenu Tam also included an exchange of poems,[37] few of his *piyutim* were included in the Ashkenazi liturgy. In one manuscript, however, the *kinah* 'Amrah tsiyon eikh yatsuni banai?' (א 5832; 'Zion said, how did my sons go out from me?') is correctly attributed to Abraham Ibn Ezra.[38] Containing the acrostic 'Abraham', this *kinah* also exhibits several Sephardi features. Attribution was further facilitated by the fact that most Ashkenazi *paytanim* named Abraham included their patronym when signing their name in acrostics to their *piyutim*. It is also possible that the text was transmitted to Ashkenaz together with the correct attribution. However, since it appears in Ashkenaz only in this lone fourteenth-century manuscript, and was not included in printed *kinot* collections, little importance can be attached to its correct attribution.

Another attribution to Abraham Ibn Ezra in an Ashkenazi manuscript concerns the previously discussed Ashkenazi Zionide, 'Zion, take all the balm of Gilead'. This information was later transmitted in printed editions of *kinot*. Apart from being labelled 'Sephardi' in some rubrics and attributed to Solomon Ibn Gabirol and to Elijah the Elder in others, this *kinah* is attributed to Abraham the Astrologer (Abraham Hahozeh) in a manuscript that contains many interesting rubrics. Modern scholarship has sought to identify this figure with Abraham Ibn Ezra, given citations from his works in texts by Eleazar of Worms and his German Pietist pupils that refer to Abraham the Astrologer.[39] Though apparently composed by an Ashkenazi author, the Zionide was attributed in the rubrics created by medieval scribes to Sephardi authors whose names they knew, such as Abraham Ibn Ezra or Solomon Ibn Gabirol. Uncertainty regarding the origin of this anonymous Zionide may account for its labelling as 'Sephardi' in a number of rubrics.[40]

'Zion, take all the balm of Gilead' is among the oldest Ashkenazi derivatives of 'Zion, will you not enquire?' and is the Ashkenazi Zionide that is most often transmitted in the manuscripts studied, appearing twenty-one times.

[36] e.g. the Hizkuni; see Kanarfogel, *The Intellectual History and Rabbinic Culture of Medieval Ashkenaz*, 121.

[37] See Luzzatto, *Ha'takot yekarot shel shu"t veshirim*. A new edition can be found in *Shirat rabenu tam*, ed. Meiseles, 140–4.

[38] Oxford, Bodleian Library MS Can. Or. 86.

[39] Y. L. Fleischer, 'How Many Rabbis Existed by the Name R. Abraham Hahozeh?' (Heb.); Abramson, 'Prophet, Visionary, and Seer' (Heb.).

[40] On the ambiguity in this Zionide that invited different attributions, see Hollender, 'Angepasste Nachdichtungen'.

Nevertheless, only eight meaningful rubrics for this *kinah* are known, of which four contain ascriptions and four comment on its Sephardi style, its melody, and its model.

In this case, however, the dating of the manuscripts that contain the rubrics sheds light on the emergence of different attributions.[41] The only dated manuscript, Oxford, Bodleian MS Mich 571 (Neubauer 1097), copied in 1289, ascribes the *kinah* to Abraham the Astrologer. The privately owned manuscript that attributes it to Solomon Ibn Gabirol (using the laconic 'Gabirol') probably dates from the late thirteenth or early fourteenth century. A rubric found in fragments from a *maḥzor* that had been used in the bindings of archival files from Cremona, dated to the same time, refers to the *kinah* as 'Sephardi'. MS Vatican, Biblioteca Apostolica ebr. 319, from the fourteenth century, contains an ascription to Rabbenu Solomon; this may refer to Solomon Ibn Gabirol or to Solomon Habavli, to whom two other Sephardi *kinot* were also attributed. Of the two manuscripts that have been dated to the fourteenth or fifteenth centuries, MS Leiden Acad. 214 points to the model of 'Zion, will you not enquire?'; Erlangen, Universitätsbibliothek MS 2601 describes the *kinah* as 'Sephardi'. Two rubrics exist in manuscripts that were copied in the fifteenth century, with Vatican, Biblioteca Apostolica ebr. 312 picking up the description as Sephardi, while Jerusalem, JNL MS Heb. 4° 6724 contains an attribution to Elijah the Elder. In the context of liturgical poetry, R. Elijah the Elder is often identified as Elijah ben Menahem of Le Mans in France, who lived during the eleventh century; he contributed to the Ashkenazi poetic tradition, and was sometimes quoted by the Tosafists.[42] Of the

[41] In the aforementioned attributions of Sephardi *kinot* to the Italian *paytan* Solomon Habavli, the dating of the manuscripts transmitting these attributions does not contribute to a better understanding of the development. In both cases Oxford, Bodleian Library, MS Opp. 12, copied in the late 13th or early 14th century, transmits a rubric with an ascription, one to Solomon Habavli and one to 'R. Solomon'. The second ascription to Solomon Habavli occurs in a 15th-century manuscript (Vatican 312) that contains many attributions to Ashkenazi *paytanim*, including some references to the occasions for which the *piyutim* were written, one correct ascription to Judah Halevi ('Zion, will you not enquire?'), and two rubrics that define *kinot* as Sephardi. The erroneous ascription of a *kinah* by the Sephardi Solomon ben Isaac Gerondi to Solomon Ibn Gabirol occurs in a 14th-century manuscript (Paris, Musée de Cluny MS 12290); it also contains a few ascriptions to Ashkenazi authors and one correct ascription to Judah Halevi ('The day of my oppression'). The evidence is too uneven to interpret.

[42] See the anecdote about one R. Elijah visiting the great Ashkenazi *paytan* Simon ben Isaac and collaborating with him on a *piyut* for Passover, discussed in Grossman, *The Early Sages of Ashkenaz* (Heb.), 93–4; id., *The Early Sages of France* (Heb.), 87–8; E. Fleischer, 'Prayer and Piyyuṭ in the Worms Maḥzor', 37–8; Hollender, *Piyyut Commentary in Medieval Ashkenaz*, 155–6. Even though the identification of R. Elijah—who was mentioned as a contemporary of

four suggested authors he is the only one who can clearly be identified as Ashkenazi, but he, too, is not the author of this *kinah*, inspired by Judah Halevi's 'Zion, will you not enquire?' Assuming that the medieval scribes considered Abraham the Astrologer to be Abraham Ibn Ezra, the earlier ascriptions are to the Andalusian poets, and only a later manuscript names the Ashkenazi sage Elijah the Elder as the author. The earlier rubrics and the majority of the later ones thus point to an identification of the *kinah* as Sephardi.

An unusual rubric, added in a later hand in a Hamburg manuscript dating from the fourteenth century, mixes attributions in a way that renders the difference between Sepharad and Ashkenaz virtually insignificant. The original rubric correctly attributes 'Sha'ali serufah be'esh' (ש 132; 'Enquire, consumed in fire') to Meir of Rothenburg and describes it as a composition written on the occasion of the burning of the Torah (*sic*!) in Paris. The later rubric, however, adds that it was 'composed by Rabbenu Solomon bar Isaac, of blessed memory, or composed by Rabbenu Moses Maimon'. Neither is correct, but Solomon bar Isaac (Rashi) did compose *piyutim*, while Moses ben Maimon (Maimonides) is not known to have written poetry. Maimonides was, indeed, cited in the *piyut* commentaries composed by figures in the circle of the German Pietists; the most famous of these was *Sefer arugat habosem*, compiled by the Bohemian scholar Abraham ben Azriel in the early thirteenth century. These commentaries referred to Maimonides both as Moses Maimon and as Mosheh Hasefaradi, a name that he himself used.[43] That the scribe who penned the rubric imagined that the author of the *kinah* could just as easily have been Rashi or Maimonides suggests that he was markedly uninterested in distinguishing between Ashkenaz and Sepharad where the authorship of liturgical poetry was concerned. This evidence is unique in the corpus studied, and it is also late. Nevertheless it helps to illustrate the ease with which Ashkenazi liturgical traditions adopted Sephardi texts and authors and incorporated them seamlessly.

In the corpus studied, erroneous attributions are made to both Judah Halevi and Solomon Ibn Gabirol; this may also have occurred in the case of Abraham Ibn Ezra, the third important Sephardi poet included in the

Simon ben Isaac—with Elijah the Elder of Le Mans is not universally accepted in modern scholarship, he is the figure who was intended by the medieval authors of the narrative and who was accepted by their audiences.

[43] On this group of *piyut* commentaries see Hollender, 'Piyyut Commentary in the Nuremberg Mahzor'.

Ashkenazi liturgy. In none of these cases does the attribution function as a marker of foreign origin.

The lack of explicit references to the 'otherness' of Sephardi poetry in the meta-texts of Ashkenazi liturgical manuscripts may come as a surprise. The texts examined above may stimulate re-evaluation of the notion that Hebrew poetry was one of the boundary-markers between the medieval subcultures of Ashkenaz and Sefarad. The inclusion of Sephardi *piyutim* in the Ashkenazi *maḥzor*, and the routine way in which the accompanying rubrics present them, attest to cultural contact between medieval Ashkenaz and Sepharad, brokered, most probably, in France. They demonstrate an Ashkenazi openness to cultural products imported from other Jewish communities. They also attest to the self-esteem of Ashkenazi *paytanim* of the late twelfth and thirteenth centuries, who did not shy away from emulating certain Sephardi models. Still, if the rubrics of medieval *piyutim* offer no evidence of boundary-markers between Ashkenaz and Sepharad, neither do they suggest that medieval Jewish authors saw themselves as members of a unified society. The subtle differences between rubrics to Sephardi and Ashkenazi *piyutim* may depend largely on the information available. Physical distance was, however, not the major impediment to cultural transfer. More important factors in the separation between Ashkenaz and Sepharad, perhaps emblematic, were their different assessments of the information deemed worthy of transmission, especially across regional boundaries. Whereas in Ashkenaz knowledge about *paytanim* was transmitted in rubrics and in *piyut* commentaries as well as in folk narratives about *paytanim*, similar knowledge was not transferred together with the Sephardi *piyutim*. The Ashkenazi authors of rubrics perceived this as a shortcoming and dealt with it in different ways.[44] Over the course of time their endeavours created a more unified image of the contributors to the Ashkenazi *maḥzor*.

[44] Among them the attribution to Ashkenazi authors and the invention of the origin of Judah Halevi's Zionide. They also used the lack of available meta-knowledge as a factor in their decision in which cultural sphere a *kinah* had originated.

Bibliography

ABRAHAM BEN AZRIEL, *Sefer arugat habosem, kolel perushim lapiyutim*, ed. E. E. Urbach, 4 vols. (Jerusalem, 1939, 1963).

ABRAMSON, SHRAGA, 'Prophet, Visionary, and Seer: R. Abraham Hahozeh' (Heb.), in David Telzner (ed.), *Jubilee Volume in Honour of R. Mordecai Kirschblum* [Sefer yovel mugash likhvod harav mordekhai kirshblum] (Jerusalem, 1983), 117–39.

BEIT-ARIÉ, MALACHI, 'Transmission of Texts by Scribes and Copyists: Unconscious and Critical Interference', *Bulletin of the John Rylands University Library of Manchester*, 75/3 (1993), 33–51.

BRENER, ANN, *Judah Halevi and His Circle of Hebrew Poets in Granada* (Leiden, 2005).

DAVIDSON, ISRAEL, *Thesaurus of Medieval Hebrew Poetry* [Otsar hashirah vehapiyut], 4 vols. (New York, 1924–33).

EMCKE, CAROLIN, *Kollektive Identitäten: Sozialphilosophische Grundlagen* (Frankfurt am Main, 2010).

FLEISCHER, EZRA, 'Issues Regarding the Poetry of the First Italian *Paytanim*' (Heb.), *Hasifrut*, 30–31 (1981), 131–67.

——'Prayer and Liturgical Poetry in the Great Amsterdam Mahzor', in Albert van der Heide and Edward van Voolen (eds.), *The Amsterdam Mahzor: History, Liturgy, Illumination* (Leiden, 1989), 26–43.

——'Prayer and Piyyut in the Worms Maḥzor', in Malachi Beit-Arié (ed.), *Worms Maḥzor: MS Jewish National and University Library Heb 4°781/1. Introductory Volume* (Jerusalem, 1985), 37–78.

FLEISCHER, YEHUDA LEIB, 'How Many Rabbis Existed by the Name R. Abraham Hahozeh?' (Heb.), *Horeb*, 11 (1951), 256–68.

FRAENKEL, AVRAHAM, 'An Ashkenazi Tradition on the Arrival of R. Judah Halevi in Jerusalem' (Heb.), *Hama'ayan*, 53/3 (2013), 5–14.

GROSSMAN, AVRAHAM, *The Early Sages of Ashkenaz: Their Lives, Leadership and Works (900–1096)* [Ḥakhmei ashkenaz harishonim: koroteihem, darkam behanhagat hatsibur, yetsiratam haruḥanit mereshit yeshivatam ve'ad ligezerat tatnu (1096)] (Jerusalem, 1981).

——*The Early Sages of France: Their Lives, Leadership and Works* [Ḥakhmei tsarfat harishonim: koroteihem, darkam behanhagat hatsibur, yetsiratam haruḥanit] (Jerusalem, 1995).

HALKIN, ABRAHAM S. (ed.), *Moses Ibn Ezra: Studies and Deliberations on Hebrew Poetry* [Mosheh ibn ezra: sefer ha'iyunim vehadiyunim al hashirah ha'ivrit] (Jerusalem, 1975).

HOLLENDER, ELISABETH, 'Adoption and Adaptation: Judah ha-Levi's ציון הלא תשאלי לשלום אסיריך in Its Ashkenazic Environment', in Elisheva Baumgarten, Ruth Karras, and Katelyn Mesler (eds.), *Entangled Histories: Knowledge, Authority, and Jewish Culture in the Thirteenth Century* (Philadelphia, 2017), 248–62.

——'Angepasste Nachdichtungen. Vom Umgang mit innerjüdischer Differenz in der mittelalterlichen liturgischen Poesie', in Stefan Alkier, Michael Schneider, and Christian Wiese (eds.), *Diversität—Differenz—Dialogizität: Religion in Pluralen Kontexten* (Berlin, 2017), 264–81.

——*Clavis Commentariorum of Hebrew Liturgical Poetry in Manuscript*, Clavis Commentariorum Antiquitatis et Medii Aevi 4 (Leiden, 2005).

—— *Piyyut Commentary in Medieval Ashkenaz*, Studia Judaica 42 (Berlin, 2008).

—— 'Piyyut Commentary in the Nuremberg Mahzor', in *The Nuremberg Mahzor* (forthcoming).

—— ' "Tsion She'arit Bne Ya'aqov": An Ashkenazic *Qina* in Sephardic Garb', in Ephraim Hazan and Avi Shmidman (eds.), *A Word of Hope: Studies in Poetry and Piyyut presented to Professor Binyamin Bar-Tikva*, Piyyut in Tradition 5–6 (Ramat Gan, 2017), *5–*21.

—— '"Zion, Will You Not Inquire After the Well-Being of Your Miserable Ones?": Medieval Qinot from Ashkenaz', in Karl E. Grözinger (ed.), *Jüdische Kultur in den SchUM-Städten: Literatur—Musik—Theater* (Wiesbaden, 2014), 261–74.

KANARFOGEL, EPHRAIM, *The Intellectual History and Rabbinic Culture of Medieval Ashkenaz* (Detroit, 2013).

LUZZATTO, SAMUEL DAVID, *Ha'atakot yekarot shel shu"t veshirim mikovtsei kitvei yad im he'arot muskalot*, *Kerem ḥemed*, 7 (1833), 19–53.

MALKIEL, DAVID J., *Reconstructing Ashkenaz. The Human Face of Franco-German Jewry, 1000–1250* (Stanford, Calif., 2009).

RASPE, LUCIA, 'Ascher ha-lewi und die Gründung des jüdischen Worms: Liturgiekommentar, Familiensinn und Geschichtsbewusstsein im mittelalterlichen Aschkenas', in Birgit E. Klein and Christiane E. Müller (eds.), *Memoria—Wege jüdischen Erinnerns* (Berlin, 2005), 133–44.

SCHORSCH, ISMAR, *From Text to Context: The Turn to History in Modern Judaism* (Hanover, 1994).

Sefer tashlum Abudraham. Vehu seder avodat yom hakipurim hameyuḥas leyosi ben yosi vegam piyutim shonim shel paytanim hagedolim im perush gadol hamefarshim rabenu david bar yosef bar david abudraham, ed. Lipman Philipp Prins (Berlin, 1900).

Shirat rabenu tam. Piyutei rabi ya'akov ben rabi me'ir, ed. Isaac Meiseles (Jerusalem, 2012).

TIMM, ERIKA, *Graphische und phonetische Struktur des Westjiddischen unter besonderer Berücksichtigung der Zeit um 1600* (Tübingen, 1987).

CHAPTER ELEVEN

Minhag and Migration: Yiddish Custom Books from Sixteenth-Century Italy

LUCIA RASPE

A MIGRATION of German Jews to Italy can be traced to the final decades of the fourteenth century; it peaked in the fifteenth, when the Jews were expelled from almost all of the German cities and many principalities, and effectively came to a close with the warfare that ravaged northern Italy in the early 1500s.[1] Settling at first in the towns and hamlets of the Friuli and the Venetian mainland, then moving on towards the Po valley, Ashkenazi Jews soon became a presence in numerous places which had not had a Jewish settlement before. It was only when their southward migration converged with a wave of indigenous Italian Jews moving north from Rome at about the same time that ethnically mixed communities came into being,[2] and it was in the sixteenth century that ghettoization, in Venice and elsewhere, forced Jews of all backgrounds—including the more recent arrivals from Iberia—into close proximity with one another.[3] Thus, over time, the peninsula was turned into a meeting ground of diverse Jewish cultures. If the newcomers from Germany had initially felt a strong need to preserve their own traditions, not least because Jewishly they were in no man's land, it was under the conditions of ghetto life that their acculturation began to make headway. At the end of the sixteenth century, when the language of Italo-Ashkenazi Jews shifted to a variety of Italian written in Latin characters used in both external and internal communication, the golden age of this first centre of German Jewish culture

Much of the initial research for this essay was carried out while I held a Yad Hanadiv/Beracha Foundation Visiting Fellowship in Jewish Studies at the Hebrew University in 2009–10, for which I remain grateful.

[1] Shulvass, 'Ashkenazic Jewry in Italy'; Bato, 'L'immigrazione degli ebrei tedeschi in Italia'; Toaff, 'Migrazioni di ebrei tedeschi'.

[2] Toaff, 'Convergenza sul Veneto di banchieri ebrei romani e tedeschi'.

[3] Roth, *The History of the Jews of Italy*, 309–28; Milano, *Storia degli ebrei in Italia*, 527–8.

beyond the borders of historical Ashkenaz came to a close.[4] By that time, however, crucial developments had occurred. The traditions brought to Italy by Ashkenazi immigrants had been enshrined in print, as it were, when the new technology took off on the peninsula from the 1470s onward. As a result, the Italian intermezzo, its relatively short duration notwithstanding, would seem to have left a distinctive mark on the shape that historical Ashkenaz took in the early modern period.

While the basic patterns of the Ashkenazi migration to, and settlement in, Italy have become fairly clear over the past decade or two, its cultural ramifications have only recently begun to come into focus. Among scholars of Yiddish, the crucial role of Italy in the emergence of a literary tradition has of course long been noted.[5] *Yiddish in Italia*, the overview recently offered by Chava Turniansky and Erika Timm, has opened new perspectives for research and identified many remaining lacunae.[6]

One area that has hardly been studied is that of *minhagim* books, a genre peculiar to Ashkenazi Jews. Situated at the intersection of learned and lay culture, *minhagim* books record both the prayer rite (*minhag*) and the customs (*minhagim*) observed in synagogue and at home over the course of the Jewish year. Two types of *minhagim* books have been distinguished in the past: works that record the conduct of exemplary scholars deemed worthy of emulation, and works that provide instruction regarding the customs specific to a particular community, especially where synagogue liturgy is concerned.[7] Although a reliance on received custom alongside written halakhah had been characteristic of Ashkenazi Judaism from early times,[8] it was in the course of the eastward expansion of Jewish settlement in Germany in the thirteenth century that liturgical *minhagim* books began to proliferate.[9] Similarly, the disruption of communal life and the discontinuity of local tradition that came in the wake of the expulsions of the fifteenth century could not have left the genre unaffected.

One example is *Sefer maharil*, the collection of customs based on the teachings of R. Jacob ben Moses Molin Halevi of Mainz (Maharil, d.1427),

[4] Shmeruk, *Yiddish Literature: Aspects of Its History* (Heb.), 73–4. For the analogous process that replaced Hebrew with Italian among Italian Jews at about the same time, see Bonfil, 'Changing Mentalities of Italian Jews'.

[5] Shmeruk, 'The Beginnings of Yiddish Narrative Prose' (Heb.); id., 'Yiddish Printing in Italy' (Heb.).

[6] Turniansky and Timm, *Yiddish in Italia*.

[7] Zimmer, 'A Book of Customs of the School of the Maharil' (Heb.), 59–62.

[8] Ta-Shma, *Early Franco-German Ritual and Custom* (Heb.), 13–105; id., 'Ashkenazi Jewry in the Eleventh Century', esp. 10–24.

[9] Mincer, 'Liturgical Minhagim Books'.

which was compiled by his student Zalman of Sankt Goar.[10] While *Sefer maharil* is often considered the epitome of Rhenish tradition, it would seem to owe more to the southward migration of its compiler than has previously been thought. Scholars had indeed suspected that Zalman of Sankt Goar might have moved to Italy at a later stage in his life. This has been confirmed in a recent dissertation, which has unravelled the complicated history of the various redactions of *Sefer maharil* that Zalman produced and circulated over a period of more than forty years following his teacher's death.[11] Not only does this history reflect the compiler's move away from the heartlands of historical Ashkenaz, it also testifies to the high demand for guides to Ashkenazi practice that his work must have met among his fellow Italo-Ashkenazi Jews.

If *Sefer maharil* was the most influential among the *minhagim* books that circulated in Italy in the mid-fifteenth century, it was by no means the only one. Two additional compilations appear to have enjoyed similar popularity among Ashkenazim south of the Alps before the advent of print. Of the *minhagim* book put together by one Zalman Yent in Treviso apparently in the 1430s, only two manuscripts are known.[12] By contrast, the collection compiled by one Samuel of Ulm in 1449 has been preserved in close to twenty codices, the great majority of them from Italy; the earliest extant copy was written in 1453 by a recent exile from Ulm to Treviso.[13]

A large part of the *minhagim* books we have in Yiddish are likewise from Italy. Although Maharil himself had vigorously opposed the translation of halakhic literature into the vernacular, wishing to leave ritual knowledge in the hands of scholars,[14] that position proved untenable over time. Many of the Ashkenazi settlements in northern Italy, especially during the formative phase of the German Jewish diaspora, were made up of no more than one or two families; that trend continued as more recent newcomers fanned out into the

[10] Zalman of Sankt Goar, *Sefer maharil*, ed. Spitzer.

[11] Pelles, 'The Book of "Maharil"' (Heb.).

[12] Edited from an early 16th-century manuscript held in Munich, Bayerische Staatsbibliothek Cod. hebr. 401 (IMHM 1237), fos. 195^{r}–199^{v}, in Tyrnau, *Sefer haminhagim*, ed. Spitzer, 169–82. A better copy has since been identified among the marginal texts in a manuscript *sidur* kept in Frankfurt am Main, Universitätsbibliothek Johann Christian Senckenberg MS hebr. oct. 227 (IMHM 23165), fos. 169^{v}–172^{r}. Its codicological features would seem to suggest that it was written in Italy, possibly no later than the mid-1430s.

[13] Zimmer, 'A Book of Customs' (Heb.). See also Ta-Shma, 'The Literary Content of the Manuscript', 47–8, 56–60.

[14] Romer-Segal, 'Yiddish Works on Women's Commandments', 39; Yuval, *Scholars in their Time* (Heb.), 312–18.

hinterland. Communities in a proper sense (*kehilot*) there were few.[15] Under these conditions, there was apparently a market for *minhagim* books not only in Hebrew but also in Yiddish. And it was in Italy that such books in each of the two languages made the move into print. The first Hebrew custumal brought to press was *Sefer maharil*, which appeared in Sabbioneta in 1556 and was twice reprinted in Cremona, in 1558 and 1568. In 1559 the *editio princeps* of the *minhagim* ascribed to Abraham Klausner was published in Riva di Trento; in 1566 the customs of Isaac Tyrnau (or Ayzik Tirna) appeared in Venice.[16] Finally, Simon Halevi Günzburg brought a Yiddish *minhagim* book to press in Venice in 1589. When it was reissued with woodcut illustrations four years later, the book became a bestseller; it was reprinted across Europe well into the nineteenth century.[17] While the woodcuts are familiar to many, the text of Günzburg's work has been given little consideration to date.[18]

Manuscripts have attracted even less attention. Of the fifteen handwritten Yiddish *minhagim* books extant in public collections that are not mere transcriptions of printed editions, seven are of Italian provenance; others appear to have been brought to Italy by their owners.[19] None of these manuscripts have been researched to date. In fact, Turniansky and Timm have identified 'a systematic recording of the contents of all the Yiddish *Minhagim* together with an examination of whether, and to what extent, the early versions depend upon the Hebrew *Minhagim* by Isaac (Ayzik) Tyrnau (around 1400), as the later printed versions do' as 'an urgent, but most demanding task'.[20] My goal here is to take first steps in that direction and to see how the Ashkenazi migration to Italy may be reflected in these manuscripts.

[15] Toaff, 'Migrazioni di ebrei tedeschi', 15–16; Bonfil, 'The Settlement of Wandering Jews' (Heb.).

[16] See Klausner, *Sefer minhagim lerabenu avraham kloizner*, ed. Dissen; Tyrnau, *Sefer haminhagim*, ed. Spitzer.

[17] For a preliminary list of editions see Shmeruk, 'The Illustrations of the Yiddish *Minhagim*' (Heb.), 35–34.

[18] A French translation of the Venice 1593 edition is currently being prepared by Jean Baumgarten (Paris). Meanwhile, see his 'The *Seyfer ha-minhogim* by Shimon ben Yehuda ha-Levi Guenzburg'.

[19] For an overview see Steinschneider, 'Jüdisch-Deutsche Litteratur und Jüdisch-Deutsch', 60–1, no. 406; 'Jüdisch-Deutsche Litteratur und Jüdisch-Deutsch 3', 136–8; cf. Wolfthal, *Picturing Yiddish*, 27–8 n. 4.

[20] Turniansky and Timm, *Yiddish in Italia*, 70. The dependence of Günzburg's printed work on Tyrnau, which is taken for granted here, is itself open to debate. I hope to return to this question in the near future. Meanwhile, see Shmeruk, 'Yiddish Printing in Italy' (Heb.), 126–7 (Eng. trans. p. 178); contrast Frakes (ed.), *Early Yiddish Texts*, 112–13, 382.

Once we examine their text it is easily apparent that the fifteen Yiddish *minhagim* manuscripts divide into families representing a number of distinct works in a fairly stable manner. Turniansky and Timm state that four of the seven Italian manuscripts appear to belong to the same family.[21] In three of these four, the *minhagim* form the bulk of the text. One manuscript, written in Soncino in 1533, apparently for a woman, concludes with a translation of the biblical book of Ruth.[22] Another, written in Casalmaggiore and undated, includes a Yiddish exposition of the Hebrew calendar and the corresponding tables.[23] A third manuscript, dated 1557, preserves the *minhagim* alongside a Yiddish work on women's commandments.[24] The same two texts also appear together in one of the most comprehensive anthologies of Old Yiddish texts extant today, a codex written in Venice during the winter of 1553/54, again for a woman.[25]

If these four manuscripts are described in *Yiddish in Italia* as closely related, my own research has shown that another two of the seven also belong to this group.[26] Although they are bound together as one manuscript,[27] they actually form two distinct codicological units, neither of which has a colophon. The assumption of their Italian provenance relies on the fact that one of the two was acquired in Venice by a woman named Fradlina (an Italianized form of the Yiddish Freydlin) in 1550;[28] the other was owned by Hanna, the wife of Salamon Puglieso in Lodi, apparently in the third quarter of the

[21] *Yiddish in Italia*, 74.

[22] MS Paris, Bibliothèque Nationale de France [BnF] héb. 587 (Institute of Microfilmed Hebrew Manuscripts [IMHM], Jerusalem, film no. 30736), fos. 1r–61v, 62r–66r. See Turniansky and Timm, *Yiddish in Italia*, 76–7, no. 37.

[23] MS Paris, BnF héb. 588 (IMHM 24838), fos. 1r–60v, 61r–85v; Turniansky and Timm, *Yiddish in Italia*, 78, no. 38.

[24] MS Paris, Alliance israélite universelle [AIU] H9A (IMHM 2745), fos. 1r–82v, 83r–107v; Turniansky and Timm, *Yiddish in Italia*, 74–5, no. 36. Cf. Fram, *My Dear Daughter*, 143.

[25] MS Oxford, Bodleian Library Canon. Or. 12 (IMHM 16677), fos. 1r–90r, 91r–109v. Of what must have been at least 397 folios, 276 have been preserved. The manuscript was commissioned by one Menahem Katz for his daughter Serlina, perhaps on the occasion of her wedding. See Neubauer, *Catalogue of the Hebrew Manuscripts in the Bodleian Library*, no. 1217; Turniansky and Timm, *Yiddish in Italia*, 96–9, no. 47; Shtif, 'A Yiddish Manuscript Library' (Yid.).

[26] As is implied in Shtif, 'A Yiddish Manuscript Library' (Yid.), 525–7.

[27] MS Berlin, Staatsbibliothek Or. Qu. 694. See Steinschneider, *Verzeichniss der hebräischen Handschriften*, ii. 16–17, no. 166; Turniansky and Timm, *Yiddish in Italia*, 79, no. 39.

[28] Steinschneider, 'Jüdisch-Deutsche Litteratur und Jüdisch-Deutsch 3', 137. Watermarks similar to those of this manuscript can be found in Briquet, *Les Filigranes: Dictionnaire historique des marques du papier*, nos. 11912 (Padua, 1515) and 11914 (Padua, 1552).

sixteenth century, and bears an Italian censorship note dated 1609.[29] Both were acquired from private hands in Italy in 1869.[30]

Thus, of the seven manuscripts of *minhagim* in Yiddish written in Italy, six preserve essentially the same work. The seventh is different.[31] Completed some time before 1503, it may well be the earliest of the group; it is better known than the others because of its highly original illustrations of Jewish life at the turn of the sixteenth century, which have recently been subjected to detailed study.[32] The text has not been given commensurate attention; however, it has long been recognized as a translation of the *minhagim* compiled by Samuel of Ulm—a first translation from the Hebrew, it would seem, judging from the relatively large number of corrections made by the translator-scribe as he went along.[33] The manuscript itself appears to have remained in the hands of the same family for a relatively long time; there is no evidence that it was ever copied. Hence Samuel of Ulm's *minhagim*, widely diffused although never printed in Hebrew, do not seem to have had much of a reception in Yiddish.[34]

The opposite may be said of the Yiddish work represented in the remaining six manuscripts from Italy. This work is based on the *minhagim* ascribed to Zalman Yent, of which only two Hebrew manuscripts have been preserved. The close connection between the Hebrew compilation and its Yiddish adaptation is evident in the overall arrangement of the material, as well as in their respective treatment of specific topics.[35] Zalman Yent's work is a bare-bones liturgical handbook. Unlike other near-contemporaneous *minhagim* compila-

[29] MS Berlin 694/2, fos. 79ʳ, 80ᵛ. For a Salomone de Poesiis (Pugliese) documented in Lodi between 1565 and 1575, see Simonsohn, *The Jews in the Duchy of Milan*, 1436, 1584, 1611. The manuscript's watermarks resemble Briquet nos. 14467, 14471, and 14472, all documented in Lombardy between 1523 and 1560.

[30] Steinschneider, 'Jüdisch-Deutsche Litteratur und Jüdisch-Deutsch 3', 130; id., 'Mittheilungen aus dem Antiquariat von Julius Benzian', 117, nos. 80–1.

[31] MS Paris, BnF héb. 586 (IMHM 27580); Turniansky and Timm, *Yiddish in Italia*, 70–3, no. 35.

[32] Wolfthal, *Picturing Yiddish*, 3–84.

[33] For one example see MS Paris 586, fo. 24ᵛ (reproduced in Wolfthal, *Picturing Yiddish*, fig. 20), where the Hebrew *ad* ('up until') preceding a specific line from a Hebrew prayer appears struck out and replaced with the Yiddish equivalent *biz gen* by the original scribe.

[34] For evidence of a second, independent translation into Yiddish, see my '*Minhagim* Books in Yiddish'.

[35] See my edition of a portion of the Yiddish text and its Hebrew source prepared for the Early Modern Workshop and available at <http://fordham.bepress.com/emw/emw2010/emw2010/4>. One telling example is the practice, recommended in both the Hebrew and the Yiddish manuscripts, of reciting the blessing 'Al hatorah' following the *haftarah* of the afternoon service on Yom Kippur, a custom specifically associated with Zalman Yent of Treviso in

tions, including that of Isaac Tyrnau,[36] it does not address weekday or regular sabbath services but works its way through the special occasions of the Jewish year. Like the Hebrew, the Yiddish adaptation notes when and how synagogue ritual diverges from everyday practice, and includes the liturgical poetry and biblical readings for each individual occasion. The listings of the liturgical poetry contained in the two Hebrew manuscripts are highly selective, however. While Zalman Yent's *minhagim* provide the incipits of specific hymns to be recited on the nights of the three pilgrimage festivals, the respective information for their morning services is uneven, and almost completely lacking for the High Holy Days.[37] Traces of a similarly uneven approach remain in the Yiddish work, underscoring its dependence on the Hebrew.[38]

One difference between Zalman Yent's Hebrew *minhagim* collection and its Yiddish adaptation lies in the fact that the Yiddish manuscripts—like many of the older Hebrew *minhagim* books—begin their overview of the Jewish year in the month of Elul, while Zalman Yent's work—like the near-contemporaneous compilations of Samuel of Ulm and Isaac Tyrnau—begins in Nisan. This may be one reason why the connection between the two works has not been noticed in the past. However, a closer look at the text reveals that the organization of the earlier Hebrew work has left traces in all six manuscripts of its Yiddish adaptation.[39]

MS Parma, Biblioteca Palatina 2857 (de Rossi 665; IMHM 14355), fo. 32ᵛ. Cf. the discussion in [Ernst] Daniel Goldschmidt's introduction to his *Maḥzor layamim hanora'im*, ii. 30–1.

36 See Shtif, 'A Yiddish Manuscript Library' (Yid.), 525–6. Shtif distinguishes Günzburg's (and Tyrnau's) 'systematic' approach from the 'chronological' approach taken in MS Oxford 1217 and its cognates.

37 As noted in Spitzer's introduction in Tyrnau, *Sefer haminhagim*, 167–8. This may suggest that what the original compiler had before him was a *sidur* of the type that contained the prayers for weekdays and the sabbath but also included *ma'arivim* (poetic pieces inserted into *ma'ariv*) for the three festivals, as well as the *hoshanot* for Sukkot, *reshuyot* for Simhat Torah, and *yotserot* and *zulatot* for the special sabbaths. The *piyutim* for the High Holy Days, on the other hand, would typically have been included in a *maḥzor*. On these distinctions see e.g. Fraenkel, 'Ashkenazi Tradition about R. Judah Halevi's Reaching Jerusalem' (Heb.), 6 n. 6.

38 While the six manuscripts fill in much of what the Hebrew lacks for the festivals, readers are expressly referred to prayer books for the *piyutim* of both Rosh Hashanah and Yom Kippur. See e.g. MS Paris 587, fos. 3ʳ, 7ʳ, 11ᵛ, 12ʳ. In the following, most of my references to the Yiddish work under discussion will be keyed to this manuscript, the earliest among those that are dated.

39 For one example see the discussion of the penitential prayers to be recited when a circumcision falls on the Fast of Esther in MS Paris 587, fo. 29ʳ; there readers are referred back to the corresponding discussion regarding 17 Tamuz, which in fact only occurs on fo. 55ᵛ. Incidentally, a similar switch—from Elul to Nisan—occurs in *Sefer maharil*, from the first revision produced after the compiler's move to Italy onwards; Pelles, 'The Book of "Maharil"' (Heb.), 182.

Another difference between the Hebrew and Yiddish manuscripts lies in the fact that the Yiddish text is significantly longer. In one of the two Hebrew manuscripts which presents a running text, Zalman Yent's work is eight—tiny—pages long.[40] In the most elaborate manuscript of its Yiddish adaptation, the text takes up seventy-nine quarto leaves.[41] Not all of this is due to the fact that Yiddish tends to be more wordy than Hebrew. What does the version preserved in Yiddish add? It fills in some of the liturgical lacunae of the Hebrew. It adds a number of domestic practices, providing information on when—and in what mood—meals should be eaten and suggesting specific foods for specific occasions. It adds the wording of blessings recited at home and information on how these change if a festival falls on a Friday or Saturday night. It includes detailed instructions on how to bake matzot, how to search for crumbs of leaven on the night before Passover, and how to conduct the Seder.[42] It also adds material aimed at more specific audiences, such as one section of several pages which explains to worshippers of priestly descent how they are to bless their fellow congregants on the various festivals.[43]

While a comparison of the two Hebrew manuscripts of Zalman Yent's compilation shows a tendency towards such expansion in the later of the two,[44] the six manuscripts of the Yiddish version are all remarkably—and somewhat disappointingly—similar to one another. One exception is MS Paris 588. While the language of that copy suggests that it is the most archaic text of the six, the quality of the scribal work unfortunately leaves much to be desired—a situation not at all rare where Old Yiddish manuscripts are concerned.[45] Whereas the other manuscripts all have a running text, MS Paris 588 here and there offers two columns.[46] This would seem to suggest that its *Vorlage* originally had a shorter text that was subsequently annotated, and the copyist did not quite know what to do with that. This detail offers insights into the ways in which Zalman Yent's text was expanded, and would make a good starting point for further investigation of the process of textual growth.

What is more, although undated, MS Paris 588 may preserve informa-

[40] MS Munich 401, fos. 195r–198v.

[41] MS Berlin 694/2, fos. 1r–79r.

[42] MS Paris 587, fos. 32r–44r.

[43] Ibid., fos. 3v–5r.

[44] MS Munich 401.

[45] The similarly poor job done by the copyist of MS Oxford 1217 (who refers to himself as a *na'ar* in the colophon on fo. 90r) has been noted by Shtif in 'A Yiddish Manuscript Library' (Yid.), 143–5. One reason for this may lie in the fact that young and inexperienced scribes sometimes practised their skills on Yiddish before they were allowed to move on to Hebrew texts, which were perceived as more sacred—much like the 17th-century compositor studied by Simon Neuberg; see 'The First Yiddish Book Printed in Amsterdam', 11.

[46] For an example see MS Paris 588, fos. 17v–18r.

tion about when the adaptation of Zalman Yent's *minhagim* was underway. As mentioned earlier, this particular manuscript also contains a work on the Jewish calendar and the corresponding tables.[47] These tables may originally have been transmitted in tandem with our Yiddish *minhagim*, since they are referred to in two of the manuscripts where they do not actually appear.[48] In MS Paris 588 they do, and they mention Rosh Hashanah of the upcoming year 5232.[49] The calendar section thus appears to have been composed in 1471; this may also be the year in which this particular adaptation of Zalman Yent's *minhagim* was written.

The above information enables us to fill some of the time gap between Zalman Yent's Hebrew *minhagim*, put together in the 1430s, and the Yiddish versions we have, of which the earliest dated manuscript was copied in 1533.[50] The date also fits the little that we know about Zalman Yent himself. While two of Israel Isserlein's responsa mention him as one of several rabbis resident in Treviso in the mid-1430s,[51] he has not been identified in archival sources to date.[52] However, a colophon in one of the two Hebrew manuscripts tells us that his *minhagim* were followed 'in the Jewish community of Treviso and in Mestre and also in all of Lombardy'.[53] While 'Lombardy' may literally refer to the region where Ashkenazi Jews were settling in growing numbers at the time, it was also used more loosely to denote Italy as a whole.[54] Indeed, a responsum cited in *Leket yosher* (*c.*1470) makes reference to Zalman Yent as the author of *minhagim* which were followed 'in all the lands of Italy'.[55] This is precisely what the relatively wide diffusion of his work in Yiddish would

[47] Ibid., fos. 61^{r}–85^{v}.

[48] MS AIU H9A, fo. 68^{r}; MS Oxford 1217, fo. 69^{v}.

[49] 1471/72 according to the Christian reckoning; MS Paris 588, fo. 64^{r}. I am grateful to Malachi Beit-Arié for pointing this out.

[50] The first outside evidence we have of *minhagim* books in Yiddish would seem to date from the early 1490s. See David Stern's remarks in Stern, Markschies, and Shalev-Eyni, *The Monk's Haggadah*, 83–5, and the text on pp. 99 (Latin), 114 (English).

[51] Israel Isserlein ben Petahya, *Sefer terumat hadeshen*, pt. II (*Pesakim ukhetavim*), 441, nos. 257–8 (I owe the date to Yacov Guggenheim). Additional sources are listed in Spitzer, 'Social and Religious Ties between the Jews of Austria and Northern Italy', 33–4.

[52] Möschter, *Juden im venezianischen Treviso*, 341, no. 173.

[53] MS Munich 401, fo. 199^{v} (בקהילת טערוז ובמעשטרי וגם בכל לומברדיאה). My reading follows that suggested in Spitzer's introduction in *Sefer haminhagim*, 167 n. 2, as against the reading given in his own edition, ibid. 182.

[54] As noted by Erika Timm in Shmeruk, *Paris and Vienna* (Heb.), 330.

[55] MS Munich, Bayerische Staatsbibliothek Cod. hebr. 405 (IMHM 1646), fo. 80^{v}. See Joseph ben Moses, *Sefer leket yosher*, ed. Freimann, i. 110, or the more recent edition, *Sefer leket yosher*, 'Oraḥ ḥayim', ed. Kinarti, 252. For the dating of the autograph see Freimann's introduction, ibid., p. xii; on Zalman Yent himself see ibid., p. xxvii, no. 38.

seem to indicate. It also confirms recent findings regarding the importance of Treviso as the pre-eminent centre of the Ashkenazi diaspora in Italy during its formative years in the first half of the fifteenth century, before a change in municipal policy led to its decline and gradual replacement by Mestre and Padua, and finally, from 1509 onward, by Venice itself.[56]

What does a study of the Yiddish versions of Zalman Yent's *minhagim* add to our understanding of the cultural history of Ashkenazi Jews in Italy? Three lines of enquiry seem especially promising. One concerns the relationship of *minhag* and migration. As mentioned above, *minhag*—certainly when it refers to a community's prayer rite—is essentially a local matter. Generally speaking, of course, Ashkenazi liturgy at large divides into two major branches: the apparently older western Ashkenazi rite, *minhag raynus* or *minhag ashkenaz* proper, and the eastern Ashkenazi variant, *minhag ostraykh*, which later came to be identified as *minhag polin*.[57] Because a majority of Ashkenazi immigrants, especially during the early phase of their settlement in Italy in the late fourteenth and early fifteenth centuries, came from the western and south-western parts of the Holy Roman Empire,[58] the prayer rite they established south of the Alps generally adhered to the western Ashkenazi variant; indeed, both Samuel of Ulm and Zalman Yent are indebted to Maharil.[59] However, the picture becomes more complex where *seliḥot* are concerned, the penitential prayers recited before and during the High Holy Days and on the various fast days over the course of the Jewish year. The liturgical poets of medieval Ashkenaz were famously prolific in this area. At the end of the Middle Ages there were literally hundreds of poems from which to choose for every occasion, and each community or region developed its own habits regarding what to recite, in what order, on which day.[60] While a full study of

[56] Möschter, *Juden im venezianischen Treviso*, esp. 262–73; cf. Toaff, 'Migrazioni di ebrei tedeschi', 15–21.

[57] See Goldschmidt, *Maḥzor layamim hanora'im*, i. 13–14; Zimmer, *Society and Its Customs* (Heb.), 216–19.

[58] Haverkamp, 'Ebrei in Italia e in Germania', 64–9.

[59] As noted by Shtif in 'A Yiddish Manuscript Library' (Yid.), 525. This would seem to be the reason why the Yiddish *minhagim* in MS Oxford 1217 are misleadingly classified as an adaptation of *Sefer maharil* in the IMHM online catalogue. See also Beit-Arié, *Catalogue of the Hebrew Manuscripts in the Bodleian Library Supplement*, s.v.

[60] On *seliḥot* and their recitation see Elbogen, *Jewish Liturgy*, 177–84, §33. A list of thirteen different *seliḥot* rites brought to press at various times in early modern eastern and western Ashkenaz can be found in Goldschmidt, *Maḥzor layamim hanora'im*, ii. 13, or at greater length in the introduction to either one of his editions of the two rites that remain in use among *ashkenazim* in Israel today, the Polish and the Lithuanian. See his *Seder seliḥot keminhag lita*, 6–8; *Seder seliḥot keminhag polin*, 6–8.

the development of these local orders of *seliḥot* recitation has not been undertaken to date and lies beyond the scope of the present study, we may note that in those cases that have left us enough evidence to follow their evolution, the local rites proved remarkably stable over time. Hence when a work of the fifteenth or sixteenth century offers a list of the *seliḥot* to be recited on the various occasions throughout the year, it hands us a key, as it were, to its own localization—and one that is far more precise than the simple distinction between east and west.

The six Yiddish *minhagim* manuscripts from Italy do exactly that, and this confirms their close relationship to the work of Zalman Yent. It is true that a full list of the *seliḥot* to be recited throughout the year is preserved only in the more recent of the two extant Hebrew manuscripts.[61] However, its authenticity is underscored by the fact that the same list, headed *seder haseliḥot beterviz* ('the order of penitential prayers according to the rite of Treviso'), also appears in an early Italian autograph of *Sefer maharil*; later redactions of that work explicitly ascribe the same selections to Zalman Yent.[62]

These lists of *seliḥot* also appear in the Yiddish versions—not as an appendix, as is the case in the Hebrew manuscript, but inserted into the text at the appropriate junctures.[63] With few exceptions, these *seliḥot* closely follow those of Zalman Yent; moreover, they correspond to what emerged as the *seder seliḥot* recited by Ashkenazim all over Italy after it first appeared in print in Piove di Sacco around 1475. In other words, the Yiddish manuscripts alert us to the fact that what became the *minhag* of Ashkenaz-in-Italy in the course of early Hebrew printing indeed goes back to what had been laid down by Zalman Yent in Treviso in the 1430s.[64]

Interestingly, this specific order of *seliḥot* does not correspond to any of the orders used elsewhere, either in the Rhineland, although Zalman Yent had studied with Maharil and shared his western Ashkenazi orientation, or in Ulm, although the *minhag* of the Ashkenazim in Italy is generally thought to be close to that of Swabia.[65] As a matter of fact, it appears that hardly any

[61] MS Munich 401, fos. 199^{r-v}.

[62] MS Oxford, Bodleian Library Mich. 292 (cat. Neubauer 907; IMHM 21866). See Pelles, 'The Book of "Maharil"' (Heb.), 13, no. 2; 182–3, nos. 9–10.

[63] See e.g. MS Paris 587, fos. 1^v (*seliḥot* for the days preceding Rosh Hashanah), 7^v–9^r (the Days of Repentance between Rosh Hashanah and Yom Kippur), 11^r–12^v (the various services on Yom Kippur), 20^{r-v} (the fast of *behab*), 23^v (10 Tevet), 28^v (the Fast of Esther), and 55^v (17 Tamuz).

[64] I discuss the Italo-Ashkenazi *seliḥot* tradition and its German Jewish antecedents in greater detail in my 'Migration of German Jews into Italy' (forthcoming).

[65] Zunz, *Die Ritus des synagogalen Gottesdienstes*, 71.

community had a fixed order of *seliḥot*, down to the very last number for each and every day of the Days of Repentance, at the time. To the extent that the matter has been studied, there seems to be a consensus that the practice of *seliḥot* recitation remained fairly fluid throughout the later Middle Ages; it was only in the age of print that it fully evolved into a multiplicity of divergent traditions.[66] If this is the case, then the Italo-Ashkenazi example would seem to indicate that what triggered this development was perhaps not the hoary antiquity of local custom. On the contrary, it seems that the experiences of exile and migration, of beginning afresh in a new land without a tradition of its own, may have played a crucial role in the process.

A second point that emerges from a study of the Yiddish versions concerns their intended audience. Several of our manuscripts—in fact, all of those that preserve information regarding their patron—were originally written for women.[67] That is by no means atypical. Although the term 'women's literature'—inspired, in part, by the blurbs that can be found on the title pages of many pre-modern Yiddish printings—has lately come into disrepute for flattening the multifaceted world of Old Yiddish literature,[68] the fact that so many of the extant manuscripts are addressed to specific women remains noteworthy; indeed, it has been singled out as a feature characteristic of Yiddish literature in Italy.[69]

What do the *minhagim* manuscripts tell us of the religious lives of Ashkenazi women in sixteenth-century Italy? On the level of content, hardly anything at all. Here and there, remarks relating to women's observances appear to have been added more or less as an afterthought. At one point the text notes that women, too, are obliged to hear the reading of Megilat Ester on Purim; at another it states that they do not have to count the *omer* between Pesach and Shavuot.[70] We also find that when a female or minor claim to have performed the search for any remaining leaven on the night before Passover, they are to be

[66] See Fraenkel and Fraenkel, 'Prayer and *Piyut* in the Nuremberg *Maḥzor*' (Heb.), 97–8, esp. 98 n. 458.

[67] This is explicitly indicated in MSS Paris 587 and Oxford 1217 and implicit in MS AIU H9A. In addition, MSS Berlin 694/1 and 694/2 were owned by women.

[68] After all, only a minority of Jewish men were able to follow the injunction to study in the Holy Tongue, while Yiddish was the vernacular accessible to all. See e.g. Berger, 'An Invitation to Buy and Read: Paratexts of Yiddish Books', 38–9; Frakes, *Early Yiddish Texts*, pp. xliii–xliv, 247. A more detailed discussion can be found in Turniansky, *Language, Education and Knowledge among East European Jews* (Heb.), 61–76.

[69] Turniansky, 'Special Traits of Yiddish Literature in Italy', 195–6. None of the Yiddish *minhagim* manuscripts preserved from outside Italy that I am aware of bear comparable dedications.

[70] MS Paris 587, fos. 29^{r}, 45^{v}.

trusted, and that women, too, lean on pillows during the Seder.[71] On the other hand, there is much in the text that can hardly have been of any practical use to women.[72] If a female readership was intended in the Yiddish text, that may be reflected primarily in the somewhat condescending tone of address. For instance the reader is told more than once that, while there are several reasons for a particular observance, there is no need to go into the details because 'for you, one explanation will do'.[73] Elsewhere, variations in practice are discussed—some people do things in a certain way, some in another—before the text concludes, 'Now you do as you like, and whatever you feel like.'[74] Whether the reader of these and similar lines is imagined to be female or not, the addressee's inability to read Hebrew appears to colour the treatment s/he receives at the hands of the writer.

This leads us to a final point, which concerns the relationship of theory and practice. To what extent were these handbooks written in order to aid their readers in the actual observance of the commandments? On the face of it, we would tend to think that this must have been their primary purpose.[75] However, there is much in the manuscripts that raises doubt. I have mentioned, for instance, that the Yiddish work typically gives the full wording of the blessing over wine recited at home, including the respective variants when a festival begins on a Friday or Saturday night. Yet what good are these texts if the scribal work is so poor that, more often than not, entire phrases are left out?[76] Even worse, there is little marginal evidence from later hands indicating that a reader actually noticed, and tried to make the text more usable. Generally speaking, the audience does not seem to have cared.[77]

A similar attitude can be detected with regard to the voluntary fast days observed by some in the community. The Yiddish work begins each month by listing the relevant days and the reason for fasting on each. What, then, are we to make of a fast intended to commemorate the death of the biblical Samuel, which is dated to 28 Iyar by one manuscript, to 8 Iyar by another, and to 8 *and* 20 Iyar by a third?[78] While the actual level of observance of these fast days

[71] Ibid., fos. 37^{r-v}, 40^{r}. All of these issues, of course, have their own history.

[72] As noted in Shtif, 'A Yiddish Manuscript Library' (Yid.), 146.

[73] MS Paris 587, fo. 35^{v} (מן זגיט מער סבורת [!] אבער דו הושט גנוג מיט דיזר סברא).

[74] MS Berlin 694/1, fo. 2^{v} (טו נון ווי דו ווילשט אונ' ווי דיר עבן איז).

[75] See e.g. Baumgarten, 'Prayer, Ritual and Practice in Ashkenazic Jewish Society', 126–31.

[76] See e.g. MS Paris 587, fo. 3^{r}; MS Oxford 1217, fo. 5^{v}.

[77] One exception is MS AIU H9A. See e.g. the corrections on fos. 41^{r}, 58^{v}, 80^{v}.

[78] MS Berlin 694/1, fo. 46^{r}; MS Berlin 694/2, fo. 69^{v}; MS Paris 587, fo. 51^{v} (עכט טג אונ' צווײנציג טג אין אייר).

among Italo-Ashkenazi Jews (or Ashkenazi Jews at large) is open to debate, the Yiddish *minhagim* manuscripts would appear to have been a highly unreliable guide for anybody so inclined.[79]

Last but not least, the Yiddish manuscripts also display a peculiar sense of humour. One blatant example appears in the section concerning the priestly blessing, which recommends that, before going up to the *dukhan*, the priests present in synagogue take off their shoes (which is indeed done to this day) and their trousers (which is not). This crudity occurs in four of the six manuscripts, although the spelling in two is so garbled that the copyists themselves may not have been aware what they were writing.[80] By contrast the scribe of MS Berlin 694/2 displayed some individuality by introducing jokes of his own. After devoting several pages of text to the intricacies of the Hebrew calendar, setting out how the four special sabbaths before and after Purim will fall, depending on whether or not the year is intercalated and on the day of the week on which Rosh Hodesh Adar falls (information that is presented in tables in the other manuscripts), he concludes, 'Parashat Hahodesh I'll let *you* work out!'[81] A few pages on, we learn that the Torah reading for the third intermediate day of Passover runs from Exodus 34: 1 to 'I don't know where'.[82] Lest we harbour any doubts as to the jocular nature of these remarks, the same scribe tells us about the liturgy of the Great Sabbath during the week before Passover that 'if Shabat Hagadol falls on a Thursday, no *yotser* is said'.[83]

This is not the place to reflect on the traditional role of the vernacular in providing outlets for scribal humour.[84] However, the playful approach evident here and elsewhere accentuates a certain incongruousness that may be inherent in the very concept of *minhagim* books in Yiddish; at the very least it complicates any notion we may have of the Yiddish handbooks serving as vehicles of instruction and guides to religious observance.

[79] For the underlying Hebrew tradition see Elizur, *Wherefore Have We Fasted?* (Heb.), esp. 177–80; cf. 230–9 for a sceptical view of actual practice.

[80] MS Paris 587, fo. 3v (זענט כהנים אין דער שולין דיא זולין איר שוך אונ' הוזין אויש טון); MS Paris 588, 5r (איר שוך . . . אונ' איר הוזן); MS AIU H9A, fo. 5v ([?] איר שוך . . . אונ' איר חונין); MS Oxford 1217, fo. 6v ([!] איר שויך . . . אונ' איר חזן). Cf. the variant unique to MS Oxford 1217, fo. 16r, regarding the eve of Yom Kippur (אונ' אידרמן ציכט זיין שויך אוייש אונ' זיין הוזן אונ' גיט שולן).

[81] MS Berlin 694/2, fo. 39r (אונ' פרשת החדש לוש איך דיך רעכענה).

[82] Ibid., fo. 66r (בון ויאמר ה' אל משה פסל לך ביש אן איך וואש ניט וואו).

[83] Ibid., fo. 50r (אונ' ווען שבת הגדול גוויל אם דורשטיג דארף מאן קיין יוצר ניט זאגין).

[84] See Rosenzweig, 'Rhymes to Sing and Rhymes to Hang Up', esp. 162–3, on the juxtaposition of religious texts and humorous material bordering on the obscene in MS Oxford 1217, a miscellany intended for a young bride. For a parallel from Judaeo-French, see Fudeman, *Vernacular Voices*, 124–50.

When Zalman Yent fixed the *minhagim* of the Ashkenazi settlement in Treviso in the 1430s, he did so because there was a need for synagogue functionaries to know how public prayer was to be conducted in a community which lacked a local tradition of its own and was made up of immigrants of diverse backgrounds. Whoever expanded his collection some four decades later had a more ambitious aim. More work is needed on the text and on its sources in order to sharpen the adaptation's profile and intention. In any event, when that adaptation was translated into Yiddish, the interests of its audience may have lain elsewhere. By the sixteenth century it had become *en vogue* among Italo-Ashkenazi bankers eager to participate in the book culture of the Italian Renaissance to commission manuscripts in the vernacular for their wives and daughters, and the much-augmented *minhagim* book of Zalman Yent was among the many works translated to cater to that market.[85] Whether or not the information it contained was relevant to the everyday life of its owners, it was apparently a good book to have, to put on the shelf, and perhaps even to leaf through on a sabbath afternoon.[86]

The discord between the several layers of the text pulling in different directions may have been one of the reasons why the Yiddish work was never consigned to print. The *Minhogim* that were printed in Venice in 1589 were a different story; as an original Yiddish work conceived as a comprehensive guide to Ashkenazi practice, they were immensely successful everywhere. The indigenous Italo-Ashkenazi tradition discussed in this essay, in contradistinction, remained on the shelf long after the Yiddish tongue had ceased to be spoken in Italy. In a sense, it remains there today so that we may probe it for what it may tell us about the efforts made by German Jewish émigrés to preserve their identity in a new land. Although this effort may have lost some of its urgency when they and their descendants began to integrate into ghetto society after all, we remain indebted to their effort for much of what we know of medieval Ashkenaz to this day.

[85] For a closer look at the social history of Yiddish manuscript production in 15th- and 16th-century Italy, see my 'Portable Homeland', 40–2.

[86] Cf. the remarks ('owned but not read') about a near-contemporaneous Yiddish work from Italy in Fox and Lewis, *Many Pious Women: Edition and Translation*, 19.

Bibliography

BATO, JOMTOV LUDOVICO, 'L'immigrazione degli ebrei tedeschi in Italia dal Trecento al Cinquecento', in Umberto Nahon (ed.), *Scritti in memoria di Sally Mayer: Saggi sull'ebraismo italiano* (Jerusalem, 1956), 19–34.

BAUMGARTEN, JEAN, 'Prayer, Ritual and Practice in Ashkenazic Jewish Society: The Tradition of Yiddish Custom Books in the Fifteenth to Eighteenth Centuries', in Shlomo Berger et al. (eds.), *Speaking Jewish—Jewish Speak: Multilingualism in Western Ashkenazic Culture*, Studia Rosenthaliana 36 (Leuven, 2003), 121–46.

——'The *Seyfer ha-minhogim* by Shimon ben Yehuda ha-Levi Guenzburg (Venice, 1593) and the Origin of an Old Yiddish Literary Tradition', in Shlomo Berger (ed.), *Between Yiddish and Hebrew*, Amsterdam Yiddish Symposium 7 (Amsterdam, 2012), 7–35.

BEIT-ARIÉ, MALACHI, *Catalogue of the Hebrew Manuscripts in the Bodleian Library: Supplement of Addenda and Corrigenda to Vol. I (A. Neubauer's Catalogue)*, ed. R. A. May (Oxford, 1994).

BERGER, SHLOMO, 'An Invitation to Buy and Read: Paratexts of Yiddish Books in Amsterdam, 1650–1800', *Book History*, 7 (2004), 31–61.

BONFIL, ROBERT, 'Changing Mentalities of Italian Jews between the Periods of the Renaissance and the Baroque', *Italia*, 11 (1994), 61–79.

——'The Settlement of Wandering Jews in Italy in the Late Middle Ages' (Heb.), in Avigdor Shinan (ed.), *Emigration and Settlement in Jewish and General History* [Hagirah vehityashvut beyisra'el uva'amim: kovets ma'amarim] (Jerusalem, 1982), 139–53.

BRIQUET, CHARLES-MOÏSE, *Les Filigranes: Dictionnaire historique des marques du papier dès leur apparition vers 1282 jusqu'en 1600*, 2nd edn. (Leipzig, 1923).

ELBOGEN, ISMAR, *Jewish Liturgy: A Comprehensive History*, trans. Raymond P. Scheindlin (Philadelphia, 1993).

ELIZUR, SHULAMIT, *Wherefore Have We Fasted? 'Megilat Ta'anit Batra' and Similar Lists of Fasts* [Lamah tsamnu? Megilat ta'anit batra ureshimot tsomot hakerovot lah] (Jerusalem, 2007).

FOX, HARRY, and JUSTIN JARON LEWIS, *Many Pious Women: Edition and Translation*, Studia Judaica 62 (Berlin, 2011).

FRAENKEL, AVRAHAM, 'Ashkenazi Tradition about R. Judah Halevi's Reaching Jerusalem' (Heb.), *Hama'ayan*, 53/3 (2013), 5–12.

——and JONAH FRAENKEL, 'Prayer and *Piyut* in the Nuremberg *Maḥzor*' (Heb.) (2008), <http://web.nli.org.il/sites/NLI/Hebrew/digitallibrary/moreshet_bareshet/Mahzor-Nuremberg/Documents/fraenkel_j_a.pdf>, accessed 27 Dec. 2016.

FRAKES, JEROLD C. (ed.), *Early Yiddish Texts: 1100–1750* (Oxford, 2004).

FRAM, EDWARD, *My Dear Daughter: Rabbi Benjamin Slonik and the Education of Jewish Women in Sixteenth-Century Poland*, Monographs of the Hebrew Union College 33 (Cincinnati, 2007).

FUDEMAN, KIRSTEN A., *Vernacular Voices: Language and Identity in Medieval French Jewish Communities*, Jewish Culture and Contexts (Philadelphia, 2010).

GOLDSCHMIDT, DANIEL, *Maḥzor layamim hanora'im lefi minhagei benei ashkenaz lekhol anfeihem*, 2 vols. (Jerusalem, 1970).

—— *Seder seliḥot keminhag lita* (Jerusalem, 1965).

—— *Seder seliḥot keminhag polin* (Jerusalem, 1965).

HAVERKAMP, ALFRED, 'Ebrei in Italia e in Germania nel tardo medioevo: Spunti per un confronto', in Uwe Israel, Robert Jütte, and Reinhold C. Mueller (eds.), *'Interstizi': Culture ebraico-cristiane a Venezia e nei suoi domini dal Medioevo all'età moderna*, Centro Tedesco di Studi Veneziani / Ricerche 5 (Rome, 2010), 47–100.

ISRAEL ISSERLEIN BEN PETAHYA, *Sefer terumat hadeshen*, ed. Shemuel Avitan (Jerusalem, 1991).

JOSEPH BEN MOSES, *Sefer leket yosher*, ed. Jacob Freimann, 2 vols. (Berlin, 1903–4).

—— *Sefer leket yosher*, 'Oraḥ ḥayim', ed. Amihai Kinarti (Jerusalem, 2010).

KLAUSNER, ABRAHAM, *Sefer minhagim lerabenu avraham kloizner*, ed. Yonah Y. Dissen (Jerusalem, 1978); 2nd edn., ed. Shlomo J. Spitzer (Jerusalem, 2006).

MILANO, ATTILIO, *Storia degli ebrei in Italia* (Turin, 1963).

MINCER, RACHEL ZOHN, 'Liturgical Minhagim Books: The Increasing Reliance on Written Texts in Late Medieval Ashkenaz', Ph.D. diss. (Jewish Theological Seminary, 2012).

MÖSCHTER, ANGELA, *Juden im venezianischen Treviso (1389–1509)*, Forschungen zur Geschichte der Juden A 19 (Hanover, 2008).

NEUBAUER, ADOLF, *Catalogue of the Hebrew Manuscripts in the Bodleian Library* (Oxford, 1886).

NEUBERG, SIMON, 'The First Yiddish Book Printed in Amsterdam: *Sefer Mismor Lethodé*', *European Journal of Jewish Studies*, 4 (2010), 7–21.

PELLES, ISRAEL M., 'The Book of "Maharil" (Customs of Maharil) According to Its Autograph Manuscripts and Its Speciality as a "Multi-Draft Versions" Work' [Sefer 'maharil' ('minhagei maharil') al pi kitvei hayad ha'otografiyim shelo veyiḥudo keḥibur merubeh arikhot], Ph.D. diss. (Bar-Ilan University, 2005).

RASPE, LUCIA, '*Minhagim* Books in Yiddish: A Tentative Taxonomy', in David Bunis, Katja Šmid, and Chava Turniansky (eds.), *Ladino and Yiddish Rabbinic Writings* (forthcoming).

—— 'Portable Homeland: The German-Jewish Diaspora in Italy and Its Impact on Ashkenazic Book Culture, 1400–1600', in Yosef Kaplan (ed.), *Early Modern Ethnic and Religious Communities in Exile* (Newcastle upon Tyne, 2017), 26–43.

—— 'The Migration of German Jews into Italy and the Emergence of Local Rites of *Seliḥot* Recitation', in Lukas Clemens and Christoph Cluse (eds.), *European Jewry around 1400: Disruption, Crisis, and Resilience* (forthcoming).

ROMER-SEGAL, AGNES, 'Yiddish Works on Women's Commandments in the Sixteenth Century', in Chava Turniansky (ed.), *Studies in Yiddish Literature and Folklore*, Research Projects of the Institute of Jewish Studies Monograph Series 7 (Jerusalem, 1986), 37–59.

ROSENZWEIG, CLAUDIA, 'Rhymes to Sing and Rhymes to Hang Up: Some Remarks on a Lampoon in Yiddish by Elye Bokher (Venice 1514)', in Shlomo

Simonsohn and Joseph Shatzmiller (eds.), *The Italia Judaica Jubilee Conference*, Brill's Series in Jewish Studies 48 (Leiden, 2013), 143–66.

ROTH, CECIL, *The History of the Jews of Italy* (Philadelphia, 1946).

SHMERUK, CHONE, 'The Beginnings of Yiddish Narrative Prose and Its Centre in Italy' (Heb.), in Daniel Carpi, Attilio Milano, and Alexander Rofé (eds.), *Scritti in memoria di Leone Carpi: Saggi sull'ebraismo italiano* (Jerusalem, 1967), 119–40.

—— 'The Illustrations of the Yiddish *Minhagim* (Venice 1593) in the Editions from Seventeenth-Century Prague' (Heb.), *Studies in Bibliography and Booklore*, 15 (1984), 52–31.

—— *Paris and Vienna*, ed., with Erika Timm [Pariz un viena: mahadurah bikortit betseruf mavo, he'arot venispaḥim] (Jerusalem, 1996).

—— *Yiddish Literature: Aspects of Its History* [Sifrut yidish: perakim letoledoteiha], Literature, Meaning, Culture 5 (Tel Aviv, 1978).

—— 'Yiddish Printing in Italy' (Heb.), *Italia*, 3 (1982), 112–75.

—— 'Yiddish Printing in Italy', in Chava Turniansky and Erika Timm, *Yiddish in Italia: Yiddish Manuscripts and Printed Books from the 15th to the 17th Century* (Milan, 2003), 171–80.

SHTIF, NOKHEM, 'A Yiddish Manuscript Library in a Jewish House in Venice in the Mid-Sixteenth Century' (Yid.), *Tsaytshrift* [Minsk], 1 (1926), 141–50; 2–3 (1928), 525–44.

SHULVASS, MOSHE, 'Ashkenazic Jewry in Italy', *YIVO Annual of Jewish Social Science*, 7 (1952), 110–31.

SIMONSOHN, SHLOMO, *The Jews in the Duchy of Milan: A Documentary History of the Jews in Italy*, 4 vols. (Jerusalem, 1982–6).

SPITZER, SHLOMO, 'Social and Religious Ties between the Jews of Austria and Northern Italy during the 15th Century', in Giacomo Todeschini and Pier Cesare Ioly Zorattini (eds.), *Il mondo ebraico: Gli ebrei tra Italia nord-orientale e Impero asburgico dal Medioevo all'età contemporanea*, Collezione Biblioteca 90 (Pordenone, 1991), 31–41.

STEINSCHNEIDER, MORITZ, 'Jüdisch-Deutsche Litteratur und Jüdisch-Deutsch', *Serapeum*, 25 (1864), 33–46, 49–62, 65–79, 81–95, 97–104.

—— 'Jüdisch-Deutsche Litteratur und Jüdisch-Deutsch. 3. Artikel: Nachträge', *Serapeum*, 30 (1869), 129–40, 145–59.

—— 'Mittheilungen aus dem Antiquariat von Julius Benzian. I. Handschriften', *Hebräische Bibliographie*, 9 (1869), 30, 60–2, 94, 117.

—— *Verzeichniss der hebräischen Handschriften*, Die Handschriften-Verzeichnisse der Königlichen Bibliothek zu Berlin 2, 2 vols. (Berlin, 1878–97).

STERN, DAVID, CHRISTOPH MARKSCHIES, and SARIT SHALEV-EYNI, *The Monk's Haggadah: A Fifteenth-Century Illuminated Codex from the Monastery of Tegernsee, with a Prologue by the Friar Erhard von Pappenheim*, Dimyonot 1 (University Park, Pa., 2015).

TA-SHMA, ISRAEL M., 'Ashkenazi Jewry in the Eleventh Century: Life and Literature', in id., *Creativity and Tradition: Studies in Medieval Rabbinic Scholarship, Literature and Thought* (Cambridge, Mass., 2006), 1–36.

——*Early Franco-German Ritual and Custom* [Minhag ashkenaz hakadmon: ḥeker ve'iyun], 2nd edn. (Jerusalem, 1994).

——'The Literary Content of the Manuscript', in *The Rothschild Miscellany: A Scholarly Commentary* (Jerusalem, 1989), 39–88.

TOAFF, ARIEL, 'Convergenza sul Veneto di banchieri ebrei romani e tedeschi nel tardo Medioevo', in Gaetano Cozzi (ed.), *Gli ebrei e Venezia, secoli XIV–XVIII* (Milan, 1987), 595–614.

——'Migrazioni di ebrei tedeschi attraverso i territori triestini e friulani fra XIV e XV secolo', in Giacomo Todeschini and Pier Cesare Ioly Zorattini (eds.), *Il mondo ebraico: Gli ebrei tra Italia nord-orientale e Impero asburgico dal Medioevo all'età contemporanea*, Collezione Biblioteca 90 (Pordenone, 1991), 3–29.

TURNIANSKY, CHAVA, *Language, Education and Knowledge among East European Jews* [Lashon, ḥinukh vehaskalah bemizraḥ eiropah: bein kodesh leḥol], The Jews of Eastern Europe: History and Culture 7 [Polin: perakim betoledot yehudei mizraḥ eiropah vetarbutam 7] (Tel Aviv, 1994).

——'Special Traits of Yiddish Literature in Italy', in Turniansky and Timm, *Yiddish in Italia*, 191–6.

——and ERIKA TIMM, with CLAUDIA ROSENZWEIG, *Yiddish in Italia: Yiddish Manuscripts and Printed Books from the 15th to the 17th Century* (Milan, 2003).

TYRNAU, ISAAC, *Sefer haminhagim*, ed. Shlomo J. Spitzer, 2nd edn. (Jerusalem, 2000).

WOLFTHAL, DIANE B., *Picturing Yiddish: Gender, Identity, and Memory in the Illustrated Yiddish Books of Renaissance Italy*, Brill's Series in Jewish Studies 36 (Leiden, 2004).

YUVAL, ISRAEL JACOB, *Scholars in Their Time: The Religious Leadership of German Jewry in the Late Middle Ages* [Ḥakhamim bedoram: hamanhigut haruḥanit shel yehudei germanyah beshilhei yemei habeinayim] (Jerusalem, 1988).

ZALMAN OF SANKT GOAR, *Sefer maharil: minhagim shel rabenu ya'akov molin*, ed. Shlomo J. Spitzer (Jerusalem, 1989).

ZIMMER, ERIC, 'A Book of Customs of the School of the Maharil' (Heb.), *Alei sefer*, 14 (1987), 59–87.

——*Society and Its Customs: Studies in the History and Metamorphosis of Jewish Customs* [Olam keminhago noheg: perakim betoledot haminhagim, hilkhoteihem vegilguleihem] (Jerusalem, 1996).

ZUNZ, LEOPOLD, *Die Ritus des synagogalen Gottesdienstes*, Die synagogale Poesie des Mittelalters 2 (Berlin, 1859).

PART IV

Cultural Content as a Marker of Jewish Regional Identities

CHAPTER TWELVE

A Collection of Jewish Philosophical Prayers

Y. TZVI LANGERMANN

INTRODUCTION: HEBREW PHILOSOPHICAL PRAYERS AND THE ROLE OF THE PARMA CODEX

The philosophical quest for God found powerful expression in medieval Hebrew poetry. Poets composed hymns in praise of the Deity and his creations, as philosophers understood them, and they poetically expressed their great thirst for the divine presence. This longing was no less powerful among the philosophically inclined than it was among mystics. Any number of poetical compositions on the soul or on the wonders of nature may be contemplated with devotional intent, but there are specific compositions whose direct address to the Deity indisputably marks them as prayers. A few philosophical prayers, most notably Solomon Ibn Gabirol's 'Keter malkhut' ('Crown of Kingship') found their way into some standard liturgies, where they remain to this day. In addition, philosophical prayers attributed to Aristotle and other non-Jews were included in Hebrew collections. Some of these compositions—'Keter malkhut' is the outstanding example—have been the subject of academic study.[1] Most philosophical prayers, however, remain unstudied and even unpublished.[2]

Beginning roughly in the twelfth century, philosophical culture and a philosophical approach to the religious life struck roots throughout the Jewish communities of the Mediterranean basin. The political, religious, and linguistic barriers which divided numerous autonomous regions were no barrier

[1] There is now a book-length study by Israel Levin, *The Crown of Kingship (Keter Malkhut) of Solomon Ibn Gabirol* (Heb.).

[2] As far as I know, there has been no study of Hebrew contributions to the genre. There are some valuable studies on the prayers of Hellenistic philosophers: van den Berg, *Proclus' Hymns*; Dillon, 'The Platonic Philosopher at Prayer'; Layne, 'Philosophical Prayer in Proclus's Commentary on Plato's Timaeus'.

at all for the spread of Jewish philosophy. Nonetheless by the fifteenth century Jewish philosophy was in retreat. External forces had emptied the great centres of Iberia and Provence of most of their Jewish inhabitants. Internally kabbalah was in the process of displacing philosophy as the dominant Jewish theological framework.[3] Still, Jewish philosophers held their own in some places, particularly in regions belonging to the Byzantine cultural orbit, even if no longer under the rule of the Byzantine emperors. The most important of these was Candia, capital of Crete. At that time the island was under Venetian rule, and connections with the Italian peninsula were particularly strong. An important entrepôt and a truly Mediterranean city, Candia was a bastion of Jewish philosophy which displayed open resistance to the kabbalah. It became a place of refuge for like-minded individuals from around the Mediterranean basin.[4]

Codex Parma De Rossi 997 is an enormous collection (394 folios) of private, occasional prayers copied in a Byzantine hand of the fifteenth century.[5] Most of the supplications are philosophical in their content and language. Although not the only codex to bring together philosophical prayers, it is by far the richest and most diverse collection of this sort. This is not an ordinary prayer book with additions; it is a collection devoted exclusively to supererogatory liturgies. To put it in the language of Jewish custom, the texts are *tefilot reshut*, prayers that may be offered at the discretion of the supplicant, rather than *tefilot keva*, mandatory prayers that must be recited at fixed times. The collection includes prayers by some Cretan authors, and it is very possible that the codex was copied in Candia or its environs; in any event, its contents certainly reflect the religious tendencies of the Candian philosophers. Authors from all around the Mediterranean are represented: Bahya Ibn Pakuda, Moses and Abraham Ibn Ezra, and Ibn Gabirol, all of whom hailed from the Iberian peninsula; members of the Ibn Tibbon clan, who inhabited Provence and Italy; and the Provençal Yedayah Hapenini, to name the most famous. Local poets include Shemaryah Ikriti, Elijah ben Eliezer, and Judah Kilti. Also represented are Sa'adyah Gaon, a native of Egypt who spent most

[3] Of course the full story is much more complex. Not all thinkers saw a conflict, or a need to choose, between the two; the situation varied much locally. However, the gradual rise of the kabbalah is noted in general histories, e.g. Sirat, *A History of Jewish Philosophy in the Middle Ages*, 273, and Goodman, 'Jewish Philosophy', 475–80.

[4] See Ravitzky, 'A Kabbalist Confutation of Philosophy' (Heb.), *Tarbiz*, 58 (1989), and the literature cited there.

[5] Also listed as Palatina 1753 and Richler 1098; see Richler, *Hebrew Manuscripts in the Biblioteca Palatina*, 286–7.

of his career in Iraq; Judah Hehasid, the German mystic; and a prayer is even ascribed to Maimonides. Strikingly, the codex also includes prayers attributed to Aristotle and Hippocrates, copied from the Hebrew translation of an Arabic gnomology by Ḥunayn b. Isḥāq (809–73).

Many different occasions for prayer are represented here, for example a prayer for the success of the standard daily prayer; dialogues with or reproofs of one's own soul; litanies based on Maimonides' so-called thirteen articles of faith.[6] In the case of most prayers, no specific time or situation is specified for their recital. One may imagine that they would have been said in private, perhaps in an isolated spot and at night, given the recognized stature of night vigils, but there is no evidence that this was the case. Several of the prayers in this collection are said to have been recited by their respective authors 'every morning'. In principle they could have been said whenever the supplicant felt the urge to do so.[7]

Before analysing the material in the Parma Codex, some clarifications are in order. I use the term 'philosopher' to refer to someone who has studied and internalized philosophical teachings, which may have been received orally, by way of books, or both. Of course a variety of philosophies were on the market, and even a single text was open to a variety of interpretations, some sharply at odds with others. Nonetheless I maintain that philosophers on the whole shared a common approach to the world and similar conceptions of the Deity. This made it possible to put together a compilation such as the Parma Codex, which comprises a diverse group of authors who might otherwise be placed in different pigeonholes. In a word, the philosophers of whom I am speaking—the consumers of the Parma Codex, as I see it—were not rigidly aligned with any particular school.

I define philosophical prayer, or the prayer of the philosopher, by its content. Philosophical prayer addresses a being recognized and revered by philosophers, for example the Cause of Causes. Prayers that express wonder over cosmic structures and processes described in philosophical texts should also be regarded as exemplars of philosophical prayer.[8] Prayers of philosophers such as Halevi and Ibn Gabirol on philosophical subjects may also be defined

[6] I say 'so-called' because Maimonides did not draw up a list of ideas in which one must 'believe'; he rather articulated a set of notions of whose truth one must convince oneself by means of ratiocination.

[7] On morning prayers see Nilsson, 'Pagan Divine Service in Late Antiquity', 63–9 *passim.* On a special corner or space for private prayers see Langermann, 'From Private Devotion to Communal Prayer', 39*–41*. On night vigils see Tanenbaum, *The Contemplative Soul*, 111–16.

[8] We have evidence for this sort of incorporation of philosophy into Jewish prayer from very

as prayers even if their content is not relayed in philosophical language. 'Keter malkhut', the prime example of this genre, was written by a philosopher and conveys many philosophical ideas, using both the specific idiom of philosophy and the language of Hebrew liturgy.[9]

The social context of philosophical prayer must be considered as well. Were these prayers said communally by a group of like-minded people? Alternatively, would their consumers have preferred to perform their devotions or text-centred meditations in private? The codex reveals nothing at all about the performance context. The late Ezra Fleischer asserted that lengthy supplications, such as Ibn Gabirol's 'Keter malkhut' and similar compositions by Bahya Ibn Pakuda and Sa'adyah Gaon, were not meant to be said as part of the communal prayer. He claimed that they were designed for the individual, at whatever moment suited him.[10] The prayers in question have no place at all in the standard liturgies of the synagogue of Cretan Jewry.[11] We can only guess by whom, when, and where they were recited.

Indeed, we have precious little information about the actual performance of supererogatory worship. That the practice existed is certain. Sherira Gaon mentions the pious custom (*minhag ḥasidut*) of reciting hymns and praises in the middle of the night.[12] A question addressed to Maimonides enquires whether 'someone who arises at night in order to offer a supererogatory prayer [*li-yatanaffula bi-l-ṣalāt*] or praise, or to recite verses or psalms until dawn', must recite beforehand the daily blessings on the Torah.[13] There is no evidence, however, that these responsa addressed philosophical prayer specifically.

Jacob ben Sheshet penned a lengthy invective against the philosophical attitude towards prayer; it was reproduced by Nahmanides' disciple, Isaac of Acre. However, the passage contains no reports of philosophers at prayer, or

early times. See Van der Horst, 'Greek Philosophical Elements in some Judaeo-Christian Prayers'.

[9] The many Arabic liturgical compositions of the Karaites which exhibit a philosophical tenor should at least be mentioned. MS D. Sofer 71 (IMHM F 72213), for example, contains 'ecstatic Sufi' prayers which, in my view, belong to the genre of philosophical prayer.

[10] See his note to Jefim Schirmann's *The History of Hebrew Poetry in Muslim Spain* (Heb.), 33 n. 410. Tanenbaum (*The Contemplative Soul*, 58) takes note of Ibn Gabirol's epigraph to 'Keter malkhut', where he explains that that piece was meant to be his own private prayer but it may also serve as an inspiration to others.

[11] Concerning the Jewish community of Crete and its liturgical history see Weinberger, *Jewish Poets in Crete*, 1985.

[12] Müller (ed.), *Responsen der Lehrer des Ostens und Westens*, no. 141.

[13] *Teshuvot harambam*, ed. Blau, ii. 342, no. 187.

of any special prayers recited by philosophers.[14] An unnamed Jew, who most probably lived in Morocco, prepared a Judaeo-Arabic paraphrase of 'Keter malkhut' at the request of a certain Judah Ibn Muyal. The translator reports that Ibn Muyal used to recite 'Keter malkhut' as a supererogatory prayer (*tanafful*) every sabbath.[15] Closer in time and place to the Parma Codex is MS Vatican 320, a late fourteenth-century copy of the Romaniote *maḥzor* used by Balkan Jews, with many additions. Noteworthy are the hymns, many of them philosophical in tenor ('Keter malkhut' included), inserted at the beginning of the prayer book, with the instruction to say them before the morning service.[16] There are also data concerning supererogatory prayers that were said at astrally auspicious times, but there is no reason to suppose that these were philosophical prayers.[17] The information concerning supererogatory kabbalistic prayer is much richer.[18]

The literary dimension of the prayers must also be considered. Stefan Sperl's analysis of three non-Jewish prayers from different religious traditions and historical circumstances provides an excellent model.[19] Structural analysis is particularly useful for comparing prayers. Limitations of space allow me to offer only brief forays into this wide-open field of enquiry.

PRAYERS ASCRIBED TO MAIMONIDES

The fact that the first two prayers in the codex are ascribed to Maimonides should come as no surprise, given his stature among Jewish philosophers. These prayers, explored by Leopold Dukes and Moritz Steinschneider, have been known to scholars for well over a century. Alexander Marx later showed that the two texts are intimately related; the second is an enlarged version, or

[14] Georges Vajda (*Recherches sur la philosophie et la kabbale*, 356–71) published a free translation, grappling as best he could with a densely embellished work of rhymed prose.

[15] Langermann, 'A Judaeo-Arabic Paraphrase of Ibn Gabirol's *Keter Malkhut*', 29.

[16] Richler, *Hebrew Manuscripts in the Vatican Library*, 262.

[17] Langermann, 'To Determine the Hour' (Heb.).

[18] Reif, *Judaism and Hebrew Prayer*, 244; the entire seventh chapter of his book is relevant to this theme. Though Reif discusses the philosophy of prayer, he does not engage philosophical prayer, certainly not of the kind explored in the present study. Also noteworthy is the combination of social and halakhic forces which are currently transforming the kabbalistic *tikunim* into mandatory prayers. The most interesting source for this phenomenon is to be found in the weekly 'sheets' distributed in Israeli synagogues. *Kol eliyahu*, 247 (1999) has a responsum from the late Mordecai Eliyahu, former Sephardi chief rabbi, who stated that someone who happens to be awake at midnight is obligated to say the *tikun*, and that everyone ought to make the effort.

[19] Sperl, 'The Literary Form of Prayer'.

amplification, of the first. Marx published an edition of both as a single text, marking off the amplifications in square brackets.[20] He noted that, in his catalogue of the manuscripts at Leyden, Steinschneider had characterized this composition 'as a philosophic contemplation ending in the form of a prayer'. This is true, insofar as the first sections take the form of a monologue. The short version begins,

> God, Creator of All;
> Principle of Principles, Secret of Secrets;
> His name is He, and He is His name;
> I will praise and glorify His name,
> Even though silence is His praise,
> And speechlessness His glorification.

Only in the final paragraph (the ninth in Marx's division) is there the direct appeal that one expects in prayer, 'O Cause of Causes'. Following additional philosophical encomia, there is a request and one of the traditional endings to Jewish prayers: 'Please deposit my surety with You, and may I be acceptable to You. For I have made an effort even where I did not perceive . . . Blessed are You, Who hears prayer.' It seems to me that for Maimonideans the distinction between prayer and contemplation is moot if at all existent. The entire composition deserves to be called a prayer.

Is this an authentic composition by Maimonides? Steinschneider thought so; Marx takes no stance. The content is certainly Maimonidean. That God and His Name are the same fits Maimonides' philosophy; no different powers within the godhead for him! The Great Eagle also emphasized that silence is the true praise—the silence of the philosopher who knows that no words are adequate in the presence of the Divine, and the speechlessness of someone struck by a true religious experience. However, given Maimonides' extreme conservatism as far as liturgy is concerned, I think it highly unlikely that he would have written a prayer of this sort, and even less likely that he would have allowed it to circulate.[21]

[20] Marx, 'Texts by and about Maimonides', section 2, pp. 381–5. Full references to the earlier studies may be found there. Marx consulted the Parma Codex; additional copies of these prayers have since been identified, but they do not alter the picture.

[21] Given his position, as summarized, for example, by Herbert Davidson (*Moses Maimonides*, 383), that worship through prayers and rituals falls short of the highest form of worship, 'to keep silent is praise'; and that the adulation of God that permeates the liturgy is 'a grudging concession to human frailty', there would be no reason for Maimonides to compose additional prayers of his own. For a somewhat different approach, which, however, would probably still reject the prayer ascribed here to him, see Reif, *Problems with Prayers*, ch. 12,

Two more prayers ascribed to Maimonides are found in the codex, and they, too, have been studied by Marx. One, a confession, has been identified by Z. Diesendruck and then described by Marx as a composition of Moses Ibn Ezra.[22] The other is a very short formula; Marx has published it and demonstrated that it is cobbled together from pieces of the end of *Guide of the Perplexed* i. 58, making use of the translations of both Ibn Tibbon and al-Harizi.[23] His comment, 'It is remarkable that a passage of the *Guide* thus directly entered the liturgy', seems a bit off the mark. The prayer-like ending of *Guide* i. 58 is a common literary device in Arabic, used to sign off a subtle metaphysical discussion. The author blesses and praises the Deity, but notes —in keeping with his metaphysical principles—that his true being is far beyond human ken, such that all attempts to describe or praise him look pitiful.

THE PRAYERS OF ARISTOTLE AND IBN TIBBON

The first of this pair of prayers is a short daily prayer ascribed to Aristotle, in Hebrew translation from an Arabic piece found in several manuscripts. The second is an amplification of the first; the Parma Codex contains the only copy known to me. The Hebrew version of Aristotle's prayer was prepared by Judah al-Harizi, part of his Hebrew translation of a collection of aphorisms compiled by Ḥunayn ibn Isḥāq, an Assyrian Christian of ninth-century Baghdad, which widely circulated under the title *Musarei hafilosofim*.[24] Just where Ḥunayn learned of the prayer is not known. The second prayer, attributed to an unnamed member of the Ibn Tibbon clan, is certainly modelled on Aristotle's text, but it is a bit longer. (One historian has gone so far as to suggest that the discovery of Aristotle's prayer in the pockets of some yeshiva students in sixteenth-century Poland led to one of the first cases of internal Jewish censorship.)[25]

'Maimonides on the Prayers'. Reif notes (214 n. 16) several responsa in which Maimonides firmly rejects liturgical poetry, thus courting controversy.

22 Marx, 'Texts by and about Maimonides', 382.

23 Note that in Harizi's numbering this is ch. 57.

24 The Arabic original is found in Ibn Isḥāq, *Ādāb al-Falāsifa*, 82. Harizi's translation was edited by Loewenthal (*Musare Hafilosofim*); the prayer is on p. 27. There are significant differences between MS Parma and Loewenthal, especially in the first hemistich. I may add that the pseudo-Aristotelian tract *De pomo* ends with a prayer ascribed to the great philosopher.

25 Yavets, *Sefer toledot yisra'el*, pt. 13, pp. 69–70.

The Parma version reads:

The Prayer of Aristotle Each Morning:

I am that I am; the Eternal that will not perish, and the Originator of everything, Save me from Your great fire.

The prayer opens with a citation from Exodus 3: 14. 'I am that I am' replaces 'O Eternal of Eternals!' (*yā azal al-azalī*) in Ḥunayn's version. Al-Harizi, a poet who composed his own philosophical liturgies, but also translated both Ḥunayn and Maimonides into Hebrew, must have had in mind Maimonides' investment in this verse, to which he devoted a lengthy chapter (i. 63) of his *Guide of the Perplexed*.[26] Thus 'I am that I am' should be taken as a direct address to a divine name. Hebrew has no equivalent to the Arabic apostrophe *yā*, 'O', but the context makes the meaning clear enough. Ever the littérateur, al-Harizi has replaced Ḥunayn's phrase with a Hebrew equivalent that, like the Arabic, repeats a word: *ehyeh asher ehyeh*. The Arabic phrase denotes God's eternality; al-Harizi's biblical substitution, mediated through its Maimonidean interpretation, stresses that the being of God is beyond description or predication.

Expanding upon this is a prayer by Ibn Tibbon (which member of the clan is not specified), also to be recited each morning:

The Prayer of Ibn Tibbon Each Morning:

Blessed be the Highest of the High, the Cause of Causes and the Agent of Agents; Who was, is and will be; Other than You, there is no God.

I implore you, for the sake of Your great, holy, and awesome Name, to save me from the misdoings of matter, which perishes without leaving a trace. May I have a share in that which emanates from the holy place, so that I may gaze into the awesome, resplendent light, and take refuge with You there. Please, Lord of all, save me from Your great and wondrous fire.

A PRAYER BY A LOCAL PHILOSOPHER, CRAFTED OUT OF EARLIER ETHICAL TEXTS

Folios 127–41 comprise a series of prayers by a local philosopher of the fourteenth century, Elijah ben Eliezer Yerushalmi of Candia, author of *Aderet emunah*, which presents a philosophy of Judaism; a commentary on Maimonides' *Guide*; an anti-kabbalistic commentary on *Sefer habahir* (one of the

[26] For this reason the reading of MS Parma must be preferred over Loewenthal's edition, which has *adir* ('magnificent') in place of *ehyeh*.

early, foundational texts of the kabbalah); and a number of treatises on logic. With the exception of the first section of *Aderet emunah*, none of these writings has been published or studied.[27]

The last in the series of prayers is a supplication that was placed at the end of *Sha'ar haperishah*, the 'Chapter on Abstinence' of what the author refers to as 'his book', that is, *Aderet emunah*. In adding a private prayer of his own composition to a chapter whose theme is the abandonment of this-worldly concerns, Yerushalmi followed in the footsteps of Bahya, who had placed two prayers at the end of his widely read *Duties of the Heart*. Bahya's first prayer is a *tokhaḥah* or admonition, in effect a scolding that one gives to oneself; the other is a *bakashah*, or supplication. In the final section of his book he recommended that both be said at night.[28] But Yerushalmi did not simply follow Bahya's lead; he lifted almost the entire prayer from the concluding section of Bahya's own *Sha'ar haperishah*, the ninth and penultimate section of his *Duties of the Heart*. In order to insert Bahya's text (in the Hebrew translation of Judah Ibn Tibbon) into a liturgical framework, Yerushalmi supplied some fairly standard formulations.

But the story does not end here. In the seventh and concluding chapter of his *Sha'ar haperishah* Bahya wrote: 'I have seen an eloquent disquisition on the meaning of abstinence by an outstanding person, who charged his son with it. I liked it, and so I made it into the final part of this section just as I found it; it is in place of an admonition of my own to you.'[29] In other words, he recounts that he had found an ethical will, possibly written by one of the Sufis from whom he liberally drew, having seen that it would make a fitting ending to one of the sections of his book.[30] This very text, then, had first been transformed from a passage in an ethical will into a coda for a section of a manual of spirituality, and from there into a prayer. It crossed two boundaries of literary form, moved from Arabic to Hebrew (or from Arabic to Judaeo-Arabic to Hebrew), and, very likely, from a Muslim setting to a Jewish one.

In its latest instantiation, as a prayer, four separate sections are visually marked off; their first words are written in bold, majuscule letters. I distinguish subsections, as indicated in the following schema:

[27] On this thinker see Rosenberg and Gershovitz, '*Aderet Emunah* of R. Eliyahu ben Eliezer Hayerushalmi' (Heb.), and the earlier studies by Rosenberg cited in n. 1 of their essay.

[28] The two prayers are appended to Kafih's bilingual edition, *Sefer torat ḥovot halevavot* (Jerusalem, 1973), 434–41.

[29] My translation from Kafih's edition, 407.

[30] Lobel, *A Sufi–Jewish Dialogue*.

Part I (22 lines)

(*a*) Opening prayer asking that the supplicant be counted among those who know, etc. (ll. 1–4).

(*b*) Complementary prayer, that the supplicant not be numbered among the errant, whose errors are described at great length (ll. 4–22).

Part II (46 lines)

A section depicting the ideal human. Appealing to the Cause of Causes, the supplicant prays that this depiction might apply to him. Yerushalmi adds an interpolation into the ethical will cited by Bahya, adding the phrase 'grant me that I be one of those whose heart You have broadened by means of Your generous spirit'. This transforms Bahya's description of an ideal into a request that one might become that type of person.

Part III (5 lines)

A short prayer beseeching God to 'put into our heart' the decision to make the correct choice before it is too late.

Part IV (9 lines)

(*a*) A short coda praying for the redemption of the Jewish people, followed by a few lines of praise.

(*b*) One of the standard, traditional signatures, from Psalm 19: 15: 'May what my mouth says and my heart thinks be pleasing before You, O God, my Creator and Redeemer.'

A LONG AND COMPLEX SUPPLICATION BY JUDAH HALEVI

Arguably the greatest Hebrew poet of all time, Halevi wrote many liturgical pieces for recitation in the synagogue or in private. 'Avarekh et adonai asher ye'atsani' ('I will bless the Lord, who has given me sound advice') is the longest prayer that he composed, running to 418 lines in Haim Brody's publication.[31] It has never been studied in any detail; my discussion here is intended as a first step only, to be followed, I hope, by a deeper look on the part of a specialist in liturgical poetry. Ibn Gabirol's 'Keter malkhut' is considered to be the model

[31] Brody (ed.), *Diwan des Jehuda ha-Levi*, iv. 138–57.

for all the long philosophical *bakashot*.[32] However, 'Avarekh' and 'Keter malkhut' share little in common beyond their length, their division into different sections, and their function as private prayers, which may or may not have been the original intention of their authors.[33] 'Avarekh' is divided into discrete sections, each accompanied by a title which at times indicates the type of prayer (e.g. *viduy* or confession), at other times the bodily posture. The prescription of specific bodily postures is unique among all supplications known to me. Some, such as prostration (*hishtaḥavayah*) and kneeling (*keri'ah*), have no place in the ordinary synagogue service, though there is evidence of their employment in private prayer.[34]

This fascinating composition was published by Brody in his edition of Halevi's *Dīwān*, then again by D. Jarden.[35] Neither Brody nor Jarden took notice of the variations in the manuscripts. Brody's version has fourteen sections, each with a caption. Jarden identifies seventeen sections; unlike Brody's edition, and unlike the version in the Parma Codex, not all of Jarden's sections have captions. Jarden's titles are taken from the opening phrase of each section, which is standard practice in the academic study of Hebrew poetry. In this case, unfortunately, the convention masks Halevi's own captions. Jarden placed the captions of the individual sections in an apparatus to the opening section, but not in the liturgy itself, as Brody did, and as ought to be done. Finally, he gave separate numbers, 45 to 61, to his seventeen sections, and he treated each of those as a separate composition—a policy that does not do justice to the unity of the piece. It is clear, nonetheless, from Jarden's explanatory note in the apparatus that he was well aware that the entire opus was meant as a single, unified *bakashah*, but this critical point is lost in his print presentation.

The Parma Codex contains a truncated version of the same prayer.

[32] Ezra Fleischer observes that 'Avarekh', in its structure and purpose, is 'a sister to "Keter malkhut" and the great *bakashot* of Bahya'; see Schirmann, *The History of Hebrew Poetry in Muslim Spain* (Heb.), 461 n. 196. Zerahyah Girondi and Judah al-Harizi also composed lengthy philosophical *bakashot*; see Maizalish, 'An Unknown Personal *Bakashah* by Rabbenu Zerahyah Halevi' (Heb.) and Fleischer, 'The Divine *Qasidas*', (Heb.). Al-Harizi's authorship of the latter is not certain, but very plausible.

[33] On the functions of 'Keter malkhut' see above; Dov Jarden (*The Liturgical Poetry of Yehuda Halevi* (Heb.), iv. 132) describes 'Avarekh' as a *bakashah* for the ten days of repentance beginning on Rosh Hashanah and culminating on Yom Kippur. While that would certainly be an appropriate time for offering this prayer, I have seen no evidence that Halevi actually designated it for that purpose.

[34] I have mustered the available sources in my 'From Private Devotion to Communal Prayer'.

[35] Jarden, *The Liturgical Poetry of Yehuda Halevi*, iv. 132–41.

It terminates at the end of line 293, the end of Brody's Section Nine; his edition has four more sections, covering about 120 lines. Moreover, one folio has fallen out of the Parma manuscript. MS Oxford Neubauer 1971, an outstanding *dīwān* studied by Joseph Yahalom, would have provided a most important witness,[36] for 'Avarekh' is listed in the table of contents. Unfortunately the quire containing this prayer is missing.

Other manuscripts display flexibility in both the arrangement of the text and the occasion of its recitation. In MS Amsterdam, *Ets ḥayim* 49 E 19, the prayer contains fifteen sections, but it is divided differently from the versions found in Brody and in the Parma manuscript; each section is marked off by a caption written in bold, majuscule letters. A copy of 'Avarekh' is found at the end of MS Moscow 1186, a collection of ethical treatises. Here the copyist has bookended the poem with two additional pieces, which do not belong to Halevi's composition—a *tokhaḥah* at the beginning (fos. 209*b*–210*a*) and a *bakashah* at the end (fo. 214*b*). In one *maḥzor* of the Italian rite (MS Vienna, Austrian National Library 29), 'Avarekh' is included among a group of confessions recited on the eve of Yom Kippur. It is also found in at least one copy of the early Ashkenazi *Maḥzor vitry* (MS Parma Palatina 2574). Finally, it was printed in a series of texts appended to an early Ashkenazi halakhic compendium, *Likutei hapardes* (Venice 5279 A.M).

Though Halevi's philosophical opus, the *Kuzari*, rejects philosophy as a way of life, he is counted by academic scholarship as a philosopher, indeed, one of the most important Jewish philosophers of the medieval period. For this reason alone, his liturgies, especially the private prayers, deserve to be included among the prayers of the philosophers. His odes to the soul in particular are suffused with philosophical teachings and vocabulary.[37] Noteworthy in this connection is Halevi's translation into Arabic of the daily morning prayer, 'Elohai, neshamah shenatata bi'—not far removed conceptually from his odes to the soul—in *Kuzari* I: 115. While the philosophical teachings in 'Avarekh' are not especially interesting, the complex and involved liturgy beautifully illustrates the ardent, almost desperate longing of the philosopher to communicate with the Deity by means of prayer—structured prayer, with fixed bodily postures to match the texts.

An almost innocent side remark in the *Kuzari* offers an interesting insight into the place of prayers, especially newly composed ones, in the religious life of the 'worshipper' (*al-muta'abbid*), an ideal Jew constructed by Halevi in

[36] Yahalom, 'Kitāb al-Šuḍūr fī al-Manẓūm wa-al-Manthūr' (Heb.).

[37] See Tanenbaum, *The Contemplative Soul*, especially ch. 8.

Kuzari III: 1. This individual

> loves to converse with God in private; to stand, to supplicate, to pray all the *taḥanunim* and *bakashot* that he can remember.[38] But he will find pleasure in the new *teḥinot* for only a few days, as long as they are new. Then, as they become rote, the soul does not respond to them. They provide no ground for submission, nor for the soul's longing.[39]

For this reason, claims Halevi, the worshipper soon abandons prayer and returns to the worldly demands of his soul: sensual delights, food and drink, and so on.

We do not know if Halevi had any specific targets in mind when he criticized the 'new *teḥinot*'. To be sure, many new supplications were made available in his time, including his own creations, which have been and remain a source of inspiration for generations of Jews. It is tempting to think, and very plausible, that the passage is autobiographical; perhaps Halevi was giving vent to *ennui* with his own compositions. Nonetheless it is surprising that, after bemoaning the fact that prayers can become rote recitations, he went on to recommend a prayer regimen focused on the canonically fixed Amidah. Because it is said three times daily (different versions are recited on sabbaths and festivals) it might easily become routine. Interestingly enough, Maimonides (*Guide* iii. 51) also targeted this traditional prayer as a focal point of his exercise in concentration. It is striking that two of the most creative Jewish thinkers of the period urged readers to learn to concentrate on the meaning of their obligatory prayers, which many Jews undoubtedly knew by heart. In the end, each in his own way regarded the daily repetition of the standard prayers as the best path towards achieving this higher goal.

'Avarekh' is definitely a private prayer, said by the supplicant on behalf of himself alone. This fact is brought out in the coda, a prayer for the redemption of the Jewish people. As a rule, the communal element is emphasized, indeed placed in the foreground, in Jewish prayer. A Jew prays as part of the community; not just on behalf of local co-religionists, or of Jews around the world, but for all Jews present and past. Halevi was the most nationalistic Hebrew poet of his age; he expressed his longing for Zion in a series of odes, and he manifested his love for his ancestral homeland when he abandoned fame and fortune in Spain for the Holy Land. He was also a very private person, and 'Avarekh' is a highly personal prayer. Only in the final section does he nod to the tradition of including all Israel in his prayer.

38 Prayer books were not common and prayers were recited from memory.

39 My translation from Halevi, *Kitāb al-Radd wa-l-Dalīl fi l-Dīn al-Dhalīl*, 91.

A PRAYER ASCRIBED TO 'ZERAHYAH', AND AGAIN TO HIPPOCRATES (AND ELSEWHERE TO SOCRATES)

This prayer appears first on folio 125*a* of the Parma Codex, with the caption 'The Prayer of Abūqārṭ [= Hippocrates] Every Morning'; then again—with some significant differences—on 167*b*, under the title 'A Pure prayer, translated by Rabbenu Zerahyah of blessed memory'. The copyist who included both either did not notice or did not care that the two are nearly identical.[40] These two prayers are, in turn, very similar (again, with some differences, not necessarily insignificant) to a prayer ascribed to Socrates, found in two other manuscripts: MS New York, Jewish Theological Seminary of America 2469, fo. 212*b*, and MS Amsterdam, *Ets ḥayim* 47 E 19, fos. 29*b*–30*b*.[41] The latter is a collection of private prayers similar to the Parma Codex, including Bahya's 'Keter malkhut' and Judah Halevi's 'Avarekh'. As Zerahyah ben She'altiel Hen is named as the translator of Socrates' prayer, it is likely that he is the author of the prayer attributed in our manuscript to Zerahyah, and that the prayer was translated from Arabic.[42]

Though Zerahyah ben She'altiel Hen is certainly the most compelling choice for the author, or translator, of these prayers, doubts remain. His translations are characterized by a dense and viscous Hebrew, not at all like the fluid language of this prayer. A possible alternative is Zerahyah Halevi, who translated from the Arabic the 'Chapters on Felicity' attributed to Maimonides. The thrust of the 'Chapters', whether or not Maimonides wrote them, is certainly closer in spirit to Socrates' prayer than anything translated by Zerahyah Hen.[43] Zerahyah Girondi, a well-known poet whose lengthy *bakashah* was mentioned above,[44] is also a candidate; his philosophical inclinations fit well with the sentiments of the prayer. Finally, one cannot rule out the Zerahyah who had authored a kabbalistic commentary on the Torah, preserved uniquely in MS Paris, AIU 146, and whose work remains unstudied. Though this man is

[40] Note, however, that sections III and IV (see below) are missing from Hippocrates' prayer; they are found in the prayer ascribed to Socrates.

[41] Leopold Zunz (*Literaturgeschichte der synagogalen Poesie*) reports that the Hebrew prayer of Socrates had been printed several times, but gives no references.

[42] On Zerahyah's activity as a translator see briefly *Aristotle's 'De Anima'*, ed. Bos, 1–4.

[43] See now for full discussion and references Manekin et al. (eds.), *Moritz Steinschneider*, i. 165. The editor of that text, H. S. Davidowitz, leaned towards identifying him with Zerahyah Hen, even though the latter is not known to have been a Levite.

[44] See n. 32.

not known to have been a translator, his interest in the letters of the alphabet, to which Moshe Idel has called attention, is a point of contact with the coda of the prayer, as we shall see.[45]

Because the prayers in the Parma Codex resemble so closely the Hebrew prayers found elsewhere and which are ascribed to Socrates, it seems useful to take a closer look at 'Socratic' prayer, especially since, as far as I know, no prayers are attributed to Hippocrates. There is, of course, the famous Hippocratic oath, and a prayer attributed to Maimonides that is often confused with it, but that is a physician's prayer for ethical guidance.[46]

Classical sources contain a few prayers, or meditations, by Socrates.[47] A short supplication of his, recorded in an Arabic source,[48] may be rendered into English as follows:

> Oh God, I approach you in the intensity of my fervour for You. I swear by Your Truth, I restrain my thoughts from gesturing in Your direction, all the more so my tongue from describing You precisely. If this, my God, is my message concerning You, then what can I say about You, in tandem with my tears that are on Your account?

Like Aristotle's prayer discussed above, this text is very brief. Its theme is the supplicant's inability to direct his thoughts towards the Deity, let alone utter any praises. The prayer is thus reduced to a confession that the supplicant is speechless and moved to tears, resonating with Maimonides' well-known opinion that awestruck silence is the ideal form of praise.[49]

The prayers of concern in this section—the two found in the Parma Codex and the prayer of Socrates—all display the same structure, content, and vocabulary. Nonetheless I would not dismiss the differences as insignificant. In particular, Zerahyah may have sanitized the prayer in order to make it fully acceptable to Jews. The two texts found in the Parma Codex are displayed below in parallel columns; in the notes I occasionally refer to the Arabic prayer of Socrates translated above, as it may help in understanding the Hebrew prayers.

[45] Idel, *Language, Torah, and Hermeneutics in Abraham Abulafia*, 144.

[46] The prayer ascribed to Maimonides is still a live issue in the medical community. See e.g. Crawshaw, 'The Hippocratic Oath is Alive and Well in North America'.

[47] Jackson, 'The Prayers of Socrates'.

[48] Gätje, *Pseudo-Aristotle*, 135.

[49] *Guide of the Perplexed*, i. 59 (trans. Pines, i. 139–40).

Zerahyah's prayer	Hippocrates' prayer
I. **Blessed** be the First of the First and the Eternal of the Eternal	I. **Blessed** be the First of the First and the Eternal of the Eternal
The Pre-eternal, Who will not disappear in the face of flowing time and ever-changing instants	The Pre-eternal, Who will not disappear in the face of flowing time and ever-changing instants
Great and holy, luminous and pure	Holy, great, and pure
Neither bound by place nor enclosed by time	Who is not contained by place or seized by time
Rather, it is He who institutes times and creates places	For She is the limpid pearl, clean and pure, first among all the divine light-emitting luminaries; they are those who sustain all the intellectual forces
Blessed are You in the supernal, eternal, and everlasting pearl[50]	And shine upon the faces of the creatures
It is the limpid pearl, clean and pure	
First among all the light-emitting luminaries	
They [denizens of the pearly realm] are the angels, they are the intellectual powers that shine upon the faces of the creatures	
Blessed is the Lord of the world, from Whom derives the life of the spiritual powers, and the angelic psychic form	**Blessed** is the Lord of the world, from Whom derives the life of the spiritual spirits [seems to be a simple scribal error, *ruḥot* instead of *koḥot*] and the angelic psychic forms
II. I beseech You, for the sake of Your eternity in everlastingness and Your unity, that You protect me[51] and rescue me[52] from the darkness of ignorance	**II. I beseech You**, for the sake of Your eternity in everlastingness and Your unity, that You protect me and save me from the darkness of ignorance that

[50] On the word 'pearl' (*peninit*) see Klatzkin, *Thesaurus Philosophicus Linguae Hebraicae*, pt. III, 196, especially the reference to 'Keter malkhut'; there, too, the angels are described as pearls. Cf. Ziai, 'Beyond Philosophy', 221, citing a cosmogonic myth that 'the first thing God created was a glowing pearl He named Intellect, *ʿaql*.

[51] I correct תפצני to תצפנני, relying on the prayer of Hippocrates.

[52] Again here I make a minor correction to the Hebrew.

Zerahyah's prayer	Hippocrates' prayer
that seethes in this world. Draw me to the clear light that issues forth from You, and I will take refuge in you.	seethes in this world [and take me] to the clear light that issues forth from You, and I will take refuge in You.
Make my share, for the sake of Your name, the share of the supernal secrets.	**Make** my share part of it [the light] for the sake of Your name,
Grant me [rule over; necessary emendation, from MS *Ets ḥayim*] natures and the reinforcement of physique, so that I may set out on the path of the intellect; the upright path by which I will merit to glow in Your light;	Transfer me from the rule of the natures and the reinforcement of lusts to the upright path of the intellect, by means of which I will attain luminescence in Your light.
And by Your differentiating me from perishable human nature and from the earthly, perishable human physique	And by Your differentiating me from perishable human nature, and the finalizing [bringing to an end] domicile
And joining me to the angelic nature, which lasts forever and maintains itself for all eternity;	Allow me to return to the angelic nature, which lasts forever and maintains itself for all eternity;
It is the domicile of the pious and God-fearing.	It is the source of the pious and God-fearing.
III. Woe is me, alas, for I have come late to my intellect, and I have not given You Your due;	
Alas, woe is me, for I have kept silent[53] and not thanked You for all the good that You have done for me. How bitter for me, how very sorry I am for my fleeting heart, for I have not understood that You lead me to high and lofty beliefs.	
Please, God, have me attain them! Support my intellect until You guide me and take me to the source of sources; it is the fountain of life and the eternity of eternities.	

[53] Isa. 6: 5, mistakenly written as *nitmeiti* rather than *nidmeiti*; the error is probably due to dictation that was not heard correctly.

Zerahyah's prayer	Hippocrates' prayer
IV. Please, God,[54] save me from the cesspools of difficult times, and from the circumstances of the moments, one upon the other; that I may have no need for, or any attraction towards, the vanities of the world, chasing after bodily lusts. Have me attain knowledge of the supernal knowledge [i.e. be united with it], which is knowledge of the separate letters [*otiyot muvdalot*], so that [my] end may not be among the letters that are like one another [*otiyot mitdamot*] in the lower world, as well as the ever-changing forms that pass on without remaining.[55] You are witness to everything, rule over all and everything, and are capable of everything.	

Both of these liturgical compositions highlight themes and characterizations favoured by the philosophers. We find declarations that God is beyond time or space and that the angelic realm is the First Light, to give just two examples. Of greater interest to the study of prayer are the supplicant's requests. He begs to be redeemed from ignorance, and to be transformed from 'nature' to 'intellect', from human to angelic being. These requests certainly reflect the type of redemption philosophers had in mind. The confessions similarly resonate with the worries of philosophers: shortcomings in praising God or in comprehending his works.

The basic structure is as follows: (I) tripartite praise; (II) first supplication; (III) confession; (IV) second supplication. Part I is further subdivided into two (Hippocrates) or three (Zerahyah) subsections, each beginning 'Blessed', as do all traditional Jewish blessings. The second supplication is also divided into two subsections, each beginning 'Please God'.

[54] Again I have made a minor correction to an obvious scribal error.

[55] *Otiyot muvdalot* is a term used in the *masorah*, the tradition that determines the correct reading of Hebrew Scripture; *otiyot mitdamot* is used by Ibn Janāḥ in *Sefer ha-Rikma, ouvrage grammatical du XIe siècle*, 142.

The prayer opens with a tripartite hymn of praise, composed of three sections, each beginning 'Blessed'. The three blessings correspond—roughly perhaps—to three worlds: divine, angelic, and a third one inhabited by beings who have vital spiritual forces and angelic psychic forms; presumably these are humans. The structure of the opening is identical to that of the Jewish Amidah prayer, which begins with three blessings of praise. However, this similarity is not carried through in the rest of the prayer.

The first supplication has two parts: a modest request, to be saved from ignorance, and a second set of increasingly grand pleas, beginning with the wish to rule over the body so as to free the mind, and culminating in the request to be annexed to the 'angelic nature'. In the prayer of Hippocrates, the act of joining the 'angelic nature' is characterized as a 'return'. There follows a short confession, in which the supplicant expresses remorse for 'coming late' to the path of the intellect. The prayer ends with a second supplication, a highly charged plea to be guided to 'the Source of Sources'. The construct form in Semitic languages often serves as a superlative; the 'source of sources' thus means, in effect, the ultimate source. Using the imagery of filth—not uncommon in the Neoplatonic and Gnostic traditions—the supplicant begs to be saved 'from the cesspools of difficult times', and ends with another request to join the highest ranks. He employs here a terminology which remains a mystery, referring to the 'supernal knowledge' as knowledge of the 'separate letters', which he contrasts to 'the letters that are like one another'. On the face of it the simple, 'separate' (that is, unattached to matter) intellects are contrasted with the compound (but the simplest of compounds, homeomerous) entities in the terrestrial realm. However, the meaning of the phrases eludes me and awaits additional content analysis.

The literary investigation of prayer, especially prayer written by and for philosophers, has yet to draw the attention of academics. I am hopeful that this brief foray, based on a rich collection put together in a late Byzantine Jewish setting, stimulates further explorations.

Bibliography

Aristotle's 'De Anima', Translated into Hebrew by Zerahyah ben Isaac ben She'altiel Hen, ed. and trans. Gerrit Bos (Leiden, 1994)

BRODY, HAIM (ed.), *Diwan des Jehuda ha-Levi*, 4 vols. (Berlin, 1801–30).

CRAWSHAW, RALPH S., 'The Hippocratic Oath Is Alive and Well in North America', *British Medical Journal*, 309 (6959) (1994), 952.

DAVIDSON, HERBERT, *Moses Maimonides: The Man and His Works* (Oxford, 2005).

DILLON, JOHN, 'The Platonic Philosopher at Prayer', in Theo Kobusch and Michael Erler (eds.), *Metaphysik und Religion* (Munich, 2002), 279–95.

FLEISCHER, EZRA, 'The Divine *Qasidas*' (Heb.), *Tarbiz*, 67 (1997), 29–102.

GÄTJE, HELMUT, *Pseudo-Aristotle: Studien zur Überlieferung der aristotelischen Psychologie im Islam* (Heidelberg, 1971).

GOODMAN, LENN E., 'Jewish Philosophy', in Edward Craig (ed.), *Shorter Routledge Encyclopedia of Philosophy* (London, 2005), 475–80.

HALEVI, JUDAH, *Kitāb al-Radd wa-l-Dalīl fī al-Dīn al-Dhalīl (Al-Kitāb al-Khazarī)* [Kuzari], ed. David H. Baneth and Haggai Ben-Shammai (Jerusalem, 1977).

IBN ISḤĀQ, ḤUNAYN, *Ādāb al-Falāsifa (Sentences des Philosophes)*, ed. A. Badawi (Kuwait, 1985).

IBN JANĀḤ, JONAH, *Sefer ha-Rikma, ouvrage grammatical du XIe siècle*, ed. Baer ben Alexander Goldberg and Raphael Kirchheim (Frankfurt am Main, 1856).

IBN PAKUDA, BAHYA, *Sefer torat ḥovot halevavot*, ed. Yosef Kafih (Jerusalem, 1973).

IDEL, MOSHE, *Language, Torah, and Hermeneutics in Abraham Abulafia* (Albany, NY, 1989).

JACKSON, DARRELL, 'The Prayers of Socrates', *Phronesis*, 16 (1971), 14–37.

JARDEN, DOV, *The Liturgical Poetry of Yehuda Halevi* [Shirei hakodesh lerabi yehudah halevi] (Jerusalem, 1978–85).

KLATZKIN, JACOB, *Thesaurus Philosophicus Linguae Hebraicae* (New York, 1968).

LANGERMANN, Y. TZVI, 'From Private Devotion to Communal Prayer: New Light on Abraham Maimonides' Synagogue Reforms', *Ginzei Qedem*, 1 (2005), 31*–49*.

—— 'A Judaeo-Arabic Paraphrase of Ibn Gabirol's *Keter Malkhut*', *Zutot* (2003), 28–33.

—— 'To Determine the Hour: Choosing Auspicious Times for Prayer by Means of the Stars' (Heb.), *Pe'amim*, 85 (2001), 76–88.

LAYNE, DANIELLE A., 'Philosophical Prayer in Proclus's Commentary on Plato's Timaeus', *The Review of Metaphysics*, 67 (2013), 345–68.

LEVIN, ISRAEL, *The Crown of Kingship (Keter Malkhut) of Solomon Ibn Gabirol* [Keter malkhut lerabi shelomoh ibn gevirol: kolel mahadurah bikortit shel keter malkhut im hakdamah, perush veḥilufei nusaḥ] (Tel Aviv, 2005).

LOBEL, DIANA, *A Sufi–Jewish Dialogue: Philosophy and Mysticism in Bahya Ibn Paquda's* Duties of the Heart (Philadelphia, 2007).

LOEWENTHAL, A., *Musare Hafilosofim (Sinnspruche der Philosophen)* (Frankfurt am Main, 1896).

MAIMONIDES, MOSES, *Guide of the Perplexed*, trans. Shlomo Pines, 2 vols. (Chicago, 1963).

—— *Teshuvot harambam*, ed. Joshua Blau, 4 vols. (Jerusalem, 1958).

MAIZALISH, YITZHAK, 'An Unknown Personal *Bakashah* by Rabbenu Zerahyah Halevi' (Heb.), *Pirkei Shirah*, 1 (1990), 47–59.

MANEKIN, CHARLES H., Y. TZVI LANGERMANN, and HANS HINRICH BIESTERFELDT (eds.), *Moritz Steinschneider. The Hebrew Translations of the Middle Ages and the Jews as Transmitters*, i: *Preface. General Remarks. Jewish Philosophers*, Amsterdam Studies in Jewish Philosophy 16 (Dordrecht, 2013).

MARX, ALEXANDER, 'Texts by and about Maimonides', *The Jewish Quarterly Review*, {NS} 25 (1935), 371–428.

MÜLLER, JOEL (ed.), *Responsen der Lehrer des Ostens und Westens* (Berlin, 1885).

NILSSON, MARTIN P., 'Pagan Divine Service in Late Antiquity', *Harvard Theological Review*, 38 (1945), 63–9.

RAVITZKY, AVIEZER, 'A Kabbalist Confutation of Philosophy—The Fifteenth-Century Debate in Candia' (Heb.), *Tarbiz*, 58 (1989), 453–82.

REIF, STEFAN, *Judaism and Hebrew Prayer: New Perspectives on Jewish Liturgical History* (Cambridge, 1995).

—— *Problems with Prayers: Studies in the Textual History of Early Rabbinic Liturgy* (Berlin, 2006).

RICHLER, BENJAMIN, *Hebrew Manuscripts in the Biblioteca Palatina in Parma* (Jerusalem, 2001).

—— *Hebrew Manuscripts in the Vatican Library* (Vatican, 2008).

ROSENBERG, SHALOM, and URI GERSHOVITZ, '*Aderet Emunah* of R. Eliyahu ben Eliezer Hayerushalmi' (Heb.), *Da'at*, 49 (2002), 47–86.

SCHIRMANN, JEFIM, *The History of Hebrew Poetry in Muslim Spain* [Toledot hashirah ha'ivrit bisefarad hamuslemit], ed. Ezra Fleischer (Jerusalem, 1995).

SIRAT, COLETTE, *A History of Jewish Philosophy in the Middle Ages* (Paris, 1985).

SPERL, STEFAN, 'The Literary Form of Prayer: Qur'an Sūra One, the Lord's Prayer and a Babylonian Prayer to the Moon God', *Bulletin of the School of Oriental and African Studies*, 57 (1994), 213–27.

TANENBAUM, ADENA, *The Contemplative Soul: Hebrew Poetry and Philosophical Theory in Medieval Spain* (Leiden, 2002).

VAJDA, GEORGES, *Recherches sur la philosophie et la kabbale dans la pensée juive du Moyen Âge* (Paris, 1972).

VAN DEN BERG, ROBERT M., *Proclus' Hymns: Essays, Translations, Commentary* (Leiden, 2001).

VAN DER HORST, PIETER W., 'Greek Philosophical Elements in some Judaeo-Christian Prayers', *Sacra Scripta*, 7 (2009), 55–64.

WEINBERGER, LEON J., *Jewish Poets in Crete* (Cincinnati, 1985).

YAHALOM, JOSEPH, 'Kitāb al-Šuḏūr fī al-Manẓūm wa-al-Manthūr: Judah Halevi's Dīwān, edited by Joshua Halevi' (Heb.), in Joshua Blau and David Doron (eds.), *Heritage and Innovation in Medieval Judaeo-Arabic Culture* [Masoret veshinuy batarbut ha'aravit-hayehudit shel yemei habeinayim] (Ramat Gan, 2000). 127–44.

YAVETS, ZE'EV, *Sefer toledot yisra'el*, pt. 13 (Tel Aviv, 1937).

ZIAI, HOSSEIN, 'Beyond Philosophy: Suhrawardi's Illuminationist Path to Wisdom', in Frank Reynolds and David Tracy (eds.), *Myth and Philosophy* (Albany, NY, 1990), 215–43.

ZUNZ, LEOPOLD, *Literaturgeschichte der synagogalen Poesie* (Berlin, 1865).

CHAPTER THIRTEEN

Prophets and Their Impact in the High Middle Ages: A Subculture of Franco-German Jewry

MOSHE IDEL

SOME MEDIEVAL INTERPRETATIONS OF PROPHECY

In one of the most intriguing statements found in the vast opus of R. Solomon Yitshaki (Rashi), he claims that '[the people of] Israel in exile, though they are not prophets, they are sons of prophets. And those and the others are behaving in accordance with beautiful and respectable custom, and custom should not be changed.'[1] Without entering into the distinction between the biblical terms 'prophets' and 'sons of prophets', their implications, or the rabbinic sources used by Rashi when referring to Jews as 'sons of prophets', I would like to highlight the centrality of custom as something that unifies all Jews in exile, and also ensures their elevated spiritual status. This means that custom is a mode of behaviour, a specific type of performance that is quintessential for maintaining the quasi-prophetic element in all Jews. However, as other scholars have pointed out, it is evident that the emphasis on the centrality of custom is a unique characteristic of Ashkenazi Jewish culture. This is the reason why no parallel statement to Rashi's assessment can be found in other centres of Jewish culture: nowhere else was custom venerated

[1] See Rashi in *Sefer hapardes*, ed. Ehrenreich, 302 and 265, discussed by Israel M. Ta-Shma in *Early Franco-German Ritual and Custom* (Heb.), 27, 29 n. 24. Ta-Shma's monograph constitutes the most comprehensive, erudite, and penetrating exposition of the crucial role played by custom in Ashkenazi culture. See also Zfatman, *From Talmudic Times to the Middle Ages* (Heb.), 462, and in more general terms Zimmer, *Society and Its Customs* (Heb.). For the source of part of this dictum see BT *Pes.* 66*a–b*, JT *Shab.* 17*a*, and following them also many other rabbinic sources. Close to Rashi is the formulation of R. Tsidkiyah ben Abraham, *Shibolei haleket*, ed. Buber, 'Semaḥot', 344, §13. The affinity between the rabbinic sources mentioned here and the rabbinic phrase *minhag nevi'im* (the custom of prophets) deserves special attention for understanding Rashi.

so much, and nowhere else were post-biblical Jews as a whole described as potential sons of prophets. In a way this claim implied continuity between the biblical and medieval times, in both a ritual and a spiritual sense.

However, at least in principle, the concept of prophecy consists of a complex of components: the personality of the prophet; the source of prophecy; the process of prophecy—which may include techniques to reach that level; the content of prophecy, be it written or oral; and, finally, the authority of those prophecies. Like many other ancient Jewish topics, prophecy was systematically interrogated in the Middle Ages as a result of the reflective mode of thought introduced by the philosophical trends that entered Judaism. Each new theological system interpreted prophecy in its specific manner and by resorting to its main concepts. This is evident in R. Sa'adyah Gaon's theory of the revelation of the Glory,[2] or in Maimonides' long discussion of prophecy, especially in his *Guide of the Perplexed*.[3] At the same time, while elaborating on his neo-Aristotelian interpretation, the Great Eagle was cautious regarding the possibility of prophetic phenomena emerging in the exilic period. Resorting to new intellectual tools in Judaism, the Neoplatonic interpretations that emerged in the Middle Ages contributed towards a much more reflective understanding of the ancient phenomena.[4] Also influential were the astral explanations of prophetic occurrences found since the twelfth century.[5] When the theosophical structure of ten *sefirot* emerged, prophecy was interpreted accordingly as related to one divine power or another.[6] With the emergence of the prophetic kabbalah, a more ecstatic understanding of prophecy was articulated, combining linguistic techniques (based mainly on divine names) with a philosophical interpretation of the phenomenon.[7] In general, these types of prophecy were not particularly concerned with the external voice as the actual medium of revelation.

Last but not least: magically inclined authors regarded ancient prophecy

[2] See Altmann, 'Saadya's Theory of Revelation'; Kreisel, *Prophecy*, 27–93.

[3] Kreisel, *Prophecy*, 148–315. For the intellectual background see Rahman, *Prophecy in Islam*; H. A. Wolfson, *Studies in the History of Philosophy and Religion*, ii. 60–119; Walzer, and 'Al-Farabi's Theory of Prophecy and Divination'; and for its impact on Maimonides see Macy, 'Prophecy in al-Farabi and Maimonides'; Eran, 'Intellectual Modifications in Maimonides' Model of Prophecy' (Heb.); and ead., 'The Diffusion of the *Hads* Theory of Avicenna' (Heb.), 71–6.

[4] Altmann and Stern, *Isaac Israeli*, 185–217; Kreisel, *Prophecy*, 103–14; Afterman, *Devekut* (Heb.), 49–51.

[5] See e.g. Ibn Malka, *Perus lesefer yetsirah*, ed. Vajda, 23, 26, 33, or the astro-magical *Sefer ha'atsamim*, mistakenly attributed to Abraham Ibn Ezra, ed. Grossberg, 13–14.

[6] See e.g. Afterman, *Devekut* (Heb.), 226 245, 255–6, 258–9; Pedaya, '*Aḥuzim bedibur*' (Heb.).

as resulting from invocations of the Divine, or of angels, by means of magical names.[8] For example R. Isaac ben Jacob Hakohen, a kabbalist living in mid-thirteenth century Castile, testified that he had visited France and learned about occult lore from magical writings that were used by anonymous Jewish sages: 'It is transmitted in the name of the ancient sages that they made [magical] use of *Shimusha deheikhalei zutartei* and of *Shimushei deshedei*. And it is the ladder to be climbed in order to reach the degrees of prophecy and its powers.'[9] Magical technique similarly informed the Ashkenazi forms of prophecy and that of Abraham Abulafia, though in different ways.

These distinctions cover a variety of explanations to mostly inner experiences, which may also vary from one case to another. Indeed, it is possible to distinguish between three main approaches to understanding prophecy in Judaism during the Middle Ages: eschatological, ethical, and ecstatic.[10] The last mentioned is predicated upon an internalization of prophecy as an inner experience which culminates in an intellectual event, and in which external dimensions, such as the voice, are left behind as inferior. This study will focus primarily on this last approach.

The philosophers, kabbalists, and astrologers who portrayed prophecy as the peak of religious experience did so in the course of commenting on ancient canonical texts, but they did not claim, at least not overtly, that they had enjoyed prophetic experiences, or even reached the status of a prophet. Nor were they understood by others to have made such claims. Seen from this point of view, their discussions did not contradict the famous rabbinic statements that prophecy had ceased among the people of Israel,[11] nor that which

[7] See Idel, *The Mystical Experience in Abraham Abulafia*, *passim*, and the important passage preserved in R. Moses of Kiev, *Shushan sodot*, 69*b*; Scholem, *On the Mystical Shape of the Godhead*, 253, 259–60, 314 n. 22; id., '*Sha'arei tsedek*: A Kabbalistic Text' (Heb.); id., 'Eine kabbalistische Erklärung der Prophetie als Selbstbegenung', 289–90; Har'ar, *Le porte della giustizia*, ed. Idel, *passim*. I would like not to enter here the complex question of the phenomenological relationship between biblical prophecy and ecstasy. See e.g. Hines, 'The Prophet as a Mystic', Wilson, 'Prophecy and Ecstasy', or Uffenheimer, *Ancient Prophecy in Israel* (Heb.), 80–224. See also Fishbane, 'Biblical Prophecy as a Religious Phenomenon'; Levison, 'Two Types of Ecstatic Prophecy According to Philo', 83–9.

[8] See the passage by R. Nehemiah the Prophet discussed in Idel, 'Incantations, Lists, and "Gates of Sermons"' (Heb.), 489–90.

[9] Scholem, *Jewish Studies* (Heb.), ii. 98. Compare also ibid. 82, 92, 98, 107, 110.

[10] See Idel, 'On Prophecy and Early Hasidism', 47–56.

[11] See BT *Meg.* 17*b*; Urbach, 'Prophet and Sage in the Jewish Heritage' (Heb.); Alexander, 'A Sixtieth Part of Prophecy'; Yadin-Israel, 'Bavli *Menah'ot* 29b and the Diminution of the Prophets', esp. 94–105; Dan, 'The End of Prophecy' (Heb.); and esp. Sommer, 'Did Prophecy Cease?' See also Glatzer, 'A Study of the Talmudic Interpretation of Prophecy'; Bamberger,

declared the sage higher than the prophet, a statement which enjoyed a long career in the Middle Ages.[12] One may debate whether or not some of the medieval writers entertained hidden self-understandings or aspirations to prophecy, as claimed in Abraham J. Heschel's pioneering studies, based on the scant evidence concerning prophecy in the Middle Ages.[13] Yet I am not attracted to the sharpness of Heschel's distinction between prophecy and ecstasy; it seems to reflect an essentialist approach to complex phenomena. In any case, a variety of prophetic manifestations are found sporadically in medieval Judaism, as in Christianity, where these phenomena similarly caused tension.[14] Nevertheless Heschel is right in observing that there is nothing totally new in the linkage between dream and prophecy.[15] Not only did the Talmud note that a dream was conceived to be a sixtieth part of prophecy, even legal discussions were at times regarded (though in a quite guarded or even dismissive manner) as *divrei nevi'ut*, words of prophecy.[16]

In the following discussion I refer to occurrences of the term *navi* in some medieval texts, excluding treatments of non-prophetic forms of revelation. Expressions of positive and negative attitudes towards people who claimed prophetic abilities have sociological implications; they may serve as a convenient benchmark for assessing the culture in which those individuals and their critics were embedded. Here I am more concerned with claims related to prophecy, that is, the forms of rhetoric and their occurrence in Jewish cultures, rather than with the experiences that are covered by the term 'prophecy'. Though the content of some prophetic experiences may be similar to those designated by terms such as 'the hovering of the Shekhinah' or 'the revelation of Elijah', my interest here lies with the actual use of the terms 'prophet' and 'prophecy', which carry more authoritative status. The possibility of regard-

'Revelations of Torah after Sinai'; and Goldreich, *Automatic Writing in Zoharic Literature and Modernism* (Heb.), 9 n. 1.

[12] Goshen-Gottstein, '"The Sage is Superior to the Prophet"'; Huss, '"A Sage is Preferable to a Prophet"' (Heb.); E. R. Wolfson, '"Sage is Preferable to Prophet"'.

[13] Heschel, *Prophetic Inspiration after the Prophets*. See also his classical contribution to this topic, *The Prophets*. As to the possibility that Heschel himself could have thought of himself as a prophet see E. K. Kaplan, *Holiness in Words*, 138–9. See also Perlman, *Abraham Heschel's Idea of Revelation*, and Idel, *Old Worlds, New Mirrors*, 217–33.

[14] See e.g. Aune, *Prophecy in Early Christianity*, or Hvuidt, *Christian Prophecy*; Arbesmann, 'Fasting and Prophecy in Pagan and Christian Antiquity'. For later prophetic phenomena in Christianity see Reeves, *The Influence of Prophecy in the Late Middle Ages*; Woods, *Mysticism and Prophecy*; McGinn, '"Trumpets of the Mysteries of God"'; and Taithe and Thornton (eds.), *Prophecy: The Power of Inspired Language in History*.

[15] Heschel, *Prophetic Inspiration after the Prophets*.

[16] See BT *Eruv*. 60*b*; *BB* 12*a*.

ing oneself as a prophet in such a society heightened the individual's self-confidence and self-esteem, and it may have triggered creativity.

WHO WERE THE PROPHETS OF THE FRANCO-GERMAN REGIONS?

I am not concerned here with the scholastic applications of mainly Greek models of thought to ancient Israelite phenomena, that is, the classical prophets, but with claims for the existence of prophecy in the Middle Ages, in a specific area, the Franco-German regions, notwithstanding the rabbinic claim that prophecy had ceased.[17] This chapter in Jewish spirituality does not depend on the new trends in medieval Jewish thought mentioned above, but on a series of names and brief discussions concerning prophets that appeared between, roughly speaking, 1150 and 1300 in a specific geographical area. In an earlier series of studies related to prophecy, I have proposed to pay special attention to the Franco-German evidence, found in a variety of sources describing experiences and techniques.[18] In line with Ludwig Wittgenstein's recommendation not to search for the precise meaning, I will here examine the very appearance of the term 'prophet' in the texts to be addressed below, in order to see its different uses.

A tentative list of five prophets, together with a figure reported to have made an ascent on high, has been compiled by Gershom Scholem,[19] and a somewhat longer one by Abraham J. Heschel, who enumerated eight

[17] For the various discussions of the similarities and differences between Jewish culture in northern France and in Germany, especially its southern provinces, see e.g. Grossman, *The Early Sages of France* (Heb.), 539–86; Kanarfogel, 'German Pietism in Northern France'; id., *The Intellectual History and Rabbinic Culture of Medieval Ashkenaz*, 537; Malkiel, *Reconstructing Ashkenaz*. For the character of the Ashkenazi culture as distinct from the Sephardi one see e.g. Zfatman, *From Talmudic Times to the Middle Ages* (Heb.), and ead., *The Jewish Tale in the Middle Ages* (Heb.). I shall not deal here with the contemporary oriental view of prophecy in the circle of Maimonides' family, influenced as they were by Sufi ideas. See e.g. Fenton, 'A Mystical Treatise on Perfection, Providence and Prophecy'; id., 'Deux écoles piétistes'; Heschel, *Prophetic Inspiration after the Prophets*, 119–25.

[18] See Idel, 'On the Metamorphosis of an Ancient Technique of Prophetic Vision' (Heb.); id., *Kabbalah: New Perspectives*, 90–1, 97–103; id., 'Gazing at the Head in Ashkenazi Hasidism'; id., *Enchanted Chains: Techniques and Rituals in Jewish Mysticism*, 109–10; id., 'Lawyers and Mystics in Judaism', 14–18, id., 'Incantations, Lists, and "Gates of Sermons"' (Heb.), 499–507; id., 'On R. Nehemiah ben Shlomo the Prophet's Commentaries' (Heb.), 157–8. See also, more recently, Lifshitz, *One God, Many Images* (Heb.), 161–82.

[19] *Origins of the Kabbalah*, 239–40, 248. See also E. R. Wolfson, *Through a Speculum that Shines*, 191–2.

prophets, though of these one is not Ashkenazi.[20] More recently, in a very erudite and critical study, Shraga Abramson has paid special attention to some occurrences of the term *navi* in medieval literature,[21] and similar issues have been examined by Amos Goldreich.[22] By combining the findings of these scholars and adding some other cases, we have at least eleven figures from the Franco-German regions who were explicitly referred to as prophet, *navi*.

1. First and foremost, the famous Rashi, active in Troyes, France, was described as a prophet by Ashkenazi authors.[23]
2. His son-in-law, R. Judah ben Nathan, was referred to as a prophet.[24]
3. R. Samuel Hanavi of Speyer, of the Kalonymus family, the father of R. Judah Hehasid, active in twelfth-century southern Germany, was also described as having ascended on high.[25] Interestingly, a tradition about the prophetic process was transmitted in his name among the members of his school.[26]
4. R. Jacob ben Meir, Rashi's grandson known as Rabbenu Tam, was referred to as a prophet by his student R. Eliezer ben Solomon.[27]
5. R. Samuel Hanavi of Rouen, active in the early thirteenth century, perhaps around 1230, is discussed immediately below.
6. R. Abraham the Prophet was, from the little we know, referred to as the source of exegetical information.[28]

[20] *Prophetic Inspiration after the Prophets*, 13–23.

[21] See Abramson, 'Prophet, Seer, Visionary' (Heb.).

[22] *Automatic Writing in Zoharic Literature and Modernism* (Heb.), *passim*.

[23] See Abramson, 'Prophet, Seer, Visionary' (Heb.), 118. See also Kanarfogel, *'Peering through the Lattices'*, 229 n. 24; Idel, 'Enquiries in the Doctrine of the Book of the Responding Entity' (Heb.), 240 and n. 289.

[24] Abramson, 'Prophet, Seer, Visionary' (Heb.), 118.

[25] See the important eschatological material collected by Marx in 'Essay on the Year of Redemption' (Heb.); Scholem, *Origins of the Kabbalah*, 248 n. 98; id., *Major Trends in Jewish Mysticism*, 374 n. 77; Heschel, *Prophetic Inspiration after the Prophets*, 13–14; Abramson, 'Prophet, Seer, Visionary' (Heb.), 119; Marcus, *Piety and Society*, 70, 163 n. 59; Wolfson, *Through a Speculum that Shines*, 191 n. 10. For most of the known information about this figure see *Kitvei avraham epstein*, ed. Haberman, i. 245–68.

[26] See Abraham ben Azriel, *Sefer arugat habosem*, ed. Urbach, i. 200.

[27] Heschel, *Prophetic Inspiration after the Prophets*, 15–19; Abramson, 'Prophet, Seer, Visionary' (Heb.), 118.

[28] Heschel, *Prophetic Inspiration after the Prophets*, 21 n. 55; Abramson, 'Prophet, Seer, Visionary' (Heb.), 121; Ta-Shma, *Collected Studies* (Heb.), i. 26 n. 12.

7. R. Isaac the Prophet is mentioned in a manuscript where material from another prophet, R. Nehemiah ben Solomon, is found.[29] At the bottom of the same page the name R. Isaac Hakohen also appears, and I surmise that they are the same person.[30] A certain R. Isaac of France is mentioned in the Ashkenazi *Perush haroke'aḥ al hatorah*, written in the mid-thirteenth century and attributed to R. Eleazar of Worms.[31] The interpretation of a biblical matter appears on the same page, described as being 'from the mouth of R. Isaac'.[32] Elsewhere in the same book there is a reference to a 'prophet from Tsarfat' who discussed a certain topic in the commentary with the commentator.[33] Later in the same commentary the author testifies that he had 'asked R. Isaac, the prophet from Tsarfat'.[34] Since it is plausible that the author of the commentary was living in Germany, we may infer that R. Isaac the Prophet went from France to Ashkenaz sometime in the mid-thirteenth century, which is why he was called 'of Tsarfat'. I assume that all those references deal with the same person, and if this is true the following portrait emerges: R. Isaac Hakohen was a prophet who came from France to Ashkenaz, was recognized as such and engaged the anonymous commentator in discussions on exegetical topics. This may be a case of prophetic hermeneutics.

8. R. Ezra, the Prophet of Moncontour, was a contemporary of R. Samuel of Rouen.[35] From the little we know about him, he can be considered an eschatological prophet, for he was depicted as having ascended on high in order to receive information regarding the date of the End. According to some sources, his prediction was checked by none other than R. Eleazar of Worms, and found to be accurate.[36] However, as he was also imagined

[29] See MS Parma-Palatina 2342, fo. 264*a*. [30] Ibid.

[31] *Perush haroke'aḥ al hatorah*, ed. Klugemann, ii. 31. On the problem of authorship of this commentary see Dan, 'The Torah Commentary of R. Eleazar of Germaiza' (Heb.), 644; id., *History of Jewish Mysticism and Esotericism* (Heb.), v. 204–6, 303–10. On the three occurrences of R. Isaac in this commentary see Dan, 'The Ashkenazi Hasidic "Gates of Wisdom"', 187; Kanarfogel, 'Rabbinic Figures in Castilian Kabbalistic Pseudepigraphy', 100 n. 80. See also Siegel, *Sefer sodei razei semukhim*, 79–80.

[32] *Perush haroke'aḥ al hatorah*, ii. 31. See also Kanarfogel, *'Peering through the Lattices'*, 195 n. 14, 211, 238 n. 49. [33] *Perush haroke'aḥ al hatorah*, ii. 221. [34] Ibid. 229.

[35] See Scholem, *Origins of the Kabbalah*, 239 n. 86, 248; Heschel, *Prophetic Inspiration after the Prophets*, 19–20; Abramson, 'Prophet, Seer, Visionary' (Heb.), 121–2; Urbach, *The Tosafists* (Heb.), i. 336–7, ii. 528; Ta-Shma, *Collected Studies* (Heb.), i. 150–1; Kanarfogel, *'Peering through the Lattices'*, 244–5 and n. 67; Yuval, *'Two Nations in Your Womb'* (Heb.), 273, 285–6.

[36] See Assaf, *Sources and Studies in Jewish History* (Heb.), 147–8, 153–4. *Nota bene* the resort to the divine name mentioned on p. 154.

to have disclosed secrets of the canonical writings, he might also be regarded as a hermeneutical prophet.

9. Last but not least: R. Nehemiah ben Solomon, also known as R. Troestlin, the Prophet of Erfurt (to be discussed below), was active between around 1225 and 1260, which means that he was part of the generation of the two previously mentioned prophets.

Two other prophets are known from the second part of the thirteenth century, one from Ashkenaz and one from France:

10. R. Abraham Axelrod of Cologne, who went to Spain, first to Barcelona and then probably also to Castile, was described as a prophet in an important document by R. Solomon ben Abraham Ibn Adret, to be discussed below.
11. An anonymous prophet active in France, probably in the last third of the thirteenth century, is mentioned by Ibn Adret in a responsum:

    And the rabbis of Ashkenaz and France did the same to that one from Cologne, and from their enquiry was revealed [to them] that which was revealed, in truth. Also today there is one [prophet] in France as it has been testified to us. Sometimes he predicts future things and some of them happen. And the rabbis promulgated what they promulgated concerning people's relation to him,[37] as I have heard.[38]

It is evident from the context that Ibn Adret speaks about an additional prophet, other than the prophet of Cologne, and that the latter should be identified with the previously mentioned R. Abraham. The fact that some modus operandi of these prophets has been established indicates that they were not ostracized by the rabbinic establishment of the two countries. Unfortunately Ibn Adret does not explain the details of the rabbinic regulations he mentions. However, we may infer from this passage the existence of a subculture of what I call the secondary elite, who may have been regulated by the primary elite, in both northern France and Germany.

Let me start with the remark that seven out of the eleven prophetic figures are of French extraction, namely numbers 1, 2, 4, 5, 7, 8, and 11. Even R. Nehemiah, active in Erfurt and cited in German sources, has some relation

[37] That is, they found a way to regulate the relationship between people and the prophet.

[38] *Teshuvot harashba*, ed. Dimitrovsky, i. 107, no. 34. This responsum is also known as no. 548, the number it was given in an earlier printed edition. See Teicher, 'The Medieval Mind'; Idel, 'Ashkenazi Esotericism and Kabbalah in Barcelona', 92–3; and Goldreich, *Automatic Writing in Zoharic Literature and Modernism* (Heb.), 174–5.

to France, for if my analysis of a certain document related to him is correct, his father was a student of the famous Tosafist R. Judah Sir Leon of Paris.[39] Thus, even if we exclude cases 1, 2, and 4 as ones in which 'prophet' was merely granted as an honorific title to one who had achieved great erudition, there are more French than German examples. Still, recourse to this honorific title is instructive, given how exceptional it is in Jewish sources from contemporary Europe. R. Elijah the Elder, an eleventh-century poet and inhabitant of France, whom Heschel referred to as a prophet, probably had nothing to do with prophecy, as pointed out by Shraga Abramson.[40] With the exception of R. Nehemiah and his circle—to be discussed below—very little is known concerning the literary heritage of the other prophets or their other activities. The little we do know suggests that their activities may somehow have been related to the preservation of the *heikhalot* literature in the centres of Jewish culture where they were active.[41] Yet even this cannot constitute the major explanation for the recurrence of the epithet 'prophet'.

The significance of the above list can be better understood when compared to the situation in other Jewish cultural centres in the same period. There may perhaps be one single piece of evidence for the epithet 'prophet' in Provence and Spain up until the seventies of the thirteenth century; this concerns R. Sheshet Benvenisti, the so-called Prince of Barcelona.[42] In Italy there is one single reference, but this is found in a book deeply immersed in Ashkenazi culture and, according to Abramson, the reference is a copyist's error and may have nothing to do with prophecy.[43] There is one reference to Maimonides as a 'prophet'.[44] R. Jacob Hanavi of Narbonne, probably active in southern France in the eleventh or early twelfth century, in what Jews called Provintsyah, may be counted as a Provençal exception.[45] Abramson has also

[39] See Idel, 'On Symmetric Histories and Their Termination' (Heb.), 94, 99. To my discussions there the treatment of Ta-Shma, *Collected Studies* (Heb.), i. 151–2 should be added.

[40] Heschel, *Prophetic Inspiration after the Prophets*, 22, but see Abramson, 'Prophet, Seer, Visionary' (Heb.), 124.

[41] On the transmission of some elements belonging to lost themes from the *heikhalot* literature in Ashkenazi writings, see Idel, 'From Italy to Germany and Back'; id., 'Holding an Orb in His Hand: The Angel 'Anfi'el', 26–8; and Scholem, *Origins of the Kabbalah*, 248. On the esoteric aspects of this school see Kanarfogel, *'Peering through the Lattices'*.

[42] Heschel, *Prophetic Inspiration after the Prophets*, 22–3; Abramson, 'Prophet, Seer, Visionary' (Heb.), 124.

[43] See Abramson, 'Prophet, Seer, Visionary' (Heb.), 119, 124; Kanarfogel, *'Peering through the Lattices'*, 231.

[44] Abramson, 'Prophet, Seer, Visionary' (Heb.), 118.

[45] See Scholem, *Origins of the Kabbalah*, 239–40, and nn. 87, 88; Abramson, 'Prophet, Seer, Visionary' (Heb.), 118–19.

drawn attention to the occurrence of the term 'prophet' in medieval poetic references to the poet, but none of these references designate a specific historical figure.[46]

The Franco-German examples thus convincingly show an incomparably greater interest in prophecy than is found in other European Jewish centres. It is against this background that the special Ashkenazi Pietist concern with R. Sa'adyah Gaon's theory of prophecy, related to the revelation of the divine Glory, should be understood. It was not merely the expression of a philosophical stance or a matter of exegetical treatment.[47] The theory itself constituted what I call a pneumatic interpretation.[48] The question I am posing here (though without proper elaboration) is whether the theory of revelation of the divine Glory adopted by Hasidei Ashkenaz may have been for them not just a matter of esoteric theology, but a theory which provided them with an experiential understanding of prophecy.[49] Discussions about the nature of prophecy proliferate in the writings of several generations of the Pietists, especially in those of R. Eleazar of Worms. But what seems to me indicative of the role played by their theological discussions is the presence, in some of their writings, of linguistic and other techniques related to prophecy. Nevertheless, with the exception of R. Samuel of Speyer, no other member of Hasidei Ashkenaz was ascribed the epithet 'prophet'.

In what follows I attempt to review in greater detail the information related to three of the above-mentioned 'prophets', emphasizing the public manifestation of prophecy and its occurrence in a synagogue setting. This framing reveals that the label 'prophet' refers not only to the inner life of the individual but to the role played by such figures on the socio-religious plane. We may assume that this public arena involved the audience in some form of

[46] Abramson, 'Prophet, Seer, Visionary' (Heb.), 122; Pagis, 'The Poet as Prophet in Medieval Hebrew Literature', 140–50.

[47] See the gist of Scholem's *Major Trends*, 80–118, but see 80–1; Dan, *The Esoteric Theology of Ashkenazi Hasidism* (Heb.), 104–68; id., *History of Jewish Mysticism and Esotericism* (Heb.), v. 209–92; or Liss, *Elazar ben Yehuda von Worms*. These Pietist perspectives are part of what I call the theologization of Jewish mysticism; see my 'On the Theologization of Kabbalah in Modern Scholarship'. Compare also to Lifshitz, *One God, Many Images* (Heb.), *passim*.

[48] *Kabbalah: New Perspectives*, 234–49; Kanarfogel, 'Approaches to Prophecy in Ashkenazic Torah Commentaries' (forthcoming).

[49] For the importance of the experiential aspects in Jewish mysticism, including Ashkenazi culture, see my *Kabbalah: New Perspectives*, 27, 91–2, 98, 323 n. 171, and *Enchanted Chains*, 110; Liebes, 'New Directions in the Study of Kabbalah' (Heb.), and E. R. Wolfson, *Through a Speculum that Shines*, *passim*, esp. 190–2, 244–5, 264–6; id., 'The Mystical Significance of Torah Study in German Pietism'; Schneider, *The Appearance of the High Priest* (Heb.), 260–1 n. 181.

participation; bystanders did not merely watch a theatrical performance in a detached manner. Given Rashi's view mentioned above, according to which ordinary Jews are the sons of prophets, might certain (exceptional) figures in his cultural environment, qualified to be labelled 'prophets', have been at the forefront of the vocal performance of the synagogue service?

R. SAMUEL, THE PROPHET OF ROUEN

A fascinating testimony is related to the figure of R. Samuel, the Prophet of Rouen (who should not be identified with the much earlier R. Samuel the Prophet, the father of R. Judah Hehasid, who lived in southern Germany).[50] According to this testimony, the angel Metatron was compelled to descend in order to solve a halakhic question that arose in the city of Rouen early in the thirteenth century. Let me translate first a pertinent part of the passage:

Let all the holy communities know that on the Wednesday after Tishah Be'av,[51] R. Samuel, the true prophet, was preaching in the attic of R. Menahem of Rouen,[52] and the rabbis who were sitting in front of him were R. Jacob of Provence and R. Isaac from the bridge of Audemer,[53] and R. Menahem and the other rabbis, and R. Abraham ben Samuel, and Rabbi Aaron ben Isaac, and R. Jacob of Cresbia, and youths who are experts,[54] and he [the prophet] was preaching about the portion of the 'Song at the Sea'.[55] At the end of the sermon R. Jacob of Provence asked the true prophet: 'My lord, ask R. Elijah of Paris[56] and Rabbenu Tam[57] how the knot of the phylacteries is to be knotted, if it should be knotted every day, or if it is possible to tighten it, or if we ought to tighten and knot it.' The prophet immediately called Metatron in front of them, and he said as follows: 'Metatron, Metatron, descend here in front of us!' He [Metatron] said: 'What do you want? I am not going to descend because Moses, our master, is in front of you and I fear to go there. But ask me and I shall answer you.' The prophet became angry and told him once again: 'Come down and bring with you R. Elijah of Paris and our master Tam!' He [Metatron] said to him: 'Rabbi Elijah of Paris cannot come because he is performing sacrifices before the Holy One, blessed be He.' The prophet said to him, 'In any case he should descend because we need his

[50] Compare to Heschel, *Prophetic Inspiration after the Prophets*, 14. Neither are the two identical to a third, and much later, R. Samuel Hanavi, who was alive in 1271/2 in Castile, as we shall see below.

[51] Or the fourth day after Tishah Be'av.

[52] On him see Golb, *Les Juifs de Rouen au Moyen Âge*, 297–304.

[53] See ibid. 304.

[54] Heb. *yodei sefer*; see ibid. 304 n. 35.

[55] Deut. 32.

[56] Perhaps it is the well-known late 12th- and early 13th-century Tosafist R. Judah Sir Leon, who was sometimes described as R. Judah of Paris. See Urbach, *The Tosafists* (Heb.), i. 323–35; Kanarfogel, 'Rabbinic Figures in Castilian Kabbalistic Pseudepigraphy', 87–8 n. 41. He died in 1224.

[57] R. Jacob ben Meir Tam was the teacher of R. Menahem's father.

learning!' Metatron told him: 'If he descends, the Shekhinah will descend with him.' The rabbis told him: 'It is prohibited to bother the Shekhinah.' And R. Jacob [of Provence] answered: 'Ask our master Moses, who is here.' And the prophet did so and asked him: 'How is the knot of the phylactery to be knotted?'[58]

The term 'prophet' occurs six times in a relatively short passage and more frequently in the ensuing discussion not translated here, and it is twice qualified by the adjective 'true'. This qualification suggests that there were also other prophets, who were not considered to be true. The scene is an attic, when the pericope concerning the Exodus from Egypt was read in public following the delivery of a sermon in front of figures described as rabbis. The prophet is, therefore, officiating in a community well known to him, and where he formally serves as a preacher. However, rather than being asked to relay prophecy, he is asked to play a more modest role in deciding between two modes of tying the knot of the phylacteries. As is clear from the continuation of the passage, this matter was the subject of a dispute between R. Tam, R. Elijah of Paris, and Moses, giver of the Torah. This topic has to do with Moses' biblical revelation, for, according to the rabbis, he saw the knot of the divine phylactery.[59]

We might assume that the mighty angel Metatron was compelled to descend when a simple formula was uttered. Unable to escape the power of the adjuration, the angel looks for a variety of excuses or pretexts for not coming down: first he notes the presence of Moses amidst the group of rabbis; then he claims that R. Elijah of Paris is performing sacrifices in the supernal Temple; finally he asserts that the descent of R. Elijah may cause the descent of the divine presence, which would be intrusive. Submitting to the group's fears about the inappropriateness of such an act, R. Samuel the Prophet, who performs the adjuration, turns to Moses and opens a discussion with him about the halakhic topic under scrutiny. The passage seems to emphasize the special status of R. Elijah of Paris, despite the fact that he is mentioned in connection with one of the most venerated halakhic figures, Rabbenu Tam. The former, and not the latter, is presented as a high priest, someone whose learning the assembled require. I wonder whether this strong affinity between R. Elijah and the divine presence does not reflect some notion of the medieval

[58] For the original Hebrew text see Kaufmann, 'La Discussion sur les philactères', 273–7, and R. Gedaliah Ibn Yahya's *Shalshelet hakabalah*, 118–20; Golb, *History and Culture of the Jews of Rouen* (Heb.), 92, 98–9, 104, as well as Kanarfogel, *'Peering through the Lattices'*, 172 and n. 98; Scholem, *Origins of the Kabbalah*, 239–40; and Idel, 'Metatron à Paris'. Compare also to Heschel, *Prophetic Inspiration after the Prophets*, 17, and Abramson, 'Prophet, Seer, Visionary' (Heb.), 121.

master's apotheosis, in the vein of the apotheosis of Enoch, who became an archangel, Metatron.

Despite the very strong magical language—'Metatron, Metatron, descend!'—and the impression that the angel can hardly escape magical coercion, both R. Samuel's initial intention and his recourse to the opinion of Moses in solving the dispute reflect a reticence towards angelic decisions in matters of halakhah. One of the reasons for finding the solution among mortals, Moses among them, is that Metatron, while willing to reveal his opinion, is unwilling to descend. By contrast, Moses descends. This descent may well have something to do with the fact that in an earthly rabbinic court the judges want to be able to see and interrogate the person involved in the legal process. Indeed, the passages that follow the above quote describe R. Elijah and R. Tam as descending and setting forth their arguments, though taking the views of Moses into consideration. And if Samuel Hanavi does not want to force the hand of Metatron and cause his descent, the angel cannot be taken seriously as a participant in the halakhic deliberations, let alone be regarded as the source of the final decision.

Metatron's first excuse for not bringing R. Elijah of Paris down in order to participate in the discussion is interesting. His portrayal as a *kohen*, a priest, is a detail that is not prominent among the historical data about him. This idiosyncratic vision is reminiscent of the description of the prophet Elijah as a high priest in the preface to a magical book, *Shimushei torah*, and to a certain extent in the biblical episode where Elijah offers sacrifices.[60] It should be remembered that Moses is also implied in the passage from *Shimushei torah*, just as in the above passage describing R. Samuel Hanavi.[61]

In fact, the legal discussion analysed above is an exception in its specific field, but reflects a wider phenomenon that had been present in Jewish mysticism since late antiquity. Its place in the history of halakhah is to be understood in the context of a struggle between the dominant halakhic school, which accepted the legalistic stance of R. Tam, and the more marginal position of R. Elijah of Paris. The entire passage describes the attempt of a peripheral individual or group to endorse R. Elijah's endeavour to modestly reform halakhah by enlisting an angelic-magical practice. In other words, according to this passage R. Samuel operates as a mantic prophet.

[59] For the history of this theme see Afterman, 'The Phylactery Knot' (Heb.).

[60] See 1 Kgs 14. See also Heschel, *Prophetic Inspiration after the Prophets*, 5 n. 7.

[61] See the introduction to *Shimushei torah*, printed under the title *Ma'ayan ḥokhmah* in Jellinek (ed.), *Bet ha-Midrasch*, i. 61.

Let me now turn to the sermon that precedes the mantic session discussed above. It focuses on a pericope that is to be read a few weeks after the date of the delivery of the sermon. In a series of instructions found in medieval manuscripts, there are many formulas entitled 'the name of [or for] the homilist'; these consist of magical names, both divine and angelic, that are believed to facilitate the delivery of a sermon.[62] Some of them are similar in style to what we find in the writings of R. Nehemiah the Prophet, to be discussed below. A recipe of this sort is found in two manuscripts replete with magical material from many periods in the history of Jewish magic. In the table of contents of MS Sassoon 290—now MS Genève and Montana, the Segre Amar Collection 145—a 'name of the homilist' is mentioned in the name of a certain R. Samuel. Though this set of instructions was part of the now lost section of the manuscript, it has been preserved in a parallel manuscript, now in the John Rylands Library in Manchester.[63] In light of the magical nature of the event described above, it seems plausible that this Samuel was identical to the prophet and homilist from Rouen. In any case, one magical recipe designed for delivery of the 'sermon' contains three mentions of the Tetragrammaton, and is addressed to God, who 'created the supernal angels, who gave the divine spirit onto the mouth of the prophets of truth'.[64] Here the homilist and the prophet almost coincide.[65] The fact that sermonic performance was oral may account for the fact that the compositions of this author are not extant.

R. NEHEMIAH (TROESTLIN) BEN SOLOMON, THE PROPHET OF ERFURT

In several thirteenth-century documents we encounter the phrases 'R. Nehemiah the Prophet'[66] and 'R. Troestlin the Prophet'.[67] Gershom Scholem

[62] See Idel, 'Incantations, Lists, and "Gates of Sermons"' (Heb.), 499–507.

[63] Olim MS Gaster 177, fo. 42*b*. See Benayahu, '*Sefer Shushan Yesod Olam* of R. Yosef Tirshom' (Heb.), 204–5, 212–13, and Goldreich, *Automatic Writing in Zoharic Literature and Modernism* (Heb.), 126 n. 72.

[64] See Scholem, *Devils, Demons, and Souls* (Heb.), 136. Scholem considered this text to be of Provençal extraction, while I consider it to be of Ashkenazi origin. See my 'Incantations, Lists, and "Gates of Sermons"' (Heb.), 494.

[65] See also the later nexus between prophecy and sermon in R. Shem Tov Ibn Gaon, *Badei ha'aron*, adduced by Goldreich in *Automatic Writing in Zoharic Literature and Modernism* (Heb.), 174 n. 14.

[66] See *Merkavah shelemah*, ed. Mussayoff, 31*b*; MS Paris BN 838, fo. 14*a*; and Marx, 'Essay on the Year of Redemption' (Heb.), 94.

[67] MS New York, JTS 8114, second part of the manuscript, fo. 17*b*, and MS Sasson 290, now MS Genève and Montana, the Segre Amar Collection 145, p. 620; Goldreich, *Automatic Writing*

has proposed that the two names refer to the same person.[68] On the basis of these references I have identified a series of short and mostly anonymous treatises, which consist mainly of commentaries on different topics, as writings belonging to that prophet and his circle.[69] So, for example, *Sefer hanavon*, printed twice as an anonymous treatise, is also entitled *Sefer nevi'im*; the sum of the numeric value of the consonants in both *hanavon* and *nevi'im* (113) equals the gematria of the name Nehemiah.[70]

Most of R. Nehemiah's writings are commentaries either on liturgical pieces[71] or on divine and angelic names.[72] It seems plausible that concentration on the latter topic had more than one aim, but it is hard to ignore the possible nexus between divine names and the epithet 'prophet', as will be discussed below. Like his contemporary R. Samuel of Rouen, R. Nehemiah was also concerned with the figure of Metatron, dedicating an entire treatise—found in different versions in many manuscripts—to his seventy names.[73]

Unparalleled among the writings of other prophets is a relatively long piece, explicitly called a prophecy, which was authored by R. Nehemiah and in which he disputes the eschatological calculations of many authorities who had written about that topic. His claim is that repentance will facilitate the

in Zoharic Literature and Modernism (Heb.), 59 n. 8, 74; Scholem, *Kabbalah: The Beginnings* (Heb.) 201–2, 206; Marx, 'Essay on the Year of Redemption' (Heb.), 198, 202; and Abramson, 'Prophet, Seer, Visionary' (Heb.), 122. Compare to Heschel, *Prophetic Inspiration after the Prophets*, 20.

[68] On his name see Scholem, *Origins of the Kabbalah*, 239 n. 86; id., *Major Trends in Jewish Mysticism*, 88, 370 n. 21; and id., *Kabbalah: The Beginnings* (Heb.), 206.

[69] See e.g. Idel, 'Some Forlorn Writings of a Forgotten Ashkenazi Prophet', 188–96; id., 'Incantations, Lists, and "Gates of Sermons"' (Heb.); id., *Ben: Sonship and Jewish Mysticism*, 218–35. For an earlier study dealing with some of his anonymous texts see Liebes, 'The Angels of the Shofar and *Yeshua sar hapanim*' (Heb.). More recently see the numerous discussions of this figure in Goldreich, *Automatic Writing in Zoharic Literature and Modernism* (Heb.), *passim*.

[70] Idel, 'Some Forlorn Writings of a Forgotten Ashkenazi Prophet', 184–6.

[71] See Idel, 'R. Nehemiah ben Solomon the Prophet's Commentary on the *Piyut* "El na le'olam tuarats"' (Heb.); id., 'An Unknown Liturgical Poem for Yom Kippur' (Heb.); id., 'The Commentaries of R. Nehemiah ben Shlomo on the *Piyut* "Ha'ohez beyad midat mishpat"' (Heb.); id., 'On the Identity of the Authors of Two Ashkenazi Commentaries' (Heb.). Cf. Soloveitchik, 'Three Themes in the *Sefer Ḥasidim*', 352.

[72] See e.g. my 'On R. Nehemiah ben Shlomo the Prophet's Commentaries on the Name of Forty-Two' (Heb.), 157–261; 'The Anonymous *Commentary on the Alphabet of Metatron*' (Heb.), 1–10; and 'R. Nehemia ben Shlomo the Prophet's Commentary on the Seventy Names of God' (Heb.), as well as several versions of commentaries on the name of seventy-two letters, extant anonymously in manuscripts, a topic that will be treated separately.

[73] See Idel, 'Some Forlorn Writings of a Forgotten Ashkenazi Prophet', 187–90; id., *Ben: Sonship and Jewish Mysticism*, 218–35.

advent of the eschaton,[74] which makes him an ethical prophet rather than an eschatological one.

R. Nehemiah's writings are replete with magical themes, particularly information concerning the combination of the letters of divine names and their magical uses, including material related to the 'name of the homilist'. However, for the time being no evidence of his public performances (including sermons) has been available. We may assume that he was not a lone figure, since one of the manuscripts refers to him as a teacher,[75] and some of his writings were expanded in more than one version and copied in a number of manuscripts.[76] He was acquainted with the technique of gazing at water in order to see the divine light, as mentioned above.[77] His extant writings are indebted to the *heikhalot* material and a variety of magical sources, but rarely refer to the nature of the prophetic process. He does, nevertheless, provide some explanations of how prophecy operates,[78] and attributes the practice of incantation of names to the prophet Ezekiel.[79] Thus, according to one of his discussions,

There is a screen of fire hanging before the Seat of Glory,[80] and it is prohibited to look anywhere but through that curtain. And [only] at the appropriate time, a stormy wind will come and elevate the screen, and if the prophet does not close his eyes immediately he will lose the light of his eyes, because of the light of the splendour of the Glory of the Shekhinah.[81]

Elsewhere, R. Nehemiah offers a rather original interpretation of a rabbinic statement regarding prophecy after the end of the prophetic period. When commenting on one of the names of the angel Metatron, Hakham, he writes:

in gematria it amounts to *hanavi*, since all the prophets were very wise . . . but now the secrets are delivered only to those whose minds are innocent, in accord with what the sages, blessed be their memory, said: 'Following the destruction of the Temple prophecy was taken from the prophets and delivered to fools.'[82] Not to complete fools, who tear apart their clothes and spend their nights in cemeteries, and walk

[74] See my 'On Symmetric Histories and Their Termination' (Heb.), 92–123.

[75] See MS Parma-Palatina 2342, fo. 266*b*.

[76] See e.g. nn. 71 and 72 above.

[77] *Commentary on the Seventy Names of the Angel of Presence*, printed as *Sefer haḥeshek*, ed. Epstein, 8*b* no. 66.

[78] Ibid. 1*a* no. 1; 3*a* no. 16; 4*a* nos. 25, 26; 7*a* no. 53.

[79] Idel, 'Incantations, Lists, and "Gates of Sermons"' (Heb.), 489–90.

[80] The Hebrew term *yeri'ah* is used to denote the screen of fire. This term plays a major role in Nehemiah's architecture of the supernal world.

[81] *Sefer haḥeshek*, 3*a* no. 16. The prophet has been prevented from seeing the light of the Glory of the Creator but can see the light of the Glory; see ibid. 8*b* no. 66.

[82] BT *BB* 12*b*.

lonely during the night, but to a simpleton, who does not know how to cheat. And he is called 'simpleton' [*peti*] and is easy to deceive since *peti* [in gematria] amounts to *tamim* [pure],[83] as it is said: 'the Lord's instruction is pure and it makes the simple wise' [Ps. 19: 8].[84]

R. Nehemiah understands the Hebrew term *edut* as a reference to secrets and prophecy. This perspective is important as it reinforces Heschel's thesis about the affinities between medieval prophecy and secrets.[85] While the talmudic rabbis had intended to wholly negate the value of supernal revelations after the end of prophecy, Nehemiah attempted to salvage the possibility of continued significant prophecy. He framed the recipient not as the intellectually perfect individual (as did Maimonides, for example); rather, he conceived the 'innocent' as the heirs to the ancient prophets. This being the case, R. Nehemiah saw no barrier to the possibility of prophecy in his own time. His use of the phrase 'but now' is quite instructive—notwithstanding the fact that elsewhere in his treatise he claimed that prophecy was 'now' removed from Israel.[86] Does this exegetical move reflect R. Nehemiah's self-understanding as a prophet? I would say that the two passages translated above share in common the identification of innocence, in some form, as part of the prophet's nature: he is one who sees through the curtain, and is a simpleton.

It is quite plausible, therefore, that in the period between 1225 and 1265 at least five different prophets were active in the Franco-German region: Samuel, Nehemiah, Ezra, Isaac, and Abraham Axelrod. Only in the case of R. Ezra of Moncontour is there an obvious eschatological prophecy, in which precise dates for redemption are mentioned. The other four prophets are not known to have entertained distinct eschatological speculations. For this reason it would be inappropriate to attribute the emergence of the entire phenomenon of prophecy in the period under discussion solely to the imminence of the year 1240, which, according to the Jewish calendar, marked the beginning of the sixth millennium.[87] In the above list of eleven figures referred to as prophets, the first four were active in the twelfth century, long before 1240. It is thus unreasonable to ascribe the emergence of these prophetic phenomena to the impact of Joachim of Fiore's prophetic approach

[83] *Peti* = 490 = *tamim*.

[84] *Sefer haḥeshek*, 7*a* no. 53.

[85] *Prophetic Inspiration after the Prophets*, 6, 19.

[86] *Sefer haḥeshek*, 6*a* no. 46. About this passage see Idel, 'R. Nehemia ben Shlomo the Prophet's Commentary on the Seventy Names of God' (Heb.), 514 and n. 76.

[87] Scholem, *Origins of the Kabbalah*, 239; Yuval, 'Jewish Messianic Expectations towards 1240'.

in the early thirteenth century, or to the messianic effervescence surrounding 1240, or to predictions about the return of prophecy in the year 1211.[88]

Scholem portrayed some of these prophets as figures who continued the practice of *merkavah* techniques:

We learn of the existence, in France and Germany of the twelfth and thirteenth centuries, of scholars who bear the surname 'the prophet.' This designation, by no means a mere honorific without specific connotation, indicates either that the persons thus named practiced Merkabah mysticism and experienced visionary journeys through the heavens like the celebrated tosafists Isaac of Dampierre and Ezra of Montcontour or Rabbi Troestlin the prophet in Erfurt; or that they actually appeared as prophets.[89]

In fact there is no evidence pertaining to R. Nehemiah's ascent on high, despite the profound influence the *heikhalot* literature had on his writings. Of course the ideal of prophecy does not occur in that literature. Scholem's assessment that these figures 'appeared as prophets' hardly sheds light on the phenomenon itself. An additional possible understanding of the term 'prophet'—as applied to certain twelfth- and thirteenth-century Ashkenazi authors—has been offered by Ivan Marcus, who suggests that it referred to 'an ability to derive exegetically the esoteric divine will'.[90] This explanation of the term would also fit the case of Rashi, and it is compatible with other hints regarding the exegetical role of the prophets.

TWO LATER ASHKENAZI DISCUSSIONS OF PROPHECY

Let me turn to two Ashkenazi figures active outside Germany. The first is R. Joseph ben Shalom, also known as R. Joseph Ashkenazi, a late thirteenth-century kabbalist who visited Barcelona. His connection to the Kalonymite family in the Rhineland is explicit; he was a descendant of the most important family in the history of Ashkenazi esotericism in Catalonia.[91] However, it is not just the Ashkenazi lineage that concerns me here, but the elements of Ashkenazi esotericism that are quite evident in his writings.[92] He was con-

[88] Heschel, *Prophetic Inspiration after the Prophets*, 116–17.

[89] Scholem, *Origins of the Kabbalah*, 239.

[90] *Piety and Society*, 163 n. 59.

[91] On this kabbalist see Scholem, 'The Real Author of the *Commentary on Sefer Yetsirah*' (Heb.); Vajda, 'Un Chapitre de l'histoire du conflict entre la kabbale et la philosophie'; Liebes, *Studies in the Zohar*, 93–5; and Idel, 'Ashkenazi Esotericism and Kabbalah in Barcelona', 100–4.

[92] See e.g. his *Perush kabali libereshit rabah*, 259. For references to Ashkenaz see also ibid. 226, 229, 247. It seems that on pp. 256–7 the impact of R. Eleazar of Worms's *Sefer hashem* is quite evident. He refers several times to the German language as *leshon ashkenaz*. Compare also his discussion of the affinity between the Tetragrammaton and the Tselem in his *Perush lesefer yetsirah*,

cerned with the importance of the divine name, and referred to it as part of a mystical technique for attaining prophecy. His discussion of the role of the Tetragrammaton in his specific method reveals a fascinating combination of the Ashkenazi emphasis on the importance of the divine name, the technique of imagining colours, and what he calls philosophical views of prophecy:[93]

The sages of the philosophers have already written on the issue of prophecy, saying that it is not improbable that there will be a person to whom matters will appear in his imaginative faculty, comparable to that which appears to the imaginative faculty in a dream. All this [could take place] while someone is awake, and all his senses will be obliterated as the letters of the Divine Name [stand] in front of his eyes,[94] in the gathered colours. Sometimes he will hear a voice, a spirit, a speech,[95] thunder, and a noise with all the organs of his hearing sense, and he will see with his imaginative faculty, with all the organs of sight, and he will smell with all the organs of smell, and he will taste with all the organs of taste, and he will touch with all the organs of touch, and he will walk and levitate.[96] All this, while the holy letters are in front of his eyes, and its [the Name's] colours are covering it; this is the 'sleep of prophecy'.[97]

In the passage that precedes the above citation, R. Joseph Ashkenazi had affirmed Maimonides' description of the psychology of prophecy, according to which the intellectual influx that reaches the human mind from cosmic intellects is translated into words and images by means of the faculty of imagination. However, R. Joseph Ashkenazi then proceeds to introduce elements that are totally alien to the thought of the Great Eagle (this may be compared to the approach of Abraham Abulafia, who inserted linguistic elements in his variants of Maimonides' definition of prophecy):

The influx will emanate onto the intellectual faculty, and from there it will emanate onto the [faculty of] imagination. And it will appear to him as if he sees the face of a man speaking with him by voice, spirit, and speech. The visions [*marotav*] of that man

in *Sefer yetsirah*, 34*c*–*d*, and his *Perush kabali libereshit rabah*, 147, 149. Similar discussions can be found in many of the writings of R. Eleazar of Worms. Cf. Idel, *Enchanted Chains*, 109–13, and id., *Golem*, 138–42.

[93] *Perush kabali libereshit rabah*, 223. See also Idel, *Kabbalah: New Perspectives*, 105. The emphasis in this passage on the power of imagination should be compared to what is written in the commentary on *Sefer habahir* entitled *Or haganuz*, printed in *Sefer habahir*, ed. Margoliot, 18, attributed by Scholem to R. Joseph Ashkenazi.

[94] Cf. Ps. 16: 8.

[95] Heb. *kol, ruaḥ vedavar*; cf. *Sefer yetsirah* 1: 9. Though the method is related to some form of visual technique, the result is a matter of voice. For more on voice and revelation see below.

[96] The verb used here is *p-r-ḥ*, which may point to levitation or floating in the air, or may even be connected to ascent. See also the various versions of *Toledot yeshu* about floating in the air by resorting to divine names.

[97] Heb. *tardemat hanevuah*; cf. *Genesis Rabbah* 17: 5.

are sometimes by means of letters [possessing] the colour [*mareh*] of copper or the colour of snow,[98] or the colour of the [man's] clothing, the *badim*,[99] or [they are] like the colour of the gold of *opaz*[100] or the colour of *tarshish*[101] or the colour of lightning[102] or like a torch of fire[103] or in the likeness of copper[104] or in the likeness of the colour of the rainbow[105] or in the likeness of *tekhelet*[106] or in the likeness of fire or in the likeness of water. Or he is running between mixtures [*ta'arovot*][107] of these colours.[108]

When describing prophetic visions, R. Joseph Ashkenazi resorts to concepts and terms he had cited earlier, in the name of the philosophers. Most remarkable in this context is his use of a phrase from *Sefer yetsirah* in both the description of the vision and in the technical passage. His invocation of the concept of letters, together with colours, points in the same direction: unlike Maimonides, who supplied some of the concepts cited here, but did not elaborate a specific technique for attaining prophecy, R. Ashkenazi describes an experience that lasts as long as the colours imagined by the aspirant are in front of his eyes—in his imagination, I assume. This passage reflects an attempt to translate the terms found in Daniel 10: 5–6 and Ezekiel 1 into paradigms for a world that the mystic can experience through his power of imagination. Like Abraham Abulafia, Ashkenazi adopted Maimonides' definition of prophecy, but connected it to a technique that has nothing to do with the Great Eagle's theory.[109]

R. Jacob ben Asher of Toledo, an eminent Ashkenazi author and younger contemporary of R. Ashkenazi, wrote in the *Arba'ah turim*, his widely influential legal code,[110] about a stance the worshipper might adopt during prayer:

Let him think as if the Shekhinah stands before him, as it is said, 'I have set God always before me',[111] and he should arouse the *kavanah* and delete all the distracting

98 This form of referring to white is found more than once in this kabbalistic school. See e.g. Idel, '*Kavvanah* and Colors', 5.

99 Cf. Dan. 10: 5.

100 Ibid.

101 Dan. 10: 6 and see also Ezek. 1: 16.

102 Dan. 10: 6.

103 Ibid.

104 Ibid.

105 Ezek. 1: 28.

106 Presumably a sort of blue.

107 This term points, on the one hand, to a mixture of colours in general, such as those related to the median *sefirot* Tiferet and Yesod, and on the other hand possibly, though less plausibly in this specific context, to the mixtures of colours as reflecting the nature of the last *sefirah*.

108 *Perush kabali libereshit rabah*, 223. For more on this passage see Idel, *Enchanted Chains*, 228–32, and id., *The Mystical Experience in Abraham Abulafia*, 32.

109 The common denominator between Abulafia and Ashkenazi—their interest in prophecy as a possible actual experience—may also have something to do with the interest in prophecy and with the existence of several figures that were designated as such in Ashkenaz in the first half of the 13th century, as seen above. See also Idel, 'Maimonides and Kabbalah', 58–9.

110 See Ta-Shma, *Collected Studies* (Heb.), ii. 167–83.

111 Ps. 16: 8.

thoughts so that his thought and intention will remain pure during his prayer . . . It is incumbent to direct one's thought because, for Him, thought is tantamount to speech . . . and the pious ones and the men of [good] deeds were concentrating their thought and directing their prayer to such an extent that they reached a [state of] divestment of their corporeality and the strengthening of their intellective spirit such that they reached [a state] close to prophecy.[112]

This passage is of paramount importance for the later development of Jewish mysticism. It represents the first explicit influence of Jewish mysticism on a major legal code, and, in this sense, the 'canonization' of a certain mystical technique, explicitly described as one that leads to an experience close to prophecy. According to this text, prophecy is not an extraordinary state of mind, infused by God in order to reveal his intention. Rather, it is the result of human initiative, as man is capable of reproducing this sublime experience at will, in the daily liturgy. Though the specific terminology used by R. Jacob indubitably points to the influence of Spanish kabbalah—and indeed he wrote his code in fourteenth-century Toledo—the fact that an Ashkenazi figure included such a passage in a legal code seems to me to be more than an accident. It follows from the special interest in prophecy shared by Ashkenazi scholars, some of whom were interested in esotericism.

This codification of a moment envisioned as prophecy reverberated in innumerable instances in and outside Jewish mysticism as it was also adopted in Joseph Karo's more influential code, which was based on that of R. Jacob ben Asher. In this sense we may speak about a turning point, for a major halakhist, Karo, adopted an ideal formulated by Jewish mystics—in my opinion under the impact of Geronese kabbalah and ecstatic or prophetic kabbalah—and incorporated it into daily ritual activity. To a great extent eighteenth-century hasidism went in this direction as well. Jacob ben Asher and Karo combined the Ashkenazi concern with prophecy as a present phenomenon with concepts imported from other modes of thought, reflecting encounters with other cultures.

[112] *Arba'ah turim*, 'Oraḥ ḥayim', 98; Heschel, *Prophetic Inspiration after the Prophets*, 26–8. For the huge impact of this passage see Werblowsky, *Joseph Karo*, 61–2, and A. Kaplan, *Meditation and Kabbalah*, 283–4, who pointed out some sources and influences of this passage. See especially a text printed in *Talmidei rabenu yonah*, on *Ber.* 5, quoted by Heschel in *Prophetic Inspiration after the Prophets*, 26–7; Idel, *Studies in Ecstatic Kabbalah*, 163–4 n. 136. On the nexus between prayer and ecstasy in early rabbinic literature see Na'eh, '"Bore niv sefatayim"' (Heb.) and Wolfish, 'Hatefilah hashogeret' (Heb.).

TECHNIQUES FOR REACHING PROPHECY IN FRANCO-GERMAN REGIONS

A linkage between the recitation of divine names and prophecy was already hinted at by R. Hai Gaon in the early part of the eleventh century, and this nexus was maintained in the Franco-German regions. Its perpetuation, which sometimes took the form of a technique, shows that the label 'prophet' in the above texts is not simply an honorary title, but was connected to some form of extraordinary experience, as we have seen in the case of R. Samuel Hanavi. In the words of R. Hai:

Likewise a 'dream question':[113] there were several elders and pious men who lived with us and who knew them [i.e. the divine names] and fasted for several days, neither eating meat nor drinking wine, [staying] in a pure place and praying and reciting great and well-known verses and [their] letters by numbers,[114] and they went to sleep and saw wondrous dreams similar to prophecy.[115]

This passage evinces a linkage between the use of the divine name of seventy-two letters as a technique and an extraordinary experience, which is itself compared to prophecy. No doubt this is a mantic type of prophecy, which is hardly part of the *heikhalot* literature, but belongs, much more, to popular magic.

Let me adduce some examples for such a nexus between divine names and prophecy in the period when the title 'prophet' recurs. In an interesting treatise entitled *Sefer haḥayim*, composed in the early thirteenth century probably in France,[116] and attributed to R. Abraham Ibn Ezra, the following is written:

A vision occurs when a man is awake and reflects upon the wonders of God, or when he does not reflect upon them but pronounces the Holy Names or those of the angels, in order that he be shown [whatever] he wishes or be informed of a hidden matter—and the Holy Spirit then reveals itself to him, and he knows that he is a worm and that his flesh is like a garment, and he trembles and shakes from the power of the Holy Spirit, and is unable to stand it. Then that man stands up like one who is faint, and he

[113] Heb. *she'elat ḥalom*. On this technique see e.g. Heschel, *Prophetic Inspiration after the Prophets*, 55–6.

[114] It seems likely that he is referring to the letters of the name of seventy-two; see Idel, *The Mystical Experience in Abraham Abulafia*, 15.

[115] Quoted in R. Judah Barceloni's *Perush sefer yetsirah*, 104; and also in Ashkenazi, *Ta'am zekenim*, 54; MS New York, JTS 1805, fo. 41*a*; *Otsar hage'onim*, ed. Levin, 'Ḥagigah', iv. 17. See also Heschel, *Prophetic Inspiration after the Prophets*, 8; Scholem, *Origins of the Kabbalah*, 322; Idel, *The Mystical Experience in Abraham Abulafia*, 15; Goldreich, *Automatic Writing in Zoharic Literature and Modernism* (Heb.), 188.

[116] See Idel, *Golem*, 86–91.

does not know where he is standing, nor does he see or hear or feel his body, but his soul sees and hears and this is called vision and sight, and this is the matter of most prophecy.[117]

Though prophecy is only one of the different terms for the experience reached by pronouncing divine names, it is nevertheless considered to be an explanation that accounts for most expressions of prophecy. A strong mantic understanding of the aim of the technique is evident in this passage. The effect of the technique is depicted as expansion of the activities of the senses, and some form of empowerment.[118] This situation is described as available in the present tense, as a positive experience, and it has nothing to do with an exegetical approach to scriptural texts.

In a mid-thirteenth-century critique of Ashkenazi thought and practices, R. Moses ben Hasdai of Taku, who was well acquainted with *Sefer haḥayim*, writes:

two of those who were lacking in knowledge [among] the schismatics [decided] to make themselves prophets, and they used to recite Holy Names, and at times performed *kavanot* during this recitation, and the soul was astounded, and the body fell down and was exhausted; but for such as these there is no barrier to the soul, and the soul becomes the principal thing [in their constitution] and sees afar; [but] after one hour, when the power of that Name which had been mentioned departs, he returns to what he was, with a confused mind.[119]

Here the use of divine names is considered to be an available and effective means of inducing experiences of clairvoyance; the passage affirms that they were used de facto by certain early thirteenth-century individuals who believed that by uttering these letters they could reach a prophetic state. The last two passages corroborate each other: during the process of reciting the names the body trembles violently, freeing the soul from its dependence upon the senses and creating a new form of consciousness. This is the only critique

[117] MS Cambridge Add. 643, fo. 19*a*; MS Oxford-Bodleiana 1574, fo. 34*b*; MS Vatican 431, fo. 39*a*, and *Sefer haḥayim*, ed. Dan, 51. This passage is quoted in the name of Ibn Ezra—with slight changes—in *Ketav tamim* by R. Moses Taku in *Otsar neḥmad*, ed. Kircheim, iii. 85, which matches the version found in MS British Library 756, fos. 170*b*–171*a*. About this work see Dan, *The Esoteric Theology of Ashkenazi Hasidism* (Heb.), 143–56.

[118] For a similar claim see Hollenbeck, *Mysticism, Experience, Response and Empowerment, passim.*

[119] *Ketav tamim*, printed in *Otsar neḥmad*, ed. Kircheim, iii. 84; Scholem, *Major Trends in Jewish Mysticism*, 102–3; Heschel, *Prophetic Inspiration after the Prophets*, 26; Idel, *The Mystical Experience in Abraham Abulafia*, 16–17; id., *Enchanted Chains*, 79; Kanarfogel, *'Peering through the Lattices'*, 211.

of matters related to prophecy as a contemporaneous phenomenon in the Ashkenazi world with which I am acquainted. However, R. Moses Taku is also critical of many other topics.

Another testimony to the connection between recitation of the divine name and prophecy is found in a brief statement of R. Moses Azriel ben Eleazar Hadarshan, the great-grandson of R. Samuel Hehasid: 'Whoever knows it [the divine name] and prays using it, the Shekhinah dwells upon him and he prophesies like the ancient prophets.'[120] According to this master, the specific context for the use of the divine name is prayer: whoever knows the divine name can activate it such that it may have a mystical and prophetic effect. In other words, R. Moses Azriel describes a licit practice in which recitation of the divine name may not have been seen as a breach of rabbinic prohibitions. Might this reference implicitly allude to the prophetic practice and experience of his great-grandfather, R. Samuel the Prophet of Speyer? (However, there were also less traditional uses of divine names among the Ashkenazi masters.)

Last but not least: an anonymous 'anti-philosophical' Provençal critique from the 1240s accused French traditionalist sages who dealt with magical uses of divine names of defining themselves as 'Masters of the Name, among the famous prophets of truth'.[121] This charge brings to mind the technique related to the divine name and a prophetic experience described by R. Joseph Ashkenazi.

All of the above quotations, excluding that of R. Joseph Ashkenazi, were formulated outside the framework of the great speculative and theological systems of their age, whether Aristotelian, Neoplatonic, or astrological. A common element that underlies the various practices—whether the dream question, the name of the homilist, the opening of the heart,[122] the creation of the golem,[123] the ascent of the soul on high,[124] or prophecy—is the recourse to

[120] See R. Moses Azriel ben Eleazar Hadarshan, *Commentary on Shiur komah*, printed by Scholem in *Kabbalah: The Beginnings* (Heb.), 222. See also Idel, *Kabbalah: New Perspectives*, 169; id., *Enchanted Chains*, 78; and E. R. Wolfson, *Through a Speculum that Shines*, 267, who suggests some form of visual revelation.

[121] Printed in Schatzmiller, 'Contributions to a Picture of the First Controversy on the Writings of Maimonides' (Heb.), 143; see also Halbertal, *Between Torah and Wisdom* (Heb.), 115. For the term 'prophet of truth' see the passage on R. Samuel of Rouen above.

[122] See e.g. *Sidur rabenu shelomoh migermaiza*, ed. Hershler, 99.

[123] For the deep impact on Abulafia's mystical techniques of R. Eleazar of Worms's method for reaching some form of pneumatic experience and for creating a golem, see Idel, *The Mystical Experience in Abraham Abulafia*, 22–3, and id., *Golem*, 99–104; for R. Joseph Ashkenazi see id., *Golem*, 119–26.

[124] See my *Ascensions on High in Jewish Mysticism*, 26–7, 54–5.

a variety of divine names. The omnipresence of divine names is one of the reasons for the vast literature devoted to this topic in Ashkenaz—in comparison to other Jewish centres—starting with R. Eleazar of Worms's comprehensive *Sefer hashem*, and R. Nehemiah's numerous commentaries on divine names.[125] They appear to have much to do with a major aspect of Ashkenazi theology, namely immanentism, the concept that God is found everywhere—*bakol*.[126]

This comprehensive understanding of the prophetic effects of the use of divine names is well represented in a passage by Abraham Abulafia:

> The other part [of the lore of kabbalah, namely the ecstatic one,] consists in the knowledge of God by means of the twenty-two letters,[127] out of which, and out of whose vowels and cantillation marks, the divine names and seals are composed.[128] They [the divine names and seals] speak to the prophets in their dreams, in the Urim and Tumim, in the Divine Spirit, and during prophecy.[129]

Abulafia's inclusive vision of prophecy as comprising a variety of states of mind induced by the hierarchically arranged divine names indicates an acquaintance with the variety of Ashkenazi views regarding prophets, as we shall see. The present-tense formulation is extremely important, as it reflects Abulafia's confidence that he is a prophet.

ABRAHAM BEN SAMUEL ABULAFIA

Ashkenazi masters started to visit Catalonia and Castile from the second half of the thirteenth century.[130] Theirs were not touristic or courtesy visits, but attempts to escape the suffering inflicted on the Jewish communities in Germany. The visiting masters left their imprint on the cultural ambiance that

[125] On the special concern with divine names in Ashkenaz see e.g. Dan, *The Esoteric Theology of Ashkenazi Hasidism* (Heb.), 74–6, 146–7, 219–20, and Idel, 'Defining Kabbalah', 101–3.

[126] See e.g. Dan, *The Esoteric Theology of Ashkenazi Hasidism* (Heb.), 171–83; Ta-Shma, *Collected Studies* (Heb.), i. 148–9 n. 23; Lifshitz, *One God, Many Images* (Heb.), *passim*.

[127] The view that the letters of the Hebrew alphabet are important vehicles for reaching knowledge of God is paramount in ecstatic kabbalah.

[128] The seals (*ḥotamot*) are different combinations of the letters of the Tetragrammaton, conceived, according to *Sefer yetsirah*, as stamping the extremities of the universe.

[129] See his epistle *Vezot liyehudah*, printed by Adolf Jellinek in *Auswahl kabbalistischer Mystik*, pt. I, p. 15, corrected according to MS New York JTS 1887, fo. 98*b*. For the context of this quote see Idel, 'Defining Kabbalah', 106–8. For more on the topic see my discussions in Har'ar, *Le porte della giustizia*, ed. Idel, 130–44. Compare this to a similar distinction between four levels of prophecy in Nahmanides' commentary on Exod. 28: 30, discussed in Heschel, *Prophetic Inspiration after the Prophets*, 3 n. 4.

[130] See Ta-Shma, 'Rabbenu Dan Ashkenazi' (Heb.), 386 (repr. in id., *Collected Studies* (Heb.), 157.

developed in Barcelona and Castile. This is quite evident in the case of R. Abraham ben Samuel Abulafia (1240–*c*.1292), a self-proclaimed prophet and messiah, who started his studies of kabbalah in Barcelona in 1270, after several years of studying the works of Maimonides and neo-Aristotelian writings. He found in Barcelona at least two treatises stemming from the main school of German Jewish esotericism, Hasidei Ashkenaz.[131] He also had access to Ashkenazi traditions that were different from those emanating from the Kalonymite family active in Worms and Regensburg,[132] and, in addition, to at least one text written by R. Nehemiah the Prophet.[133] This can be discerned in several of Abulafia's discussions of his approach to prophecy, as, for instance, in the following passage:

> Behold this sublime name, written in an explicit manner, combined in an appropriate way . . . and whoever knows how to permute it in an adequate manner, the divine spirit will certainly envelop him, or the efflux of wisdom will emanate upon him, and guide his intellect to [understand] the essence of reality in a sudden manner . . . and all these names are combined here, in order to explain the secrets of these seventy-two letters, from which the life of the World to Come is attained by those who prophesy.[134]

Abulafia's synthesis between the linguistic techniques he found in the aforementioned treatises and in their underlying sources—such as R. Hai Gaon's testimony and Maimonides' neo-Aristotelian understanding of prophecy—contributed much to his definitions of prophecy and to the history of kabbalah in general.[135] He proclaimed himself a prophet several times in his writings, and this self-perception is further confirmed by the critique of R. Solomon Ibn Adret.[136] Interestingly enough, Abulafia speaks about a student who received from him some kabbalistic traditions around 1271/2 in Medinat Celim, a town in Castile, and refers to him as R. Samuel the Prophet.[137] He unfortunately provides no more details about this prophet (whose appearance may be related to the impact of the Ashkenazi prophetic subculture in that region). On the other hand, Abulafia also identified another

[131] See Idel, '*Sefer Yetsirah* and Its Commentaries' (Heb.), 485. See also Afterman, *The Intention of Prayers in Early Ecstatic Kabbalah* (Heb.), 115–17.

[132] For the affinity between the technique of Abulafia to reach prophecy by means of divine names and similar earlier phenomena in Ashkenaz see Idel, *The Mystical Experience in Abraham Abulafia*, 16–24.

[133] On this issue see Idel, 'From Italy to Germany and Back', 47–94.

[134] MS Paris, Bibliothèque Nationale 777, fos. 108*b*–109*a*.

[135] Idel, 'Definitions of Prophecy' (Heb.), 14–15, 19–25. See also E. R. Wolfson, *Abraham Abulafia*, or Hames, 'A Seal within a Seal', 153–72.

[136] See *Teshuvot harashba*, vol. i, no. 34 (Dimitrovsky edn.); vol. i, no. 548 (earlier edn.).

[137] See Abulafia, *Otsar eden ganuz*, ed. Gross (Jerusalem, 2000), 369.

student he had in Castile, and who was not from Ashkenaz, R. Moses ben Simeon of Burgos. This famous kabbalist's description of the prophetic method combines recitations of divine names and intellectual depictions, reflecting a process of interiorizing the prophetic event.[138]

Between the years 1270 and 1295 there were in Castile three different prophets of Sephardi extraction—Abraham Abulafia, Samuel, and Nisim (to be discussed shortly)—whereas none had existed there earlier. While the first two were in contact, it seems that the latter constitutes a totally separate phenomenon. Were the latter two, like the former, influenced by the arrival of Ashkenazi emigrants in Castile? In the absence of textual evidence, it is hard to know, but we may tentatively ask why they appeared in the precise period when Ashkenazi figures made their way to Castile. Is it a sheer historical coincidence? It would be reasonable to assume that there was a surge of creativity among what I call the 'secondary elites' in Catalonia in the late 1260s; from the early seventies Abulafia also became part of that revival.[139]

R. Solomon Ibn Adret's attempts to impose a rather centralistic attitude to religious knowledge can be seen both in his sharp critique of Abulafia and in his more moderate though conspicuous reservations concerning the young Nisim ben Abraham, the so-called Prophet of Avila,[140] as well as in his decisive role in the controversy over the study of philosophy, in which he advocated that it be limited to individuals older than 25.[141] That is, as a religious leader Ibn Adret was far less tolerant than is suggested by the intellectual diversity of his writings, in which Neoplatonism, neo-Aristotelianism, talismanic magic, Ashkenazi traditions, and theosophical-theurgical kabbalah coexist on different levels—and, I assume, within a hierarchical structure. (This is somewhat reminiscent of the approach of his disciple, R. Bahya ben Asher.) In search of religious stability, the leader from Barcelona had to marginalize other forms of religious or philosophical knowledge lest they be employed in a manner subversive of rabbinic authority. This certainly was the case when he rejected the prophetic and messianic aspirations of Abraham Abulafia, and the latter's self-perception.

[138] See *The Mystical Experience in Abraham Abulafia*, 19.

[139] Cf. my 'Kabbalah and Elites in Thirteenth-Century Spain', and 'Nahmanides: Kabbalah, Halakhah and Spiritual Leadership'. See also Kanarfogel, *The Intellectual History and Rabbinic Culture of Medieval Ashkenaz*, 23, 537.

[140] See Idel, 'R. Shlomo Ibn Adret and Abraham Abulafia' (Heb.). See now Goldreich's analysis in *Automatic Writing in Zoharic Literature and Modernism* (Heb.), 174, 294, 329–33.

[141] See Ben Shalom, 'The Ban Placed by the Community of Barcelona on the Study of Philosophy', where the earlier bibliography is adduced.

Though it is plausible that Abulafia's first prophetic, ecstatic revelation in 1270 Barcelona had messianic overtones,[142] neither messianism nor prophetism gained ground in that city in the lifetime of Ibn Adret or his disciples. Indeed, prophetism was debated by Ibn Adret in a famous responsum, as will be seen. This was not the case among kabbalists in Castile, however, where both R. Isaac ben Jacob Hakohen[143] and the zoharic literature[144] displayed distinct types of messianic consciousness. The messianism and prophetism that were so central to Abulafia's ecstatic kabbalah were even more pronounced in the traditions that were committed to writing and disseminated in Sicily.

THE SYNAGOGUE AS A BACKGROUND FOR THE MYSTICISM OF THE PROPHETS

The Franco-German Jewish prophets belong to a subculture that should be understood within wider Ashkenazi culture. What was it in this culture that could allow, or even encourage, the emergence and flourishing of prophets? The answer appears in my earlier discussion of the scene concerning R. Samuel, the prophet of Rouen. The event described, the prophet's performance, took place in an attic, in circumstances similar to a synagogue, and was triggered by the presence of a learned audience. There is no evidence of protest or tension in the report. Such reports should be seen in the larger context of Ashkenazi culture, depicted by Haym Soloveitchik as possessing a 'profound sense of its own religiosity' and as reflecting an 'intense religiosity'.[145]

The above examples are by no means exceptions, since paranormal experiences in synagogues were also reported elsewhere in the regions under scrutiny here. Recently Jeffrey R. Woolf has referred to the 'experiential quality of medieval Ashkenazi God awareness', highlighting the role played by the synagogue itself.[146] Woolf collected a range of testimonies that refer not to specific prophetic experiences but to more general experiences of the divine presence, such as the Shekhinah or the Holy Spirit, during prayer. He concludes by saying that 'God's Presence in the synagogue was experienced by medieval Ashkenazim in an immediate, material mode'.[147] The data adduced in his study is totally independent of my earlier treatments of the prophets,

[142] See Idel, *Messianic Mystics*, 58–100, and Berger, 'The Messianic Self-Consciousness of Abraham Abulafia', 55–61.

[143] See Dan, 'The Emergence of Messianic Mythology'.

[144] See Liebes, *Studies in the Zohar*, 1–84.

[145] 'Religious Law and Change', 211–12.

[146] See his 'And I shall dwell in their midst', 302; Rodov, 'Revisiting the "Blind Synagogue"', 83–94; and Shalev-Eyni, 'The Aural-Visual Experience in the Ashkenazi Ritual Domain'.

[147] See Woolf, 'And I shall dwell in their midst', 322.

and the picture he has produced supplements some of the findings in my studies, fleshing out the background of my claims. Three additional examples that corroborate each other may be adduced, one of which specifically relates to a prophetic figure.

Ibn Adret refers, in his above-mentioned responsum, to two prophets who are, roughly speaking, contemporaries. One of them, whose name is unknown, was mentioned as no. 11 in my list above and was briefly discussed there. The other one is the enigmatic figure, R. Abraham Axelrod of Cologne,[148] referred to by Ibn Adret as the 'prophet . . . of Cologne'. Despite his reservations concerning the character of R. Abraham, Ibn Adret reports the following:

I saw a man from Ashkenaz and his name was Abraham of Cologne, and he passed by way of our land to the king of Castile, the father of the current reigning king.[149] And he changed his name to Nathan in order to disguise himself. And he was standing in the synagogue of Cologne at the west [wing] and a voice came out of the east wing from above the ark, where the Torah scroll is deposited.[150] And he was asked about every topic and he answered. And that voice delivered a sermon better than any sage of Israel. And this Abraham was saying that the voice was that of Elijah, of blessed memory. And I heard from an elderly, wise, and honourable person who was in the house of my master, my father, that on a sabbath day he [Abraham] was in front of him. And several rabbis who had gathered together from the land were there, for him. And he delivered a sermon on the pericope 'Vayehi kekhalot'.[151]

Repulsion and admiration are mixed in this highly illuminating passage. Ibn Adret reports two main aspects of R. Abraham's practices: one is the mantic one—his answering the queries of the public. The other practice, more elitist, consists in delivering wonderful sermons that are portrayed as unparalleled in Spain. In both cases the performance itself emanates from the Torah ark and

[148] See Scholem, *Origins of the Kabbalah*, 240 n. 87; Idel, 'Ashkenazi Esotericism and Kabbalah in Barcelona', 86–100; id., *Golem*, 137–8; Abrams, 'From Germany to Spain', 89–90; Goldreich, *Automatic Writing in Zoharic Literature and Modernism* (Heb.), 117, 175, 286, 295, 325, 331.

[149] That is, at the time of Alfonso Sabio, which means sometime between 1265 and 1284, but probably in the earlier part of this span of time.

[150] On the ark of the covenant, reminiscent of the Torah ark, as the locus of revelation see the view of Ibn Adret (*Teshuvot harashba*, ed. Dimitrovsky, i, no. 94); Heschel, *Prophetic Inspiration after the Prophets*, 99–100 n. 94; and, in similar contexts, Goldreich, *Automatic Writing in Zoharic Literature and Modernism* (Heb.), 101 n. 12, 117 n. 17. See also the view that the Temple can refer to Scripture in Wieder, '"Sanctuary" as a Metaphor for Scripture', 165–75. For voice as hypostasis in ancient Jewish sources see Yadin-Israel, 'קול as Hypostasis in the Hebrew Bible'; Charlesworth, 'The Jewish Roots of Christology'; Orlov, 'Praxis of the Voice'.

[151] *Teshuvot harashba*, ed. Dimitrovsky, i, no. 35.

is, according to the Cologne prophet, in the voice of the prophet Elijah. The combination of sermon and some form of mantic operation in this account calls to mind the passage describing the earlier R. Samuel, the prophet of Rouen, discussed above. Moreover, in both cases rabbis were present during the homiletical performance. The two operations mentioned by Ibn Adret have their parallels in three other testimonies from his time in Ashkenaz. Just before the cited passage, he adduces another testimony instructive for our topic:

There are those who [magically] use the Name. And reliable people have told me[152] that they have seen in the land of Ashkenaz an upright person who was delivering sermons in public, before the great men of Torah, [saying] wonderful things. And those sermons are not matched by all the great [men] in the land.[153] And it is done by use of the Name that is designated as 'the name of the homilist'.[154]

Whether the magical name was used by both R. Abraham and the anonymous Ashkenazi man is not clear. But Ibn Adret is amazed by the testimonies, in both accounts, about the extraordinary quality of the sermons. Though the second testimony is unrelated to a prophet, it reveals the domain in which Ashkenazim were imagined to excel, namely, homiletical sermons induced by magical practices and carried out in the presence of rabbinic figures. This seems consistent with the unusual number of thirteenth-century Ashkenazi commentaries on the Pentateuch that are grounded in radical hermeneutical forms, especially in a variety of gematria devices.[155]

A different testimony parallels another aspect of the report about R. Abraham of Cologne's conversation with the prophet Elijah. It is found in a passage concerning an ordinary Jew and which Joseph Dan dates to the lifetime of R. Judah Hehasid: 'A Jew used to [encounter] an angel exiting from the holy ark, in order to speak with him.'[156] The phrase *hayah ragil* (used to) suggests that this was a rather frequent experience, and in the Middle

[152] It is not clear whether those 'reliable people' were Sephardi Jews who visited Cologne and returned, or Ashkenazi Jews who had immigrated to Barcelona.

[153] It is not clear whether Ibn Adret means Catalonia or Ashkenaz here.

[154] *Teshuvot harashba*, ed. Dimitrovsky, 105, and Goldreich, *Automatic Writing in Zoharic Literature and Modernism* (Heb.), 116 n. 17.

[155] See Abrams and Ta-Shma's preface to their edition of *Sefer gematriyot lerabi yehudah heḥasid*, 1–4; Kanarfogel, *Jewish Education and Society*, 86–99; id., *The Intellectual History and Rabbinic Culture of Medieval Ashkenaz*, 289–374; Marcus, 'Exegesis for the Few and for the Many', 1–24; and my 'On Angels and Biblical Exegesis', 216–26.

[156] See Dan, *Studies in Ashkenazi-Hasidic Literature* (Heb.), 23. See also Lifshitz, *One God, Many Images* (Heb.), 183–214.

Ages Elijah was considered to be an angel. This recurring experience differs from the claim in some contemporary sources (mainly Ashkenazi, it appears) regarding the revelation of Elijah from one Day of Atonement to another.[157] Whether those reports have anything to do with the much earlier technique of summoning the so-called Sar Hatorah in order to receive some form of information is an open question.[158]

The third testimony consists of few words, but they are crucial for our discussion. The testimony is found in an anonymous commentary on poems written in Germany in the last decades of the thirteenth century:

> I have found that they heard from the mouth of the voice in Cologne. And by its revelation in the future it will be revealed to everyone, as it is said:[159] 'Therefore my people shall know my name'.[160]

The reference to the 'voice' from Cologne in this passage strongly parallels Ibn Adret's depiction of R. Abraham Axelrod's performance in the very same town. Moreover, the way in which the divine name is mentioned here is extremely important: while the revelation being described appears to have been limited to one individual, the passage asserts that a future revelation will be public. The connection between the pronunciation of the name and the voice seems significant to me. As Avraham Grossman has pointed out, this anonymous commentary is replete with themes that are close to those discussed in the works of Hasidei Ashkenaz.[161]

The above testimonies are short (perhaps truncated) reports, and, as in the case of Ibn Adret's responsum, they are not always approving. The prophets themselves were less inclined to commit to writing their 'inspired' sermonic performances. While it is quite plausible that R. Abraham Axelrod, who was interested in prophecy, had an impact on Abulafia's kabbalah,[162] the latter's approach to the role of the synagogue, and, to a certain extent, to prayer in an ideal religious life, was much more reserved. Abulafia emphasized the importance of solitude as a necessary condition for attaining the state of prophecy.[163]

[157] See above the material referred to in n. 64. I cannot address here the traditions concerning the revelation of kabbalah in the mid-12th century to members of the family of Rabad. See Heschel, *Prophetic Inspiration after the Prophets*, 32–7, and Scholem, *Origins of the Kabbalah*, 241–3. None of those early kabbalists has been designated as a prophet.

[158] See Idel, *Absorbing Perfections*, 140–2, 145–6, 173–8, 381, and the accompanying endnotes.

[159] Isa. 52: 6.

[160] MS Oxford-Bodleiana 1209, fo. 44*b*, printed by Avraham Grossman in 'The Commentary on the Poems of R. Aharon ben Hayim Hakohen' (Heb.), 467 n. 36.

[161] Ibid. 467.

[162] See Idel, 'Ashkenazi Esotericism and Kabbalah in Barcelona', 86–100.

[163] See my *The Mystical Experience in Abraham Abulafia*, 37–41, and *Le porte della giustizia*,

THE RITUAL VOICE, THEURGY, AND VOCAL REVELATION

As is evident from a long series of recent studies, the experiential dimension of synagogal life is related to the special role attributed to prayer in Ashkenazi religious practice.[164] The existence of lengthy commentaries on the daily liturgy and on a series of liturgical poems, incomparably more than in the Italian or Spanish Jewish traditions, bears witness to this proclivity. Following certain earlier sources, some Ashkenazi masters considered efficacious prayer to be the crown on the head of the divinity, and liturgical activities as the daily installation of the king,[165] while others regarded prayer as contributing to the expansion of the Divine Glory.[166] Though markedly different,[167] both trends have rabbinic roots. Another interesting source for the Ashkenazi understanding of a certain moment in prayer is found in a *heikhalot* passage, where God and prayer look at one another during the recitation of the Trisagion 'Kadosh, kadosh, kadosh'.[168] It thus seems that there are different types of direct contact with the Divine: the theurgical one—basically aural—and the ocular one, and in both cases some form of anthropomorphism is implied.[169] This confirms Woolf's emphasis on the 'immediate, material mode' of Ashkenazi religiosity,[170] which I would call pre-axial. I use this term in keeping

117–24. See especially his discussion on prayer in a synagogue: *Sefer haḥeshek*, ed. Gross, 50, 64; *Otsar eden ganuz*, ed. Gross, 171–2; and in one of his epistles, *Matsref lakesef*, in *Matsref hasekhel*, ed. Gross, 105.

164 See Ta-Shma, *Early Ashkenazi Prayer* (Heb.); id., 'The Minor Temple' (Heb.); Dan, 'The Emergence of Mystical Prayer'; id., *History of Jewish Mysticism and Esotericism* (Heb.), v. 293–326; R. Abraham ben Azriel, *Sefer arugat habosem*; Grossman, *The Early Sages of France* (Heb.), 507–38; Kanarfogel, *'Peering through the Lattices'*, 93–130; id., 'Esotericism and Magic in Ashkenazi Prayer'; id., *The Intellectual History and Rabbinic Culture of Medieval Ashkenaz*, 375–444; Fishman, 'Rhineland Pietist Approaches to Prayer'; Abrams, 'The Secret of All Secrets' (Heb.); id., 'The Shekhinah Prays before God' (Heb.); E. R. Wolfson, 'Sacred Space and Mental Iconography'; Kogman-Appel, *A Mahzor from Worms*; Hollender, *Piyyut Commentary in Medieval Ashkenaz*; and ead., *Clavis Commentariorum of Hebrew Liturgical Poetry*.

165 See my *Kabbalah: New Perspectives*, 191–7; Farber-Ginat, 'The Concept of the Merkavah' (Heb.), 231–44 n. 40, 609; Green, *Keter: The Crown of God in Early Jewish Mysticism*.

166 See my *Kabbalah: New Perspectives*, 160–1, and at length in my 'On the Identity of the Authors of Two Ashkenazi Commentaries' (Heb.).

167 See my 'On the Identity of the Authors of Two Ashkenazi Commentaries' (Heb.).

168 See Idel, 'The *Qedushah* and the Observation of the Heavenly Chariot' (Heb.), 7–15.

169 See Kanarfogel, 'Varieties of Belief in Medieval Ashkenaz', and Idel, 'R. Nehemiah ben Solomon the Prophet's Commentary on the *Piyut* "El na le'olam tuarats"' (Heb.), 19–25.

170 See his 'And I shall dwell in their midst', 322. See also Lifshitz, *One God, Many Images* (Heb.), 123–54.

with Karl Jaspers's notion that certain periods of human history were 'axial ages', in which people developed a more abstract and universal understanding of religion and the universe.

The emphasis on the importance of loud prayer in this passage from the *heikhalot* has much to do with the intensification of the religious effort.[171] It demands not only a more focused type of activity but also a more intense one, and is related to a sense of importance of one's religious acts. It is this heightened sense that can encourage more extraordinary performances, basically aural and much less grounded in intellectual effort. The belief that loud prayer may be efficacious was shared by the community.

Of course, loud study of the Torah was also found in Germany. Towards the end of the thirteenth century R. Moses Azriel, a descendant of R. Samuel the Prophet, wrote:

> An explanation of 'Those who busy themselves with Torah with their 248 limbs, they will be remembered.' And so one is to learn out loud [in a loud voice] with 248 limbs, in order that all of his limbs may fulfil this commandment, as it is written, 'Death and life are in the power of the tongue' [Prov. 18: 21]. For this refers to Torah study and this is what is written, 'Ordered in all things and secured' [2 Sam. 23: 5]. An explanation of 'secured': It is secured for him in the supernal realm and he will be remembered for a good remembrance in the supernal realm. And this [refers to] those who learn out loud, for it is written, 'Death and life are in the power of the tongue'. For this death and life are more in the power of the tongue than of the other limbs, for it is taught that good demons sit beside the man in order to hear Torah from his mouth. If he learns out loud so that they are able to hear, they will bless him and request the Holy One to lengthen his days. And if they are unable to hear they will harm him. And this is what is written, 'For they are life for those that find them' [Prov. 4: 22]—for those that find by way of the mouth, as it says, 'In her right hand is length of days; in her left, riches and honour' [Prov. 3: 16].[172]

I wonder whether there is such a strong emphasis on loud vocal performance elsewhere in Judaism.[173] This loudness is part of the archaic, pre-axial aspects of religion preserved in Ashkenaz; one which did not undergo axial reinterpretation by means of philosophical apparatus.[174] The above emphasis on

[171] See Idel, 'Performance, Intensification, and Experience in Jewish Mysticism'.

[172] Printed in Scholem, *Kabbalah: The Beginnings* (Heb.), 236.

[173] See my *Enchanted Chains*, 221–3, and 'The Voiced Torah and Sonorous Communities'.

[174] See the interpretation of the audible voice as part of a mystical technique and as referring to an intellectual influx in an anonymous commentary on liturgy written in the 1260s and edited by Afterman in id., *The Intention of Prayers in Early Ecstatic Kabbalah* (Heb.), 112–14. This preference for the voice as an allegory for the intellectual influx is a case of axial interpretation of a pre-axial approach.

liturgy and voice should be seen as complementary to the notion of revelation as a vocal exchange between the human and divine realms. It may plausibly reflect some form of reciprocity—an idea that found special expression in the writings of R. Eleazar of Worms. He portrayed liturgy as a gift of the community to God, a double crown or diadem which God will return to Israel at the end of time.[175] The prophet who delivers a sermon to his audience brings the revelation of supernal forces to the community; I have described this elsewhere as a 'sonorous community'.[176] This is explicitly so in the cases of R. Samuel of Rouen and R. Abraham Axelrod of Cologne.

SOME CONCLUSIONS

Let me extend the discussion of prophecy in Ashkenaz beyond considerations of the synagogue mystique and powers of liturgical performance. Compared with other forms of Jewish culture, the Jewish culture of Ashkenaz was quite open to the miraculous; this may be seen in the positive role played by dreams,[177] and from the presence there of the theme of the Golem.[178] Together with techniques for attaining prophecy—especially by means of the recitation of divine and angelic names—we may speak about dreams and techniques to create Golems as part of an anomian tendency in Ashkenaz.[179] This culture operated with a more enchanted universe than did other contemporary Jewish communities in Europe, and this is the reason for the richness of magical material in the countries that hosted Ashkenazi culture. Its enchanted world-view is also reflected in two other beliefs: the assumption of an occult relationship between the canonical texts—the Hebrew Bible and liturgy—and the structure of the universe,[180] and the possibility of heavenly ascent, an undertaking practised by R. Ezra, the Prophet of Moncontour. Components that were vital to some dimensions of Ashkenazi culture were

[175] See Idel, 'On the Identity of the Authors of Two Ashkenazi Commentaries' (Heb.), 125–9.

[176] See Idel, *Enchanted Chains*, 221–3.

[177] Harris, 'Dreams in *Sefer Hasidim*'; Dan, 'On the Pietists' Notion of the Dream' (Heb.), 288–93; Kanarfogel, 'Dreams as a Determinant of Jewish Law and Practice'; id., *'Peering through the Lattices'*, 164–5, 216–17, 228; Alexander-Frizer, *The Pious Sinner*, 91–7. See also Idel, 'On *She'elat Halom* in Hasidei Ashkenaz'; id., *Les Kabbalistes de la nuit*; and Heschel, *Prophetic Inspiration after the Prophets*, *passim*.

[178] See Idel, *Golem*, 54–95.

[179] On anomian techniques see Idel, *Kabbalah: New Perspectives*, pp. xvi–xvii; id., *Enchanted Chains*, 70, 100–1, 122, 198; Har'ar, *Le porte della giustizia*, ed. Idel, 113–16.

[180] See Dan, *The Esoteric Theology of Ashkenazi Hasidism* (Heb.), 84–104; id., *History of Jewish Mysticism and Esotericism* (Heb.), v. 393–422; Lifshitz, *One God, Many Images* (Heb.), 123–53.

marginal in the Provençal and Spanish milieux up to around 1270, including the two major forms of kabbalah that developed there.

However, in the period between the years 1270 and 1290, Spanish Jewish culture experienced a spiritual renascence, which I have described elsewhere as having opened a window of opportunities for kabbalah.[181] To be sure, the dramatic expansion of this literature, especially in Castile, had more than one reason; I cited as possible contributions to the formation of the Zohar the arrival in Spain of pieces of ancient Jewish literature,[182] the creativity generated by the Castilian Spanish Renaissance related to King Alfonso X, and the encounters between several different forms of Jewish esotericism that had existed beforehand elsewhere in the region.[183] The assumption of my study was that the medieval Ashkenazi texts discussed above had found their way to Spain, and to Castile in particular; there they contributed to the cultural flourishing that culminated in the emergence of the zoharic literature. A number of contemporary scholars have noted the impact of Ashkenazi esotericism on both Catalan and Castilian kabbalah.[184] For example the arrival in Castile of magical recipes, most probably of Ashkenazi origin, must be counted among the factors that caused the unparalleled creativity that preceded the composition of zoharic literature. One of these recipes, discussed by Amos Goldreich, was entitled 'the name of the writer' (*shem hakotev*),[185] and another one 'the name of the homilist' (*shem hadoresh*).[186] The earlier history of the magical

[181] 'The Kabbalah's "Window of Opportunities" 1270–1290' (Heb.).

[182] See my *Ben: Sonship and Jewish Mysticism*, 410–17, and 'Enoch is Metatron' (Heb.), 99–100.

[183] *Kabbalah: New Perspectives*, 211, 215. See also my 'On European Cultural Renaissances and Jewish Mysticism' (Heb.), 55–64.

[184] Farber-Ginat, 'The Concept of the Merkavah' (Heb.), *passim*, e.g. 128; Abrams, 'From Germany to Spain'; id., '"The Book of Illumination" of R. Jacob ben Jacob Hakohen', esp. 57, 61, 85, 111, 247; id., 'Special Angelic Figures'; Idel, 'Ashkenazi Esotericism and Kabbalah in Barcelona'; id., 'The Anonymous *Commentary on the Alphabet of Metatron*' (Heb.), 258–9; id., 'R. Nehemiah ben Shlomo the Prophet and MS London, British Library 752' (Heb.), 10; and Goldreich, *Automatic Writing in Zoharic Literature and Modernism* (Heb.), *passim*. For the impact of the Ashkenazi treatments of some motifs on R. Bahya ben Asher see also E. R. Wolfson, *Along the Path*, 152 n. 209, and esp. 155 n. 224, where again an Ashkenazi tradition is adduced by Bahya ben Asher as 'kabbalah', and p. 175 n. 328. See also Kanarfogel, 'Rabbinic Figures in Castilian Kabbalistic Pseudepigraphy'; id., *The Intellectual History and Rabbinic Culture of Medieval Ashkenaz*, 539. The presence of R. Joseph Ashkenazi in Barcelona, and perhaps in Castile, should also be taken into consideration in this context. See e.g. Liebes, *Studies in the Zohar*, 93–5, 104, 130. See, however, the view of Joseph Dan in 'The Vicissitudes of the Esoterism of German Hasidism' (Heb.).

[185] Goldreich, *Automatic Writing in Zoharic Literature and Modernism* (Heb.), 43–94.

[186] See my 'Incantations, Lists, and "Gates of Sermons"' (Heb.).

recipes has been documented meticulously in Goldreich's rich study mentioned above;[187] my accent here is less on the techniques themselves and much more on the prophetic valences related to them. The present explanation of the shift in the nature of kabbalah from the first half to the last quarter of the thirteenth century resonates with Israel M. Ta-Shma's findings regarding the infiltration of certain Ashkenazi customs into zoharic literature,[188] and, in more general terms, with the ascent of Ashkenazi halakhah in Catalonia and Castile.[189] The openness to the veracity of dreams in zoharic approaches is also consonant with Ashkenazi culture.[190] Moreover, in the later kabbalistic writings of R. Moses de León and R. Joseph Gikatilla (and even later, in the early fourteenth century, those of R. Joseph Angelet) there are explicit discussions of a technique mentioned in earlier Ashkenazi sources for attaining a visionary experience of the divine chariot through contemplation of water or oil.[191] The same technique is described in a zoharic discussion.[192] Whether it was actually practised by those kabbalists, or whether it related to some form of interpretation of the account of Ezekiel's chariot, on which they were commenting, is, for the time being, an open question. What is evident, however, is that both de León and Gikatilla actually interpreted the details of the technique as symbolically referring to different powers and intra-divine processes.[193]

In this context it is worth pointing out that Charles Mopsik's proposal to attribute a strong prophetic valence to some of the writings of de León and Gikatilla could serve my general point here. However, it has been criticized, convincingly in my opinion, by Yehuda Liebes.[194] Firstly, neither de León nor

[187] *Automatic Writing in Zoharic Literature and Modernism* (Heb.), 277–333.

[188] See his *Ha-Nigle She-Ba-Nistar* (Heb.).

[189] Ta-Shma, *Collected Studies* (Heb.), ii. 109–80, especially the first study, entitled 'Ashkenazi Hasidism in Spain', which deals with the Catalan halakhic master R. Jonah Gerondi (d.1263), and Kanarfogel, *The Intellectual History and Rabbinic Culture of Medieval Ashkenaz*, 538–9.

[190] See Yisraeli, *The Interpretation of Secrets and the Secret of Interpretation* (Heb.), 255–9.

[191] See Idel, 'On the Metamorphosis of an Ancient Technique' (Heb.), 4–7. For the earlier sources of this technique see Gruenwald, 'Mirrors and the Technique of Prophetic and Apocalyptic Vision' (Heb.), 95–7. I hope to elaborate on my study on the basis of a number of additional sources and the scholarship written since its publication.

[192] See Idel, 'On the Metamorphosis of an Ancient Technique' (Heb.), 5–6, discussing a passage quoted from *Zohar ḥadash*, ed. Margoliot, 39*d*.

[193] See Idel, 'On the Metamorphosis of an Ancient Technique' (Heb.), 4–5.

[194] See Mopsik's preface to his edition of R. Moses de León's *Sefer shekel hakodesh*, 6–8, and Hellner-Eshed, *A River Flows from Eden*, 322–3; Liebes' review essay, 'Charles Mopsik, *Moses de León's Sefer shekel hakodesh*' (Heb.), and Mopsik's response in *Kabbalah*, 3 (1998), 210–14. See also

Gikatilla used the terms 'prophet' or 'prophecy' in depicting their own writings, activities, or self-understanding. Secondly, no one later regarded either of them as a prophet, as was the case with earlier Ashkenazi figures. The writings of de León and Gikatilla lack any eschatological messages, claims about heavenly ascents, or the manipulation of divine names. Their mention of the technique of gazing at water, discussed earlier, is a repetition of Ashkenazi material. It should be noted, nevertheless, that in an early, short treatise of Gikatilla's the topic of prophecy is found—though without any claim to his own prophecy. His discussion seems to reflect the early phase of his thought, when he was influenced by Abraham Abulafia, one of his first teachers. While his later theosophical writings contain a theory of prophecy, they do not reflect a more concentrated interest in the subject.[195]

There can be no doubt as to Abraham Abulafia's Sephardi extraction, or regarding the impact of Ashkenazi literature on his prophetic thought and on some of his techniques. Yet given the Zohar's basically Sephardi character, a serious scholar may discern openness to pneumatic phenomena in Castile as well. The existence of Samuel the Prophet in the town of Medinat Celim—a small place where Gikatilla was also then living—and of the young prophet active later in the city of Avila, together with Abulafia's stay in Castile, show that this pneumatic factor, which was new in that cultural region, should be weighed seriously when attempting to explain how the vast and more innovative zoharic literature emerged. If R. Abraham Axelrod was also present in Castile (as can be reasonably inferred from Ibn Adret's passage quoted above), this would reinforce such a hypothesis. The impact of yet another prophet, R. Nehemiah, can also be discerned in the writings of some Castilian kabbalists.[196] Even such a towering Sephardi figure as Ibn Adret was impressed by the inspired sermons offered by Ashkenazi homilists, and the high esteem in which kabbalists in Barcelona held Ashkenazi esoteric knowledge, especially concerning divine names, is widely documented.[197]

It is not clear whether or not Ashkenazi techniques were put to work in composing zoharic literature, as Goldreich suggested in his treatment of 'the name of the writer', and as is the case, to a certain extent, in Abulafia's other

Liebes, 'Zohar and Eros' (Heb.). I, too, find Mopsik's arguments less than convincing and this is the reason that I did not engage them in my foreword to his Hebrew edition.

[195] See Goetschel, 'The Conception of Prophecy in the Works of R. Moses de León and R. Joseph Gikatilla' (Heb.), and my 'Incantations, Lists, and "Gates of Sermons"' (Heb.), 499–501.

[196] See my 'On *Magen David* and the Name *Taftafiah*' (Heb.), 18–32.

[197] See my 'Ashkenazi Esotericism and Kabbalah in Barcelona'.

techniques, some of which are of Ashkenazi origin.[198] While the zoharic literature has strong homiletical dimensions, texts pertaining to 'the name of the writer' also refer to acquiring the capability of fast copying, and to the generation of newly written compositions. As Goldreich has explained, in some cases the two magical names may be related to prophetic self-consciousness.[199]

The answer, I believe, is not a matter of either/or. What seems more reasonable is to speak about some form of osmosis that resulted from the encounters between Ashkenazi and Sephardi thinkers, and led to the imitation of the sermonic genre; after all, the zoharic literature is, at least partly, a series of sermons. However, unlike the Ashkenazi-type sermons, which (like Ashkenazi commentaries on the Torah) are replete with a variety of radical forms of numerical exegesis, zoharic-type sermons are grounded in a more veiled, symbolic mode, closer to the style of the earlier kabbalistic literature. Interestingly enough, the zoharic corpus is predicated upon the imitation of a rabbinic type of culture, at least rhetorically, avoiding claims of prophecy; this feature may explain its smooth reception.

In other words, the prophetic mode is a trigger for creativity that operates by removing mental inhibitions in order to enable the individual to create or to innovate. In this sense the Ashkenazi traditions contributed more than specific techniques. Late thirteenth-century Castilian forms of kabbalah, such as that of Abraham Abulafia, were less concerned with the faithful oral transmission of secrets, with the sources of reliable traditions, or with close literary exegesis than was the case with Nahmanides' kabbalistic school active in Catalonia. Castilian kabbalists were much more open to an experiential and pneumatic approach to the interpretation of canonical texts and to the generation of new texts.[200] The more philological orientation of the Andalusian exegetical tradition was marginalized in the innovative kabbalah of Castile, just as the plain sense of the Bible according to Rashi and his followers, the *pashtanim*, was neglected in most of the thirteenth-century Ashkenazi commentaries on the Pentateuch. However, while the Ashkenazi traditions were, from a conceptual point of view, incomparably poorer than the approaches found in many places among Jews in Spain, the partial integration of those Ashkenazi traditions, and especially of the technical ones, bolstered the creativity that related to more systematic approaches and more abstract in-

[198] However, the meaning offered to prophecy in Abulafia's works depends dramatically on the intellectual framework of the neo-Aristotelian tradition, which is, conceptually speaking, far away from the Ashkenazi theories of prophecy.

[199] *Automatic Writing in Zoharic Literature and Modernism* (Heb.), 9 n. 1.

[200] See Idel, 'We Have No Kabbalistic Tradition on This'.

tellectual concepts, whether Maimonidean, Neoplatonic, or theosophical. In emphasizing these influences, I do not suggest that other possible influences on kabbalah be neglected or underestimated, whether Hermetic, Christian, or of some Muslim variety. Yet I doubt if any one of these, or all of them together, can explain the explosion of writing in this very specific period of time.

Whereas in Ashkenaz, as we have seen, two kinds of elite—rabbis and prophets—coexisted, the situation in Spain was different, as evinced by Ibn Adret's responsum discussed above. Abraham Abulafia, the only significant Sephardi prophet of the thirteenth century, most of whose numerous writings have reached us, was excommunicated despite the fact that he was active in Sicily, that is, far away from Barcelona. It is essential to emphasize that only a very small part of Abulafia's writings was lost; the vast majority of them are found in manuscripts in non-Sephardi handwritings. This may be contrasted with the writings of R. Nisim ben Abraham, the young prophet of Avila, which were revealed by an angel, who also dictated a lengthy commentary on them. These texts had once circulated in Spain—as some were sent by R. Nisim's father to Ibn Adret—yet they are now entirely lost.

Finally, the nexus between some forms of prophecy, prophetic inspiration, and creativity is also evident in other decisive moments in the development of Jewish mysticism. This was the case in Shabateanism, especially where R. Nathan of Gaza was concerned,[201] and in eighteenth-century hasidism, where there are explicit references to prophecy.[202] It is further reflected in twentieth-century researchers' interest in prophecy.[203] Without a sense of self-confidence and self-esteem—which can easily turn into megalomania as has indeed sometimes happened—it is difficult to be creative while remaining

[201] An interesting parallel may be drawn between Ibn Adret's response and one of the fiercest critics of Shabateanism, R. Jacob Sasportas, who was aware of Ibn Adret's views found in the response. See also Rapoport-Albert, *Women and the Messianic Heresy of Sabbetai Zevi*.

[202] See Scholem, *Major Trends in Jewish Mysticism*, 334; id., 'The First Two Testimonies on Hasidic Confraternities and the Besht' (Heb.), 239; Tishby, 'The Messianic Idea and Messianic Trends in the Growth of Hasidism' (Heb.), 40; Heschel, *The Circle of the Ba'al Shem Tov*, 20; Weiss, *Studies in Eastern European Jewish Mysticism*, 27–42; id., 'Beginnings of the Flourishing of the Hasidic Way' (Heb.), 60–2; Etkes, *Ba'al Hashem: The Besht* (Heb.), 171–2; Goldish, *The Sabbatean Prophets*; Mark, *Mysticism and Madness*, *passim*; Idel, 'On Prophecy and Magic in Sabbateanism' (Heb.), 7–50; id., 'The Besht as Prophet and as Talismanic Magician' (Heb.); id., 'On Prophecy and Early Hasidism'; id., 'Lawyers and Mystics in Judaism', 29–36; id., 'Abraham Abulafia, Gershom Scholem and R. David Hakohen (Hanazir), on Prophecy' (Heb.).

[203] See Schweid, *Prophets to Their People and Humanity* (Heb.); Cherlow, 'The Image of the Prophetic Halakhah' (Heb.); Rosenak, *The Prophetic Halakhah* (Heb.); Wachs, *The Flame of the Holy Fire* (Heb.), 209–40.

within the framework of a traditional society. This may also be the case where some other major intellectual and religious phenomena are concerned.[204]

[204] See e.g. Toussaint, 'L'individuo estatico'; Reeves, *The Influence of Prophecy*; Barnes, *Prophecy and Gnosis*; Potesta (ed.), *Il profetismo gioachimita tra Quattrocento e Cinquecento*; Schwartz, *The French Prophets*.

Bibliography

ABRAHAM BEN AZRIEL, *Sefer arugat habosem*, ed. E. E. Urbach, 4 vols. (Jerusalem, 1939).

ABRAMS, DANIEL, '"The Book of Illumination" of R. Jacob ben Jacob Hakohen', Ph.D. diss. (New York University, 1994).

—— 'From Germany to Spain: Numerology as a Mystical Technique', *JJS*, 47 (1996), 85–101.

—— 'The Secret of All Secrets: The Conception of the Glory and of the Intention of Prayer in the Writings of Eleazar of Worms' (Heb.), *Da'at*, 34 (1995), 61–82.

—— 'The Shekhinah Prays before God: A New Source for the Theosophical Concept of Hasidei Ashkenaz and their View of the Transmission of Secrets' (Heb.), *Tarbiz*, 63 (1994), 509–32.

—— 'Special Angelic Figures: The Career of the Beasts of the Throne-World in Hekhalot Literature, German Pietism and Early Kabbalistic Literature', *REJ*, 155 (1996), 363–86.

—— and ISRAEL M. TA-SHMA, *Sefer gematriyot lerabi yehudah heḥasid* (Los Angeles, 1998).

ABRAMSON, SHRAGA, 'Prophet, Seer, Visionary—Rabbi Abraham the Visionary' (Heb.), in D. Telzner (ed.), *Jubilee Volume in Honour of Rabbi Mordecai Kirshblum* [Sefer yovel mugash likhvod harav mordekhai kirshblum] (Jerusalem, 1983), 117–39.

ABULAFIA, ABRAHAM, *Matsref lakesef*, in *Matsref hasekhel*, ed. A. Gross (Jerusalem, 2001).

—— *Otsar eden ganuz*, ed. A. Gross (Jerusalem, 2000).

—— *Vezot liyehudah*, in Adolf Jellinek (ed.), *Auswahl kabbalistischer Mystik*, pt. I (Leipzig, 1853).

AFTERMAN, ADAM, *Devekut: Mystical Intimacy in Medieval Jewish Thought* [Devekut: hitkashrut intimit bein adam lamakom bahagut hayehudit biyemei habeinayim] (Los Angeles, 2011).

—— *The Intention of Prayers in Early Ecstatic Kabbalah* [Kavanat hamevarekh lemakom hama'aseh: iyunim beperush kabali latefilot min hame'ah hashelosh-esreh] (Los Angeles, 2004).

—— 'The Phylactery Knot: The History of a Jewish Icon' (Heb.), in G. Bohak et al.

(eds.), *Myth, Ritual and Mysticism: Studies in Honor of Professor Ithamar Gruenwald* (= *Te'udah*, xxvi) (Tel Aviv, 2014), 441–80.

ALEXANDER, PHILIP S., 'A Sixtieth Part of Prophecy: The Problem of Continuing Revelation in Judaism', in J. Davies, G. Harvey, and W. G. E. Watson (eds.), *Words Remembered, Texts Renewed: Essays in Honour of John F. A. Sawyer*, Journal for the Study of the Old Testament Supplement Series 195 (Sheffield, 1995), 414–33.

ALEXANDER-FRIZER, TAMAR, *The Pious Sinner: Ethics and Aesthetics in the Medieval Hasidic Narrative* (Tübingen, 1991).

ALTMANN, ALEXANDER, 'Saadya's Theory of Revelation: Its Origin and Background', in E. I. Rosenthal (ed.), *Saadya Studies* (Manchester, 1943), 4–25.

—— and SAMUEL STERN, *Isaac Israeli* (Oxford, 1958).

ARBESMANN, RUDOLF, 'Fasting and Prophecy in Pagan and Christian Antiquity', *Traditio*, 7 (1949), 1–71.

ASHKENAZI, E., *Ta'am zekenim* (Frankfurt am Main, 1855).

ASSAF, SIMHAH, *Sources and Studies in Jewish History* [Mekorot umeḥkarim betoledot yisra'el] (Jerusalem, 1946).

AUNE, DAVID EDWARD, *Prophecy in Early Christianity and the Ancient Mediterranean World* (Grand Rapids, 1983).

BAMBERGER, B. J., 'Revelations of Torah after Sinai', *HUCA*, 16 (1941), 97–113.

BARNES, ROBIN BRUCE, *Prophecy and Gnosis: Apocalypticism in the Wake of the Lutheran Reformation* (Stanford, 1988).

BENAYAHU, MEIR, '*Sefer shushan yesod ha'olam* of R. Joseph Tirshom' (Heb.), *Temirin*, 1 (Jerusalem, 1971/2), 187–269.

BEN SHALOM, RAM, 'The Ban Placed by the Community of Barcelona on the Study of Philosophy and Allegorical Preaching—A New Study', *Revue des Études Juives*, 159 (2000), 387–404.

BERGER, ABRAHAM, 'The Messianic Self-Consciousness of Abraham Abulafia—A Tentative Evaluation', in Joseph Blau (ed.), *Essays on Jewish Life and Thought Presented in Honor of Salo Wittmayer Baron* (New York, 1959), 55–61.

CHARLESWORTH, JAMES H., 'The Jewish Roots of Christology: The Discovery of the Hypostatic Voice', *Scottish Journal of Theology*, 39 (1986), 19–41.

CHERLOW, YUVAL, 'The Image of the Prophetic Halakhah' (Heb.), *Akdamot*, 12 (2002), 7–48.

DAN, JOSEPH, 'The Ashkenazi Hasidic "Gates of Wisdom"', in G. Nahon and Ch. Touati (eds.), *Hommage à Georges Vajda* (Louvain, 1980), 183–9.

—— 'The Emergence of Messianic Mythology in 13th Century Kabbalah in Spain', in *Occident and Orient: A Tribute to the Memory of A. Schreiber* (Leiden, 1988), 57–68.

—— 'The Emergence of Mystical Prayer', in J. Dan and F. Talmage (eds.), *Studies in Jewish Mysticism* (Cambridge, Mass., 1982), 85–121.

DAN, JOSEPH, 'The End of Prophecy and Its Significance to Jewish Thought' (Heb.), *Alppayyim*, 30 (2007), 257–88.

—— *The Esoteric Theology of Ashkenazi Hasidism* [Torat hasod shel ḥasidei ashkenaz] (Jerusalem, 1968).

—— *History of Jewish Mysticism and Esotericism* [Toledot torat hasod ha'ivrit], 11 vols. (Jerusalem, 2008–2015).

—— 'On the Dream Theories of the German Pietists' (Heb.), *Sinai*, 68 (1971), 288–93.

—— *Studies in Ashkenazi-Hasidic Literature* [Iyunim betorat hasod shel ḥasidut ashkenaz] (Ramat Gan, 1975).

—— 'The Torah Commentary of R. Eleazar of Germaiza' (Heb.), *Kiryat sefer*, 59 (1984), 644.

—— 'The Vicissitudes of the Esoterism of German Hasidism' (Heb.), in *Studies in Mysticism and Religion presented to Gershom Scholem* (Eng. and Heb.) (Jerusalem, 1967), 87–100.

ERAN, AMIRA, 'The Diffusion of the *Hads* Theory of Avicenna from Maimonides to Rabbi Nahman of Bratzlav' (Heb.), in A. Elqayam and D. Schwartz (eds.), *Maimonides and Mysticism: Presented to Moshe Hallamish on the Occasion of His Retirement* [Ḥilḥulah shel hatefisah hasekhilah hanevu'it shel ibn sina min haparshanut hamistit larambam ad lerabi naḥman mibraslav] (Ramat Gan, 2009), 71–6.

—— 'Intellectual Modifications in Maimonides' Model of Prophecy' (Heb.), *Terumah*, 12 (2002), 149–61.

ETKES, IMMANUEL, *Ba'al Hashem: The Besht, Magic, Mysticism, Leadership* [Ba'al hashem: habesht—magyah, mistikah, hanhagah] (Jerusalem, 2000).

FARBER-GINAT, ASSI, 'The Concept of the Merkavah in the Thirteenth-Century Jewish Esotericism—"Sod ha'egoz" and Its Development' [Tefisat hamerkavah betorat hasod bame'ah hashelosh-esreh—'Sod ha'egoz' vetoledotav], Ph.D. diss. (Hebrew University of Jerusalem, 1986).

FENTON, PAUL, 'Deux écoles piétistes: Les "Hasidei Ashkenaz" et les soufis juifs d'Egypte', in S. Trigano (ed.), *La Société juive à travers l'histoire* (Paris, 1992), i. 200–25.

—— 'A Mystical Treatise on Perfection: Providence and Prophecy from the Jewish Sufi Circle', in D. Frank (ed.), *The Jews in Medieval Islam* (Leiden, 1995), 301–34.

FISHBANE, MICHAEL, 'Biblical Prophecy as a Religious Phenomenon', in Arthur Green (ed.), *Jewish Spirituality* (New York, 1986), i. 62–81.

FISHMAN, TALYA, 'Rhineland Pietist Approaches to Prayer and the Textualization of Rabbinic Culture in Medieval Northern Europe', *JSQ*, 11 (2004), 313–31.

GLATZER, N. N., 'A Study of the Talmudic Interpretation of Prophecy', *Review of Religion*, 10 (1945), 115–37.

GOETSCHEL, ROLAND, 'The Conception of Prophecy in the Works of R. Moses de León and R. Joseph Gikatilla' (Heb.), in J. Dan (ed.), *The Age of the Zohar* [Sefer hazohar vedoro] (Jerusalem, 1989), 217–37.

GOLB, NAHUM (NORMAN), *History and Culture of the Jews of Rouen in the Middle Ages* [Toledot hayehudim be'ir rouen biyemei habeinayim] (Tel Aviv, 1976).

—— *Les Juifs de Rouen au Moyen Âge: Portrait d'une culture oubliée* (Rouen, 1985).

GOLDISH, MATT, *The Sabbatean Prophets* (Cambridge, Mass., 2004).

GOLDREICH, AMOS, *Automatic Writing in Zoharic Literature and Modernism* [Shem hakotev ukhetivah otomatit besifrut hazohar uvemodernizm] (Los Angeles, 2010).

GOSHEN-GOTTSTEIN, ALON, '"The Sage is Superior to the Prophet": The Conception of Torah through the Prism of the History of Jewish Exegesis', in Howard Kreisel (ed.), *Study and Knowledge in Jewish Thought* (Beer Sheva, 2006), ii. 37–77.

GREEN, ARTHUR I., *Keter: The Crown of God in Early Jewish Mysticism* (Princeton, NJ, 1997).

GROSSMAN, AVRAHAM, 'The Commentary on the Poems of R. Aharon ben Hayim Hakohen' (Heb.), in Zvi Malachi (ed.), *Be'oraḥ mada: Studies in Jewish Culture Dedicated to Aharon Mirsky* [Be'oraḥ mada: meḥkarim betarbut yisra'el mugashim le'aharon mirsky] (Lud, 1986), 451–68.

—— *The Early Sages of France: Their Lives, Leadership and Works* [Ḥakhmei tsarfat harishonim: koroteihem, darkam behanhagat hatsibur, yetsiratam haruḥanit] (Jerusalem, 1995).

GRUENWALD, ITHAMAR, 'Mirrors and the Technique of Prophetic and Apocalyptic Vision' (Heb.), *Beit mikra*, 40 (1970), 95–7.

HALBERTAL, MOSHE, *Between Torah and Wisdom: Rabbi Menahem Hame'iri and the Maimonidean Halakhists of Provence* [Bein torah leḥokhmah: rabi menaḥem hame'iri uva'alei hahalakhah hamaymonim beprovans] (Jerusalem, 2000).

HAMES, HARVEY, 'A Seal within a Seal: The Imprint of Sufism in Abraham Abulafia's Teachings', *Medieval Encounters*, 2 (2006), 153–72.

HAR'AR, NATAN BEN SA'ADYAH, *Le porte della giustizia*, ed. Moshe Idel (Milan, 2001).

HARRIS, MONFORD, 'Dreams in *Sefer Hasidim*', *PAAJR*, 31 (1963), 51–80.

HELLNER-ESHED, MELILAH, *A River Flows from Eden: The Language of the Mystical Experience in the Zohar*, trans. N. Wolski (Palo Alto, 2009).

HESCHEL, ABRAHAM J., *The Circle of the Ba'al Shem Tov—Studies in Hasidism*, ed. S. H. Dresner (Chicago, 1985).

—— *Prophetic Inspiration after the Prophets: Maimonides and Other Medieval Authorities*, ed. M. M. Faierstein (Hoboken, NJ, 1996).

—— *The Prophets* (New York, 1962).

HINES, H. W., 'The Prophet as a Mystic', *American Journal of Semitic Languages and Literature*, 40–41 (1923–4), 37–71.

HOLLENBECK, JESS B., *Mysticism, Experience, Response and Empowerment* (University Park, Pa., 1996).

HOLLENDER, ELISABETH, *Clavis Commentariorum of Hebrew Liturgical Poetry in Manuscript*, Clavis Commentariorum Antiquitatis et Medii Aevi 4 (Leiden, 2005).

——*Piyyut Commentary in Medieval Ashkenaz* (Berlin, 2008).

HUSS, BOAZ, '"A Sage is Preferable to a Prophet": Rabbi Shimon Bar Yohai and Moses in the Zohar' (Heb.), *Kabbalah*, 4 (1999), 103–39.

HVUIDT, NIELS CHRISTIAN, *Christian Prophecy, The Post-Biblical Tradition* (Oxford, 2007).

IBN ADRET, SOLOMON, *Teshuvot harashba* [responsa], ed. C. Z. Dimitrovsky, 2 vols. (Jerusalem, 1990).

IBN MALKA, JUDAH, *Perush lesefer yetsirah*, ed. G. Vajda (Ramat Gan, 1974).

IBN YAHYA, GEDALIAH, *Shalshelet hakabalah* (Jerusalem, 1962).

IDEL, MOSHE, 'Abraham Abulafia, Gershom Scholem and R. David Hakohen (Hanazir) on Prophecy' (Heb.), in Y. Amir (ed.), *Derekh haruaḥ: Jubilee Volume in Honour of Eliezer Schweid* [Derekh haruaḥ: sefer yovel le'eliezer schweid] (Jerusalem, 2005), ii. 787–802.

——*Absorbing Perfections: Kabbalah and Interpretation* (New Haven, 2002).

——'The Anonymous *Commentary on the Alphabet of Metatron*—An Additional Treatise of R. Nehemiah ben Shlomo the Prophet' (Heb.), *Tarbiz*, 76 (2006), 255–64.

——*Ascensions on High in Jewish Mysticism: Pillars, Lines, Ladder* (Budapest, 2005).

——'Ashkenazi Esotericism and Kabbalah in Barcelona', *Hispania Judaica Bulletin*, 5 (2007), 69–113.

——*Ben: Sonship and Jewish Mysticism* (London, 2007).

——'The Besht as Prophet and as Talismanic Magician', in A. Lipsker and R. Kushelevsky (eds.), *Studies in Jewish Narrative: Ma'aseh Sipur, Presented to Yoav Elstein* [Ma'aseh sipur: meḥkarim besiporet hayehudit mugashim leyoav elshtein] (Ramat Gan, 2006), 122–33.

——'The Commentaries of R. Nehemiah ben Shlomo on the *Piyut* "Ha'ohez beyad midat mishpat"' (Heb.), *Kabbalah*, 26 (2012), 165–201.

——'Defining Kabbalah: The Kabbalah of the Divine Names', in R. A. Herrera (ed.), *Mystics of the Book: Themes, Topics, and Typology* (New York, 1993), 97–122.

——'Definitions of Prophecy—Maimonides and Abulafia', in A. Elqayam and D. Schwartz (eds.), *Maimonides and Mysticism, Presented to Moshe Hallamish* (Ramat Gan, 2009), 1–36.

——*Enchanted Chains: Techniques and Rituals in Jewish Mysticism* (Los Angeles, 2005).

——'Enoch is Metatron' (Heb.), repr. in id., *The Angelic World: Apotheosis and Theophany* [Olam hamalakhim: bein hitgalut lehitalut] (Tel Aviv, 2008).

——'Enquiries in the Doctrine of the Book of the Responding Entity' (Heb.), *Sefunot*, 17 [NS 2] (1985).

——'From Italy to Germany and Back: On the Circulation of Jewish Esoteric Traditions', *Kabbalah*, 14 (2006), 47–71.

——'Gazing at the Head in Ashkenazi Hasidism', *Journal of Jewish Thought and Philosophy*, 6/2 (1997), 265–300.

——*Golem: Jewish Magical and Mystical Traditions on the Artificial Anthropoid* (Albany, NY, 1990).

——'Holding an Orb in his Hand: The Angel 'Anfi'el and a Late Antiquity Helios Mosaic', *Ars Judaica*, 9 (2013), 19–44.

——'Incantations, Lists, and "Gates of Sermons" in the Circle of Rabbi Nehemiah ben Shlomo the Prophet, and their Influences' (Heb.), *Tarbiz*, 77 (2008), 499–507.

——'Kabbalah and Elites in Thirteenth-Century Spain', *Mediterranean Historical Review*, 9 (1994), 5–19.

——*Kabbalah: New Perspectives* (New Haven, 1988).

——'The Kabbalah's "Window of Opportunities" 1270–1290', in E. Fleischer et al. (eds.), *Me'ah She'arim: Studies in Medieval Jewish Spiritual Life, in Memory of Isadore Twersky* [Me'ah she'arim: sefer hazikaron liprof. yitsḥak twersky] (Jerusalem 2001), 171–208.

——*Les Kabbalistes de la nuit*, trans. O. Sedeyn (Paris, 2003).

——'*Kavvanah* and Colors: A Neglected Kabbalistic Responsum', in Moshe Idel, Devorah Dimant, and Shalom Rosenberg (eds.), *Tribute to Sara: Studies in Jewish Philosophy and Kabbalah Presented to Professor Sara O. Heller Wilensky* [Minḥah lesarah] (Jerusalem, 1994).

——'Lawyers and Mystics in Judaism: A Prolegomenon for a Study of Prophecy in Jewish Mysticism', *Straus Working Papers*, 10/10 (New York, 2010), 14–18.

——'Maimonides and Kabbalah', in I. Twersky (ed.), *Studies in Maimonides* (Cambridge, Mass., 1990), 31–81.

——*Messianic Mystics* (New Haven, 1998).

——'Metatron à Paris', in H. Bresc and B. Grevin (eds.), *Les anges et la magie au Moyen Âge* (Rome, 2002), 701–10.

——*The Mystical Experience in Abraham Abulafia*, trans. J. Chipman (Albany, NY, 1988).

——'Nahmanides: Kabbalah, Halakhah and Spiritual Leadership', in M. Idel and M. Ostow (eds.), *Jewish Mystical Leaders and Leadership in the 13th Century* (Lanham, Md. 1998), 15–92.

——*Old Worlds, New Mirrors: On Jewish Mysticism and Twentieth-Century Thought* (Philadelphia, 2010), 217–33.

——'On Angels and Biblical Exegesis in Thirteenth-Century Ashkenaz', in D. A. Green and L. S. Lieber (eds.), *Scriptural Exegesis: The Shapes of Culture and the Religious Imagination: Essays in Honour of Michael Fishbane* (Oxford, 2009), 211–44.

IDEL, MOSHE, 'On European Cultural Renaissances and Jewish Mysticism', *Kabbalah*, 13 (2005), 43–78.
——'On the Identity of the Authors of Two Ashkenazi Commentaries on the Poem *Ha'aderet veha'emunah*, and on the Views of Theurgy and *Kavod* in R. Eleazar of Worms' (Heb.), *Kabbalah*, 29 (2013), 67–208.
——'On *Magen David* and the Name *Taftafiah*: From Jewish Magic to Practical and Theoretical Kabbalah' (Heb.), in A. Reiner et al. (eds.) *Ta-Shma: Studies in Judaica in Memory of Israel M. Ta-Shma* [Ta-shema: sefer zikaron le-y. m. ta-shma] (Alon Shvut, 2011), i. 18–32.
——'On the Metamorphosis of an Ancient Technique of Prophetic Vision in the Middle Ages' (Heb.), *Sinai*, 86 (1980), 1–7.
——'On Prophecy and Early Hasidism', in M. Sharon (ed.), *Studies in Modern Religions, Religious Movements, and the Babi-Baha'i Faiths* (Leiden, 2004), 41–75.
——'On Prophecy and Magic in Sabbateanism', *Kabbalah*, 8 (2003), 7–50.
——'On R. Nehemiah ben Shlomo the Prophet's Commentaries on the Name of Forty-Two and *Sefer haḥokhmah* Attributed to R. Eleazar of Worms' (Heb.), *Kabbalah*, 14 (2006), 157–261.
——'On *She'elat Halom* in Hasidei Ashkenaz: Sources and Influences', *Materia Judaica*, 10 (2005), 99–109.
——'On Symmetric Histories and Their Termination: On the Prophecy of R. Nehemiah ben Shlomo the Prophet in an Anonymous Messianic Document' (Heb.), in Y. Ben-Naeh et al. (eds.), *Studies in Jewish History Presented to Joseph Hacker* [Asufah leyosef: kovets meḥkarim shai leyosef Hacker] (Jerusalem, 2014).
——'On the Theologization of Kabbalah in Modern Scholarship', in Y. Schwartz and V. Krech (eds.), *Religious Apologetics—Philosophical Argumentation* (Tübingen, 2004), 123–74.
——'Performance, Intensification, and Experience in Jewish Mysticism', *Archaeus*, 13 (2009), 95–136.
——'The *Qedushah* and the Observation of the Heavenly Chariot', in J. Tabori (ed.), *From Qumran to Cairo: Studies in the History of Prayer* [Mikumran lekahir: meḥkarim betoledot hatefilah] (Jerusalem, 1999), 7–15.
——'R. Nehemiah ben Shlomo the Prophet and MS London, British Library 752' (Heb.), *Igeret ha'akademyah hale'umit hayisra'elit lemada'im*, 29 (Jerusalem, 2007), 10–12.
——'R. Nehemiah ben Shlomo the Prophet's Commentary on the Seventy Names of God and the Threefold Narrative' (Heb.), in M. Bar Asher et al. (eds.), *Meir Benayahu Memorial Volume* (Jerusalem, 2016), 499–546.
——'R. Nehemiah ben Solomon the Prophet's Commentary on the *Piyut* "El na le'olam tuarats"' (Heb.), *Moreshet Yisra'el*, 2 (2006), 5–41.
——'R. Shlomo Ibn Adret and Abraham Abulafia: For the History of a Neglected Polemic' (Heb.), in D. Boyarin et al. (eds.), *Atara leḥayim: Studies in the Talmud*

and Medieval Rabbinic Literature in Honour of Professor Haim Zalman Dimitrovsky [Atara leḥayim: meḥkarim betalmud uvesifrut harabanit shel yemei habeinyaim likhvod profesor ḥayim zalman dimitrovsky] (Jerusalem, 2000), 235–51.

——'*Sefer Yetsirah* and Its Commentaries in the Writings of R. Abraham Abulafia, and the Remnants of R. Isaac Bedershi's Commentary and Their Impact' (Heb.), *Tarbiz*, 79 (2011), 471–566.

——'Some Forlorn Writings of a Forgotten Ashkenazi Prophet: R. Nehemiah b. Shlomo ha-Navi', *Jewish Quarterly Review*, 96 (2005), 183–96.

——*Studies in Ecstatic Kabbalah* (Albany, NY, 1989).

——'An Unknown Liturgical Poem for Yom Kippur by R. Nehemiah ben Shlomo the Prophet', in J. R. Hacker et al. (eds.), *From Sages to Savants: Studies Presented to Avraham Grossman* [Rishonim ve'aḥaronim: meḥkarim betoledot yisra'el mugashim le'avraham grossman] (Jerusalem, 2010), 237–61.

——'The Voiced Torah and Sonorous Communities in Jewish Mysticism', *Deutsche Vierteljahrsschrift für Literaturwissenschaft und Geistesgeschichte*, 68 [Sonderheft] (1994), 145–66.

——'We Have No Kabbalistic Tradition on This', in I. Twersky (ed.), *Rabbi Moses Nahmanides (Ramban): Explorations in His Religious and Literary Virtuosity* (Cambridge, Mass., 1983), 51–73.

JOSEPH BEN SHALOM ASHKENAZI, *Perush kabali libereshit rabah*, ed. M. Hallamish (Jerusalem, 1984).

——*Perush lesefer yetsirah*, in *Sefer yetsirah* (Jerusalem, 1961).

JUDAH AL-BARCELONI, *Perush sefer yetsirah* (Berlin, 1885).

KANARFOGEL, EPHRAIM, 'Approaches to Prophecy in Ashkenazic Torah Commentaries', in *Richard Steiner Festschrift* (forthcoming).

——'Dreams as a Determinant of Jewish Law and Practice in Northern Europe during the High Middle Ages', in D. Angel et al. (eds.), *Studies in Medieval Jewish Intellectual and Social History: Festschrift in Honor of Robert Chazan* (Leiden, 2012), 111–43.

——'Esotericism and Magic in Ashkenazi Prayer During the Tosafist Period' (Heb.), in G. Bacon, D. Sperber, and A. Gaimani (eds.), *Studies on the History of the Jews of Ashkenaz, Presented to Eric Zimmer* [Meḥkarim betoledot yehudei ashkenaz: sefer yovel likhvod yitsḥak zimmer] (Ramat Gan, 2008), 202–16.

——'German Pietism in Northern France: The Case of R. Isaac of Corbeil', in G. S. Gurock (ed.), *Hazon Nahum: Studies in Jewish Law, Thought, and History Presented to Dr. Norman Lamm on the Occasion of His Seventieth Birthday* (New York, 1998), 207–27.

——*The Intellectual History and Rabbinic Culture of Medieval Ashkenaz* (Detroit, 2013).

——*Jewish Education and Society in the High Middle Ages* (Detroit, 1992).

KANARFOGEL, EPHRAIM, *'Peering through the Lattices': Mystical, Magical and Pietistic Dimensions in the Tosafist Period* (Detroit, 2000).
——'Rabbinic Figures in Castilian Kabbalistic Pseudepigraphy: R. Yehudah he-Hasid and R. Elhanan of Corbeil', *Journal of Jewish Thought and Philosophy*, 3/1 (1993), 77–109.
——'Varieties of Belief in Medieval Ashkenaz: The Case of Anthropomorphism', in D. Frank and M. Goldish (eds.), *Rabbinic Culture and Its Critics* (Detroit, 2008), 117–59.
KAPLAN, ARYEH, *Meditation and Kabbalah* (York Beach, 1985).
KAPLAN, EDWARD K., *Holiness in Words: Abraham Joshua Heschel's Poetics of Piety* (Albany, NY, 1996).
KAUFMANN, DAVID, 'La Discussion sur les philactères', *REJ*, 5 (1882), 273–7.
Kitvei avraham epstein, ed. A. M. Haberman, 2 vols. (Jerusalem, 1949/50; 1956/7).
KOGMAN-APPEL, KATRIN, *A Mahzor from Worms: Art and Religion in a Medieval Jewish Community* (Cambridge, Mass., 2012).
KREISEL, HOWARD, *Prophecy: The History of an Idea in Medieval Jewish Philosophy* (Dordrecht, 2001).
LEVISON, JOHN R., 'Two Types of Ecstatic Prophecy According to Philo', *Studia Philonica Annual*, 6 (1994), 83–9.
LIEBES, YEHUDA, 'The Angels of the Shofar and *Yeshua sar hapanim*' (Heb.), in J. Dan (ed.), *Early Jewish Mysticism* [Hamistikah hakedumah] (Jerusalem, 1987), 171–96.
——'New Directions in the Study of Kabbalah' (Heb.), *Pe'amim*, 50 (1992), 150–70.
——Review essay, 'Charles Mopsik, *Moses de León's Sefer shekel hakodesh*' (Heb.), *Kabbalah*, 2 (1997), 284–5.
——*Studies in the Zohar*, trans. A. Schwartz, S. Nakache, and P. Peli (Albany, NY, 1993).
——'Zohar and Eros' (Heb.), *Alppayyim*, 9 (1994), 67–119.
LIFSHITZ, JOSEPH ISAAC, *One God, Many Images: Dialectical Thought in Hasidei Ashkenaz* [Eḥad bekhol dimyonot: hagutam hadialektit shel ḥasidei ashkenaz] (Tel Aviv, 2015).
LISS, HANNA, *Elazar ben Yehuda von Worms: Hilkhot ha-Kavod. Die Lehrsätze von der Herrlichkeit Gottes* (Tübingen, 1997).
Ma'ayan ḥokhmah, in A. Jellinek (ed.), *Bet ha-Midrasch* (Jerusalem, 1967).
MCGINN, BERNARD, '"Trumpets of the Mysteries of God": Prophetesses in Late Medieval Christianity', in T. Schabert and M. Riedl (eds.), *Propheten und Prophezeiungen / Prophets and Prophecies* (Würzburg, 2005), 125–40.
MACY, JEFFREY, 'Prophecy in al-Farabi and Maimonides: The Imaginative and the Rational Faculties', in S. Pines and Y. Yovel (eds.), *Maimonides and Philosophy* (Dordrecht, 1986), 185–92.
MALKIEL, DAVID, *Reconstructing Ashkenaz: The Human Face of Franco-German Jewry, 1000–1250* (Stanford, 2008).

MARCUS, IVAN, 'Exegesis for the Few and for the Many', *Jerusalem Studies in Jewish Thought*, 8 (1989), 1–24.

—— *Piety and Society: The Jewish Pietists of Medieval Germany* (Leiden, 1981).

MARK, ZVI, *Mysticism and Madness: The Religious Thought of Rabbi Nachman of Bratzlav* (London, 2009).

MARX, ALEXANDER, 'Essay on the Year of Redemption' (Heb.), *Hatsofeh leḥokhmat yisra'el*, 5 (1921), 194–202.

Merkavah shelemah, ed. S. Mussayoff (Jerusalem, 1921).

MOSES DE LEÓN, *Sefer shekel hakodesh*, ed. C. Mopsik (Los Angeles, 1996).

MOSES OF KIEV, *Shushan sodot* (Korets, 1784).

NA'EH, SHLOMO, '"Bore niv sefatayim": A Chapter in the Phenomenology of Prayer According to Mishnah Berakhot 4: 3, 5: 5' (Heb.), *Tarbiz*, 63 (1994), 185–218.

Or haganuz, in *Sefer habahir*, ed. R. Margoliot (Jerusalem, 1978).

ORLOV, ANDREI A., 'Praxis of the Voice: The Divine Name Traditions in the Apocalypse of Abraham', *JBL*, 127/1 (2008), 53–70.

Otsar hage'onim, ed. B. Levin, 13 vols. (Haifa, 1928–49).

PAGIS, DAN, 'The Poet as Prophet in Medieval Hebrew Literature', in J. L. Kugel (ed.), *Poetry and Prophecy: The Beginnings of a Literary Tradition* (Ithaca, NY, 1990), 140–50.

PEDAYA, HAVIVA, '*Aḥuzim bedibur*: For the Clarification of a Prophetic-Ecstatic Type in Early Kabbalah' (Heb.), in Haviva Pedaya, *Vision and Speech: Models of Revelatory Experience in Jewish Mysticism* [Hamareh vehadibur: iyun betiva shel ḥavayat hahitgalut bamistorin hayehudi] (Los Angeles, 2002), 137–207.

PERLMAN, LAWRENCE, *Abraham Heschel's Idea of Revelation* (Atlanta, 1989).

Perush haroke'aḥ al hatorah lerabi eleazar migermaiza, ed. J. Klugemann, 2 vols. (Benei Berak, 1978).

POTESTA, GIAN LUCA (ed.), *Il profetismo gioachimita tra Quattrocento e Cinquecento* (Genoa, 1991).

RAHMAN, FALZUR, *Prophecy in Islam* (London, 1958).

RAPOPORT-ALBERT, ADA, *Women and the Messianic Heresy of Sabbetai Zevi, 1666–1816* (Oxford, 2011).

REEVES, MARJORIE, *The Influence of Prophecy in the Late Middle Ages: A Study in Joachimism* (Notre Dame, 1993).

RODOV, ILIA, 'Revisiting the "Blind Synagogue": Vision and Voice in Double-Nave Prayer Halls', in Aliza Cohen-Mushlin (ed.), *Jewish Architecture in Europe: New Sources and Approaches* (St Petersburg, 2015), 83–94.

ROSENAK, AVINOAM, *The Prophetic Halakhah: Rabbi A. I. H. Kook's Philosophy of Halakhah* [Hahalakhah hanevu'it: hafilosofyah shel hahalakhah bemishnat harav a. i. kook] (Jerusalem, 2007).

SCHATZMILLER, JOSEPH, 'Contributions for a Picture of the First Controversy on the Writings of Maimonides', *Zion*, 34 (1969), 126–44.

SCHNEIDER, MICHAEL, *The Appearance of the High Priest, Theophany, Apotheosis and Binitarian Theology From Priestly Tradition of the Second Temple Period through Ancient Jewish Mysticism* [Mareh kohen: teofanyah, apote'ozah veteologyah binarit bein hehagut hakohanit bitekufat habayit hasheni levein hamistikah hayehudit hakedumah] (Los Angeles, 2010).

SCHOLEM, GERSHOM G., *Devils, Demons, and Souls: Essays on Demonology by Gershom Scholem* [Shedim, ruḥot uneshamot: meḥkarim bedemonologyah me'et gershom sholem], ed. E. Liebes (Jerusalem, 2004).

——'Eine kabbalistische Erklärung der Prophetie als Selbstbegenung', *MGWJ*, 74 (1930), 289–90.

——'The First Two Testimonies on Hasidic Confraternities and the Besht' (Heb.), *Tarbiz*, 20 (1950), 228–40.

——*Jewish Studies* [*Mada'ei hayahadut*] 2 vols. (Jerusalem, 1927).

——*Kabbalah: The Beginnings* [Reshit hakabalah beprovens] (Jerusalem, 1948).

——*Major Trends in Jewish Mysticism* (New York, 1941).

——*On the Mystical Shape of the Godhead* (New York, 1991).

——*Origins of the Kabbalah*, trans. A. Arkush, ed. R. Z. J. Werblowsky (Philadelphia, 1987).

——'The Real Author of the *Commentary on Sefer Yetsirah* Attributed to R. Abraham ben David and His Works' (Heb.), J. ben Shlomo and M. Idel (eds.), *Studies in Kabbalah* 1 (Tel Aviv, 1998), 112–36.

——'*Sha'arei tsedek*: a Kabbalistic Text from the School of R. Abraham Abulafia, Attributed to R. Shem Tov (Ibn Gaon?)' (Heb.), *Kiryat sefer*, 1 (1924–5), 127–39.

SCHWARTZ, HILLEL, *The French Prophets: The History of a Millenarian Group in Eighteenth-Century England* (Berkeley, 1980).

SCHWEID, ELIEZER, *Prophets to Their People and Humanity: Prophecy and Prophets in Twentieth-Century Jewish Thought* [Nev'im le'amam vela'enoshut: nevu'ah unevi'im behagut hayehudim shel hame'ah ha'esrim] (Jerusalem, 1999).

Sefer ha'atsamim, ed. M. Grossberg (London, 1901).

Sefer haḥayim, ed. J. Dan (Jerusalem, 1973).

Sefer haḥeshek, ed. I. M. Epstein (Lemberg, 1865).

Sefer hapardes, ed. H. L. Ehrenreich (Budapest, 1934).

SHALEV-EYNI, SARIT, 'The Aural-Visual Experience in the Ashkenazi Ritual Domain of the Middle Ages', in S. Boynton and D. J. Reilly (eds.), *Resounding Images: Medieval Intersections of Art, Music and Sound* (Turnhout, 2015), 189–204.

Sidur rabenu shelomoh migermaiza, ed. M. Hershler (Jerusalem, 1972).

SIEGEL, DAVID MATATYAHU HALEVI, *Sefer sodei razei semukhim*, 2nd edn. (Jerusalem, 2001).

SOLOVEITCHIK, HAYM, 'Religious Law and Change: The Medieval Ashkenazi Example', *AJS Review*, 12 (1987), 205–23.

——'Three Themes in the *Sefer Ḥasidim*', *AJS review*, 1 (1976), 339–54.

SOMMER, BENJAMIN D., 'Did Prophecy Cease? Evaluating a Reevaluation', *Journal of Biblical Literature*, 115/1 (1996), 31–47.

TAITHE, BERTRAND, and TIM THORNTON (eds.), *Prophecy: The Power of Inspired Language in History 1300–2000* (Stroud, 1997).

TAKU, MOSES, *Ketav tamim*, in *Otsar neḥmad*, vol. iii, ed. R. Kircheim (1850), 58–99.

TA-SHMA, ISRAEL M., *Collected Studies in Medieval Rabbinic Literature* [Keneset meḥkarim: iyunim besifrut harabanim biyemei habeinayim], 3 vols. (Jerusalem, 2004).

——*Early Ashkenazi Prayer* [Hatefilah ha'ashkenazit hakedumah] (Jerusalem, 2003).

——*Early Franco-German Ritual and Custom* [Minhag ashkenaz hakadmon] (Jerusalem, 1999).

——*Hanigleh shebanistar: The Halakhic Residue in the Zohar—A Contribution to the Study of the Zohar* [Hanigleh shebanistar: leḥeker sheki'ei hahalakhah besefer hazohar], 2nd edn. (Tel Aviv, 2001).

——'The Minor Temple [of the Synagogue]: Its Representation and Its Essence' (Heb.), in S. Elitzur et al. (eds.), *Keneset Ezra: Literature and Life in the Synagogue. A Collection of Articles Offered to Ezra Fleischer* [Keneset ezra: sifrut veḥayim beveit hakeneset: asupat ma'amarim mugeshet le'ezra fleischer] (Jerusalem, 1995), 351–64.

——'Rabbenu Dan Ashkenazi' (Heb.), in J. Dan and J. Hacker (eds.), *Studies in Jewish Mysticism, Philosophy and Ethical Literature Presented to Isaiah Tishby* [Meḥkarim bekabalah, befilosofyah yehudit uvesifrut hamusar vehehagut mugashim liyeshayah tishby] (Jerusalem, 1986), 385–94.

TEICHER, JACOB L., 'The Medieval Mind', *Journal of Jewish Studies*, 6 (1955), 1–13.

TISHBY, ISAIAH, 'The Messianic Idea and Messianic Trends in the Growth of Hasidism' (Heb.), *Zion*, 32 (1967), 40.

TOUSSAINT, STÉPHANE, 'L'individuo estatico: tecniche profetiche in Marsilio Ficino e Giovanni Pico della Mirandola', *Bruniana & Campanelliana: Ricerche filosofice e materiali storico-testuali*, 6/2 (2000), 531–379.

TSIDKIYAH BEN ABRAHAM, *Shibolei haleket*, ed. S. Buber (Vilna, 1889).

UFFENHEIMER, BENJAMIN, *Ancient Prophecy in Israel* [Hanevuah hakedumah beyisra'el] (Jerusalem, 2001).

URBACH, EPHRAIM ELIMELEKH, 'Prophet and Sage in the Jewish Heritage' (Heb.), in E. E. Urbach, *The World of the Sages* [Me'olamam shel ḥakhamim] (Jerusalem, 1988), 9–20.

——*The Tosafists: Their History, Writings, and Method* [Ba'alei hatosafot: toledoteihem, ḥibureihem, shitatam], 2 vols. (Jerusalem, 1980).

VAJDA, GEORGE, 'Un chapitre de l'histoire du conflit entre la kabbale et la philosophie', *Archives d'histoire doctrinale et littéraire du Moyen Âge*, 31 (1956), 45–127.

WACHS, RON, *The Flame of the Holy Fire: Perspectives on the Teachings of Rabbi Kalonymus Kalmish Shapiro of Piacenza* [Lehavat esh kodesh: she'arim letorato shel ha'admor mipiaseczna] (Gush Etzion, 2010).

WALZER, RICHARD, 'Al-Farabi's Theory of Prophecy and Divination', in id., *Greek into Arabic: Essays on Islamic Philosophy* (Oxford, 1962), 206–19.

WEISS, JOSEPH, 'The Beginnings of the Development of the Hasidic Way' (Heb.), *Zion*, 16 (1961), 46–105.

—— *Studies in Eastern European Jewish Mysticism*, trans. and ed. D. Goldstein (Oxford, 1985).

WERBLOWSKY, R. J. ZWI, *Joseph Karo: Lawyer and Mystic* (Philadelphia, 1977).

WIEDER, NAFTALI, '"Sanctuary" as a Metaphor for Scripture', *JJS*, 8–9 (1957–8), 165–75.

WILSON, ROBERT R., 'Prophecy and Ecstasy: A Reexamination', *Journal of Biblical Literature*, 98/3 (1979), 321–37.

WOLFISH, A., 'Hatefilah hashogeret' (Heb.), *Tarbiz*, 65 (1996), 301–14.

WOLFSON, ELLIOT R., *Abraham Abulafia: Kabbalist and Prophet, Hermeneutics, Theosophy, and Theurgy* (Los Angeles, 2000).

—— *Along the Path* (Albany, NY, 1995).

—— 'The Mystical Significance of Torah Study in German Pietism', *Jewish Quarterly Review*, 84 (1993), 43–77.

—— 'Sacred Space and Mental Iconography: "*Imago Templi*" and Contemplation in Rhineland Jewish Pietism', in R. Chazan et al. (eds.), *Studies in Honor of Baruch A. Levine* (Winona Lake, Ind., 1999), 593–634.

—— '"Sage is Preferable to Prophet": Revisioning Midrashic Imagination', in Deborah A. Green and Laura S. Lieber (eds.), *Scriptural Exegesis: The Shapes of Culture and the Religious Imagination. Essays in Honour of Michael Fishbane* (Oxford, 2009), 186–210.

—— *Through a Speculum that Shines* (Princeton, NJ, 1994).

WOLFSON, HARRY A., *Studies in the History of Philosophy and Religion*, ed. I. Twersky and G. H. Williams, 2 vols. (Cambridge, Mass., 1977).

WOODS, RICHARD, *Mysticism and Prophecy: The Dominican Tradition* (London, 1998).

WOOLF, JEFFREY R., 'And I Shall Dwell in Their Midst: God's Presence in the Medieval Ashkenazi Synagogue', *JJS*, 65 (2014), 302–22.

YADIN-ISRAEL, AZZAN, 'Bavli *Menaḥot* 29*b* and the Diminution of the Prophets', *Journal of Ancient Judaism*, 5 (2014), 85–105.

—— 'קול as Hypostasis in the Hebrew Bible', *JBL*, 122/4 (2003), 601–26.

YISRAELI, ODED, *The Interpretation of Secrets and the Secret of Interpretation: Midrashic and Hermeneutic Strategies in Saba demishpatim of the Zohar* [Parshanut hasod vesod haparshanut: megamot midrashiyot vehermeneutiyot besaba demishpatim shebazohar] (Los Angeles, 2005).

YUVAL, ISRAEL JACOB, 'Jewish Messianic Expectations toward 1240 and Christian Reactions', in P. Schäfer and Mark R. Cohen (eds.), *Toward the Millennium: Messianic Expectations from the Bible to Waco* (Leiden, 1998), 105–22.

—— *'Two Nations in Your Womb': Perceptions of Jews and Christians* ['Shenei goyim bevitnekh': yehudim venotsrim—dimuyim hadadiyim] (Tel Aviv, 2000).

ZFATMAN, SARA, *From Talmudic Times to the Middle Ages: The Establishment of Leadership in Jewish Literature* [Rosh verishon: yisud manhigut besifrut yisra'el] (Jerusalem, 2010).

—— *The Jewish Tale in the Middle Ages: Between Ashkenaz and Sepharad* [Bein ashkenaz lisefarad: letoledot hasipur hayehudi biyemei habeinayim] (Jerusalem, 1993).

ZIMMER, ERIC, *Society and Its Customs: Studies in the History and Metamorphosis of Jewish Customs* [Olam keminhago noheg: perakim betoledot haminhagim] (Jerusalem, 1996).

Zohar ḥadash, ed. R. Margoliot (Jerusalem, 1978).

Index